Paths into American Culture

Psychology, Medicine, and Morals

American Civilization

A series edited by Allen F. Davis

Paths into American Culture

Psychology, Medicine, and Morals

John C. Burnham

TEMPLE UNIVERSITY PRESS

PHILADELPHIA

Temple University Press, Philadelphia 19122
Copyright © 1988 by Temple University. All rights reserved
Published 1988
Printed in the United States of America
The paper used in this publication meets the minimum
requirements of American National Standard for Information
Sciences—Permanence of Paper for Printed Library Materials,
ANSI Z39.48-1984

Library of Congress Cataloging-in-Publication Data
Burnham, John C. (John Chynoweth), 1929–
    Paths into American culture.
    (American civilization)
    Includes index.
    1. Psychology—United States—History—20th century.
2. United States—Moral conditions.   3. Medicine—
United States—History—20th century.   4. Psychoanalysis
and culture.   I. Title.   II. Series.   [DNLM: 1. Culture.
2. Morals.   3. Psychology—trends—United States.
BF 38.5 B966p]
BF108.U5B87   1987   306'.0973   87-7068
ISBN 0-87722-505-2 (alk. paper)

To Marjorie

Contents

Preface

Some years ago Merle Curti suggested to me that I collect my papers for publication, and other friends have since urged me to do so. I finally decided that at least some of my publications would fit together in a book that focused on the history of American culture, and so I was able to respond to the urging of Allen F. Davis to make some of my articles more easily accessible to interested readers with the thought that, in juxtaposition, they might add up to a statement.

The following chapters appeared as articles in various places over a number of years. Except for standardizing note format, I have not attempted to tinker with them, not even to correct for their being designed for different audiences. But I have added brief editorial comments to introduce the chapters and indicate the continuity in this book. Moreover, after each essay I have, where appropriate, appended paragraphs describing some of the relevant historical work that has appeared since I wrote. In one case I have used an unpublished paper as a whole chapter to finish the story. I hope that the comments and bibliography of the new matrix will make the volume useful beyond the constructive function that any collection can serve.

* * *

I am grateful to the editors and publishers acknowledged in the notes for each essay for permission to republish. I am also grateful to Philip Pauly and Allen Davis for helpful comments.

Several of the papers, as indicated elsewhere herein, were written with the aid of NIH grant LM 02539 from the National Library of Medicine. In addition, part of the research and writing of other papers was supported by the Foundations' Fund for Research in Psychiatry, by released time from

San Francisco State College, and for a number of years by released time and other support from the Ohio State University. Finally, part of the preparation of the present volume was supported by an Ohio State University Faculty Professional Leave.

Paths into American Culture

Psychology, Medicine, and Morals

Introduction

The avenues to understanding American culture are many, and most of them come at least part of the way through history. Within history, a number of approaches even today are relatively unexplored, or at least little traveled. The essays that follow suggest that some seldom-used routes provide, in the end, important access to the events and meaning of cultural change.

Historians' ideas have changed since the earliest of these papers was published. While I have never had any interest in historiography, I am aware of both change and the intellectual traditions that nourished the kind of historical writing that I have been doing.

The overarching framework was and is the Western civilization tradition that flourished in the 1930's and 1940's.[1] This tradition lasted among many historians until approximately the 1960's, when narrow technicians and new-style presentists (or so-called activists) turned their backs on the tradition and indeed eventually tried to rewrite history to deny that the discipline—much less society—ever benefited from the concept of Western civilization.[2]

The Western civilization idea was successful because it provided American intellectuals with a coherent set of traditions and standards to defend in the face of totalitarianism, both foreign and domestic, before and after World War II. Moreover, the concept embodied the idea that intellectual and artistic achievement were the marks of civilization and that the special hallmark of Western civilization was, in addition, respect for the dignity of the individual.[3]

One of the functions of the historian who worked under the Western civilization idea was to record the contributions of that civilization—to make a record that might inspire or even assist the thinking of future generations

or the people of another civilization. This agenda became particularly urgent in the face of Naziism and, especially later in the United States, McCarthyism, television, and other challenges that threatened to obscure and destroy human achievements.[4] It should come as no surprise, then, that the essays in this book describe both the ideals and thoughtful accomplishments of some of the better people in American, and parts of European, society. Not least among them were those who believed in the civilizing force of scientific rationalism.

In the 1940's, another tradition was flourishing in symbiosis with the Western civilization idea: American intellectual history, chiefly in the tradition of "intellectual and social" history. Intellectual and social historians particularly traced their roots to the new history of the early twentieth century, and my own two chief teachers, George Harmon Knoles and Merle Curti, consciously worked in the tradition of the "new history," especially as articulated by Frederick Jackson Turner.[5]

Such historians believed that civilization functioned as a whole, and as the culture concept in anthropology took on the meaning that no part of the culture changed without simultaneous and synchronous changes in all other parts of the culture, many of us called ourselves cultural historians. Later historians who were not intimately familiar with the social-intellectual approach agonized over "internal" versus "external" history and even took up a new term, hermeneutics, which in practice added nothing to the careful combination of textual critique and cultural contextualizing that many of us had learned years before as cultural, or social and intellectual, history.[6]

The tradition in which the following essays were written therefore not only suggested that thinkers were part of the achievements of civilization and responded to changes in the culture; the tradition led on to a belief that ideas have consequences (to quote the title of an important popular book of 1941).[7] This approach differed from that of old-fashioned Marxists who held that material and organizational aspects of the culture determined intellectual expression; and it differed also from those who reduced thinking to the level of ideology in power struggles.

The combination of the instrumental and direct power of ideas that cultural historians embraced by custom directed their investigations toward attempts to reform and uplift both society and individuals. Many of the essays herein in fact do address aspects of the reform tradition in American history. Yet in so doing, the essays also focus upon a number of the most exciting and distinctive insights and contributions of American thinkers. Using the standards of the civilization concept, and the interrelatedness of social developments of the culture concept, the role of such work as mine in American historiography has been to help call attention to important determining events and forces that have escaped others—particularly writers who believe that history is past politics and that ideas of trendy journalists constitute an adequate basis for interpreting the United States as a social, never mind his-

torical, unit. Sometimes, as in the case of morals, the perspective supplied by material from the history of technical endeavors can change the way in which one sees major social and even political events. At other times, the narrowly technical (as in psychotherapy) turns out in fact to be of great moment in the lives of large parts—or all—of the population.

I have never started out to develop a new subject matter area or a different perspective. All of my work has grown out of specific, monographic-level inquiry and concrete, detailed findings. But working in the tradition of the new history of the early twentieth century and under the inspiration of mid- to late-twentieth-century cultural historians, I often found myself, as these essays show, carried far beyond the particular and sometimes technical inquiries with which I started. It cannot be otherwise when one begins looking for obvious links to the rest of the culture.

The three roads that I explore in these essays are the history of morals, the history of the medical profession, and the history of psychiatry and psychology, including and embracing what are now called the neurosciences. Much of my work has been in the last area, and the first two groups of essays—Parts I and II—introduce this subject matter by dealing with the relationship between culture and ideas about the mind as both the culture and such ideas evolved. Chapters emphasizing the history of ideas thus provide background for explicit explorations of cultural impact. The material is arranged roughly chronologically, as well as logically, starting with the soul and moving into the mind-body problem that was general in the West and then into other intellectual, scientific, and medical trends that culminated in behaviorism and the general psychological theory of psychoanalysis. The unifying theme in this intellectual history is the development of reductionistic thinking.

In Part II, I address directly the cultural impact of such ideas. The obvious phenomenon with direct effects on American life and thinking was the "new psychology" of the 1920's, ramifications of which were still evident a half-century and more afterward. The key element in the new psychology was psychoanalysis, and the final essay in this section summarizes the impact of Freud's teachings upon American culture.

At that point, the focus turns back to social history, and especially the phenomena of human sexuality and sexual and other moral standards—about which psychologists and physicians even in their professional capacities had much to say, with substantial consequences for society. Sexual subjects are frequently misunderstood; therefore, discussion of the historiography of sexuality provides background and introduction. Then the actual history of moral standards is explored from the late nineteenth century through the Progressive era. Temperance and prohibition reform, which represented closely related social forces and which on other grounds convulsed the entire society, suggest still another facet in the changes that were taking place in values and standards in the new century.

The full implications of morals, psychology and the neurosciences, and medicine for American culture are explored in chapters that converge on the Progressive movement. The final essay indeed argues the cultural point of view strongly—at the expense of more conventional but less satisfactory interpretations—and through the example of Progressivism suggests once more that intellectual and social, and particularly psychological and medical, developments were not peripheral but were central to the history of American society. Not only did they interact with the activities of other Americans—not to mention the rest of the world—but they constituted some of the better intellectual and humanitarian enterprises for which the civilization should be remembered.

PART I

Intellectual Background

This opening essay was designed for a symposium in which the participants explored the history and present status of knowledge about dissociated thinking. Dissociated thinking in the extreme case would take the form of the "multiple personality" that can develop in one person, or the dual personalities that appeared as a literary convention in Joseph Conrad's "The Secret Sharer" and in other fiction of lower quality.* But this first chapter also serves to introduce the theme of reductionistic thinking: where it came from and the kinds of elements to which thinkers reduced human phenomena.[†]

Reductionistic thinking, as I shall explain, involves rationalizing and attempting to control life phenomena, the central characteristic, as many historians have noted, of what has often been labeled modernization.[‡] In such a role, then, this history of ideas therefore also anticipates later discussions of cultural impact.

In a very specific way, the essay introduces the idea of fundamental units to which life and thought could be reduced, units that appear here in an organized as well as elemental context. Implicit in this context was an animal model, and, as Hamilton

---

* For background, see the entire symposium, Jacques M. Quen, ed., *Split Minds/Split Brains: Historical and Current Perspectives* (New York: New York University Press, 1986); Eric T. Carlson, "The History of Multiple Personality in the United States: Mary Reynolds and Her Subsequent Reputation," *Bulletin of the History of Medicine*, 58 (1984), 72–82.

† The soul and reductionism also appear in another context in John C. Burnham, "The Encounter of Christian Theology with Deterministic Psychology and Psychoanalysis," *Bulletin of the Menninger Clinic*, 49 (1985), 321–352. See also Edward M. Brown, "Neurology and Spiritualism in the 1870s," *Bulletin of the History of Medicine*, 57 (1983), 563–577.

‡ Here and elsewhere I shall not attempt to develop the relationship of what I am describing to the idea of modernization, although I shall later allude to aspects of it, particularly widespread orientation toward future goals and belief in cause and effect. The literature is now so extensive that a discussion would be distracting; the issues are covered in various writings of Richard Jensen about applying the idea to American history. Yet it is also only fair to note that much of the change that I am describing can be conceptualized in terms of modernizing, and I have tried to present opportunities for readers so inclined to do so. T. J. Jackson Lears, *No Place of Grace: Antimodernism and the Transformation of American Culture, 1880–1920* (New York: Pantheon Books, 1981), is a notable attempt to embrace not only the idea of modernization but recent Marxist attempts to accommodate cultural history; Lears indeed touches in quite different ways on some of my themes.

Cravens points out, the biological concept of "characteristic" in animals had implications for psychology and society as well as technical genetics when it showed up in the thinking of scientific students of inheritance.[§] As I shall now proceed to suggest, however, thinking in terms of biological units established a pattern that went far beyond biology.

[§] Hamilton Cravens, *The Triumph of Evolution: American Scientists and the Heredity-Environment Controversy 1900–1941* (Philadelphia: University of Pennsylvania Press, 1978), p. 15 and passim. A recent discussion pertinent to much of this book is Robert L. Woodfolk and Frank C. Richardson, "Behavior Therapy and the Ideology of Modernity," *American Psychologist*, July, 1984, pp. 777–786.

CHAPTER ONE

The Fragmenting of the Soul

Intellectual Prerequisites

for Ideas of

Dissociation in the United States

At the beginning of the twentieth century, when the original, explicit concept of dissociation was at high tide, other distinctive concepts also appeared prominently in American intellectual and scientific discussions. The most significant concepts were those involved in attempts to demystify the soma as well as the psyche. Within the sciences of physiology, chemistry, and physics, wrote a New York scientist in 1914, "a complete explanation is to be found" for the phenomena of life.[1] This type of analysis, which led in the direction of materialistic explanation, provided not only contemporaneous intellectual context for ideas of dissociation but also evidence showing how and why those ideas evolved as they did.

It is not possible in the space of this chapter even to sketch the complete intellectual history over a century that would provide a full background for the growth of ideas of dissociation in the United States. Anyway, such a project would be superfluous, because we have Merle Curti's recent history of ideas about human nature in America, and it is just such ideas that are essential in understanding the history of dissociation. Curti shows how the rationalism of the Enlightenment gave way in the nineteenth century to more romantic ideas about humans and their emotions and irrationalities. Finally, Curti traces the development of scientific thinking about human nature in both the natural and social sciences. Like other intellectual historians, he

"The Fragmenting of the Soul: Intellectual Prerequisites for Ideas of Dissociation in the United States" is reprinted from Jacques M. Quen, ed., *Split Minds/Split Brains: Historical and Current Perspectives* (New York: New York University Press, 1986), pp. 61–83, with the kind permission of Jacques M. Quen and The Section on the History of Psychiatry, Cornell University Medical School.

places ideas of dissociation and the subconscious in a context of, first, romantic interest in affective experiences and, then, clinical/scientific interest in individuality and abnormality. Almost all of this thinking among American intellectuals had European roots, but the Americans, as Curti shows, often gave Old World ideas a stamp of their own and by the turn of the twentieth century were sending original findings back across the Atlantic.[2]

The special subject of dissociation, however, brings into focus the particular type of basic thinking about humans to which I have already referred, one usually known as reductionism. It was a type that was essential not only to ideas about dissociation but to concepts of all human thought and behavior as well as physiological processes. I therefore propose to argue in this chapter that the idea of dissociative phenomena is best understood as one of the mainstreams of nineteenth- and twentieth-century reductionism. Indeed, it can be contended that reductionism was the major intellectual strategy of the nineteenth and early twentieth centuries. Sometimes it was disguised as merely explanation, but when thinkers *explained* events, those thinkers almost always meant by "explaining" to account for the phenomenon in terms of events on a lower level, as people then understood it.[3] Reductionism was not just substituting regular natural laws for divine dispensations, then, nor chemical and physical explanations for the vital or biological. Reductionism was a relentless pursuit of the idea that knowledge of components led to knowledge of causes. In this context, I propose to show how, in the psychological-medical realm, the initial concept was the soul, and the final intellectual product was dissociative phenomena.

This narrative is timely because from one point of view psychiatrists of the late twentieth century have reanimated the old phrenology debate: Can a therapist treat just parts of a person or must that therapist treat the whole human being? Can treatment target functions that are localized, in one sense or another, or must the therapist, as in both behavioral and other psychotherapies, work with the entire organism? Moreover, finally, can the functioning of the whole organism be divided into meaningful fragments? But it was not just recently that these problems arose. The question of how to dissect a person's mind in order to understand him or her runs throughout both technical and more broadly cultural thinking about mental functioning and malfunctioning, from phrenology and neurophysiology to various psychological divisions and even whole multiple personalities. All were explanatory reductions.

In the nineteenth century, as I have already suggested, it was the soul that was being anatomized, either literally or figuratively. In the eighteenth and early nineteenth centuries, when well-educated Americans talked about the soul, they usually thought in very conventional terms, largely right out of Aristotle. They accepted the hierarchy of the vegetative, animal, and human souls. Then, in addition, they knew that the soul was coeval with life, or the life principle. (This aspect of the concept became the basis of vitalism,

which functioned as the antithesis of one version of reductionism.) Finally, they often believed that the soul was the essence of the individual.[4]

As the nineteenth century wore on, many different thinkers struggled to maintain the idea of the soul. In a general way, the soul served to place man in the universe, and so comforting an idea therefore was not likely to be surrendered easily.[5] But in the United States two kinds of motives for trying to preserve belief in the soul stood out—the religious and moral, on the one hand, and, on the other hand, the psychological.

The religious and moral stake in the human soul was in turn twofold. First, the concept of the soul was necessary in any conventional idea of an afterlife. As George Bush, a New York University professor, explained in 1845, it was customary to "recognize the tripartite distinction of man's nature into *spirit, soul,* and *body*—that when the body is forsaken at death the *spiritual* and the *psychical* elements survive in coexistence together and constitute the *true man,* which in actual usage is commonly designated by the single term *soul.*" Bush himself used both scripture and etymology to establish the closeness of psyche and spirit, and his focus was on what survived after the body was cut loose.[6]

The other aspect of the religious and moral belief in the soul was the fact that the concept of sin depended upon the idea that a single agent was necessary to carry the burden of guilt or innocence. However complicated a person might be, however numerous the constituents of his or her being, in the end he or she—the agent—either sinned or did not sin. Everyone, in those simpler times, understood that the soul was ultimately responsible for a person's actions. The soul was the essence of that person, that part of the person to which conscience and right reason spoke. Everyone knew that a person could not escape guilt simply by saying, "My hand did it," for the hand by itself had no soul but was merely subservient to the whole person's soul. "When I yield to my anger and speak a bitter word," wrote Lyman Abbott as late as 1885, "I am conscious that I have done wrong, not that some thing in me has done wrong, but that the whole I has sinned. . . . It is the soul that sins, not a faculty in the soul."[7] For conscientious folk, the soul was particularly important, then, because if there were no soul, there could be no sin. That is why I have been careful to speak of "the religious and moral" point of view, because even without religion, as in a secularizing society, the soul was still necessary to give meaning to the idea of right and wrong, for it served as the agent that decided to do right or wrong.

Psychological thinkers as well as religious writers therefore had a moral stake in maintaining the concept of the soul. But the psychological writers also had a technical interest in the concept. In so far as they dealt with thinking, the soul was the agent that did the thinking. As a consequence, virtually any conventional psychological belief was based upon the idea of the soul.

Psychological writers could, in fact, cite empirical evidence of the

existence of the soul. The evidence was consciousness, which, however interpreted—as perception, usually, or will—nevertheless provided a person with a sense of his or her unitary existence, the "I" or the "me" (philosophers were already arguing about the difference), but subjective awareness at any rate, even beyond "I think, therefore I am."[8]

One change did occur in this traditional and valuable concept. By the mid–nineteenth century, psychological writers tended to use the term "mind" in the place of "soul." A transitional English thinker of that period, George Moore, spelled out the common assumption about terminology: "To avoid confusion," he wrote, "the words soul, mind, and spirit will be employed as synonymous." What he was talking about was, in any case, as he put it, "that which is conscious of acting, thinking, and willing."[9]

Everyone knew that the unitary soul, or mind, operated through various divisions. Thomas Upham, professor of moral and mental philosophy at Bowdoin, expressed the general belief in 1840, although he still used soul and mind as functional synonyms:

> It is undoubtedly true, that the human soul is to be regarded as constituting a nature which is one and indivisible; but still there is abundant reason for asserting that its nature can never be fully understood by contemplating it solely and exclusively under one aspect. There are, accordingly, three prominent and well-defined points of view in which the mind may be contemplated, viz., the Intellect, the Sensibilities, and the Will; otherwise expressed by the phrases INTELLECTUAL, SENSITIVE OR SENTIENT, and VOLUNTARY states of mind.[10]

Regardless of the terminology, thinkers had traditionally established various such categories of mental operations, which they, like Upham, referred to as aspects of the mind or sometimes even divisions of the mind. But even divisions of the mind would have no meaningful context without the unifying soul.

The usual divisions through which the soul operated were the faculties. Like Upham, most thinkers followed the traditional divisions of cognitive, appetitive, and volitional, or intellect, feelings, and will; and most again tended to agree on at least the cognitive faculties: sensation, perception, imagination, reflection, understanding, reason, and judgment. The appetitive and volitional faculties varied more according to the different writers. But all of these divisions of the mind were still only modes through which the soul operated. As Joseph Haven explained in 1857, "Mental activity is, strictly speaking, one and indivisible. The mind is not a complex substance, composed of parts, but single and one." He went on to say that the mind worked in many ways, and upon different classes of objects. "The mind," he continued, therefore "has as many distinct faculties, as it has distinct powers of action, distinct functions, distinct modes and spheres of activity."[11]

Americans were largely old-fashioned in their conceptualizations and beliefs about the soul. In Europe, already in the eighteenth century the Romantics and pre-Romantics were beginning to secularize the concept of the soul, not only into the mind, but into the self. The self indeed turned out to be functionally the same as the soul, but now conceptualized upon secular considerations. And, eventually, this change in ideas did penetrate even into American intellectual life.

Historians of ideas who have traced the concept of the modern self note that a number of streams, including confessional and other Romantic litera-ture and Kantian philosophy, came together in the mid– and late eighteenth century, so that by the early nineteenth century the notion of selfhood was available as a commonplace in Western thinking. This self did have attributes and emphases: Each self was distinctive and original; no other one had de-veloped in the same way. Moreover, the new self was unique in time and belonged to a historical, not a static, world. Finally, the self was separate and private, known fully only to the one person. This separateness eventually led to an identity separate from society; in a more traditional society, the person and the society merged into one. By the mid–nineteenth century, distanc-ing the self from society had given rise to still another term, individualism. At first, individualism had the negative connotation of anti-social and rebel-lious, and then later a positive connotation, especially in the United States, of the political and economic individualism that went along with political and economic liberty. The concept of individuality was resoundingly secular. By 1900, geologist Nathaniel Shaler could trace the process of universal individ-uation into every aspect of nature: "It is evident," he wrote, "that in Nature various impulses concur to establish more or less enduring assemblages of actions at certain points in the realm"; Shaler's general language of course reflects the fact that he did not distinguish the principle of individuality in molecules from that in humans. All were "enduring assemblages." [12]

Now it was true that even before the soul was converted into the self, Americans tended to emphasize separateness and individuality. In 1856, for example, clergyman Richard S. Storrs, Jr., explained that God "not only communicates life to the soul, and the highest life of which we can conceive, but he separates that life by a complete inward division, from every other. He creates the soul a self-conscious Person, by the motion of his [God's] will. He endows it with its separate faculties and being. He makes it, in every case, an individual agent." [13]

When, therefore, nineteenth-century Americans spoke of the indi-vidual self, they used the term interchangeably with the soul, which, too, was unitary and distinctive as well as private. Even secularizing the soul, then, did not suggest that it could be divided, not as self and not even when the term "mind" was used in a noncommittal way to refer to the soul—as in fact it was, continuously, in treatises on philosophical psychology.

The secularizing of terms was confusing in one area, literature. Tra-

ditionally one of the major concerns in modern Western writing was the internal struggle of evil, or the demonic, with the forces of right and decency in a person. This struggle was of course a struggle for possession of the soul, and the conflicting internal forces did not represent fragmentation in either European or American literature. When Whitman wrote, for example, "I am large, I contain multitudes," he still maintained the "I" that contained the multitudes. Only later was the convention of the fragmented self—or at least a radical refocusing on independent conflicting elements inside the person— conspicuous in letters. And by that time, usually the twentieth century, reductionistic psychology was often a factor in authors' conceptualizations of a split or fragmented self, although as Masao Miyoshi points out, throughout the nineteenth century thinkers had more and more reason to feel torn asunder because they had to make choices—choices between belief and atheism, between political alternatives, between one way of life or another—and this pressure was particularly remarked on in the United States.[14]

In their more technical conceptualizations, educated Americans of the nineteenth century commonly employed two psychologies simultaneously or separately: Scottish commonsense moral philosophy, and association psychology. Both utilized the soul concept. In the Scottish school, moral sense communicated itself directly to the soul, which otherwise operated in a conventional way through faculties. And likewise the associationists, from John Locke on, assumed that there was a soul or self to entertain the ideas that they believed became associated.[15]

The first challenge to the unitary soul came, then, from a source quite outside traditional academic psychology and philosophy, namely, phrenology. Historians of medicine, psychology, and culture have all noted the large numbers of American thinkers who took up phrenology, or at least took it very seriously at some point. The evidence was quite plain. J. G. Spurzheim died in Boston in 1832 at the peak of an extraordinary public reception of his lectures there. George Combe made a remarkably successful tour of the United States from 1838 to 1840, drawing consistently large crowds of the best-educated people. Even more significant, however, was the fact that for decades a whole new group of native professionals who called themselves phrenologists brought Gall's teachings to the generality of citizens everywhere, both educated and uneducated.[16]

Among leading thinkers, phrenology tended to die out by mid-century. One very important reason was that a number of articulate opponents attacked the phrenologists specifically because they divided the soul. Phrenological spokespersons denied that their ideas in any way impaired conventional religious beliefs; rather, these advocates asserted that the anatomical, on which phrenology was founded, could not impinge on the spiritual.[17]

It is true that phrenologists did use conventional psychological concepts, specifically the faculties and powers. They had, according to physician Charles Caldwell, delivered thinkers from Hume's skepticism about the mind

by presenting, as Caldwell put it, "a rational and intelligible exposition of the mental powers, and . . . their relations to the moral, organic, and physical laws." But unfortunately Caldwell and others also talked about human propensities and even instincts that were rooted in particular "organs," or divisions, of the brain. Since the propensities were, everyone assumed, therefore inherited along with the physical constitution in which they were based, the phrenologists either wittingly or unwittingly involved in their ideas fatalism, or mechanistic determinism, as well as materialism. That moralistic Americans generally came to think that a person could cultivate and alter his or her phrenological propensities turned out to be of little moment for those interested in ideas and theory. The issue that phrenology raised was, if the brain was material and divided, the soul was in danger. Materialism and division were but two aspects of the same problem. With phrenology, wrote a critic of Caldwell, "the beautiful region of mental philosophy is to be converted into a barren *Golgotha*, or place of skulls. . . . The brain . . . is divided into several compartments, each of which exercises a separate function, producing a corresponding manifestation of the moral or intellectual faculties," by implication without the intervention of the soul. Another opponent of phrenology, writing in 1848, noted that if faulty behavior grew out of physical defects, the exact way in which the brain functioned was of little moment: "If Phrenology be true, the conduct of each individual is simply the result of a perpetual war among his organs; and the course of society the result of the conflicting organs of different heads! Let its principles prevail, and social and civil order disappear, and immorality in all its forms prevails."[18] To such critics, it made little difference if materialism opened the way to division of the soul or if fragmentation into organs led to materialism. The result was the same: denial of moral responsibility.

Even if phrenology in itself did not last, the pattern of thinking of people's behavior in terms of independent units based on brain divisions did persist, and it was central to reductionistic thinking about the mind or soul. As reductionism evolved in the nineteenth century, materialism and mechanism came to represent two independent lines of reductionists' strategies. Materialism proceeded particularly through neuroanatomy and neurophysiology, a line of inquiry that people at the time explicitly called the new phrenology because it involved another version of localizing brain function. An interest in speech, sometimes classified as a "faculty," provided the major initial impetus for the new studies using anatomy and physiology to destroy the idea of the unity of the mind. While the work of Broca and others is well known, it is worthwhile pointing out that one of the world pioneers of this exciting research that seemed to confirm brain sites for specific functions was the iconoclastic Cincinnati physician, Roberts Bartholow. Few Americans, even in science, were as dedicated as he was to materialistic reductionism, but they were well aware of materialistic ideas, both of the German philosophical variety and the more practical kind represented by Bartholow or the

widely cited English psychiatrist, Henry Maudsley. Other devotees of neurology applied an equally enthusiastic naturalism to devise neurophysiological, reflex explanations for mysterious segmented behavior such as catalepsy, somnambulism, and even spiritualism.[19] But in truth neither philosophical nor practical materialism had a wide appeal in the United States. Instead, Americans tended to avoid the issue of materialism and to think rather in terms of mechanism.

Mechanism, however, was complex. Association psychology represented one common approach to mechanism, whether it was purely psychological or translated into a reflex equivalent of the association process (which presumably bypassed the soul). Oliver Wendell Holmes, for example, was well known for his interest in mechanism and fatalism. An even more pertinent example is another, younger Boston physician, Morton Prince, who in 1885 explicated a psychopathology based on association/reflex equivalents in which, as he wrote, "ideas, sensations, etc., are the ultimates, the final terms to which phenomena can be reduced." Prince went on to describe even ego or self as but the aggregation of sensations associated together, and he concluded harshly, "There are no more grounds for the assumption of an autocratic Ego than there formerly [were] for assuming a spiritual entity for an explanation of mind." For Prince, a mix of motives in a person was sufficient to explain the (false) appearance of a single, willing unit, the soul or mind.[20] His dynamic outlook, of course, later made Prince a pioneer of dynamic psychiatry—and incidentally of dissociation.

A second approach to mechanism in Americans' thinking lay in the way in which they conceptualized the whole human organism, namely, as a machine. Now it is true that sometimes, as in popularizations and elementary school textbooks, the authors, to remove the mystery from life processes, compared human beings to steam engines. The most frequent comparisons of course depended on the fact that both children and locomotives burned fuel for energy. But as Charles Rosenberg has pointed out, nineteenth-century thinkers did not merely view humans as machines occasionally for explanatory purposes. Rather, the very language increasingly spawned mechanical metaphors for human activity, with the clear implication that human actions were understandable as mechanical events. In particular, writers, both popular and technical, employed physical and chemical language for the most mysterious part of human activity, nervous system functioning. As early as 1872, an American commentator was concluding, "Chemistry teaches that thought-force, like muscle-force, comes from food; and demonstrates that the force evolved by the brain, like that produced by the muscle, comes not from the disintegration of its own tissue, but is the converted energy of burning carbon. Can we longer doubt, then, that the brain, too, is a machine for the conversion of energy?"[21] By the late nineteenth century, in short, Americans more and more were conceptualizing the body as a fuel-consuming locomotive with limbs that moved like levers and pulleys, governed by a ner-

vous system that worked like a telegraph or, later on, a telephone exchange system.

Now at this point it may appear that I have departed from my subject, namely, the intellectual background of the idea of dissociation; having brought it up, surely one ought to stick to the central topic of association psychology as such, upon which the notion of dissociation was based, rather than pursuing far afield only the mechanistic aspects of association. The explanation is, to begin with, even today everyone knows at least some of the associationist beliefs that were so common seventy-five or a hundred years ago, and to dwell upon them would be gratuitous. But more important, what gave dissociation its special significance was what happened in the realm of mechanism and reductionism. Let me therefore show that I am not digressing.

Most reductionism initially came out of nineteenth-century medicine. The drive of scientists to understand disease led directly to their emphasis on anatomy and structure. Physicians, in struggling to perfect both diagnosis and cure, sought the rational cause of the disease, and at first structural defect stood out.[22] When virtually everyone repeatedly spoke of the complex machinery of the human body, and anatomical pathology seemed so promising, it was no wonder that the medical reinforced the mechanical, and one important direction of development was to see human biology directly in terms of physics and chemistry, as symbolized, for example, in the turn-of-the-century work of Jacques Loeb.

But already in the late nineteenth century another type of thinking began to develop, one generally identified as the rise of physiology. In this type of thinking, reductionists came to utilize an intermediate unit, that is, a generalized physiological unit. These units came to be conceptualized as analogous to atoms existing in a moving but balanced system.

The first step in developing this new viewpoint was emphasizing the idea that the body was made up of protoplasm and divided into cells, each cell in turn comparable to an amoeba or other single-celled organism. Exactly how all of these cells worked together was not clear, but that each one had a function, no one doubted. Thus was born the new atomism, or what Frederick Kilgour has called atomicity and Garland Allen holistic materialism.[23]

Dynamic atomicity represented a major step beyond the older ideas of mechanism. Where, before, the ultimate purpose of the machine—typically the body—was to function automatically in overall terms of the environment or even the soul, in the new viewpoint each elemental unit came to have its own existence and own set of goals, creating within an entire system a dynamic equilibrium, such as Claude Bernard spoke of as the *milieu intérieur* and the American physiologist, Walter Cannon, in the twentieth century popularized as homeostasis.[24] The relationships between the various units in the atomistic system permitted investigators and popularizers alike to talk about meaningful actions and interactions within a set of relationships

that could be virtually infinitely complex because of the number of units involved—a conceptualization of natural processes that permitted indefinite extension and was used for many decades thereafter.[25]

The "cell doctrine," as it was called in the nineteenth century, flourished in the Western world just when post-Daltonian chemistry was emphasizing the idea of atomistic thinking. From the beginning, as botanist Charles F. Cox shrewdly observed in 1890, the vitality of each cell in the body refuted the existence of a more general vital force such as was often identified with the soul. Moreover, the functioning of each cell had explanatory power even when the exact processes involved were as yet unknown. The authors of an 1899 school textbook, for example, concluded, "Thus we see that the health of our bodies depends on the nourishment and health of each separate cell. If we burn our hands, some of the cells are destroyed, and those lying near go to work to form new cellular tissue to take their place."[26]

By the end of the nineteenth century, the idea of the independence of the cell had developed substantially. The most spectacular extension was the germ theory of disease and the accompanying phagocyte theory, in which writers, now under the influence of Darwinism, pictured microscopic units locked in a miniature struggle for existence within the body.[27] By the twentieth century, other elements joined the cells, the germs, and the phagocytes in these internal dramas taking place in everyone's body. In 1916 physiologist J. J. R. MacLeod of Western Reserve, for example, after summarizing the extremely complex and sensitive interactions of physiological elements in the body, characterized the new outlook as one in which attention had shifted from simple physicochemical reductionism to a new reductionism, in which the constituent elements would be the interactions of what MacLeod called "normal" physiological events—the chemical and physical responses of reactive cells—or, as he put it, "the working and interdependence of the various functions which go to make up the normal." Such thinkers as MacLeod did not deny the importance of physics and chemistry, nor did they embrace any sort of vitalism. But they saw that available units, that is to say, units useful in reductionism, existed because there was in living organisms a complexity that could be resolved in terms of the very reactions carried out in the organism—each reaction with a direction or tendency and operating in a rapidly shifting environment. At the same time each reaction in turn constituted part of that environment. In effect, when investigators defined a function (or a "process" or "subsystem"), they had made an explanation.[28]

At first the elements in the new reductionism tended to be cellular, such as the gene, which came in the twentieth century to appear to determine so much of life. But soon particular complex chemicals joined the dynamic forces. By the 1890's bacteriologists were convinced that both chemical elements in the blood and phagocytes were involved in the defense against hostile microbes, and at about the same time other substances appeared on the scene, substances that could explain an enormous array of

physiological events. The most conspicuous of these chemical units were the hormones and vitamins, each of which seemed to have a function, a target, and some regulatory mechanism based on other units.

Finally, as Robert E. Kohler, Jr., points out, when attention shifted in the early twentieth century from protoplasm to enzymes in the cells, a new term came into use, namely, biochemistry. Moreover, people sometimes spoke at first of "dynamic biochemistry," and even as the explicit word "dynamic" was dropped, the word "biochemistry" continued to carry the connotation of units in dynamic relationship with one another.[29]

The nervous system held a central place in this new dynamic atomicity, both because of the supposed integrative functions of nervous system elements and the continued fascination with biological determinism of human events. With the rise of the neurone theory in the 1890's, each nerve cell came to have an independent existence, with a significance greater than just any cell because it might make a much more significant, or possibly original, contribution to the whole system. Soon reflexes were recognized as physiological units, and, of course, then, conditioned reflexes. It was not enough, complained a biochemist in 1928, for him to be a chemical, a mechanical, and, finally, an electrical engineer; he would ultimately also have to be a psychologist to make a full explanation of life processes. So far had functional units developed by that time. Indeed, when in 1912 psychologist Shepherd Ivory Franz wrote explicitly about the "new phrenology" of brain localization, he criticized localizers not only because they were not clear about what localization meant but also because "mental processes" and "mental states"— the new units of the twentieth century—were just not mechanical enough to be localized.[30]

Around the turn of the twentieth century, then, thinkers who talked about dissociation had not only conventional mechanistic association theory on which to draw but a pattern of thinking in which the functional units of the human machine each had an independent existence and purpose of their own; the implied anthropomorphism in this description is true to the language thinkers used, as, for example, transparently, in the term multiple personality. Moreover, neither function nor purpose was under the control of the organism, whether animal, or man with a soul. Nor was the organism— or human—aware except derivatively of the battles of the germ and white blood cell or the urgent messages of the hormones. When, then, psychological elements became dissociated, they took on significance because, commonly, well-informed and technically trained people already tended to think in terms of a dynamic atomicity. Indeed, the connection between medical background and interest in dynamic psychological thinking in the United States has been remarked on frequently. Perhaps on another occasion I can point out further in concrete detail how in fact physicians and scientists who among their peers were distinctive for their interest in dynamic psychiatry or psychology had earlier taken a remarkable and conspicuous interest in the

germ theory of disease and in chemical determinants. For the time being I shall simply mention Stephen Y. Wilkerson's recent vivid case history of James J. Putnam of Boston.[31]

To underline the connection between dynamic atomicity and dissociation, let me cite one particularly homely example, namely, Worcester, McComb, and Coriat's famous 1908 book, *Religion and Medicine*. To illustrate dissociation, they used an independent group of memories such as would constitute a posthypnotic suggestion. And when they wished to account for the effects of certain associative phenomena (at that time frequently characterized after Bernheim as "suggestion"), the three authors appealed to physiological knowledge. In the case of "somatic changes" and dissociation in hysteria, they observed:

> It is obvious that effects of this character point to a psychic cause. . . . It is equally evident that this mind functions otherwise than our ordinary waking consciousness, for not only are its activities unattended by a sense of effort and conscious attention which characterizes the latter, but it operates in a field whither consciousness cannot follow it, attaining its results through the instrumentality of the sympathetic nervous system, the unstriped muscles, vaso-motors, glands, etc., which lie outside the sphere of consciousness and over which conscious volition has no control. Moreover, it is to be remembered that these phenomena take place not as the result of mechanical nerve stimulation, but by suggestion.[32]

This suggestion, of course, operated through association.

One ultimate product of this kind of thinking was the "complex"—a dissociated group of memories that influenced thinking and behavior in a very distinctive way because of the emotion tied to them. Another was, naturally, as I have suggested, the multiple personality, in which a whole personality, again, with its own purposes, influenced the person. (And I shall not here explore the striking parallel of belief in individualism with belief in the individual existence of functional units in physiology and psychology.)

Finally, the great interest in instincts in the early twentieth century provided still another obvious version of this same type of independent unit. Instinct theorists suggested that inside the organism were drives, each one aimed in some direction or another and opposed by other drives and still other physiological constraints. So the instinct psychologists, such as William McDougall, commanded audiences conditioned not by mechanical models but by patterns out of the new reductionism of dynamic atomicity.

By the twentieth century, the very idea of mind was no longer equivalent to the notion of some sort of unity in a person—much less the spirituality of a soul. "Mind" had ceased to be a surrogate for a unified and responsible person. In psychologist James R. Angell's textbook of psychology, for exam-

ple, a relatively conservative document, Angell explicity disclaimed the soul, because it implied, he said, "something above and beyond the thoughts and feelings." But Angell went on also to disclaim similarly "the science of mind," because "the word *mind* ordinarily implies a certain continuity, unity, and personality, which is, indeed, characteristic of normal human beings; but which may, for all we can see, be wholly lacking in certain unusual psychical experiences."[33] Secularization, in short, did not save the soul, and, as I have already suggested, the more adventurous thinkers who worked with ideas of dissociation went much further than Angell in disbelieving the unity of the mind.

Over several decades, ideas of dissociation evolved in both the technical and popular literature of American medicine and psychology, especially through interest in hypnosis and allied phenomena. It has not been my task here to trace the way in which this happened. Rather, my object has been to suggest briefly the context of ideas that permitted the concept of dissociation to rise and flourish. But let me cite just one turn-of-the-century technical work to illustrate the pertinence to dissociation of my account of the way that Americans came to utilize the idea of a fragmented soul or mind. The example is a 1904 book by Boris Sidis and Simon P. Goodhart, *Multiple Personality*. The two authors not only employed physical science models with "constituent elements" and the "freedom of the individual elements" but equated "dissociated systems" with "neurone systems." However constrained their dynamic scheme, dissociation was part and parcel of their whole way of viewing nature as well as mind, and they, like other well-informed Americans, thought in terms of dynamic atomicity.[34]

As I indicated at the beginning, I have not mentioned a number of other aspects of American thought that were involved in ideas about dissociation. None seems to me to compare in fundamental importance and relevance with the fragmenting of the soul. Let me note for illustrative purposes the heredity-environment controversies of the late nineteenth and early twentieth centuries.[35] These controversies were of substantial importance in shaping some of the details in various thinkers' ideas, but dissociationists could come down on either side of the nature-nurture debate. Sidis and Goodhart, for example, employed the traditional European notion from Charcot and Janet that physical, that is, nervous system, degeneration was a precondition for dissociation to occur. Others came to believe that environmental occurrences—akin to hypnotism—sufficed to initiate the splitting off of psychological units. But in either case what dissociation most basically involved was the destruction of the unity of the person's thinking and willing.

The immediate successor to the first specific ideas of dissociation was, as I have already suggested, a widespread belief in determination of thought and action in which the determiners were not known to a person's consciousness. In the early twentieth century, American thinkers came to be thoroughly familiar with the idea of independent "hidden motives" in a per-

son, motives that, like germs and phagocytes, were locked in mortal combat to determine what would happen in the organism. Of course, throughout the twentieth century, the idea of hidden motives had consequences for both intellectual and social developments about which historians are still writing.[36]

It remains to be observed that the traditional notion of the conscious, unitary, and even spiritual soul did not die out immediately. As late as 1908, for example, a writer in a popular magazine, Frank Marshall White, described New York psychiatrist Frederick Peterson's psychogalvanic version of the Jungian word association test as a "soul machine." Although the term "complex" appeared in the article, the writer never did employ the idea of dynamic, possibly conflicting psychological elements; in his view, the subconscious revealed by the machine was still an integral part of the person whom the "soul" represented.[37]

But such examples of persistence of the traditional soul became increasingly unusual among educated Americans, not to mention scientists. The best evidence of how much had changed is the birth of personality theory in the 1930's, explicitly a reaction against the way that scientific psychologists had fragmented the person, a reaction against reductionism. Gordon Allport, the author of a classic pioneer work in the field, for instance, stressed the individuality of the person, but he ended up with a definition of personality that was right out of dynamic atomicity: "Personality is the dynamic organization within the individual of those psychophysical systems that determine his unique adjustments to his environment." Because of Allport's stress on the individual, indeed, the self, this unifying personality concept may have been a late-model, secularized version of the early nineteenth-century soul, but clearly the dynamic elements in it were a world away from traditional faculties.[38] It might be hard to see even the ghosts of phrenological propensities in the new definition, but the concept of independent elements of thought and impulse was clear indeed. How much, in turn, the 1930's definition owed to specific ideas of dissociation, the product of the process of reductionism, I leave to my colleagues to suggest, since it is outside the scope of this chapter.

In 1910, William James concluded that in philosophy and psychology, "souls have worn out both themselves and their welcome, that is the plain truth."[39] His efforts in the face of that truth, like the efforts of others of his generation, involved attempting to salvage moral responsibility from the complex and mechanistic universe that reductionistic thinking had suggested. Analysis of that complexity into dissociated elements helped make sense of what might have appeared irrational in terms of the older psychology of the soul.

The theme of dynamic atomicity in psychological thinking appears again in this next chapter, in which I extend the story of the mind-body problem farther into the twentieth century and note the European background more explicitly. Turn-of-the-century writers knew the standard philosophical categories, and they often viewed new developments in terms of conventional formulations, of which the most relevant, and often most distorting, was the classic discussion of soma and psyche. Yet findings in neurophysiology, psychology, and other sciences continued to force thinkers to search for new units of reductionism and so transform the mind-body problem.

The mind-body problem also serves to suggest that the psychological and neurosciences went through a transitional period in approximately the 1930's—the cutoff point of this next chapter. And the very fact that chronological divisions are possible shows that a substantial consensus existed among thinkers on at least the general strategy with which to approach mind-body issues. Meantime the importance of behaviorism and psychoanalysis in the early twentieth century—subjects of subsequent chapters— became evident. The significance of both can be understood only as the transformations in the Anglo-American concern with somatic correlates of thinking are kept in mind.

CHAPTER TWO

The Mind-Body Problem in the Early Twentieth Century

During the second half of the twentieth century, scientific advances in a number of areas revived a lively interest in an ancient philosophical concern, the mind-body problem.[1]

While writers in the very recent era are often aware of the classic formulations of the soma-psyche debate, they are often unaware of aspects of the more recent history of this problem, and ghosts from those days still haunt current discussions. The entire history of the problem as well as modern concerns become clearer in the light of changes that took place in the early twentieth century. Observers at that time and later historians have both provided materials, a sampling of which suggests the validity and usefulness of a clarifying periodization.

"Early twentieth century" is the best designation for the years between about 1890 and the 1930's that constituted this distinct era in the history of ideas about the mind-body problem. The era was defined by changes in science rather than in philosophy, and the terminal date in particular represents the confluence of a number of independent developments in disparate lines of thinking. The period began when neurophysiologists invoked the concept of the neurone and the synapse to complete the nineteenth-century sensorimotor model of the nervous system. The era ended with the rise of personality theory and biochemistry.

"The Mind-Body Problem in the Early Twentieth Century" is reprinted from *Perspectives in Biology and Medicine*, 20 (1977), 271–284, with the kind permission of the University of Chicago Press. ©1977 By The University of Chicago. All rights reserved.

Work on this paper was supported in part by NIH grant LM 02539 from the National Library of Medicine. The paper was originally presented as a lecture in the Allan McLane Hamilton Seminar Series at the Cornell–New York Hospital Medical Center, June 1975.

In the early twentieth century, a time of intellectual flowering in many parts of the Western world, professional philosophers provided little outstanding metaphysical, epistemological, or logical work on the mind-body problem. The periodic *Psychological Bulletin* summaries of the world literature on the subject, for example, revealed an aridity that was surprising, particularly because of the continued inclusion of psychology under chairs or departments of philosophy in many places in both Europe and America. The basic models of parallelism, interactionism, and double-aspect theory persisted without serious modification. Exciting events in medicine and physiology effected no substantial changes in the views of philosophical psychologists. When the American Philosophical Association set the mind-body as the theme of the 1916 meetings, for example, participants expected and witnessed lively debate. Yet afterward, when some weeks had passed so that cool judgment could prevail, the meeting reporter, Albert G. A. Balz, concluded that the entire effort had produced but "familiar notions in a new garb." "The recasting of philosophical problems in the language of science," he noted, "is not a solution of the problem."[2]

Scientists who discussed the relationship between soma and psyche did tend to use the philosopher's traditional formulations, even when attempting innovation.[3] But in fact formal and programmatic discussions tended to disappear from the scientific literature soon after the turn of the century, even in Europe, where intellectuals self-consciously used traditional philosophical categories and took traditional stances. In this physical-psychical area of thinking, professional philosophers were not speaking to problems that scientific investigators faced.

Among the philosophers themselves, the mind-body question was engendering an untoward and increasing amount of confusion.[4] Major publications such as the 1911 book, *Body and Mind*,[5] by the English physician-psychologist William McDougall had kept interest in the subject alive. McDougall, however, was but a British representative of a number of thinkers led by Hans Driesch who tended to confuse the mind-body problem with the classical Continental debate of vitalism versus materialism. The attempt to retain a soul in either psychology or physiology was in fact largely ignored by scientists as the years rolled on. The philosophers, however, often took neovitalism seriously, and they were moreover further confused by new experiments and literature introducing behaviorism. The behaviorists questioned the reality, validity, or usefulness of consciousness. Indeed, followers of this new schema published research and theory that essentially questioned the existence of what most people had thought was the "mind" part of the mind-body problem.

Since professional philosophers were more bemused than helpful, the new and exciting contributions in the early twentieth century came instead from scientists, primarily in the areas of neurophysiology and psychology. But once again there was a group being eclipsed, in this case scientists who

were filling in and extending the paradigm that was new at the turn of the century. Neither they nor their colleagues could see that in the future their work would be used in ways that they did not anticipate. These losers were investigators in classical neuroanatomy (and a few aspects of neurophysiology). Thinkers in all relevant fields tended to assume that the scientific findings offered merely detailed confirmation of earlier general views. Only in the 1930's and after did some experts begin to sense the theoretical implications of parts of post–World War I neuroanatomy and closely associated physiological work.[6] Meanwhile the shifting of attention in the twentieth century away from precisely the area that had generated the greatest interest in the nineteenth constitutes powerful evidence that the new century did indeed bring fresh viewpoints.

Just at the end of the nineteenth century, a number of workers suggested that nerve cells were independent units, both anatomically and functionally. The units came to be called neurones; the connectors between the neurones, synapses. The neurone and synapse theories represented the completion of the sensorimotor model of nervous-system functioning initiated by Bell's anatomical and Magendie's physiological distinction between efferent and afferent nerves.[7] The picture of the sensorimotor mechanism was complete as the twentieth century opened—the triumph of microscope technology, experiment, and an often considerable enthusiasm for materialism. The picture offered by such workers was described, with only some exaggeration, by C. D. Broad in 1925 in this way:

> They think of the mind as sitting somewhere in a hole in the brain, surrounded by telephones. And they think of the afferent disturbance as coming to an end at one of these telephones and there affecting the mind. The mind is then supposed to respond by sending an [efferent] impulse down another of these telephones. As no such hole, with afferent nerves stopping at its walls and [efferent] nerves starting from them, can be found, they conclude that the mind can play no part in the transaction. . . . The mistake is to confuse a gap in an explanation with a spatio-temporal gap, and to argue from the absence of the latter to the absence of the former.[8]

Despite such criticism, workers in the field were excited, and while the neurone theory remained controversial for some years, the model was so useful that opposition tended to vanish.[9] The reflex now had a firm anatomical basis and could serve as the fundamental unit of thinking. In 1928 clinician R. J. A. Berry of Melbourne summarized the new materialism in a negative dictum: *"No neurone, no mind."*[10]

Shortly after the turn of the century, in 1906, the English physiologist C. S. Sherrington made a synthesis of the new neurophysiological viewpoint in his classic, *The Integrative Action of the Nervous System*. Sherrington de-

scribed how developed and compounded constellations of reflex arcs gave an animal organism unity by integrating the actions of the organism's organs and processes. There were mechanical and chemical agencies with integrative functions, said Sherrington,

> but the integrative action of the nervous system is different from these, in that its agent is not mere intercellular material, as in connective tissue, nor the transference of material in mass, as by the circulation; it works through living lines of stationary cells along which it despatches waves of physico-chemical disturbance, and these act as releasing forces in distant organs where they finally impinge. Hence it is not surprising that nervous integration has the feature of relatively high *speed*, a feature peculiarly distinctive of integrative correlation in animals as contrasted with that of plants, the latter having no nervous system in the ordinary sense of the word.[11]

What Sherrington was describing was later recognized in part with the term "feedback," which made both mechanism and materialism credible in the face of very great complexity.

Despite the complexity glimpsed by Sherrington and his followers, the enthusiasm generated by the combination of histological and neurological evidence led a number of workers to believe that they could, or were just about to, demonstrate the material basis for every type of mental functioning, not only in reflexes but in localization of cerebral activity as well. According to such eminent scientists as the pre–World War I Berlin neurologist K. Brodmann, for example, the principle of brain localization of mental operations had been established, and only the details needed to be worked out.[12] Presumably, for each mental function a particular area could be found, and after each innervation a material trace would remain.

Rather than confirmation, however, the new century brought increasing doubt. By 1914 another neurophysiologist was saying that practical considerations forced workers to continue to speak in terms of localization of some functions, but in fact so many anomalous exceptions had appeared that all generalizations seemed to be undergoing modification. "Cerebral relations," he wrote, "are not becoming complex in the sense that more areas with definite functions are being discovered, but in the sense that many functional variations are being recorded," especially, he said, in cases of brain lesion.[13] By 1929 Karl Lashley could summarize his own and others' conclusions:

> There is no evidence to support this belief in identity of nervous elements. On the contrary, it is very doubtful if the same neurons or synapses are involved even in two similar reactions to the same stimulus. Our data seem to prove that the structural elements are relatively

> unimportant for integration and that the common elements must be some sort of dynamic patterns, determined by the relations or ratios among the parts of the system and not by the specific neurons activated. If this be true, we cannot, on the basis of our present knowledge of the nervous system, set any limit to the kinds or amount of transfer possible or to the sort of relations which may be directly recognized.[14]

The idea that brain functioning was not easily reducible to the reflex arc and, especially, localized cells had many facets. One was that, as the century progressed, scientific work in both psychology and physiology tended to emphasize function as opposed to structure. Another was evidence that some workers might try to discard the idea of a material basis for mind altogether. And finally, since the material elements were no longer clear, the mental elements too appeared no longer as viable as they once had.

The psychologists, the scientists of the mind, seemed curiously enough to be the group most affected by this crisis in anatomy and physiology. For decades most psychologists had been associationists and had equated the reflex arc with an association process.[15] Now in 1912 Shepherd Ivory Franz, the leading American psychologist working in neurophysiology, could assert that he was not certain that "all of the mental processes are associational."[16] Models of thinking other than the associational had been rare indeed until Gestalt came along in the first decades of the century. But even then the Gestaltists were interested in finding brain mechanisms, mechanisms that they hoped would correspond to the relatively complex concepts of fields and insights introduced by that school of thinking (Goldstein's work[17] is the best-known example).

The changing knowledge about the nervous system had affected psychology in two ways. First, the neural unit, the reflex, attracted an extraordinary amount of attention among investigators of the mind. Some, such as the Russian physiologist I. P. Pavlov, attempted to study the basic unit, the reflex as such. Others such as the introspectionists tried to find units of observation in thinking that corresponded to the neurological elements. These introspectionists therefore concentrated on simple perceptions in hopes of staying as close as possible to neurophysiology. Much of what was developed in the twentieth century as self-conscious innovation—like Gestalt and behaviorism—represented at least in part a revolt against being forced to restrict one's studies to the simplest elements when in fact thinking and behavior are extremely complicated.

Still another consequence of new ways of understanding nervous functioning grew out of the relationship between psychology and neurology/neurophysiology. For two generations after Bain, psychologists had taken great interest in the developing neurophysiological model and the organic events that they believed corresponded to psychological events. When new psychological theories developed, very often the inventors of the new systems

or concepts felt constrained to invent new neuroanatomical or physiological processes corresponding to the psychology—somatic processes neither provable nor disprovable but functioning as myth. In 1922 J. R. Kantor of Indiana University summarized somewhat disdainfully the problems that such mythologists had brought into psychology: "Among the conditions presumably explained by the neural apparatus is the manner in which the 'psychic,' whether conceived as stuff or process, can operate in a factual world. And so the nervous system is taken to be (1) the tangible counterpart of the intangible psychic; or (2) it serves merely to fill gaps (subconscious and association theories) between the functioning of mental (awareness) processes; (3) or further, it is made to operate as the complete substitution for consciousness in cases where no awareness is presumed to be present." [18]

Not all thinkers fell into this trap of positing fictitious neurological substrates. One type of psychologist flourishing in the early twentieth century was an investigator who in effect attempted to avoid the mind-body problem. The most notable of these evaders were the behaviorists, but many others who stressed a biological approach to psychology and psychiatry shared the same basic strategy. In part the biological approach involved a shift in emphasis to the environment of the organism, as opposed to the internal processes of the organism. The result was to focus upon what E. Stanley Abbot of McLean Hospital in 1916 called the person's "total reaction to his total environment." [19] The psychological unit, in short, became the reaction, but included within the "total reaction" was a great deal of the physiology of the organism as well as what might be called mental.

Like others, the biologically oriented continued to base their thinking on traditional neuroanatomical and neurophysiological models. These were, of course, biological models, but the holism to which Abbot and others referred tended to make behaviorists and their colleagues think at the neural level in terms of reflex but at the behavioral level in terms of the more complex response or reaction with complications such as those suggested by Sherrington.[20] While thus caught in the dilemma of building upon the reflex very simple psychological units, still the biological psychologists working on human psychology tended to follow the paradigm of workers in the field of animal behavior. In practice this meant using the model of stimulus and response, which did leave out the intervening psychical apparatus and emphasize the environment and the behavior, in the manner of experimenters with infrahuman, nonverbal organisms.

Most of the behaviorists were at heart physicalistic reductionists, like the generality of other scientists, and they continued to be distracted by the belief that the reflex unit promised a chemical/physical explanation of life and of thinking. They found the work of Pavlov and especially of Bekterev in conditioning reflexes a substantial step toward reducing mind to body.[21] Pavlov himself, of course, always believed in "higher mental processes," as he called them, but many of the biologically minded investigators retained their

associationist assumptions and continued to find the reflex arc and conditioning but a physiological equivalent of association of ideas. With the biological viewpoint, however, responses or reaction and stimulus or environment could be substituted for ideas in the associationist schema—thus practically eliminating the mind from the mind-body problem. But the erosion was not so easily effected.

The behaviorists, including the original behaviorist, John B. Watson,[22] joined various kinds of mentalists in going beyond the conventional associationist model and continuing to utilize one type of the influence of the body on the mind, namely, the instincts or instinctual drives. Three approaches to the instinct problem flourished, but what was most significant initially was the fact that the highly intellectualistic association psychology that dominated late-nineteenth-century psychology, or even faculty psychology, no longer sufficed in the new century to explain mental events.

The revived interest in instincts grew not out of psychology but out of cytology and a changing theory of heredity. After the work of August Weismann and particularly after the rediscovery of Mendelian genetics and the innovations of T. H. Morgan, scientists understood that what humans inherited was both fixed and definite. Some of the inheritance was understood to be structural—one's constitution—but another part was supposed to be dynamic—the instincts. By and large the instincts hypothesized by the various theorists were assumed to be adaptive animal traits with survival value. These instincts influenced behavior. They were inherited by way of some somatic mechanism, as part of the body, and yet they changed the course of a person's thought and conduct. Once brought into science, the instincts were a part of the mind-body problem, for it was necessary to determine by what mechanism the instinctual part of the organism influenced mind and behavior.[23]

The best-known theorist of instinct at first was McDougall, who, as noted above, also wrote explicitly, but unfortunately irrelevantly, on the mind-body problem. McDougall cited expressions of emotions as evidence that human behavior was influenced by instincts—instincts that he defined by the social effects that the instincts produced. While he assumed that instincts went through the regular neurophysiological channels, he did not try to explain what he called the "psycho-physical" processes. His problem, he believed, was to correct the work of traditional psychologists who ignored motivated and impulsive behavior. Although never eschewing introspection, McDougall in fact concentrated upon behavior, and his basic evidence came from the actions of animals and children.[24]

The behaviorists utilized instinct in a much more restricted way, as suggested before, in terms of specific repeated responses that could be understood to be consistent with reflex reductionism. Such innate responses were easily integrated with habits and emotional responses (also innate) to form complex human behavior as understood by the behaviorists.

The most successful instinct theorist of the twentieth century was Sigmund Freud.[25] He was also the most precise in using instinct as a nexus between mind and body, and his care in separating the psychical from the physiological constituted one of the strengths of his theory. Freud tried to avoid altogether any neurophysiological complications in his psychological schema, leaving his neurological model of the 1890's unpublished. Instead, he wrote about the "psychical apparatus" and tried, with considerable success, to maintain a purely psychological level of discourse. The only point at which the body touched the Freudian mind was in the somatic needs that provided "internal stimuli," which Freud conceptualized sometimes as the sources of a person's psychic energy, but at all times as instinctual drives. For each instinctual drive, Freud stipulated that there existed somatic sites, sources, and needs. For the rest of his portrait of mental functioning, he did not constrain himself with anatomical structure, although implicitly the correlation of association connectionism with the sensorimotor neurophysiological model affected him as well as his contemporaries.[26]

The instinct theorists all tended to introduce emotions as one of the mediate phenomena between body and mind. In McDougall's instinct theory, emotions were central; and Watson, as has been mentioned, felt that emotional reactions were in practice indistinguishable from instinctual reactions. In Freud's psychology, emotions signaled the presence of somatic pressure in the form of an instinctual drive. With each theorist, emotion represented a potent phenomenon through which the soma could affect the psyche. And as the twentieth century advanced, the claims of emotional factors on scientists' attention grew because of new discoveries. As Watson said in 1919, "We have tried to connect emotional activity with physiological processes because it seems that such formulations are now practical and no longer purely speculative."[27] What had impressed Watson and many other thinkers all over the world was physiological work on internal secretions and the autonomic nervous system.

The emphasis on the body at the expense of mind—indeed, the annihilation of mind—noted in the behaviorists, especially, reached a high point in the endocrine enthusiasm that developed in the early twentieth century. By means of anatomical, pathological, and chemical studies during the preceding century, the stage had been set for what became in some parts of medicine and popular thinking a fad, especially in the 1920's, when there was much excitement about therapeutic successes of various endocrine products.

Most of the endocrine glands had been identified many decades earlier, and Berthold, who worked with rooster testes, and others had shown that the presence or absence of glands could have dramatic effects, even though for some years the mechanisms involved were not understood. By the late nineteenth century, the gross pathology of myxedema and Addison's disease was well known, and in 1889 Brown-Séquard initiated therapeutic efforts

with a report of his own self-treatment. Where the instincts of Berthold's roosters had been affected by the presence and absence of testes, now Brown-Séquard reported that testicular substance changed human sexual feelings— essentially and effectively equating man with beasts. What Brown-Séquard instigated was, first, intense interest, for he was already 72 years old; and, second, the full-blown doctrine of internal secretions, namely that each endocrine body secreted into the blood specific substances necessary for normal functioning and even life. During the early twentieth century, the doctrine of internal secretions affected fundamentally ideas in both physiology and psychology.[28]

Although most workers in the field of endocrinology described the organic changes caused by endocrine substances, such writers tended to insist on the importance of internal secretions in mental processes also. Psychotic states accompanying gross dysfunction, as in thyroid conditions, had long been known,[29] and Brown-Séquard made scientists aware of possible influence on normal instinctual drives. By 1920 S. W. Bandler, a New York gynecologist and one of the enthusiasts, could include a great deal more: "The physician should be able and must be able to understand the difference between normality and abnormality in the innumerable deviations of body, mind and psyche associated with and due to the ductless glands. They are the underlying factors in heredity; they have to do with growth and development of body and mind; they have to do with instincts and emotions; they have to do with normal and abnormal psychic and mental states."[30] Even more sophisticated endocrinologists of the next decade such as Walter Timme, the Columbia neurologist, believed that endocrines greatly influenced both physical and "psychic make-up," that is, both constitution and personality.[31]

Partly the endocrine enthusiasts' arguments rested on simple empiricism: Certain conditions brought about certain behavior. Thus, like the behaviorists, the endocrinologists avoided the mind-body problem. Bandler, for example, utilized clinical evidence—case histories—to support his point of view. Other evidence for the influence of internal secretions involved experiments upon laboratory animals and was therefore necessarily entirely behavioral.[32]

But the enthusiasm for endocrines grew also out of the same underlying materialism that had inspired so many neurophysiologists for generations. Following up sensational accounts of the effects of adrenin, R. G. Hoskins, a leading U.S. experimental physiologist, for example, spent much of the 1920's testing whether internal secretions made experimental animals more vigorous than those without such secretions.[33] Even in the absence of detailed information about the precise mechanisms involved, such data were infinitely more satisfying to the hard-headed or tough-minded than, say, Freud's theoretical construct of psychical energy.

Much of the excitement in physiology was jointly the product of endocrinology and of new work on the autonomic nervous system, a term intro-

duced just at the beginning of the century.[34] The autonomic nervous system was generally understood to operate without the intervention of will and even, in part, without consciousness; it was therefore the site of complicated nervous system activity that could hardly be described as mind. Once again, the basic unit in terms of which investigators understood their material was the reflex arc; and once again, expanding the importance of the autonomic nervous system necessarily diminished the area in which the mental, properly speaking, could be understood to operate.

In the early decades of the century, a number of very clever scientists greatly advanced knowledge of the autonomic nervous system, particularly by means of severing one or another segment of the system and then observing what happened.[35] The most remarkable findings were those reported and summarized by Cannon, an American physiologist. Cannon made a number of experiments showing the physiological changes that occurred in animals when presumably hungry and, again, when stimulated to what were interpreted as emotional reactions. Among other conclusions that he drew were that hunger consisted basically of stomach contractions, as if to validate Freud's model of instinctual drive with a somatic base, and that the physiological accompaniments of strong emotion were undifferentiated, regardless of the emotion. In both cases, the primacy of the body by way of emotions and instincts tended to suggest in effect that any mental contents were at best mere epiphenomena and in any case perhaps inaccurate. And yet what Cannon was advocating was in fact the view that mental stimulation was of unrealized importance in physiological functioning, especially in autonomic nervous system processes. Indeed he started his classic volume by citing the similar work of the Russian Pavlov, who found perceptual stimuli that had somatic effects.[36]

The whole burden of this physiological work, then, was to show that, while the body, by means of gland secretions and nervous system, could affect mind, still the mind—or at least environmental stimuli—by means of innervation of the autonomic nervous apparatus could have the most profound effects upon the body, thus reversing the reductionistic belief that body affects mind. A fair amount of consternation followed the publication of the researches of such physiologists as Pavlov and Cannon, whose findings had to be integrated into a number of belief systems.

To begin with, theories of emotion had to be reviewed and revised. The James-Lange theory did not long survive evidence that, rather than emotion following bodily changes, endocrine secretion was instigated—at least sometimes—by sympathetic nervous system innervations. Moreover, the long-standing interest of turn-of-the-century scientists and public in the action of mind on body was stimulated. Mesmerism and faith healing now appeared to have a firmer material basis, and just where emotional involvement in illness might stop was uncertain. The popular vogue of New Thought—essentially the power of positive thinking—received no discouragement from

materialists such as the surgeon George W. Crile, who argued the clinical applicability of new knowledge about the emotions, using in medical practice both emotional states to affect endocrine functions and thyroid extract to alter emotions.[37]

Clearly the definition of mind itself tended to change. Traditional thinkers could still speak in terms of perception, cognition, feeling, and will; but the new material considerations and details and the new complexity of interacting factors were leading to a fresh view of humans and their mental and physical functioning. Not the least of the innovations was the emergence of what came to be known as psychosomatic medicine,[38] which has often been traced to Freud's idea of conversion hysteria.

In all of these shifts, adaptations, and discoveries, what started out in 1900 as a relatively straightforward problem with a standard history and niche in Western thought took on a most distressing protean quality. Both mind and body were being transformed in the early twentieth century. Under pressure from behaviorism and dynamics, psychology was, as wits of the day observed, losing consciousness; indeed, they continued, in the face of behaviorism psychology was in danger of losing its mind altogether. This tendency to deny mentation or at least to deny the possibility of studying mentation directly or scientifically represented a generally successful evasion of the mind-body problem. Yet the main thrust of the new view of mind was to introduce and emphasize affective determinants, either by means of the instincts or chemical and reflex actions. In a time when such phenomena as mental illness and the unreasonable conduct of the leaders of civilization in World War I seemed to demand explanation, such a shift in the study of man to irrational determinants was both appropriate and expectable. One of the great discoveries of Freud, as the premier Swiss psychiatrist Bleuler pointed out, was to detach affectivity from specific ideas in the psychical apparatus.[39] Mind, therefore, in the early twentieth century could be understood to consist of at least, and perhaps primarily, mobile emotions acting on their own and possibly, and perhaps secondarily, depending on the writer, of the traditional constituents, ideas or mental processes.

At the same time, the body aspect of the mind-body problem was changing too, for, as the English physiologist J. S. Haldane observed in 1913, the central nervous system was no longer the center of interest in science.[40] Instead, the autonomic nervous system and the endocrines attracted the attention of the scientists who were interested in the mind-body problem. They had not for the most part changed from the physicalistic reductionism that led to the dramatic progress in nineteenth-century physiology. Only the focus of work in the field had changed.

The most important change, however, was the way in which twentieth-century workers abandoned the simple mechanism of nineteenth-century reductionism in favor of a complex systems model. Taking Claude Bernard's neglected idea of an internal milieu, such investigators as Cannon now spoke

of the homeostasis maintained among the many elements of the body—elements only recently recognized as such.[41]

It was just after the turn of the century that the new atomic model gained hegemony in the biological sciences—and obviously in a way parallel to the physical sciences.[42] The germ, the gene, the instinct, the affect, and finally the neurone and the endocrine—each one operated independently within the body. Sherrington's attempt to suggest mechanisms by which the nervous system regulates itself was imitated by other workers who tried to establish the methods by which the internal secretions stay in balance and, indeed, how all of the various systems and elements interact with and counteract each other. Mechanical materialism was replaced by what Garland Allen[43] has described as dynamic materialism—a system of interactions so complex as to suggest that control of the multifarious interchanges is not likely to occur easily or soon. This was an ironical outcome of the research of so many dedicated mechanists.

The most curious part of the story, however, is the conclusion. The era of the early twentieth century came to an end with a tendency of mental and physical functioning to be separated again. On the somatic side, the elemental units were yielding to new techniques and new technologies such as the electron microscope. The endocrine era of therapy and theory, as Diana Long Hall[44] has shown, gave way in the 1930's to the biochemical era, and it was not long before biochemistry was also bringing new life to the study of neuroanatomy and neurophysiology.

The psychological aspects of man went in the opposite direction, away from elementism of all kinds and toward integration of the systems in the flowering of personality theory, again in the 1930's.[45] Building on the earlier work, personality theorists attempted to integrate the psychological processes with the changing external environment of the organism. Not only were the emotions utilized in the new viewpoints, but affect, often in the form of instinctual-drive theory, was integrated with stimulus-response, environmental-learning theories. These developments in the non-somatic aspects of man were fully anticipated by the early-twentieth-century workers discussed above; but with the addition of epigenetic factors in the 1930's, psychology, like physiology, slipped into another era. This more recent period represented by both personality and biochemistry/histology moved the mind-body problem in many ways much closer to the neurobiology of the 1970's than to the exciting scientific discussions of the early twentieth century.

With this intellectual background emphasizing thinkers' refocusing on physiology, behavior, and instinct (as opposed to mentation) and ending with dynamic-atomistic models, it is now possible to move more directly into the cultural influences that fed into behaviorism and psychoanalysis, the dominating innovations of the twentieth century; and this narrative sets the stage for inquiring, in turn, into the impact of behaviorism and psychoanalysis in the United States—and, indeed, in the Western world. Since I first wrote, other historians have continued to mine both the general and specific materials that three or four generations ago shaped mind-body discussions. Kurt Danziger, for example, has explored the ways in which reductionists transformed experimental psychology, and Merle Curti and Hamilton Cravens have each furnished extensive insights and context beyond what appears in foregoing and subsequent chapters here. Laurence D. Smith has even pointed out that by about 1930 the new positivist philosophy helped move the neo-behaviorists in psychology to interact more extensively with sophisticated ideas of being and interaction, and this type of influence was exciting to later generations of investigators.*

New scientific information potentially applicable to mind-body problems has also continued to appear and to demand new perspectives on the history of the relationship. Computer technology and the "cognitive revolution" in psychology, for example, led Karl Pribram to trace the roots of reconceptualizations of mind-brain issues back to the World War I–era positivists and phenomenologists in philosophy as well as the behaviorists important

---

* Kurt Danziger, "The Materialist Repudiation of Wundt," *Journal of the History of the Behavioral Sciences*, 15 (1979), 205–230. Merle Curti, *Human Nature in American Thought: A History* (Madison: University of Wisconsin Press, 1980). Hamilton Cravens, *The Triumph of Evolution: American Scientists and the Heredity-Environment Controversy 1900–1941* (Philadelphia: University of Pennsylvania Press, 1978). Laurence D. Smith, "Psychology and Philosophy: Toward a Realignment, 1905–1925," *Journal of the History of the Behavioral Sciences*, 17 (1981), 28–37; this argument is expanded in Laurence D. Smith, *Behaviorism and Logical Positivism: A Reassessment of the Alliance* (Stanford, CA: Stanford University Press, 1986). The interaction of logical positivism and behaviorism is also explored in K. D. Irani, "Conceptual Changes in the Problem of the Mind-Body Relation," in R. W. Rieber, ed., *Body and Mind: Past, Present, and Future* (New York: Academic Press, 1980), especially pp. 58–63.

in the last chapter and featured in the next.[†] Other scientific discoveries, particularly in the realm of biochemistry, have also contributed to ideas about non-cognitive interactions on some level or another and segmentally. Usually such discussions also still show intellectual continuity with the old instinct theories that are taken up later in this section.

These various technical developments of the second half of the twentieth century facilitated the rebirth of aggressive—if sophisticated—materialistic monism. Scientific and philosophical workers in this renewed tradition of monism tended to ignore the mind-body discussions of the early twentieth century that I described in the previous chapter. Indeed, up until the middle of the century, for reasons that I have indicated, scholars and scientists tended to ignore or evade the entire problem. "For the most part," writes Mario Bunge, "neurophysiologists, psychologists, and philosophers have been either indifferent (or perhaps just cautious), or dualists—like Sherrington, Freud, and Popper. Some recognized the problem but thought it insoluble. Others failed to see it because they had no use for the nervous system: this was the case with behaviorists and psychoanalysts. . . . And some philosophers . . . declared that the mind-body problem was really a pseudoproblem."[‡]

The irony is, of course, that the thinkers of the early twentieth century were in fact laying the foundation for what became the neurosciences—those sciences that gave life to the recent renewal of mind-body concerns. Perhaps in another generation the progenitors, from Sherrington to Cannon and others who flourished in the early twentieth century, will win recognition from descendants who will not be so close to the inspiration provided by those who lived in the decades just after 1900.[§]

Where the earlier behaviorists appeared in mind-body discussions chiefly in a negative role, as thinkers who attempted to bypass the argument about neurological substrates, when the whole

---

[†] Steve Heims, "Encounter of Behavioral Sciences with New Machine-Organism Analogies in the 1940's," *Journal of the History of the Behavioral Sciences*, 11 (1975), 368–373. Karl Pribram, "The Cognitive Revolution and Mind/Brain Issues," *American Psychologist*, 41 (1986), 507–520. See, from another point of view, Howard Gardner, *The Mind's New Science: A History of the Cognitive Revolution* (New York: Basic Books, Inc., 1985).

[‡] Mario Bunge, *The Mind-Body Problem: A Psychobiological Approach* (Oxford: Pergamon Press, 1980), p. 29.

[§] Ibid.

context of behaviorism is considered, the movement turned out to represent major cultural as well as purely intellectual forces. The interplay between culture and psychological investigators reveals that behaviorism embodied a complex set of forces. The importance of behaviorism indeed increased as the cultural ties appeared more multifarious and complicated. In such a situation, where the position and significance of a phenomenon needs clarification, an obvious tactic suggests itself to the historian, namely, seeking beginnings. And, in fact, as with many historical questions, tracing the origins of behaviorism as precisely as possible does clarify the importance of the whole movement.

On the Origins of Behaviorism

In recent years, historians of psychology, in evaluating the significance of the advent of behaviorism early in the twentieth century, have tended to raise their estimate of its importance. Gustav Bergmann, for example, has emphasized the methodological innovations of John B. Watson, founder of behaviorism, while Albert E. Goss has called attention to Watson's theory of verbal mediating responses in language and thought.[1] Such writers diverge considerably not only in the particular emphases that they give behaviorism but in their views of its origins—when it began and what its antecedents were. Earlier writers, particularly, have called into question the role of Watson and his originality.

There has, indeed, been so much controversy about the prehistory of behaviorism that the issues various writers have raised have to be explored before a general history can be written. Having once established when the phenomenon of behaviorism appeared, and who was responsible for its initial form and development, a more momentous question can be taken up, namely, what historical forces behaviorism embodied.

Much light is thrown on the significance of the coming of behaviorism by applying to it Thomas S. Kuhn's sociological model of scientific innovation.[2] Discussions of anticipations of Watson's ideas and of the influences that gave rise to behaviorism take on levels of meaning beyond mere antiquarian and partisan inquiries when predecessors and similarities of conception are fitted into Kuhn's scheme. Precursors as such, according to Kuhn, are symp-

"On the Origins of Behaviorism" is reprinted from the *Journal of the History of the Behavioral Sciences*, 4 (1968), 143–151, with the kind permission of the *Journal of the History of the Behavioral Sciences*.

toms of the gestation of scientific progress. Intellectual influences, he shows, can be detected in the characteristic reactions of the scientific community. In the case of behaviorism, careful chronology and a traditional historical analysis clear up many questions raised by past writers. But beyond the usual analysis, understanding of the significance of behaviorism in the history of psychology—and the behavioral sciences—will be incomplete until the origins of the movement are viewed in a fresh way such as Kuhn's model of innovation provides.

E. G. Boring in his standard history of experimental psychology dates behaviorism from the appearance of Watson's paper, "Psychology as the Behaviorist Views It," which was printed in the *Psychological Review* in 1913.[3] There Watson, a professor of psychology at Johns Hopkins University, and not yet 35, outlined a psychology substantially different from that conventionally accepted. Rejecting the psychophysical associationism that dominated the discipline, Watson called for a psychology that would be "a purely objective experimental branch of natural science," modeled on the physical and biological sciences. The purpose of behavioristic psychology, Watson made clear, was to predict and control behavior. The animal psychologists were already using the objective observation of animal behavior in a controlled environment. Unless human psychology took heed of the methods of these comparative psychologists, said Watson, the behaviorists proposed to extend their work and develop a purely observational experimental human psychology and thus render obsolete introspective psychology with its categories of mental elements and functions.

Watson was not just criticizing but was offering a constructive program that he had thought out in considerable detail. While he accepted associative learning as a pattern observable in all animals, he suggested that it is best to view the so-called higher thought processes as implicit movements rather than to attempt to translate them into images and similar types of mental contents. By and large, Watson's manifesto included all of the later program of behaviorism, although one of the most important parts of it, his insistence on controlling not only the immediate environment but the entire development of the experimental animal, has seldom had the attention that it deserves.[4]

Despite the fact that Watson was both explicit and clear in explaining what he was about, over the years accounts of the beginnings of behaviorism have varied widely. A number of commentators have disagreed with Boring's contention that this date of 1913, the time of the printed appearance of Watson's manifesto, signaled the appearance of behaviorism. That paper itself, or some version of it, first made a marked impression on psychologists when a number of them heard it read in at least two and possibly more public presentations in the New York area in the fall and winter of 1912–1913, primarily as one of a series of lectures at Columbia University. This lecture presentation was too close to publication—within a few months—to gener-

ate a meaningful distinction between the spoken and printed word. But a number of commentators have asserted that Watson's views were well known in the profession much earlier—that he had, for example, expressed them in 1908 in a seminar at Chicago before he left for Johns Hopkins (Gardner Murphy, undocumented); in a lecture before the psychology department at Yale sometime in 1908 (Paul Hanly Furfey, 1928); and so on.[5] Watson himself traced his ideas back as far as 1904.[6]

The date of Watson's formulation of behaviorism becomes of considerable moment because, despite Bergmann and Goss, most writers about behaviorism have attempted to show that Watson was not original in his ideas. Critics of Watsonian behaviorism have indeed tried to discredit it with the ancient argument that it really was not new anyway.[7] E. B. Titchener of Cornell, chief spokesman for the orthodox experimental psychology of his day, led the attack along this line immediately, in 1913. By the use of striking quotations, Titchener traced Watson's idea of an observational rather than introspective approach back to Comte and Cournot, both of whom had published programmatic statements more than half a century earlier. Real experimental psychologists, Titchener pointed out, had long ago and for good reason consciously rejected this traditional type of objective approach, and Watson was, therefore, naive in believing that he had discovered a new and better method of solving the problems of psychology. (Titchener asserted that behaviorism was simply not relevant to psychology and made any differences primarily a matter of definition anyway.)[8] Other critics of behaviorism tried to avoid confronting it by asserting—patronizingly—that it was but another version of one side in a classical debate in philosophy, usually the materialistic or mind-body controversies, so that Watson's views required no special attention but could be dismissed by allusion to standard arguments in philosophy.

Critics of behaviorism missed the point that Watson's originality did not consist of simply his conception of verbal mediating responses, his interest in social control, and his application of the methods and concepts of animal psychology to humans. Watson combined these elements into a synthesis, the whole of which was greater than its parts. André Tilquin, a systematic student of behaviorism, has shown that a whole panoply of "postulates" underlies it, each one with its own set of antecedents. Understandably, then, commentators could pick out any aspect of behaviorism, assert its fundamental nature, and trace its history: materialistic monism, adaptation, the reflex arc model of nervous functioning, the practicality of psychology, or organic holism, for instance.[9] Because all of these ideas were current in one form or another in Watson's formative period, compilations of rival "founders" of behaviorism who might have influenced him are particularly damaging to any claims of originality for him.

Obviously Watson could have utilized contemporary thinking, perhaps without being aware of it. But the question of originality brings with it the

question of "precursors"—why were some formulations of an idea unrecognized by contemporaries and others fully recognized? Indeed, did the "precursors" actually influence anyone?

Two depreciating commentators on Watsonianism, A. A. Roback and Robert S. Woodworth, both made long, fascinating lists of men who uttered behavioristic sentiments in the decade or so before 1913.[10] The list of "behaviorists before Watson" whom Roback and Woodworth and others have assembled includes, among others: William James, of course (1890 and especially 1904);[11] James McKeen Cattell (1904);[12] the distinguished zoologist, Herbert S. Jennings (1906 and perhaps earlier);[13] Knight Dunlap, Watson's colleague at Hopkins (around 1908); Max Meyer, who in 1911 published a remarkable book, *The Fundamental Laws of Human Behavior*;[14] and William McDougall, the English physician and psychologist, who in 1905 spoke of psychology as the science of conduct and later, in 1912, used the word, "behavior," itself.[15] Of this list of alleged precursors only two are of particular importance because only in their cases is there evidence beyond similarity of ideas to indicate that they exerted influence on Watson's thinking.[16] These men are Dunlap and Jennings, with whom Watson was thrown in contact when he went from Chicago to Johns Hopkins in 1908.

Donald D. Jensen has recently pointed out that Watson while at Chicago, in 1904 and 1907, had reviewed Jennings's work on invertebrate behavior but found it inadequate from a psychological viewpoint. After moving to Hopkins, Watson not only came to know Jennings but took a course under him. "By 1914," writes Jensen, Watson "had adopted a point of view which differed little in principle from that of Jennings, if much in style." Jensen concludes that Jacques Loeb, who taught Watson at Chicago, and Jennings were the true founders of behaviorism and that Watson merely took their ideas—especially Jennings's after 1908—and extended them to higher animals and man.[17]

On the face of it, Jensen's discovery of Jennings as the founder of behaviorism is very persuasive. Two difficulties, however, present themselves. First, the critical document, Watson's 1907 review of Jennings's book, has to be read in the light of Watson's other work and private letters. The review was not, as Jensen—most reasonably—alleges, mentalistic and anti-reductionistic, but relatively quite the opposite.[18] Second, Jennings was not by any stretch of the imagination himself a behaviorist but held quite different views.

Jennings was an extreme reductionist and never surrendered his allegiance to neuromechanism. As late as 1909 he himself drew a sharp distinction between the experimental study of complex behavior, on the one hand, and, on the other hand, the explanation of behavior—necessarily simple behavior—by physico-chemical reduction of nervous impulses. A frequent error of commentators like Jensen has been to equate behaviorism with neuromechanism, which it emphatically is not. Jennings's loyalty, as he himself

made clear, was to neuromechanism. Still imbued with nineteenth-century attitudes, Jennings rejected the essentials of behaviorism because in the hands of such men as Hans Driesch, the vitalist, they had in the past led to non-materialistic lines of thought.[19]

Watson's relationship to his old teacher, Loeb, illustrates well how he stood in regard to this line of thinking. Loeb was, like Jennings, a reductionist, and his life work was an attempt to make reductionism viable.[20] Again, Watson's ideas have often been attributed to Loeb, but their chief similarity lay in their rhetoric. Early in January, 1914, for example, Watson wrote to Loeb apologizing for his forthcoming book, *Behavior*. Very gently Watson pointed out how his views differed from Loeb's. Although they both believed that behavior can be analyzed into reflex action, Watson wrote, "I feel that your scheme is a little too simple as it now stands. . . . I do not see any other way of getting at the phenomena of behavior except to consider them as simple reflexes. I am sure our one point of difference would be the extent to which analysis has gone."[21] The truth, had Watson spelled it out with less tact (as he did privately in letters and in a review of Loeb in 1907), is that Watson despaired of waiting for a nervous system model of behavior that could be demonstrated physiologically.[22] Watson believed that it is possible to investigate complex units of behavior without waiting for the discovery of their physical and chemical equivalents and explanations.

The differences between Jennings's and Loeb's views and those of Watson are not the only objection to Jensen's attempt to credit Jennings for behaviorism: There are alternative explanations for the development of Watson's ideas. That is, granted that Watson came under Jennings's influence after 1908 at Hopkins, were there not other men with whom Watson associated at that time who were as influential on him, perhaps even more influential, than Jennings? Watson himself mentioned also not only his old friend, James Mark Baldwin, but A. O. Lovejoy, the philosopher; Dunlap; and the psychiatrist, Adolf Meyer.[23] On the face of it, for example, Meyer, director of the Phipps Clinic, should have the title of grandfather of behaviorism. Not only was Meyer later host to Watson's laboratory, located in the Clinic, but he was far more prestigious—and probably impressive—than Jennings. Moreover, Meyer, who possessed an original mind, had for years been advocating the study of human behavior without imposing on it presumed internal categories and artificial intellectualistic classifications. His approach to psychiatry was strictly biological—the same approach that won Watson fame in experimental psychology.

In the case of Dunlap we are relieved somewhat from using similarity of ideas to infer his influence on Watson. Unfortunately, however, we have to rely instead upon unsupported retrospective reports, which are not satisfying, either. Writing in his autobiography many years later, Dunlap claimed credit for behaviorism. Behaviorism was, he said, Watson's extreme version of his own ideas, which had greatly influenced Watson, who had, up until

then, been orthodox in his use of mental elements. Dunlap said flatly that it was he who directed Watson's attention to the study of behavior as such. It is true that the two men not only worked together professionally but were personally compatible. Dunlap's assertion carries particular weight because Watson, in his own short autobiography, blandly endorsed Dunlap's claim to credit. The only difficulty is, as Dunlap himself admitted, not one shred of evidence exists that at the time, he held psychological opinions that could have given rise to behaviorism.[24]

The fact is that Watson's gentlemanly acknowledgment is not consistent with his own account of behaviorism. In his autobiography Watson expressed his distaste for using human subjects in experiments and his pleasure in using animals, who, as he used to remark, were never late for experimental sessions. "With animals," wrote Watson, "I was at home. I felt that, in studying them, I was keeping close to biology with my feet on the ground. More and more the thought presented itself: Can't I find out by watching their behavior everything that the other students are finding out by using O's? [introspective Observers, as opposed to Subjects]. . . . I broached this to my colleagues, as early as 1904, but received little encouragement."[25] In this statement and elsewhere, Watson apparently established two facts concerning behaviorism: that he had had the idea as early as 1904 and that it grew primarily out of animal psychology or, at least, experimentation with animals. Given the inaccuracies and omissions of this autobiographical sketch, both of Watson's contentions require careful verification. One may also wish to question later on whether Watson was the best judge of what constituted the basic elements of behaviorism.

Fortunately, there is considerable evidence with which to establish a chronology of Watson's thinking along behavioristic lines. The date that he mentions, 1904, is, as he pointed out, the time when he heard Cattell give the St. Louis address that made him one of the precursors of behaviorism.[26] If anyone is to be characterized as the grandfather of Watson's behaviorism, the best case can probably be made for Cattell.[27] The similarity of Cattell's statement at St. Louis to Watson's, almost a decade later, is striking. Cattell not only rejected introspection as the major source of psychological knowledge but spoke in the same terms that Watson later used of control as the goal of psychology: "Control of the physical world," Cattell asserted, "is secondary to the control of ourselves and of our fellow men."

This concept of control had been present in Watson's work at least as early as 1906; it is directly involved in the new animal psychology. At that time he wrote of the difficulties in dealing with the reactions of experimental animals and declared his desire to be "in a position to devote more continuous time to them and to watch and to control their early development. . . . The effect of continued tuition upon the behavior of the individual of a given species is a general problem which must be solved before we are upon firm ground in our interpretations of specific results."[28] The idea that fascinated

Watson was the possibility of controlling and observing the total environment of experimental animals from the beginning, that is, from birth. By 1907, in reviewing the work of Jennings and Loeb, Watson emphasized the total reaction of the organism as opposed to the emphasis of Jennings and Loeb on physiological processes.[29]

By 1908 Watson had formulated many of the basic ideas and attitudes that constituted behaviorism. As early as October, 1907, he noted in a letter that he was trying to use the phrase "afferent control" in animals instead of "consciousness." His correspondence during the winter of 1907–1908 reveals that he had been drawing further conclusions about psychology, and at the end of 1908 he presented a paper embodying them at the Southern Society of Philosophy and Psychology entitled, "A Point of View in Comparative Psychology."[30] The long abstract of the paper indicates that its content would justify the claims of Murphy and Furfey that Watson had formulated behaviorism sometime earlier that same year. Watson asserted in this paper that ascribing any mental content to experimental animals was valueless for both theory and actual investigation. With the increasing ability of the psychologist to control and record experimental conditions, said Watson, introspection was becoming less necessary for the psychologist.[31]

Years later Watson characterized behaviorism explicitly as an extension of animal psychology attitudes and techniques to the realm of human psychology: "Behaviorism, as I tried to develop it in my lectures at Columbia in 1912 and in my earliest writings, was an attempt to do one thing—to apply to the experimental study of man the same kind of procedure and the same language of description that many research men had found useful for so many years in the study of animals lower than man."[32] This was Watson's basic contribution. Many strongly objective animal workers refused to follow behaviorism because they did not believe that man should be studied—or controlled—like an animal. But in Watson's 1908 paper it was clear that he already had in mind applying the objective observation of the new comparative psychology to human psychology.

The question has to be raised, therefore, why the behaviorist manifesto came in 1913 rather than in 1908. At least two reasons are obvious. First—if his popular article published in *Harper's* in 1910, "The New Science of Animal Behavior," is an accurate reflection of the development of his thinking at that time—Watson had not yet solved the problem of the higher thought processes.[33] By 1913, he had developed at least the outline of a stimulus-response model of implicit speech mechanisms in associative memory. It is this contribution of Watson that Goss emphasizes as one of the basic elements of behaviorism—so basic that the movement could not have existed without it.

But even if some sort of behaviorism had been possible without a theory of thinking, a second type of evidence shows that behaviorism of any kind was not possible until around 1913: the actions of the psychological community.

Watson's pronouncements over the course of several years had engendered no particular response from his colleagues. Then his lectures in the winter of 1912–1913 elicited a violent reaction. As Kuhn suggests, the real significance of scientific innovation lies in its effect upon the innovator's audience, his peers. Behaviorism as such, in fact, was created in 1912–1913 by psychology as a self-conscious discipline, not by Watson.

Watson himself of course noted the furor he aroused that winter. He commented innocently to his friend, Harvard psychologist Robert M. Yerkes, that although his material was not on a popular level, his audiences at his Columbia lectures were very large indeed.[34] Clearly, he was making a sensation.

Within a few months after the lectures, F. L. Wells, a psychologist at McLean Hospital and the most acute and objective observer of his own profession in those years, spelled out exactly what Watson's manifesto meant: "It is," he wrote, "an unusually concrete statement of a central idea that has always claimed certain adherents among us, at least as an idea. Therefore the way in which so many have received it seems to be due not so much to either its source or content as to a changed attitude in those who read its words."[35] Seldom do we possess such explicit evidence that an intellectual statement "crystallized thinking." Watson himself later depicted the events as a "crystallization of the behavioristic trend" in psychology.[36] The evidence shows that, in the end, Boring is correct in dating behaviorism from the presentation and publication of Watson's paper in 1912–1913, not earlier.

The application of Kuhn's model of the process of scientific innovation shows that the sudden crystallizing of behaviorism as a movement in 1913 represents a real moment of change.[37] Thus it may be true that Watson's ideas grew out of animal psychology, for the most part, and that Cattell inspired him. But the evolution of Watson's thinking, on the one hand, is not necessarily relevant to the origins of behaviorism, on the other hand.

The psychologists who reacted to Watson's manifesto were not all comparative psychologists but included men, like Wells, of every possible background in the discipline. Presumably they tended to be the younger men in the profession, and their number is traditionally credited for Watson's election as president of the American Psychological Association in 1915. Kuhn's model raises the question not of the origins of Watson's ideas but of the general condition of psychological thinking that made behaviorism possible and, presumably, inevitable. To date no one has satisfactorily explored the anomalies—such as the idea of imageless thought—or the false starts in theoretical breakthrough—presumably represented by the much heralded precursors of behaviorism—that represent Kuhn's "crisis" stage—the one immediately preceding a scientific revolution.[38]

In such a context, it is necessary to restate Watson's role in behaviorism. Rather than founder, Watson is better viewed as the charismatic leader of behaviorism. This role he played well. He was intelligent and handsome,

and his charm is legendary. Despite his youth, he had for some years been part of the ruling inner circle of the American psychological profession. Although it was not immediately evident, he had all his life sought publicity, even sensational publicity, and gloried in it. It was Titchener who at once realized the part that Watson was playing: that of the reformer, in a hurry for change.[39] As in the case of other scientific developments in America during the Progressive era, the origins of behaviorism lie no doubt not only in the science and in the profession but in society at large, where the idea of control, for example, so central in Watsonian behaviorism, was already having momentous effects in other reform endeavors.[40]

The relationship of behaviorism to social control and Progressivism appears again later in this book, but the suggestion here that behaviorism was a social as well as an intellectual movement has been developed by other authors. John O'Donnell argues that behaviorism as Watson articulated it drew on American psychologists' widespread activities in applied fields, especially education, in which not only individual differences and adaptations were important but in which the subject matter was, in fact, behavior. Acknowledging the special relationship of behaviorism to animal psychology, O'Donnell goes on to show both how the comparative psychologists were forced into applied work and how Watson himself emphasized not just general social control but application. Altogether, O'Donnell concludes, the profession consisted of enough psychologists who were doing work that was essentially behavioral, such as paper-and-pencil tests for children, that a "silent majority" like Wells supported perhaps not a strict Watsonian behaviorism but a strongly behavioristic orientation.[*]

The majority in psychology was, however, for the time being remarkably silent. Franz Samelson found distressingly little evidence of either verbal support or experimental investigation between 1913 and the 1920's that would suggest that behaviorism had made any impact on American psychologists—at least those who spoke for the psychological community. Watson's manifesto remained, Samelson shows, purely programmatic. Only as a later generation of investigators and teachers came to refer to Watson's radical stance to express the approach they took to psychology did the 1913 date come into the published record of the discipline. Samelson went on, however, to show that Watson had raised basic questions of orientation and procedure so that in the 1920's many psychologists had indeed become in one sense or another behaviorists—enough so that, for example, they contributed to the demise of old ideas of instinct.[†]

---

[*] John M. O'Donnell, *The Origins of Behaviorism: American Psychology, 1870–1920* (New York: New York University Press, 1985). Kurt Danziger, "The History of Introspection Reconsidered," *Journal of the History of the Behavioral Sciences*, 16 (1980), 241–262, for example, connected Watson's stand on introspection with his interest in application.

[†] Franz Samelson, "The Struggle for Scientific Authority: The Reception of Watson's Behaviorism, 1913–1920," *Journal of the History of the Behavioral Sciences*, 17 (1981), 399–425. Franz Samelson, "Organizing for the Kingdom of Be-

A number of scholars have filled in the details of Watson's efforts, and others have discussed the significance of behaviorism in the history of psychology and of thought in general.[‡] Clearly the issues raised between 1913 and 1915—and in 1968—are not yet settled. O'Donnell claims, however, that the foregoing chapter "set the terms of the debate for the historical problem of behaviorism."[§]

The relationship of human beings to other animals continued to offer a focus for many of the major psychological issues. In particular this question added to the mind-body problem the heredity versus environment controversy.[||] The next chapter includes not only psychoanalysis but the focal point of the nature-nurture and animal-human problems: instinct. This version of instinct survived the narrowly scientific attack of the behaviorists and their allies. Moreover, instinct, or more precisely as in Freud's thinking, instinctual drive, constituted a central element in thinking about culture. Here the medical as well as the psychological world contributed to a major set of ideas that interacted importantly with European and American civilization.

havior: Academic Battles and Organizational Policies in the Twenties," *Journal of the History of the Behavioral Sciences*, 21 (1985), 33–47.

‡ See, for example, on different levels of discussion, Darryl Bruce, "Lashley's Shift from Bacteriology to Neuropsychology, 1910–1917, and the Influence of Jennings, Watson, and Franz," *Journal of the History of the Behavioral Sciences*, 22 (1986), 27–44; Kerry W. Buckley, "Behaviorism and the Professionalization of American Psychology" (doctoral dissertation, University of Massachusetts, 1982); Brian D. Mackenzie, *Behaviourism and the Limits of Scientific Method* (London: Routledge, 1977); Paul Creelan, "Religion, Language, and Sexuality in J. B. Watson," *Journal of Humanistic Psychology*, 15 (1975), 55–78; and Michael M. Sokal, "The Gestalt Psychologists in Behaviorist America," *American Historical Review*, 89 (1984), 1240–1263.

§ O'Donnell, *The Origins of Behaviorism*, p. xi. Philip J. Pauly, "The Loeb-Jennings Debate and the Science of Animal Behavior," *Journal of the History of the Behavioral Sciences*, 17 (1981), 504–515.

|| The standard source is Hamilton Cravens, *The Triumph of Evolution: American Scientists and the Heredity-Environment Controversy 1900–1941* (Philadelphia: University of Pennsylvania Press, 1978).

The Medical Origins
and Cultural Use
of Freud's
Instinctual Drive Theory

Freud's instinctual drive theory is counted as one of his most important and distinctive contributions.[1] In the late nineteenth century when he began to formulate what ultimately became psychoanalysis, the idea of instinct was conspicuous in Western scientific thinking. Yet Freud did not utilize his contemporaries' biological and psychological work; instead he drew on an independent and distinctive medical tradition for his conceptualization. Although his thinking was insulated from the lively interest in instinct that developed in biology and related disciplines around the turn of the century, his teachings survived other theories because his contributions to the science of man fitted the needs of the new century's social organization.

Freud began theorizing at a time when his practice in Vienna had brought to his attention human sexual phenomena in their many manifestations.[2] As his letters to Wilhelm Fliess and his papers of the 1890's show, Freud was at first concerned particularly with the ways in which somatic conditions influence sexual phenomena.[3] His description of the anxiety neurosis involved, in an explicit way, purely physical concomitants of sexual phenomena. And in his early work on hysteria, Freud took pains to explain that a memory that is sexual in nature could have profound effects, both physical and mental. Then when he had formulated the concept of the wish, Freud tended to abandon physiological levels of explanation and to try to think in terms of logically consistent, purely psychological explanations.[4] By 1900 he had developed his ideas sufficiently to set forth a relatively complete human

"The Medical Origins and Cultural Use of Freud's Instinctual Drive Theory" is reprinted from the *Psychoanalytic Quarterly*, 43 (1974), 193–217, with the kind permission of the *Psychoanalytic Quarterly*.

psychology (compare chapter 7 of *The Interpretation of Dreams*). There he characterized the wish as a mental representative of internal somatic pressures upon the organism. Although he pictured the organic re-enforcement of the unconscious wish as the energizing of the primary process (the dynamic unconscious), not until 1905 in *Three Essays on the Theory of Sexuality* did he describe explicitly the somatically based instinctual drive in the form in which it has had such profound effects upon Western thinking.[5]

In Freud's works subsequent to the *Three Essays*, the concept of instinctual drive encompasses the only area in which physiology impinges directly upon psychology. Freud was aware of the fact that most physiological characteristics are presumed to be inherited. He and his contemporaries considered instincts to be necessarily a part of a person's heredity because they are physiological phenomena. An examination of Freud's conceptualization of instinctual drive, combining physiology and heredity, therefore permits an extension of the work of Amacher and Ritvo upon these two aspects of his thinking. Amacher has examined the neurophysiological beliefs of Freud's teachers upon which the founder of psychoanalysis was able to draw, and Ritvo has called attention to aspects of Freud's assumptions concerning hereditary givens.[6] These two lines of inquiry need to be brought together in connection with other scientific and medical writings of Freud's time to indicate what Freud contributed and how his work was understood.

By the last decades of the nineteenth century, the concept of instinct had been refined into several models.[7] The most common scientifically acceptable, that is, parsimonious, definition was "compound reflex action." Instinctive action was believed to consist of a series of patterned responses to a stimulus. Such a definition was essentially physiological or even materialistic without necessarily involving, for example, either biological or social purposiveness. Liddell and others have shown how the conceptualization of reflex developed in that century and grew steadily more sophisticated as neurophysiological knowledge increased.[8] Freud in his Project and, implicitly, in his general psychology drew upon both this reflex concept and the association psychology that paralleled and re-enforced it. By 1900 his teachings embodied an essentially reductionistic reflex model of the psyche in which he took account of endogenous stimuli that he later designated "instinctual drives." Rather than discussing reflexes on a physiological level, Freud utilized the psychological equivalent, association (although as Holt points out, the neurophysiological model contained elements that continued to show up as contaminants in Freud's psychological writings).[9] Until Freud's time it had been customary in science to include all behavior and thinking within association psychology, a psychological schema that, as should be emphasized, the neurophysiological model (at least until the end of the 1890's) paralleled and re-enforced. "All behavior and thinking" included even that which Freud pictured as growing out of endogenous stimuli. His contribution, indeed, was to suggest how those stimuli are integrated into association processes.

Although the Englishman, Alexander Bain, and other associationists occasionally discussed aspects of motivation and always took up the feelings, association psychology itself ostensibly had no need of instinct beyond the reflex. Many associationists nevertheless tended to employ some common-sense system of instincts for explaining aspects of both human and animal behavior, without regard for theoretical consistency. When Freud, then, transformed the primary process and began to speak in terms of endogenous instinctual drive, *Trieb*, as such, although still an associationist he became entangled in all of the conceptions of instinct current at the time that did not depend upon the reflex concept.[10]

The various conceptions of instinct that survived even a few years into the twentieth century included both the scientific and the traditional. On the Continent, common-sense instinct theory tended to be Aristotelian—a hierarchy of passions and appetites sufficient to explain any behavior. French science and medicine, for example, were so dominated by Aristotelian thinking that a more reductionistic or environmentalist (that is, sensationalist) psychology could not flourish there.[11] In Enlightenment times, the human (as opposed to animal) passions had been fairly well defined for all of Europe, but they were social in nature—pride, love of power, and the like.[12] It was this culturally derived scheme of explanation for human behavior that most association psychologists utilized even as they taught that all conduct could be interpreted in terms of a mechanistic series of associations initiated by external stimuli.

Any approach to applying the idea of instinct to human beings was complicated by the fact that since antiquity animals in particular were understood to be guided in their actions by instincts. Rather generally in the nineteenth century instinct was therefore understood to be not only physiological and inherited but animal rather than human. In English the word was ambiguous. German-speaking scientists such as Freud, however, were able to distinguish between *Instinkt*, instinct in animals, and *Trieb*, drive in humans, the latter word having the connotation of impulse and involving at some point, at least, thought processes, rather than being purely automatic or reflex in nature. Freud, like most nineteenth-century scientists, in his writings reserved the mechanical *Instinkt* for animals and very seldom equated *Trieb* with *Instinkt*.[13] Those using traditional categories to describe mental processes, such as sensations and feelings, tended to restrict human appetites and impulses to those that could be classified under the general heading of will, that is, susceptible of conscious control.

Freud's care to use *Trieb*, and the care of others (such as the classic historian of instinct, Wilm) to restrict "instinct" to animals, reflects in general the difference between a psychological and a biological level of discourse. One of the strengths of Freud's work was his attempt at logical consistency, noted above, in dealing with the psychological without confusing it with

biological or physiological points of view (although he was, of course, vividly aware of the latter and, as has been noted, not always able to exclude it).[14]

All of the nice distinctions between human and animal, biological and psychological, however, were breaking down just when Freud was working out his psychology, and many of his contemporaries did not maintain them. For example, W. T. Preyer, professor of physiology at Jena whose famous work on the developmental behavior of infants was known to Freud, utilized the term *Instinct* in connection with children. Preyer explicitly compared the instincts of animals with those of children. And, to cite another instance, Freud's teacher, Sigmund Exner, whose thinking paralleled Freud's in the 1890's, also used the term *Instinct* in connection with a neurophysiological explanation of human behavior and thinking.[15] In short, in a period of Darwinian thinking, the identification of human attributes with those of animals had become common. Sometimes the theorists simply assumed that man is another animal. At other times the theory of recapitulation was invoked, that is, the belief that man in his various developmental stages duplicates the stages through which his ancestors went as they evolved from single cells into primates. Although Freud resorted to animal parallels and recapitulation theory markedly less frequently than his contemporaries, still he did share with them the tendency to view man in terms of an animal nature.[16]

At the same time that the distinctions between human and animal instincts were breaking down in those years around the turn of the twentieth century, a new interest in man's instinctual drives developed, the interest that ultimately gave currency to Freud's ideas on the subject far beyond any interest in psychoanalysis. This renaissance of instinct derived not from physiological knowledge or psychological theory about instincts but from the fact, alluded to above, that instincts and instinctual tendencies were understood to be hereditary in nature. The precipitating event was the advent of Weismannism, the first step in the development of modern genetics. August Weismann, himself a distinguished German cytologist until he turned to biological theorizing in the 1880's, taught that the germ plasm is passed on unchanged from generation to generation and is not affected by the life history of any particular individual organism transmitting the plasm. It was Weismann who effectively challenged the prevailing idea of the inheritance of acquired characteristics, called at the time Neo-Lamarckianism.[17]

All through the late 1880's and the 1890's and even after, there raged in the world of biology and science in general a debate over whether or not Weismann was correct. The stakes in this scientific controversy were high, for if Weismann prevailed, every major theory of social improvement was affected fundamentally. As Karl Pearson wrote in his famous *Grammar of Science* concerning the implications of Weismann's theories: "Strange as it may seem, the laboratory experiments of a biologist may have greater weight than all the theories of the state from Plato to Hegel!"[18]

The opponents of Weismann, the Neo-Lamarckians, maintained that it is difficult if not impossible to distinguish between the factors of heredity and environment, especially in the case of man, whose will and training were supposed over the years to modify his inherited tendencies and habits anyway. Neo-Lamarckian beliefs basically were that the life history of an organism would by means of inheritance be reflected in the native givens of descendants of the organism. What was inherited, then, was only a generation or two previously (the number of generations and other circumstances varied with different writers) not inherent, but, on the contrary, environmental. Man, in the Lamarckian view, was of such a protean and idiosyncratic nature that studying him scientifically was either hazardous or entirely out of the question.

Weismann, by contrast, opened the door to the scientific study of man by suggesting that constant and observable, specifically human traits are carried from generation to generation unaltered and therefore are suitable objects of research. In the aftermath of the impact of Weismannism, writers such as the English biologist C. Lloyd Morgan and especially the American psychologist James Mark Baldwin began to differentiate two problems: social heredity, or culture (civilization it was often called in those days), on the one hand, and, on the other hand, inherited human nature.[19] The quest to ascertain the latter, man's inherited nature, was the chief source of the renaissance in human instinct theory in Freud's time: The instincts represented the most important of the eternal human traits. Before Weismann, instincts were seen to have their origins in the habits developed by one's ancestors; afterward, each instinct was assumed to be a distinctive and stable biological racial trait.

The renewed inquiry in the wake of Weismann's assertions brought forth a number of attempts to define just what those traits might be. The resulting lists of human instincts that various thinkers compiled were almost invariably traditional and very often circular. Mostly the instincts were used to explain the existence of recognized social institutions. The best-known such inventory was that of William McDougall (1909), who on empirical grounds postulated, for example, an instinct of pugnacity, which explains war and other combative behavior. Man was often known to be pugnacious in his conduct, and the existence of an instinct for pugnacity—an unchanging hereditary trait—could therefore not be doubted. Needless to say, sooner or later, beginning especially in the 1910's, this type of instinct theory became discredited. Hard-headed young professionals, such as the social psychologist L. L. Bernard, applied devastating logic to the instinct literature of the post-Weismann period, and the entire concept became untenable in science for some time. Only with difficulty did a single theory of instinct survive the debacle: the instinctual drive theory of Freud.[20]

Freud therefore presents a paradox: He was, as Ritvo has shown, a convinced Lamarckian to the end of his days. Yet in a scientific world dominated by Weismannism, the instinct theory that survived best was his.[21] Two

questions have therefore to be separated. One is the origin of Freud's ideas and how he articulated them into a system. The other, and independent, question is the uses that his audience made of his ideas.

It should be noted that over the years Freud frequently confronted and rejected Weismannian ideas of inheritance. In 1908, for example, Ehrenfels brought the subject up at a meeting of the Vienna Psychoanalytic Society over which Freud, as usual, presided. Indeed, as late as the World War I period Freud proposed to Otto Rank that they collaborate in writing a vindication of Lamarckianism, a project that ultimately came to nothing.[22] Weismannism also came to Freud's attention specifically in his reading on the question of instincts. Through the student of Weismann, zoologist H. E. Ziegler, the eminent Swiss psychologist Karl Groos came to the conclusion that instinctive reactions are species-specific traits transmitted unaffected by environmental influences.[23] Freud early knew Groos's work, if not Ziegler's. He cited Groos, for instance, for the instinctual drives (*Triebe*) that lead to children's discovering in the course of play the pleasurable economy of psychical energy derived from repetition of the similar or familiar.[24]

In spite of his exposure to Weismannian ideas of inheritance and instinct, Freud clung stubbornly to his Lamarckian beliefs. His interest in maintaining the validity of the phylogenetic nature of inborn acquired characteristics was connected primarily with his concern that civilization and cognate repressive forces be understood to be phylogenetic. His successors and interpreters tended to accept Weismannism and did not find the hypothesis of phylogenesis necessary for advocating and explicating psychoanalysis. Freud, it is true, urged searching for ontogenetic factors in a clinical case before attempting to invoke the phylogenetic. And what his followers found essential in both theory and clinic was the organic basis of the human instinctual drives. Nor was their reading particularly strained. Even Freud pictured as the irreducible physical-hereditary factors in psychoanalytic theory only faulty function (as opposed to content) of the nervous system, and somatic determinants of instinctual drives.[25] Neither factor necessarily committed a Freudian to either Weismannism or Lamarckianism. He could treat the instinctual drive as a representative of the somatic without getting involved in biological questions.

Freud's teachings about human instincts, as a matter of fact, had an origin independent of biological theory such as would have become involved in the Weismannism-Lamarckianism controversy. Freud as a physician had available to him from the literature of medicine an alternative view of heredity, a view more directly relevant to human instinct theory than that growing out of theoretical and experimental biology. Physicians, whatever their systematic speculations about heredity, had always tended to assume that traits persisted from one generation to another and that those traits were generally manifested in entire races. The medical men, whether or not Lamarckians in the abstract, in practice had to adhere to the old dogma,

"Like begets like." From ancient times inherited defect and familial taran-
tism were known, and the study of hemophilia, color blindness, and other
such diseases was accelerated as clinical and familial statistical studies were
accumulated during the nineteenth century.[26]

Particularly were specialists in nervous and mental diseases interested
in inheritance. Since the etiology of most of these illnesses was at best un-
clear, studies that showed tendencies of such afflictions to run in families
suggested to clinicians that they were dealing with patients suffering from
an inherent defect. Because of the social implications of such inheritances,
late-nineteenth-century medical writers devoted a great deal of attention to
the inheritance of defect, disease, predisposition to disease, general physical weakness, and all kinds of mental and moral tendencies. Most of these
physicians tended to speak of Daltonism and brachydactyly but in fact were
basically preoccupied with mental illness, inebriety, and criminality. Thus
even in medicine in this period social questions preconditioned the channel-
ing of scientific energies.[27]

For the Aristotelian physicians of that day, "mind" could in some metaphysical way be inherited. But for those like Freud, tending to physicalistic
explanations of life and even of human phenomena, it was the inheritance
of organic weakness of the nervous system that explained the failures of a
patient to react in normal ways, especially under unfavorable circumstances
when the physical vulnerability could be expected to show up. These hy-
potheses of native infirmities of course applied as well to tubercular patients,
whose malady could be shown to run in families, as to nervous patients,
where a similar ancestral taint could likewise often be detected. Such inheritances were viewed sometimes as inherited traits, sometimes as a loosely
defined, more or less inherited degeneracy, that is, a defect in the function
of the process of endowing progeny with traits (and often a slipshod empirical version of Lamarckianism). Freud throughout his life believed that his
patients suffered from congenital neuropathic constitutions, although he also
held that the derivation of the individual patient's tendency to fall ill is of
little consequence in the clinic except as it might suggest to the physician
how to shape a therapeutic regime.[28]

Yet Freud and other physicians were led to posit and deal with one
piece of inheritance that appeared regularly in practice: It was the sexual instinct, and in medical treatises, whatever the author's ethical-social stance or
psychological theory, this instinct was admitted to be general, inherited, and
human as well as animal. Conceivably, medical writers could have used psychology or biology to explain the generative instinct away, for example in associationist or Lamarckian terms, as other instincts were diluted or ignored.[29]
But in medicine the sexual instinct was dealt with directly. Furthermore,
by the turn of the century specialists in nervous and mental diseases had
already undertaken substantial investigations of the clinical manifestations of
this instinct.

Since Freud's experience with patients in the 1890's had already convinced him of the overwhelming importance of libidinal strivings in the psychical apparatus, he was of course familiar with psychiatric-neurological writings on sexuality. It was only natural, therefore, that in his general psychological theory he employed the familiar sexual instinct as the paradigm for instinctual drive.[30] Indeed, in the *Three Essays on the Theory of Sexuality* in which the instinctual drive concept was introduced as such, Freud in his first footnote mentioned that he expected his readers to be familiar with his ideas: "The information contained in this first essay," he wrote, and he might have included large parts of the other two essays, "is derived from the well-known writings of Krafft-Ebing, Moll, Moebius, Havelock Ellis, Schrenck-Notzing, Loewenfeld, Eulenburg, Bloch and Hirschfeld, and from the Jahrbuch für sexuelle Zwischenstufen."[31]

By the time of his essay, "Instincts and Their Vicissitudes," Freud had made his conception more systematic. He listed there four aspects of an instinct: its pressure (presumably quantitative); its aim, that is, satisfaction by reducing stimulation; the object of the instinct through which satisfaction can be gained; and the somatic source of the instinct. This model of an instinct is distinctive in two important respects. First, unlike biological or simple reflex models, it tends to avoid the stimulus-response pattern and, instead, to introduce one much more useful for the explanation and exploration of both normal and pathological behavior. Second, the basic components—pressure, source, aim, and object—were already well worked out in connection with a specific instinct.[32]

The great psychiatrist Krafft-Ebing serves as the superlative example of writers on whom Freud could and, as he said explicitly, did draw for his conceptualization of a human instinct.[33] Krafft-Ebing was professor at the University of Vienna and an academic sponsor of Freud for some years. He was also a leader in the scientific study of human sexual phenomena. In his monumental *Textbook of Insanity*, Krafft-Ebing noted that there are two kinds of instincts (*Triebe*) known from physiology: self-preservation and sex ("*einen Erhaltungs- und einen Geschlechtstrieb*"). In the clinic, he said, one can see these instinctual drives increased, decreased, and perverted. As he developed the place of instincts in abnormal behavior, Krafft-Ebing discussed the pathological deflections from the aim and object of the sexual instinct (*Trieb*), and in this classic text and elsewhere he made it clear that the instinct had an organic basis existing antecedent to any possible external stimulus.[34]

Within the field of medical sexology, Krafft-Ebing was and is best known for his *Psychopathia Sexualis*, a descriptive work giving the details of various sexual perversions and classifying them. In his descriptions, Krafft-Ebing included some theoretical discussions incidentally, and it was such material that Freud assumed that his readers were acquainted with. From the standard sexological literature of the day, Krafft-Ebing incorporated the

idea of actions symbolic of sexual deeds, the notion of erogenous zones, and other concepts (such as moral masochism) that were frequently known in later years from the writings of Freud rather than from the original body of science and scholarship with which Freud, as he said, started.[35]

Krafft-Ebing is only one example; one can find similar ideas in other authors who wrote on sexual subjects before 1900 and who were cited by Freud. The works of standard general psychiatric writers, such as Emil Kraepelin, are of particular importance to illustrate how well known such thinking was in medicine. Kraepelin explicitly spoke of transformations of the sexual instinctual drive (*die Umwandlungen des Geschlechtstriebes*) comparable to the vicissitudes of the drive (*Triebschicksale*) described by Freud, and suggested that such variations belong to the realm of compulsive actions. Kraepelin and most of his colleagues utilized a psychiatric psychology consonant with traditional academic psychology—he was, after all, a student of Wilhelm Wundt—that is, he conceptualized psychical operations in terms of cognition, feelings, and will.[36] But virtually all of the medical writers whom Freud was likely to have read, like Kraepelin, treated the sexual instinctual drive as a special case of one kind or another. They spoke of its quantitative strength and weakness, its aim or means of satisfaction as plastic and changeable, and what were appropriate and inappropriate objects.[37] Krafft-Ebing was simply the most comprehensive and consistent of the medical writers before Freud.[38]

Ellenberger and others have, therefore, not surprisingly found many nineteenth-century anticipations of Freud's systematic teachings about sex, and especially about the instinctual aspects of sexual phenomena. To a large extent such critics miss the significance of their own data: namely, that which Freud really did contribute can be sorted out from that which was familiar. He did not discover the perversions, for example, or even childhood sexuality, although he did effectively suggest that infants' behavior was essentially sexual in nature.[39]

What Freud did do was to articulate a well-known model of instinct into a reductionistic association psychology—a feat his teacher Meynert thought impossible—and into a concomitant well-developed theory of psychopathology.[40] Eventually, especially in 1920 and thereafter, Freud, while still following the basic paradigm, carried the concept of instinctual drive much further, utilizing, of course, refinements suggested by Karl Abraham and others.[41] But even in the earlier years Freud contributed important components to the instinctual drive theory, most notably the concept of repression and its corollary sequelae.

Freud could never have made such contributions had he not sharpened the instinct model that he adopted and adapted from the medical literature. Krafft-Ebing and his congeners talked about sexual drive (*Trieb*) in descriptive and functional terms—how people felt and what actions the drives led to, and what subjective feelings were involved. Freud tried to speak in psycho-

logical terms—how the mental apparatus operated to give instinctual drives expression.[42] The result was a shift of emphasis. Where Krafft-Ebing and others tended to think of sexual pathology as the instinct somehow changed or gone wrong, either because of heredity or environmental influence, Freud pictured pathology as the result of malfunctioning in the psychic apparatus through which the drive passed (not malfunctioning of the drive itself) so that aim or object, for instance, not the drive, was abnormal or inappropriate. Etiology and treatment in the Freudian schema, therefore, could center on the psychical apparatus rather than having to involve an unpredictable, changeable instinct. The result was both a psychology and a psychopathology that lent themselves to rational control and prediction on the presumption of a fixed structure (the psychical apparatus) and mechanical reactions, however complex and complicated.

Although Freud drew on a well-established medical tradition for his instinctual drive theory, most of his contemporaries and successors saw his work in a different context, as ordinary scientific instinct theory. Yet for them, too, familiarity with the literature of psychiatry and medical sexology made it easier to understand and accept Freud's formulations. The psychoanalytic instinctual drive concept was therefore largely familiar; all that was necessary to assimilate it was to extend the concept to drives other than sex. Freud, indeed, soon subdivided the "sexual" instinctual drive into a number of component drives.[43] Other writers to a remarkable extent believed that the Freudians thought that man is motivated by only one instinct, sex. Still, given the familiarity of intellectuals of the early twentieth century with the medical concept, it is little wonder that they confused the original operational model with other varieties of instinctual drives. This very familiarity with a model, however, furthered the influence of Freud when other investigators, too, endeavored to find a workable conceptualization of the whole range of human instincts. Even in contemporary discussions, the libidinal instinctual drive remains central and modal and presents grave intellectual problems for those who attempt to fit aggression, for example, into the original pattern.[44]

Freud is best viewed, then, not so much as an innovator in instinct theory as a creative transitional figure who stood midway between the sexologists and later instinct theorists such as the ego psychologists of our own time. He took an existing concept of instinct and refined it so that it would serve both psychology and psychopathology. But in the process he shifted the emphasis within the customary conceptualization.[45] As Wettley and Leibbrand point out, Krafft-Ebing and the sexologists emphasized the sexual object, the person's ultimate behavior, but Freud emphasized the sexual aim.[46] For Freud and the twentieth century, the focus of interest and investigation became the operation of the instinct itself, but only as it passed through the psychical apparatus.

Freud's teachings about instinctual drives fitted the needs of other thinkers of the new century in many ways. That he himself was not touched

by new scientific thinking after 1900 and that he worked independently of most contemporaneous writers on instinct theory, is of course irrelevant to the logic and actual process of the dispersion of his ideas. Up to then the amount of confusion engendered by the instinct concept rendered it useless in scientific explanation. Albert Moll, for example, the eminent physician who was himself working to refine sexual drive theory, complained in 1898 of the "confusion" about *Instinct* in the psychological literature. At that time most instinct theory was teleological in nature, emphasizing the adaptive or survival value of any given inherited reaction or tendency, which was consonant with the equating of human drives with animal instincts noted above. When, then, Freud continued to try to maintain a purely human psychological model in discussing instinctual drive, he showed how to avoid many of the problems that conventional conceptualizations generated, particularly evolutionary purpose.[47]

By 1915, Freud could acknowledge that his Lamarckian, phylogenetic explanations of the repressive force of civilization were not essential to his paradigm of an instinctual drive.[48] Other thinkers could and did utilize his model of an instinct in a Weismannian context simply by assuming that society by environmental influence gave form to the repressive forces. Perhaps the most striking evidence that Freud's ideas could be adapted to non-Lamarckian theory is the fact that Freud's own teachers, with whom he shared many basic assumptions, to a surprising extent found their work compatible with a Weismannian view of instincts. Ziegler, for example, cited both Carl Claus, with whom Freud studied biology, and Theodor Meynert as examples of eminent scientists who were early sympathetic to Weismann's arguments. Meynert is of special interest because it was his work that Ziegler cited to show the compatibility of the idea of fixed, inherited instincts with a radical physicalistic reductionism. Other of Freud's contemporaries, such as the Vienna-trained Swiss psychiatrist-biologist, Auguste Forel, showed a similar affinity for Weismann's viewpoint.[49]

There was, after all, no necessary connection between the sexologists' idea of sexual instinct and the Weismannism that led to the early-twentieth-century interest in instincts in general. Freud's consistent Lamarckianism provides an excellent example. Still another striking instance is found in Moll's work. In 1898 he devoted an entire book to the nature of *libido sexualis*. There he cited Weismann extensively on cytology and the process of human generation. But in discussing the question of how much and how the sex instinct (*Trieb*) is inherited in both men and animals, Moll explicitly rejected Weismannism and argued that conscious sexual choice has been inherited.[50]

Yet increasingly thinkers of the day showed that Weismann's views could well accommodate ideas about instinctual drives that were modeled on the "sexual instinct" as known from medicine. The most dramatic instance is provided by Orschansky, who discussed the sexual instinct specifically as a

human trait inherited according to Weismannian principles. He then went on to suggest incidentally that all human instincts were inherited, unmodified by any Lamarckian factors, and that they operated like the sexual.[51]

Such thinkers as Orschansky raise the question as to why their works fell into obscurity and why those of Freud did not. Initially it is obvious that Freud's instinctual drive theory was subsequently extremely important in the arena from which it was derived, medicine. Freud's teachings helped psychopathologists turn their attention to the workings of instinctual forces within the patient's mind, typically the mechanisms by which drives gain symbolic expression.[52] In broader biological and social theory, Weismann's teachings created a need for a model of instinct that was similarly useful. When the first endeavors to identify a series of instincts in the human species failed, Freud's work provided the model that was useful. Many writers, without making a distinction between drive and instinct, borrowed Freudian instinctual drive as a convenient equivalent to concepts and conceptualizations with other origins. As noted above, both familiarity with the old medical concept of human sexual instinct and the care with which Freud worked out his concept contributed to the pragmatic way in which writers used his work (and often ignored more unfamiliar material). Freud's later structural refinements included an impressive portrayal of a combination of a person's adaptation to both reality and instinctual drive, a *tour de force* that further strengthened the intellectual appeal of Freudian formulations.[53]

Wilfrid Trotter, Ernest Jones's brother-in-law, provides an explicit example of the kind of need that Freud's instinctual drive concept met in Western culture. In his book, *Instincts of the Herd in Peace and War*, Trotter spoke about his belief that psychology, "especially when studied in relation to other branches of biology, . . . is capable of becoming a guide in the actual affairs of life and of giving an understanding of the human mind such as may enable us in a practical and useful way to foretell some of the course of human behaviour." Trotter hoped that a "scientific statecraft" would develop to bring about permanent social progress. "Such a statecraft," he said, "would recognize how fully man is an instinctive being." And instincts Trotter believed to be hereditary units. It is hardly to be wondered at that Trotter adopted Freud's model of instinctual drive to suggest the way in which instincts operate among humans.[54]

Trotter's suggestion that knowledge and manipulation of human instincts could be made the basis of a new societal order represented an unusually clear statement of the social usefulness of a viable instinct theory in the early twentieth century. Many thinkers, especially in England and America, quickly perceived the implications of Weismann's suggestion that the biological basis of human behavior is fixed from generation to generation. And as the new century progressed, the urgency of understanding men's actions increased.

Max Weber and many of his successors have pointed out that Western

European and American society more and more in the *fin de siècle* period was becoming industrialized and bureaucratic. Human beings in this bureaucratic society became extremely dependent upon one another, and the behavior of a person therefore took on momentous consequences because he could affect the lives of so many others. Managers of such societies had to put great premium upon the predictability and control of human conduct.[55] As Pearson and Trotter and many others saw, Weismannism promised hard information about the traits of the people who had to be controlled. It was in this context, then, that Freud's instinctual drive theory with psychical structures became part of the knowledge by means of which the social managers thought that they could anticipate and limit the behavior of men. Under these circumstances Freud's theory, which had the advantage of being both familiar in part and very well thought out, was widely disseminated, and segments of his thinking became familiar to most well-read members of Western society.[56]

The technical history of instinct theory continues to attract scholars. Robert J. Richards has added both detail and intellectual context to the brief history of instinct theory sketched above by pointing out that technical biological thinkers found that Weismannism introduced complications into instinct theory that led to their tending to equate instinct and reflex, sometimes without assuming a neurological substrate.* In America, as Hamilton Cravens has shown, there were independent attacks on instinct from sociologists and psychologists, each from a separate point of departure.†

Such developments influenced events on the more popular level, but other, additional, determinants were also operating there. At the end of Chapter 4 I suggested that modern versions of Freud's instinct theory were compatible with the bureaucratic (or organizational) society that was developing in Europe and especially the United States in the early twentieth century. In a similar way, in Chapter 3, a history of the scientific aspects of behaviorism led me to observe that the social control element in behaviorism synchronized with the quest for social order and organization. Now in the chapters in the next part I explore the direct and specific cultural impact of the neurosciences and psychoanalysis.

The literature on the history of psychoanalysis itself continues to proliferate. Most of it (excluding that which is antiquarian), however, is directed to the history of ideas other than the instinctual drive theory.

---

* Robert J. Richards, "Lloyd Morgan's Theory of Instinct: From Darwinism to Neo-Darwinism," *Journal of the History of the Behavioral Sciences*, 13 (1977), 12–32.

† Hamilton Cravens, *The Triumph of Evolution: American Scientists and the Heredity-Environment Controversy 1900–1941* (Philadelphia: University of Pennsylvania Press, 1978), especially chap. 6. See also Hamilton Cravens and John C. Burnham, "Psychology and Evolutionary Naturalism in American Thought, 1890–1940," *American Quarterly*, 23 (1971), 635–657.

PART II

The Cultural Impact of Psychology

The first chapter in this section uses cultural history to establish a periodization in American history more accurate and important than one based on politics and journalism, that is, a periodization applicable to the culture in general. This effort is similar to that later made by J. Meredith Neil to establish logical periods before and after 1955, again using primarily cultural (in his work often high-culture) rather than media/political signposts.* Here I take popular interpretations of the neurosciences, rather than the arts, as a point of departure. Because of their connections to fundamental social assumptions and institutions, those special sciences had multifarious additional broad significances that reveal the major trends in the culture—as the fact that they engender a periodization shows.

* J. Meredith Neil, "1955: The Beginning of Our Own Times," paper presented to the meetings of the Organization of American Historians, New Orleans, April 15, 1971.

CHAPTER FIVE

The New Psychology

From Narcissism to Social Control

In 1931 Frederick Lewis Allen in his delightful book *Only Yesterday* synthesized a now familiar picture of the decade of the 1920's.[1] He characterized as a unit the period that began with the end of the Great War and closed with the spectacular signals of the onset of the Great Depression. Although Allen focused on changes in American life during the 1920's, his portrait of those years has left the indelible impression that they constituted a unit in terms of both public mood and the style of living to which readers of middle class and mass media appeared to aspire.

As historical analysis of the 1920's has proceeded, Allen's image of the decade as a unit has become increasingly untenable. In spite of the impact of the war and the depression, the decade now appears to have encompassed a period of critical change in American life. Instead of constituting a unit, it was a watershed. On one side were the Progressive years and the rebellion of the intellectuals that began about 1912.[2] On the other side came a period when spokesmen for their generation frankly embraced a mass, bureaucratic society and perhaps even the elements of the welfare state. Images from Allen's narrative will continue to permeate discussions of the Jazz Age, but the new periodization gives a more accurate idea of the direction in which American history was moving in the first decades of the twentieth century.

During the 1920's one of the most crucial changes occurred in precisely the area that Allen depicted most effectively: public mood and style of life.

"The New Psychology: From Narcissism to Social Control" is reprinted from John Braeman, Robert H. Bremner, and David Brody, eds., *Change and Continuity in Twentieth-Century America: The 1920's* (Columbus: Ohio State University Press, 1968), pp. 351–398, with the kind permission of the Ohio State University Press.

The phenomenon of the decade that gave the best intellectual representation of the change was the "new psychology." The new psychology was a popularization of conceptions of the human animal and his motives. Although its elements had been present since about 1912 or even earlier, only in the 1920's did the new psychology become one of the characteristic fads of the age and at the same time both symptom and cause of critical social change.[3]

In the early 1920's the new psychology was of great interest because of its relationship to the cult of the self in which Jazz Age Americans were caught up. In a remarkable reversal from an earlier day, social norms produced not only self-centered attitudes but self-indulgent behavior. To this narcissistic preoccupation the new psychology contributed both the idea of the hidden self, with its many ramifications, and a rationalization for the self-indulgent behavior.

In the later years of the decade expositors of the new psychology became involved in an interest in social control that was taking a turn different from an earlier interest in the same subject. Because the new psychology provided information about the instincts, drives, and wants of men, it suggested new ways in which they might be controlled. "The belief that we are at last on the track of psychological laws for controlling the minds of our fellow men," wrote Abram Lipsky in 1925, "has brought about a revolution in the popular attitude towards the science that teaches how to do it. . . . Out of this change has sprung the universal interest in psychoanalysis, psychotherapy, hypnotism, character-analysis, mob-psychology, salesmanship,—all connoting a technique with which one may control the minds of others."[4]

The Phenomenon

The book that gave its name to the movement, *The New Psychology and Its Relation to Life*, was written by an Englishman, A. G. Tansley.[5] An earlier generation of Americans had known another "new psychology"; indeed, E. W. Scripture of Yale had written a book in 1897 bearing that title.[6] The new psychology of Scripture and his contemporaries was an experimental physiological psychology. It consisted primarily of exploring the functioning of sensory processes in normal adult humans. The new psychology of the 1920's represented a revolt against this "dry, academic" psychology, and Tansley, for example, meant explicitly by the term "new psychology," psychoanalysis.

Psychoanalysis represented the first of three phases through which the new psychology went. After psychoanalysis came an emphasis on endocrine glands, and after the glands, behaviorism. Regardless of its changing face, however, there was a distinctive continuity in the new psychology. Tansley, for example, recognized that he was not speaking of psychoanalysis in

any narrow sense; he wanted basically to present a "'biological' view of the mind."[7]

Although behaviorism and the glands had, like Freudianism, come into American technical and *avant-garde* literature about 1912, psychoanalysis clearly dominated the first phase of the new psychology.[8] In an incredible number of publications the literate public had endless opportunities to learn about Freud's psychological theory: the unconscious, the psychic censor, repression, the instincts (especially the sex instinct), and the psychological mechanisms and symbols by means of which drives can gain indirect expression in thought and behavior. Likewise, abnormalities, psychoses and neuroses, significant slips of the tongue and pen, the curative powers of self-awareness, and various facets of psychoanalytic therapy gained publicity. Although the output of more or less popular books and articles on psychoanalysis was beginning to decline perceptibly by the middle 1920's, its influence persisted. Attacks, if not so many expositions, continued to appear. The impact of psychoanalytic ideas on literature, another index of influence, seemed to be cumulative during the decade.[9] The later decrease in expositions of Freud's teachings, in short, reflected their assimilation into popular thinking. Writers of the new psychology representing both glandular and behavioristic points of view, as a matter of fact, usually incorporated, and thereby perpetuated, psychoanalysis in the new psychology.[10]

Competent, professional psychoanalysis was not involved in the new psychology. There were a few full-time analysts left from before the war, such as A. A. Brill in New York, and in the 1920's a small but growing number of young physicians took up analysis. Many of them went abroad for special training.[11] Between them and the denizens of Greenwich Village and intellectual salons there was considerable intercourse, both professional and social, but neither the Bohemians nor the analysts were usually involved in the flurry of publications about the new psychology. The fact is that the specialists, when confronted with popular writers' distortions and dilutions of Freud's ideas, usually reacted with either silence or agonized protest.[12]

Relatively early in the 1920's, a few very active publicists established glandular theories of personality as a part of the new psychology.[13] The shift was quite noticeable, and one observer commented at the time on the sudden change: "How swiftly the spotlight of popular interest shifts from one part of the stage to another! The eyes of distressed humanity turn eagerly toward any quarter that appears to promise health and happiness. . . . Those who recently were reading Freud and Jung have now taken up with Berman and Harrow. Those who formerly were rushing to have complexes extracted are now anxious to have glands implanted."[14]

Following the example of a young New York internist, Louis Berman, these gland enthusiasts exploited not only the established knowledge that gland dysfunction can cause certain diseases and severe personality changes

but the recent work of physiologists who had shown the connection between emotion and glandular secretions. The connection between libido and the glands was of course well known; but gland psychology suggested that one's entire personality depended upon the balance of body chemicals. Specific secretions, according to the theory, can produce indolence and agitation, depression and megalomania. The public at large knew little of the general theory but fed eagerly on sensational stories about treatment with gland extract and gland transplantation. Even well-informed intellectuals took the exaggerated claims of the endocrine enthusiasts surprisingly seriously.[15]

Relatively late in the decade, the new psychology came more and more to emphasize behaviorism. Behaviorism was a mechanistic stimulus-response psychology. Behavioral investigators, using human and animal subjects alike, avoided traditional psychological concepts such as consciousness, cognition, and will. Instead, they carried out severely scientific experiments on how organisms in a carefully controlled environment react to specific stimuli. For some years behaviorism had included as a fundamental unit of explanation the Pavlovian conditioned reflex. Behaviorism had been a serious reform movement within professional psychology since 1913. In the 1920's, especially after 1925, its founder and chief exponent, John B. Watson, who was himself a distinguished experimentalist, had taken to publicizing behaviorism flamboyantly. Behaviorism, like psychoanalysis, had a number of implications, many of them iconoclastic, and generated an intense opposition.[16]

The new psychology in all of its phases was a distinctly popular phenomenon and was therefore subject to both extreme oversimplification and sensationalism. The competence of its expositors varied, but in popularization even the most capable seldom maintained high levels of scientific precision. Many were flatly incompetent to present more than a grossly distorted version of the ideas about which, allegedly, they were writing. Psychoanalysis, particularly, suffered from emasculation and misrepresentation. With all of their intellectual imprecision, however, the general ideas in the new psychology are discernible and can be discussed on that level.

Because it was a popular phenomenon in the period when, as Allen pointed out, ballyhoo reigned, the new psychology was bound to contain at least an element of faddism. Yet the waxing and waning of psychoanalysis, gland psychology, and behaviorism was not entirely a matter of public whim. The proof lies in the great exception, Couéism, which, in contrast to the rest of the new psychology, was ephemeral because it lacked scientific support sufficient to sustain it.

In November, 1921, the Swiss physician who founded the movement that bore his name, Emile Coué, made a triumphal tour of England. Americans immediately imported Couéism from England, and in January, 1923, Coué himself came to the United States. He received a ballyhoo welcome from midwestern as well as New York journalists that gave his message a currency along with mah-jongg. Coué was viewed essentially as a secular faith

healer. His technique was vulgarized into a person's repeating to himself, "Day by day, in every way [emphasize the every], I'm getting better and better." Supposedly, this "auto-suggestion" cured both physical and psychological difficulties and improved the character. A rhymster for *Life* suggested the enthusiasm and exaggeration of the publicity:

> Would you be freed from every kind
>   Of woe and make your forces double?
> Bamboozle dark Subconscious Mind,
>   That ever-present source of trouble.
>
> No matter what your goal or aim,
>   You must not doubt yourself a minute,
> But say, "Of course I'll win the game!"—
>   Subconscious Mind will make you win it.[17]

Coué based his work on the standard psychology of suggestion, which in turn had been inferred largely from the phenomenon of hypnosis (at the time thought to be suggestion in an extreme form). In addition to the conscious mind, so the theory goes, there is a subconscious mind that helps determine behavior. A repeated suggestion aimed at the subconscious will eventually influence it. This had been a well-known theory for many years before the 1920's, and a type of psychotherapy consisting of suggestions made by the physician was frequently employed. The idea of do-it-yourself suggestion, however, was relatively new on the popular level. This novelty made autosuggestion susceptible to ballyhoo, and the scientific aura of the panacea gave it a respectability lacking in other faith cures.[18] For years afterward expositors of the new psychology often mentioned Couéism, along with suggestion, in eclectic treatises; but for the most part, it, like any other fad, disappeared without a trace.[19]

The Background

Contributing to both the acceptance and the image of the new psychology throughout the twenties were the mental testing and mental hygiene movements. Each had its own existence but interacted with the new psychology in important ways. Mental testing was largely intelligence testing. The public, alerted before the war to the dangers of feeble-mindedness, was entertained in the postwar period by the concept of one's mental—as opposed to chronological—age (IQ). Statistical standardization of the tests and their use by the Army in the war gave them added social significance. Intelligence and other mental tests appeared to offer a way in which scientific study of man could be really useful. Up until then psychology had been for the most part a science remarkable because of its lack of potential for practical

application. The tests were of great importance because they suggested that psychology had practical value. This cult of practicability carried over to all of the components that went into the new psychology and eventually guided it in a direction that could not then have been foreseen.[20]

Mental hygiene was a more complex movement. It grew out of both the psychotherapy movement of the prewar period and the discovery of shell shock by physicians and the public, a discovery that had any number of consequences. The psychotherapy movement began about 1906 and infiltrated both medicine and popular thinking. Fields as disparate as literature, politics, and religion felt the impact of the movement. Psychotherapists of the time assumed that environment—and especially social environment—is very important in determining both normal and abnormal human behavior. The success of the physicians using psychological or "moral" means to treat mental illnesses suggested that a more general reform of society and the individuals in it was possible.[21] Like many other aspects of Progressive thought, the psychotherapy movement did not survive the experience of World War I in a recognizable form. It simply vanished, either absorbed or replaced by the mental hygiene movement. Indeed, many of the leaders of the psychotherapy movement were also leaders of the mental hygiene movement.

Because psychoanalysis had been introduced as, and continued to be, an important part of the psychotherapy movement, it is paradoxical that while psychotherapy as a movement withered, psychoanalysis flourished after the war. The Freudian phase of the new psychology is the more surprising because World War I had had a devastating effect upon the growth of psychoanalysis within American medicine. Freudianism, an Austrian import, was suspect because of its supposed Teutonic origins. In the backwash of anti-German feeling, the American Psychoanalytic Association almost disbanded itself in 1919.[22] The phenomenon of shell shock and its consequences heighten the paradox of the fad of psychoanalysis.

Physicians had seen "shell shock" as early as the Russo-Japanese War of 1904–1905, but the trench warfare of World War I caused the malady to appear with sometimes epidemic frequency. Soldiers—and good soldiers—often developed severe symptoms of mental illness, such as hysterical (i.e., psychosomatic) blindness, paralysis, tremors, terrors, and even hallucinations, that rendered them unfit for fighting. As the name implies, the disease was at first ascribed to shock caused by the concussion of exploding shells. The shock presumably disrupted the normal functioning of the nervous system. When careful inquiry revealed that shell shock was more common among troops who had not been exposed to shelling (or, indeed, any action at all) than among those at the front, physicians concluded that shell shock was a common neurosis, a mental illness without any apparent physical cause. The term persisted, however, partly to mask the fact that these ill war heroes had "weak nerves"; that is, were either constitutionally inferior or mildly mentally ill without any reference to war experiences.

The shell shock diseases called attention to environmental causes—as well as to environmental types of treatment—and therefore tended to vindicate the belief of the psychotherapists that these illnesses were, at least functionally, psychological in nature. (Many prominent practitioners, of course, insisted in the name of theoretical materialism that there were real physical changes that just were not discernible by methods then available.) As knowledge about shell shock spread, the public became increasingly aware that one's mind could play tricks on one and produce neurotic symptoms and uncontrollable behavior. Even those of the public for whom shell shock represented physical injury to the nerves necessarily became aware of how common and agonizing nervous diseases could be. By turning the neurosis into a war wound, the experience of World War I mitigated public attitudes toward mental illnesses more effectively than years of humanitarian propaganda.[23]

The war also created a profession to treat these illnesses outside of the mental hospitals'. The specialists in nervous and mental diseases had divided themselves by function into two distinct groups: the neurologists and the hospital physicians. The neurologists concentrated on organic diseases of the nervous system, but many of them participated in the psychotherapy movement and did some outpatient psychotherapy. The mental hospital physicians tended to keep to their asylums where they did more managing of the patients than curing them. Both neurologists and hospital physicians appeared before the public as alienists, or expert witnesses in legal proceedings. After World War I the new specialist, the neuropsychiatrist or psychiatrist, appeared. No longer exclusively a hospital physician or legal expert, the psychiatrist became in the twenties a healer, in either a hospital or an outpatient setting. It is significant, for example, that in keeping with this changing image the *American Journal of Insanity* changed its name in 1921 to *American Journal of Psychiatry*.

This popular conception of the psychiatrist resulted largely from the work of the mental hygiene movement.[24] The mental hygiene movement had been launched in 1908 by Clifford Beers, a former mental patient who enlisted the support of the country's leading specialists in nervous and mental diseases in a diffuse movement to improve the treatment of mental patients and in general foster mental health. As it became clear that the United States would probably become involved in World War I, the newly formed National Committee for Mental Hygiene approached the surgeon general and requested to be included in the war effort. A special committee of leading psychiatrists urged the Army Medical Department to create a special staff and service for nervous and mental diseases. The committee cited not only the statistics of increases in mental illnesses among European soldiers but the fact that "mental diseases were approximately three times as prevalent among the troops on the Mexican border last summer as among the adult civil population." The Army eventually accepted the program of the committee.[25]

By the end of the war several hundred specialists had been enlisted and several hundred more trained to operate a special neuropsychiatric service within the Army Medical Department.[26] Because of the low caliber of many hospital physicians, other doctors had often regarded the entire specialty with some contempt. In the war, however, psychiatrists found themselves fully recognized and appreciated for the first time. The recognition, acquired so abruptly, led these ambitious men to expect, and rightly so, that they could do even better in the 1920's.[27]

The relationship of the psychiatrists, their patients, and their admirers to the new psychology is reflected in the movement that had so successfully infiltrated psychiatry into the Army. During the 1920's and even the early 1930's mental hygiene flourished and grew.[28] It had something for everybody: neurologist, psychotherapist, psychologist, social worker. The key to its scientific and medical success—as well as its political expediency—was the team approach.

The team approach grew out of the work of William Healy, the neurologist who founded the child guidance movement. In the 1900's he had been approached by a number of reformers in Chicago, led by Jane Addams, who were concerned about juvenile delinquents. The reformers believed that science ought to be applied in order to discover why the children had gone wrong. In 1909, therefore, they commissioned Healy to carry out comprehensive studies—psychiatric, physical, psychological—of individual offenders brought before the Chicago juvenile court. Healy did the medical and psychiatric studies himself but also employed a psychologist (primarily to administer mental tests). The two of them, of course, discussed the cases informally and often conferred with social workers from other agencies. After 1917, when Healy moved his operations to Boston, he added social workers to his own staff and instituted the formal case conference to bring together the opinions of experts with different competences, each of whom had studied the same individual case. Healy used as a model the medical case conference of specialists, in which each one presented his particular view of the case and then the group together tried to reach a diagnosis.[29]

The team absorbed and tended to obliterate the special approaches of the neurologist, the psychiatrist, the psychologist or clinical psychologist, and the social worker. A psychiatrist at Buffalo State Hospital thus observed in 1924 that within a few years a remarkable change had taken place in that psychotherapy could no longer be distinguished from psychiatry.[30] Whenever a new emphasis or technique appeared, the mental hygienists could incorporate it and call it their own; such was the fate in the 1920's of Couéism, of gland therapy, of the mental testing movement, of both theoretical and applied behaviorism. Each was absorbed by adding it to the team.[31]

With democratic egalitarianism (or perhaps it was lack of discrimination), the movement welcomed not only medicine, psychopathology, and neuropathology but "psychology, sociology, education, and other fields hav-

ing to do with human behavior and the conduct of life."[32] If the members of the mental hygiene team were united on any point besides the value of co-operation, it was this: They all studied the adaptation, both physical and mental, or, more accurately, "biological," of the individual. In this emphasis they came close to the view of the dominant school in American psychiatry, eclectic dynamic psychiatry. Dynamic psychiatrists, in addition to emphasizing individual life patterns and their adaptive function, included important elements from psychoanalytic psychology.[33]

One further aspect of the mental hygiene movement deserves special notice: its emphasis on child mental hygiene and child rearing generally. Within psychiatry—and typically, dynamic psychiatry—the idea of the importance of early life was traceable directly to the influence of Freud, although popular attitudes that created the "age of the child" had other, equally important determinants.[34] Observers at the time remarked on the unbelievable growth of both medical and popular literature about childhood and child rearing during the 1920's, a proliferation that lasted well into the 1930's.[35]

The dominance of the mental hygiene movement in the Jazz Age raises again the paradox of the psychoanalytic phase of the new psychology. Not only did mental hygiene almost completely supersede psychotherapy but the mental hygienists were not necessarily friendly to psychoanalysis. Even shell shock was used commonly to demonstrate the unsoundness of Freud's beliefs—or what were imagined to be Freud's beliefs. A good example is Sidney I. Schwab, a St. Louis neurologist who in 1906 had been the first person to introduce the term "psychoanalysis" into the United States. In 1920 he asserted that the war neuroses, which clearly had no sexual determinants, had shown Freud to have been basically mistaken.[36] The secret of the success of popularized psychoanalysis lay in the cult of the self and its sequel. That is, a significant part of the literate American public discovered in Freud's teachings (and their distortions) ideas that fitted in with, first, their preoccupation with self and, second, their interest in the controllability of man. That these narcissism and control themes occurred also in the gland and behavioristic phases of the new psychology is a remarkable demonstration of the new psychology phenomenon.

The Cult of the Self

It is ironic that people who viewed their own times as an "Age of Crowds" should see the rise of a strong sense of the urgency of finding one's self. Or perhaps the irony reflects the reality that in the mass society of the twenties depersonalization called forth compensatory attitudes from a large proportion of the atoms of the faceless—and presumably lonely—multitude.

One of the striking developments of the 1920's was the culmination on

a mass scale of public interest in personal, introspective accounts of private experiences. A mass market for popularized personal documents grew primarily out of two sources: the lovelorn column of the newspaper and the cult of physical, that is, bodily, development.[37] As a matter of fact, it was the editors of *Physical Culture*, the Macfudden Company's health and exercise magazine, who initiated the phenomenon. Their offices had been flooded by unsolicited letters of an essentially confessional nature that contained the details of intimate secrets. The editors got the idea of publishing them, and *True Story Magazine* was born. Its success was immediate and unbelievable, and a host of imitators sprang up.[38]

These cheap magazines appealed, as the editors of *True Confessions* observed in 1924, to readers whose reaction was that "that experience is very like my own."[39] Another aspect of this appeal of the confession magazines was the fact that the material in them tended to be guilt-laden or aberrant in some way so that variations from mass society conformity appeared more common—and easier for the reader to deal with in himself—than might otherwise have been the case. It is very much to the point, therefore, that candid and confessional autobiographical fragments were central in popular expositions of psychoanalysis. Psychopathologists often observed that the neurotic's memories in effect caused his illness, and the case reports in the new psychology literature had all the appeal—and more—of true confessions. The relatively frequent, often didactic, use of psychoanalysis in fiction and drama as a device not only for characterizing but for suggesting dramatic problems (mother-son relationships, for example) is testimony to the interest generated by personal revelation.[40]

In other ways, however, psychoanalysis as set forth by the writers of the new psychology tended to diminish the personal and to reinforce the loss of identity and the sense of unreality fostered (presumably) by mass society. In the new psychology the apparent was not the real, and the real was never apparent. One leading exposition was entitled *Unmasking Our Minds*; the author's purpose was explicitly to help the reader discover his real self, under the assumption that it was not obvious.[41] How the new psychology led to confusion of appearances and realities was caught by the writer of a satiric "Nutshell Novel" of 1924 of the variety, "A Psycho-Analytical Idyll":

> Zachariah Hardshell and his beautiful daughter, Clammie, lived on a small farm where they struggled with Poverty and Boll Weevils. Trillion Plunks, the village banker, had warts on his nose, a mortgage on the farm, and designs on Clammie. But Clammie hated him. So Trillion dumped them into the county road. He was very cruel. He often kicked dogs, especially in the motion picture version of the novel.
>
> Byron Keats came along, playing his violin, and found them in the road. He was kind to them. He picked some wild flowers for Clammie. She loved him.

But she couldn't marry him. At first she didn't know why. Then it Dawned Upon her. She didn't love him. She hated him for being a Softie. She loved Trillion because he was a Brute.

She married Trillion and he beat her. That made her happy. But Trillion hated her for letting him get away with it. That made him miserable. Thus was poor old Zachariah avenged. He spent his old age Gloating.

Byron Keats picked some more flowers. He didn't amount to much anyway. He had a complex on destruction. 'Way down inside of him he was bloodthirsty. That was what made him such a Softie.[42]

The themes of deceptive appearance and concern with self came together in the idea of the hidden self. Popular expositions of psychoanalysis confirmed and extended the widely held belief that each person has a real self deep inside, the discovery of which, for some reason, may be desirable. "Dark hidden things," wrote Sherwood Anderson, describing the effects of psychoanalysis, "came out and found expression for themselves, and the miracle was that, expressed, they became often very beautiful." One of the better-known documents of the new psychology, for example, was called *Your Inner Self*. "Self-exploration," wrote David Seabury in 1924, in *Unmasking Our Minds*, "may suggest some answer to such questions as: 'What am I like? What are my strong and weak points? What unconscious conditions suppress and injure me? How can I understand my family, my children, my friends? What effect does my own nature have on health, happiness, marriage, career? How can I solve these problems?' "[43] As Seabury suggested, literate Americans of the Jazz Age typically considered knowledge about the interior self—and cognate understanding of others—to be of the greatest importance.

In literature, obsession with the unobvious and unconscious aspects of personality was destructive of artistic effectiveness. In attempting to portray the flow of free associations, for example, writers often lost the inner consistency that gives characterization its convincing—and interesting—quality. Novelists, for instance, tended to write about their inner feelings and emphasize impulses that they imagined had origins deep in the unconscious. Authors described, sometimes directly, sometimes symbolically, polymorphous perverse and other primitive elements in behavior or motivation as if they conveyed to the reader more meaning than was really the case.[44] In addition to deliberate obscurantism, from the concept of the hidden self writers developed the literary device of a character's being saved by the revelation of his inner self. That is, either some shock or circumstance brought about significant self-understanding, or else the dramatic action was resolved by the *deus ex clinica*.[45] Literature of the decade was strewn with the wreckage of stories and plays in which the psychiatrist offered a clumsy means (often an overnight psychoanalysis) of resolving the dramatic conflicts. If the new psy-

chology provided inspiration and technical details for the literary exponents of searching-for-the-self, they, in turn, contributed to popular knowledge of the new psychology, usually within the context of a sentimental narcissism.

One impetus to the fervent search for the hidden self was the idea that one's *real* self had potential that the everyday one did not. James Oppenheim, a former poet and lay analyst who wrote for a Los Angeles newspaper, used Jungian psychology[46] in his book on *Your Hidden Powers*: "Every human being has hidden powers which must be brought to light and used. . . . Not only is a knowledge of human nature a great power, because we can more successfully deal with others, but it is all essential in learning how to deal with ourselves, how to solve our problems and develop ourselves for the sake of our happiness, our health and our well being."[47]

The chief purveyors of the new psychology, such as Oppenheim, asserted that man's potential—and particularly their own—was seldom fulfilled. If they were not great artists, the fault lay in external circumstances rather than in personal shortcomings. Influenced by Marx, for example, many intellectuals had spoken of the tyrannies of society that held creativity and intellectuality in chains. When the intellectuals realized that early-twentieth-century society was not oppressing them, they found—in part through the new psychology—that it was their interior psyche, the internalization of conventional upbringing, that constrained their actions and withered originality.[48] In this context a person could realize the hidden powers of his self—discoverable through psychoanalysis—not so much by simple revelation of the hidden powers as by unmasking and breaking the interior chains.[49]

In the behavioristic phase of the new psychology, the idea of internalization of external inhibitions persisted, but often in a simplistic form. The behaviorists viewed the personality as the congeries of habit systems built up by conditioned reflexes. Where the behavioristic view was not just a translation of psychoanalytic concepts, the Watsonians suggested that the traditional association psychology served to explain how habit systems of adults originated.[50] Except in so far as the behaviorists emphasized a few primitive fear and sex reactions, their extreme environmentalism tended to change the emphasis of the new psychology from searching for the inner self to finding out how a person got to be the way he was.[51]

The new psychology expositions of the early 1920's had shifted remarkably in emphasis from comparable writings of the prewar period. For years there had been any number of books and articles addressed to the "nervous." The tone of these Progressive period tracts was embodied in two motifs: self-improvement (the authors were generous with exhortation) and, either directly or indirectly, social improvement and service. Expositors of psychoanalysis before the war, for example, often stressed the idea of sublimating one's primitive desires into useful social activity.[52] In the twenties the authors of the rapidly proliferating literature of the new psychology changed the

emphasis from self-improvement to self-justification; they moved from the progressive idea of service to the postwar idea of discovering one's wants, needs, and desires (usually in the hidden self or primitive chemical and reflex systems) and gratifying them.[53]

The method of justifying one's present condition was simple: No matter what you do, according to the new psychologists, your motives are impure. Therefore, why improve? Behind every action the new writers found a base motive. "Don't you even know, Mother," said Claire, the flapper daughter in John Howard Lawson's *Loudspeaker*, "that everybody's thoughts are obscenely vile? That's psychology."[54] André Tridon, a lay analyst in New York and prolific publicizer, in one chapter showed that people who talk about the weather are inhibited, "poor, weak, underdeveloped human beings . . . not daring to love and admire violently anything or anybody"; that pompous persons have a tendency to schizophrenia and "compensate for their intellectual inferiority by unbearably good manners and an annoying form of accuracy"; that snobs are "neurotics afraid of life and of competition," regressed in their exclusiveness "to the prenatal level in which the child is protected against all of life's problems but death"; that those who begrudge praising others are trying "unconsciously to kill those who [unlike themselves] do create by never mentioning them"; that superstitious people, besides having inadequate nerve and gland stimulation, "are obsessed by a sense of guilt, which, unfortunately, has a solid foundation of fact [in the unconscious], and they fear retribution"; that those who go to watch the spectacle of a destructive fire are envious sadists—"everyone is at heart a jealous brute who enjoys whatever damage is inflicted upon someone else's person or property." Tridon went on to analyze, similarly, animal lovers, busybodies, conservatives, and cardplayers, among others.[55]

The popular pseudo-Freudians reserved their sharpest scorn for the reformer, a contrast to the prewar psychoanalytic writers' tendency to urge social reform. It was explained that moral superiority originated in a most unrighteous secret self that was in danger of breaking loose. The "puritan" who was sensitive to sexual subjects suffered from "suppressed Pornophilia" and probably was hypersexual in nature. "We are told of certain professional reformers," wrote new psychologist William J. Fielding, "who have large collections of obscene pictures."[56]

When the gland psychology came in to supplement and supplant psychoanalysis, the wicked unconscious in each of us acquired palpable reality. Writers of the gland epoch attributed virtually every characteristic action to impulses generated by the chemicals secreted by the ductless glands.[57] Even the mental testing and IQ craze was utilized as a justification for not changing one's self. Because intelligence tests had suggested that feeble-mindedness was a major—and often unobvious—factor in criminal and other abnormal behavior, the IQ was often incorporated into the concept of the hidden self (and the public, it turned out, tended to confuse mental subnormality with

abnormality). Unsuspected brilliance could also be discovered in the real self. As a Yale psychologist, Howard W. Haggard, wrote, *'Tisn't What You Know But Are You Intelligent?* "Intelligence," he said, "is the capability to do productive thinking." It is not necessary to know "what Leonardo da Vinci's two most famous paintings are." Or who wrote *Carmen*. Or, apparently, to do any disciplined thinking at all.[58] One could, in short, justify his lack of self-improvement simply by pointing out his potential—a remarkable reversal of prewar devotion to acquiring character and culture.

When behaviorism came to supplement and replace psychoanalysis and the glands in the make-up of the new psychology, one's present behavior was ascribed to the accident of environmental conditioning as well as one's gut reactions. In this way the idea of self-justification continued to be a basic theme in the new psychology. It was easy to trace one's character to the circumstances and automatic emotional reactions that conditioned and gave rise to his "habit systems." As Ross L. Finney of the University of Minnesota pointed out in a book attacking behaviorism, behavioristic mechanism implied that one experience—and the conditioning that results—is as good as another. There was therefore, again, no serious motivation to change oneself.[59]

Watson himself offered the most convincing evidence of the conservative nature of behaviorism. Although he was famous for his dictum that by manipulating environment he could make any infant develop into any specified kind of person, from beggarman to lawyer or chief, Watson always in fact qualified the assertion. By 1928 he confessed that although theoretically even adults should be able to change their personalities by reconditioning, modern man lacked the necessary means of thoroughgoing control to effect a significant reconditioning. People were too spineless, too lazy and careless, said Watson, to be able to change themselves. As he grew older, he said, he became convinced that "the zebra can as easily change his stripes as the adult his personality."[60]

Regardless of specific content, the behaviorists in their popularizations echoed the same iconoclastic tone as the vulgarizers of psychoanalysis. Where the psychoanalytic writers ruthlessly showed the real self to be found in the mind, the behaviorists were talking about the real self of the gut, that is, reflex actions.[61]

The expositors of the new psychology in centering on the self almost invariably spoke in terms of motives. This preoccupation with motives was one of the marks of the age.[62] Psychoanalysis and its successors revealed that the cause of even the most innocent, everyday behavior could be shown to be impulses that were clearly improper and immoral, or at least uncivilized, in nature. H. M. Kallen, who knew both Academia and Bohemia in New York, asserted about his own times that "men have ceased to be clear in their hearts about their own motives and actions, and have become suspicious of those of their fellows."[63] The hidden, even unconscious, motive was known long before, in the writings of eighteenth-century political philosophers, for

example, and the *avant-garde* had for some time used Marxian insights to discredit the motives of apparently altruistic contemporaries. The new psychology emphasized a far more primitive type of motive and the ways in which a man rationalized and hid such motives from himself.

Even in Marxist analysis, the motives of men had some rational goal in terms of the function of the individual within the social system of production. The new psychology tended to emphasize the irrational, to deny at all the efficacy of reason on the level of motive.[64] A long period of intellectual preparation, including currents such as naturalism, decadence, and primitivism, the writings of Zola, Nietzsche, and Marx, had effectively introduced ideas of the irrationality and animality of man.[65] In a time of general disillusionment after World War I, the new psychologists, too, expressed disenchantment with the nature of man. Two immediate factors also helped account for the success of the disillusionist aspect of the new psychology: the war experience, when cherished beliefs turned out to be propaganda, and the popular impact of science, especially evolutionary thinking. One acute contemporary observer listed three propositions that were in vogue in the 1920's: "that men are moved by the same instincts as the lower species; that instinctive conduct is mechanically determined; and that the reasons conventionally given for conduct are mostly sophisticated 'rationalizations'."[66]

It was during the 1920's that the famous instinct controversy in sociology and psychology occurred, and its contents and resolution were often included in expositions of the new psychology. One of the chief aspects of the development of the psychology of motivation was the appearance of dynamic psychologies, in which the concept of instinct was used to account for the actions of man.[67] Among the lists of human instincts that various writers suggested, those of Freud and William McDougall predominated. It was in the eventual defeat of McDougall's viewpoint that the new psychology reflected most interestingly the spirit of its times.

McDougall, writing originally in 1908, had explained human behavior in terms of a number of instincts—such as the acquisitive and the gregarious —that he found expressed in well-refined adult human ways and, specifically, in civilized institutions.[68] The new psychology tended either to analyze all behavior back into instincts that are strictly animal, in a traditional sense, such as sex and hunger; or, as in behaviorism, instinct was largely discarded and man's behavior construed to be the result of accidental associations of primitive visceral and behavioral reactions. It was no accident that behaviorism grew out of non-verbal, biological animal psychology. Where specifically human drives did show up in the new psychology, they tended to have amoral connotations, such as the will to power or narcissistic self-love. The glands, as Theodore Dreiser illustrated very well, suggested a somatic concomitant for both blind, reflex action and primitive instincts as determinants of supposedly adult, civilized actions. What he had once referred to as "chemisms" took by 1925 the form in the hero of "the Efrit of his own darker self."[69]

That man has bestial passions was of course an ancient idea. In addition, Nietzsche and other writers had made common the idea that the supposedly compensatory noble instincts of man—as posited by many nineteenth-century thinkers—were in truth only myths. But this early-twentieth-century conception of man's passions, emphasizing his irrationality, differed from Hobbes's conception of man in modifying the familiar idea of hedonism and introducing an element of wilful impulsiveness uncommon for some time in Western thinking on man's nature. "The gorilla in us," wrote Tridon in 1924, "is starved for fresh air, exercise, wild motions, explosive manifestations of mirth. And the gorilla in us now and then avenges himself by compelling us, in neurotic attacks, to act like a gorilla."[70] This emphasis on the animality of man, however, did not give the new psychology its distinctive tone. The bestial passions tended, in actual exposition, to be rather boringly conventional passions; and the will to power, for instance, was surprisingly well articulated and adult. The new psychology had its impact in emphasizing not the bestial so much as the infantile and the abnormal.

Like other elements of the new psychology, the emphasis on the persistence of childish elements in adult behavior had developed in the period before World War I. As reflected in education and in other areas, America had "discovered the child," although in a culture long known for its indulgence of children, the child-centered school could hardly be described as a surprising development. Biological thinking of the day suggested that the process of growing and maturing—and adapting to the environment—both foreshadowed and determined adult patterns of life. Freud's assertions that early life patterns would persist into adulthood found a receptive audience. The behaviorists gloried in bringing infants into the laboratory, using infantile behavior patterns to fill out their general psychology. Where in the Progressive period the perspective had tended to be backward, tracing back the ways in which violations of the supposedly natural course of childhood had produced effects in adults, in the 1920's the perspective was forward looking: The environment and experiences that were provided for the child were of overwhelming importance because of their influence on later life.[71]

The cult of child rearing and child mental hygiene that was so typical of the twenties signified the concern of the age with the childish—and more specifically, the infantile—elements in the hidden self.[72] The educators especially seized upon the idea of self-expressionism in order to foster creativity in children and, presumably, adults. "The creative impulse is within the child himself," wrote the authors of a major pedagogical document of the period.[73] This idea of course sounded very much like some traditional romantic ideas, but it appeared—not always with logical consistency—in the "scientific" context of psychoanalysis and behaviorism.[74]

Since both the animality and infantilism of man were emphatically "natural," the deliciously rebellious flavor of the new psychology showed up best in the harping of its expositors upon the pervasive existence of ab-

normality in supposedly innocent human actions. "Civilization is a study in pathology and perversion," asserted one new psychologist.[75] (Nor, it should be added, is there any more effective argument justifying one's shortcomings than pointing out the prevalence of the same or worse in the population in general.) For some, the very exposure of the forbidden subject of abnormality was, perhaps understandably, unpleasant. "It is certainly somewhat trying," remarked the Jesuit psychologist E. Boyd Barrett, "to be reminded in every new book on psychology of the abnormal characteristics of pyromaniacs and homosexuals." The appeal of the new psychology, he asserted, did not need to rest on a morbid curiosity about side-show freaks.[76]

Yet the writers of the new psychology in all its phases did exploit—in however sugar-coated a form—expositions of abnormality. Tridon in writing thirty-one chapters on *Psychoanalysis and Love* spent two chapters on fetishism, two on neurotic lovers, two on non-monogamous love, two on jealousy, two on homosexuality, three on sadism-masochism, and one each (emphasizing abnormality) on virginity, modesty, and prostitution. Additional chapters likewise contain subheadings such as "Having Her Fixation-Fling."[77] The more urbane of the rebellious writers could find in every traditional human institution an amazing amount of abnormality. One such author, Samuel D. Schmalhausen, must have come close to establishing a record in a chapter he entitled "Family Life: A Study in Pathology." He not only contended that the "family is the cradle of incest" but pictured it as holding its members in "neurotic bondage." Parents continuously, he asserted, "are predisposing their children to neurotic and psychotic breakdown, to social maladjustment and misery, by preventing them from achieving ego-adequacy." And he concluded pessimistically about marriage: "When two human beings, . . . loaded with defect and derangement [as are all modern couples], attempt to bring to one another sexual joy and ego-tranquillity and human fellowship, one need not be an expert either in statistical reasoning or in psychopathology to realize with a start how very few the chances of harmony and beauty and fulfillment."[78]

The simultaneous interest in self and interest in the abnormal reflected the common concern of the time about "normality." The public in general had become vividly aware of the idea of normality when intelligence tests became standardized and widely publicized. The idea of deviation in the form of feeble-mindedness was refined to include personality traits. Not surprisingly, therefore, in the 1920's a number of personality tests appeared, designed to detect personality deviations. So great was the concern about normality that a discipline known as industrial psychiatry grew up to try to eliminate misfits from industry just as they had been screened out of the Army. The mental hygiene movement similarly popularized this concern about abnormalities of every kind: Eccentricities could in a rather romantic way take on the quality of portending sinister events in the hidden self. The possibility that abnormality might include most people—which fasci-

nated the self-centered—grew not only out of the discovery of abnormality in garden-variety aspects of life but out of the publicity about shell shock, which underlined the well-established idea in popularized psychiatry that it is difficult to draw a line between normal and abnormal.[79]

As the new psychologists introduced both primitive passions and abnormal behavior into their expositions, they inevitably and characteristically gave much attention to sex. The new psychology popularized two ideas: first, the importance of sexual desires and drives, and, second, the presence of sexual factors in a wide variety of supposedly non-sexual phenomena. One psychiatrist in the mental hygiene movement, Arthur G. Lane, admitted candidly, "The new psychology . . . has created unwarranted antagonism in many minds, and morbid curiosity in many others, because of the prominence given to the sexual instinct as the main driving force that motivates all human conduct."[80]

The new psychology, with its high sexual content, paralleled the sex education movement and the change in moral standards traditionally associated with the new freedom of women and World War I.[81] What was notable about the sex content of the new psychology was its adolescent character—adolescent in consciously sexualizing not only the hidden self but all human phenomena, and adolescent in using the sexual content for purposes of expressing a more general rebelliousness.

To a surprising extent the very freedom to talk about sexual matters generated a great deal of energy devoted to testing that freedom, and expositions of the new psychology provided a vehicle for discussing in a scientific or reasonable guise matters that otherwise would have been considered offensive, forbidden, or just plain puerile. Pornography was hidden in the case history; any word could appear in print as long as "neurosis" or "complex" appeared with it.

As disillusionment became an end in itself for the intellectual rebels and their followers, the iconoclasts found that imputing sexual qualities and motives to people's actions was an effective way to discredit them. The Marxists had, of course, for a long time used the conception of marriage as legalized prostitution to attack capitalism. In the 1920's such general attacks on institutions because of their effects on the relations between the sexes—and now with a tithe of abnormalities thrown in—flourished. Writer Floyd Dell, in his well-informed and sensitive essay on *Love in the Machine Age*, for example, condemned any number of social and economic institutions because of their undesirable effects on love making.[82] The religious establishment was especially vulnerable to sexual analysis. The pious naturally reacted with anguished objections. Barrett, the Jesuit, for example, denounced the idea that religion was simply a disguised expression of sexual instincts. "This blasphemous theory has, unfortunately, made its way into current literature," he admitted. "Hints and innuendos inspired by it are dropped here and there. Religious ritual is likened to pagan orgies. Devout and pious believers are

described as neurotic, and in a veiled way it is suggested that they are homosexual. Heaven is spoken of as a disguised sex-dream. Religious symbols are spoken of as *phallic.*"[83]

The connection between sexual emancipation and the new psychology was clear to everyone. Ben Hecht, testing the limits of emancipation, provided a good example by dedicating his work to

> the reformers—the psychopathic ones who publicly and shamelessly belabor their own unfortunate impulses; to the reformers (once again)— the psychopathic ones trying forever to drown their own obscene desires in ear-splitting prayers for their fellowman's welfare; to the reformers—the Freudian dervishes who masturbate with Purity Leagues, who achieve involved orgasms denouncing the depravities of others; to the reformers . . . the psychopathic ones who seek to vindicate their own sexual impotencies by padlocking the national vagina, who find relief for constipation in forbidding their neighbors the water closet.[84]

Nor was sexual rebelliousness the exclusive domain of psychoanalysis and its close relatives. The fact that popularizers of the influence of the glands devoted a large part of their expositions to the gonads testified not only to their business sense but to the beliefs of both the writers and their readers. Similarly, behaviorism, in the laboratory more purely "scientific" than was tolerable to many psychologists, in the hands of Watson and other popularizers sounded essentially the same as vulgarized psychoanalysis in stressing the importance of proper sexual education and the extreme importance of sex in all life matters.

It was psychoanalysis, nevertheless, that bore most of the burden of the common popular association between the new psychology and sex. The usual belief was that Freud had shown that (1) repressions—presumably sexual in nature—were at the root of many nervous illnesses; and (2) the less repressed a person was, therefore, the healthier he was. This popular conception coincided in time with a widespread belief that sexual mores were changing and led to the conclusion that psychoanalysis and the whole new psychology were partly responsible for the change in moral standards.

Liberated spokesmen for the Jazz Age as well as their critics shared this belief. "We studied Freud, argued Jung, checked out dreams by Havelock Ellis, and toyed lightly with Adler," asserted a precocious teen-age writer. "And all these authorities warned us of the danger in repressing our normal instincts and desires." Playwright Rachel Crothers, in her heavy-handed satire *Expressing Willie*,[85] recognized the common belief with the song lyrics, "Express Yo'se'f My Chile," in which one is warned not to suppress himself but to let all his emotions "rise to the top." Playwright Crothers explicitly contrasted the injunction of 1924 to "*Express yo'se'f*" with the type of child training and advice to young ladies known in a former time and embodied

in exhortations to suppress one's feelings and impulses. Expositors of the new psychology such as Tridon implied continuously that expressing one's true self—more than was customary—would be the royal road to health and happiness.[86]

The extent of the change wrought by the new psychologists' tender concern about repression is reflected best in the sex education movement. During the 1920's the sex educators played down their customary emphasis on abstinence for the sake of preventing disease from fear of causing too much repression. One critic of the new psychology, for example, who charged that Schmalhausen's book *Why We Misbehave* deserved to be called *Why We Should Misbehave*, still showed himself remarkably timid about asserting that a little repression, at least, is harmless.[87]

Unreconstructed critics of the new psychology alone remained relatively unconcerned about repression, possibly because they understood the fundamental issues. One of the most vitriolic, Harvey Wickham, recognized the similarity between popularized psychoanalysis and behaviorism. Both are materialistic, he wrote, and both are mechanistic. "The two philosophies," he continued, "have but one effect—to sanction *laissez-faire* in matters of sex. A verbalized but otherwise unconditioned 'gut-reaction' is but a conscious 'libido' freed from the suppression which might create a 'complex.' Dr. Watson's superiority lies in his insistence upon education where sex is not involved. Freud's superiority is literary."[88]

Even the sexual emphases of the new psychology, in the context of emphasizing man's wants rather than his duties, were often understood to be self-indulgent, or at the least self-centered.[89] This theme of egocentricity flourished especially in the psychoanalytic period of the new psychology. The behaviorists also incorporated it by emphasizing, for example, the uniqueness of each organism. With the behavioristic phase, however, came the second characteristic of the new psychology, one that set popularized psychology of the later 1920's off from the immediate postwar period and, in one way, connected it to the 1930's. This was the theme of control—social control.

Social Control

When the psychologists used the mental test in World War I to bring attention to the usefulness of psychology, they gave impetus to the development of an important aspect of modern bureaucratic society.[90] In the 1920's the mental tests were used primarily in the schools, but as part of the new psychology were also applied to industry. During the war the military had adopted three devices from the psychologists: the intelligence tests to weed out those whom it was not worthwhile to train; systems of rating subordinates so as to introduce a semblance of objectivity; and aptitude tests. After the

war, segments of industry, with much encouragement from psychologists, ostentatiously adopted or at least experimented with the three devices.[91]

The industrial use of psychological tests reflected a major shift in attempts at scientific management. Scientific management had, in the Progressive period, typically focused on the job, as exemplified in the Taylorization, or rationalization, of industry and time-motion study. Gradually the conception grew that centering attention on the worker rather than the job might turn up ways to increase output. From the one-best-way approach to a task, the new thinking turned to a recognition of individual differences in the workers. Thus personnel work, with its own literature, scientific management, and paternalism in industry, with its dual goals of increasing production and killing unionism with kindness, all called attention to the importance of the worker. After stable employment conditions replaced the high labor turnover period of the immediate postwar years, and after the evident failure of much of the testing to achieve practical results—around 1925—interest in mental tests declined. But the basic quest of industry for a practical industrial psychology remained.[92]

The new psychology, as a psychology of motivation, had great potential for any applied psychology. As one professional psychologist noted at the time, "A rather insistent demand for an adequate psychology of motivation has always been made by those who are interested in the control of human nature. It has come from economists, sociologists, educators, advertisers, scout masters, and investigators of crime."[93] The businessmen, especially, because of their interest in controlling human nature, wanted to know how to predict it. As Loren Baritz has pointed out, with the growth of large bureaucratic organizations, managers needed to avoid the unpredictable, even the unpredictable human element. "The goal was to create an organization so perfect that . . . it would be run by law, not men."[94]

In the first stage of the attempts to apply the new psychology as such to industry, writers suggested that industrialists take into account the instinctual drives of their employees. Ordway Tead, for example, produced a book on *Instincts in Industry* in which, for the sake of completeness, he even took up "the sex instinct" as applied to the factory. Since Tead (who used primarily McDougall's conception of instincts) spoke chiefly in terms of the direct expression of instincts, the chapter dealt mostly with seduction and stands as a parody on itself and the not uncommon idea of applying general concepts of instincts directly to the problem of control of labor.[95]

Meanwhile, the psychology of advertising and selling had developed early in the century as one of the first areas in which psychology could be applied.[96] For some time the standard motivations of man appeared in the literature of both psychology and business as elements to which advertisers and salesmen could appeal. Then in the period of the new psychology, while the basic idea of appealing to men's wants remained the same, advertising psychologists largely abandoned the concept of human instincts as such and

turned instead to the specific, determinable wants of men. As Henry C. Link, an advertising psychologist, explained, the new psychology of selling led to "studying people's wants and buying habits as the best clue to what they *will* buy, in contrast with the older emphasis on overcoming their sales resistance to articles which we think they *should* buy." To Link the market survey was fundamentally behavioristic, and certainly this departure represented the applied psychology version of the movement—again, largely behavioristic— to avoid speaking in terms of theoretical human instincts.[97]

A similar development, a second stage, within industrial psychology was even more revealing. The personnel specialists began to talk about the specific wants of the individual workers rather than generalizing about them. Control of the workers and preclusion of "labor problems" was now thought of in terms of dealing with the concrete and immediate set of desires of each worker. The wants could either be satisfied or they could be tempered, diverted, or otherwise controlled. Although writers on industrial psychology tended to assert that they had the workers' good at heart, control obviously could lead to exploitation.[98]

When Benjamin Stolberg, a well-known Marxist writer, denounced psychology for its sellout to capitalism, he could present a strong case. Not only had a group of leading scientific psychologists formed their own corporation—The Psychological Corporation—to spread the use of psychology by businessmen (at considerable profit to the psychologists, as it turned out), but industrial psychological consultants were making effective use of the idea of dealing with immediate wants of workers so as to prevent either a major problem or any questioning of the situation. The worker was supposed to be at fault, not the system, and he was supposed to adjust to it. "The key-word of psychology today," asserted Mary Parker Follett, one of the best-known writers on industrial psychology, "is desire." She developed a system of solving labor problems by open and candid analysis of the wants and desires of the parties involved, during which process the reduction of the conflict to simple, specific elements took much of the fight out of both sides. A smart manager, she said, would study habits and reaction patterns and anticipate them, thereby bringing them under control.[99]

Perhaps it was appropriate that in the "business civilization" of the 1920's the concept of social control should have had experimental application in industry and that important techniques in the bureaucratic manipulation of people should have been pioneered by business. The idea of social control was an old one. Originally the concept had centered on the informal controls that society exercises over the individual, the mores or folkways. Out of the possibility of manipulating these informal controls rather than, say, laws or orders, came the idea of social management.[100]

After the war, many intellectuals sensed that old social patterns had disintegrated or were in the process of doing so. Many of these thinkers

therefore eliminated the concept of determining social patterns from among the major underpinnings of their world views; such thinkers instead began utilizing the new psychology of the inner self.[101] It was inevitable, then, that the new psychology, while replacing the older assumptions on which previous ideas of social control had been based, would contribute new approaches to the subject. The behaviorists, especially, explicitly emphasized the idea of predicting behavior in order to control it. Advocates of the new objective psychology were acutely aware of what one *avant-garde* writer discovered only in 1924: its "crying and significant social meanings." [102]

In the new psychology, writers did find aspects of the individual that might be used for purposes of social control. "The disillusioned—not disheartened—liberalism of today," observed William Ernest Hocking, a Harvard University philosopher, in explaining contemporary interest in the problem of human nature, "turns itself heart and soul to psychological enquiry. It perceives that there is a human nature which invites the use of the same principle that Bacon applied to physical nature,—something having laws of its own which must be obediently examined before we can hope to control it." [103] It was in searching for means of control that the postwar thinkers found the irrational. In 1925, in his book describing *Means of Social Control*, sociologist F. E. Lumley expressed this fact in his conclusion that "control by the methods discussed has been accompanied by and charged with a very large .amount of primitive or childish *feeling*." And Lipsky, in his *Man the Puppet: The Art of Controlling Minds*, remarked on "the growing realization" that knowing "the nature of the psychological dispositions . . . make[s] control possible." [104]

Just as the businessman found that direct appeals to basic human nature would not lead to control, so thoughtful Americans learned from the use of propaganda during the war the way in which the irrational in man can be manipulated. Walter Lippmann, in *Public Opinion*,[105] one of the most influential books of the decade, stated the common conclusion that predictability does not follow from knowing the basic drives and interests; what was needed for social control was the knowledge of how each individual will perceive a situation, how his conceptualization of reality as he knows it will in turn activate his drives and instincts, not in their primitive form but in their practical, habitual, and adult form. In business the market survey provided one model; in public life, public opinion polls. The test of validity was not hypothetical drives but actual behavior.

The new psychology contributed, therefore, in many ways to the preoccupation of the people of the 1920's with controlling other people. An outstanding example was H. A. Overstreet's famous book *Influencing Human Behavior*.[106] Here was a chapter, "The Appeal to Wants." Here was the idea of changing people by changing their habit systems. Here were explanations of behavior such as "rationalization." All of them were synthesized in a

context of common sense to the end of enlarging the individual's feeling of power and control, on the one hand, and on the other hand, self-valuation and self-importance.

It is easy to show how the new psychology reflected and exemplified main currents in American society and culture in the 1920's: how self-centered, self-indulgent attitudes and an emphasis on men's desires laid the foundation for social control, how the search for the interior self led to attempts at external control of people.[107] At first used by business in the twenties, the new psychology emphasis on social control portended much for the 1930's.

The new psychology was involved in the expression of many phenomena and attitudes distinctive to the twenties. It was part and parcel of the change in manners and morals that F. Scott Fitzgerald and Frederick Lewis Allen portrayed so vividly. And the new psychology was also involved in trends of the decade that may eventually appear more significant than changing moral standards (such as, for example, the remarkable intellectual assault on the institution of motherhood) but which scholars have thus far hardly explored.[108] In most of these examples the role of the new psychology was no greater than that of other cultural forces, such as the popular discovery of primitive cultures through the work of such anthropologists as Margaret Mead. The new psychology was so involved in cultural changes of the 1920's as ultimately to raise the question whether its importance can be determined with any precision or even suggested meaningfully.

But important as it was as the mirror and index to an era, the new psychology provided, if not the tool for cultural change, at least the avenue of its expression. The new psychology suggested a meaningful way to work out in practice the relatively vague concepts of social control that had developed in the Progressive period.

The new social control movement adopted from the health crusades of an earlier period the concept of improving the world not by social action but by a patient program of individual treatment of large numbers of people. As tuberculosis and syphilis were fought not primarily by general laws but by curing everyone who was sick, so the mental hygienists and other new psychologists wanted to change the social mass—one atom at a time. The change can be epitomized in the shift from general prohibition laws to the individual treatment of the alcoholic by a psychiatrist—or Alcoholics Anonymous.

More clearly than even the businessmen, the social workers showed the impact of the new psychology in their emphasis upon individual therapy and adjustment and its use as a melioristic device. Social workers had been a powerful and important element in the prewar Progressive movement and in harmony with that movement had emphasized the role of environment in the lives of their clients. As a consequence, the social workers gave much attention to general social reform measures as well as to the dependent people with whom they worked directly. By the late twenties casework,

under the influence of psychiatry, tended to abstract the client from his "environmental and cultural milieu" and to emphasize his internal attitudes and even his emotional life. The inner man, not the outer environment, was to be adjusted.[109] By offering the technique of conditioning, the behaviorists, too, furnished a concrete method whereby their aspirations for social control could be worked out in practice, case by case, person by person, without any troublesome recourse to general social reform.

The new psychology of the twenties, whether in the form of mental hygiene, psychiatric social work, or business personnel and welfare practices, provided the technique for modern bureaucratic society.[110] In addition to control through mass movements, advertising, the propaganda and voluntary actions typical of, say, World War I, now there was control through the bureaucratic society in which the inner need, the individual desire, was carefully manipulated and indulged, person by person, so as to prevent the childish, brutal, perverse, or savage in any man's hidden self from disrupting the predictability of civilization.[111]

The agencies of control in bureaucratic society were still the experts, as in the Progressive period, but now their expertise was directed toward individuals rather than general problems. Floyd Dell, who typified the intellectuals of the early twentieth century, reflected the sentiment generated by the new psychology in suggesting that social salvation lay in the *deus ex clinica*, the psychiatric treatment of everyone.[112] More typical of the extravagant bureaucratic society to come was the team approach, the committee of experts, looking not for desirable social changes, but trying to help the individual in a world taken as given.

On the popular level, then, the technical interest in instinct theory had a counterpart in the idea of motives. Intellectuals in general expanded their vision from the idea that human nature was animal to the idea that it was also infantile and abnormal. And clearly two areas of applied psychology/psychiatry made a substantial impact on the middle-class "public": intelligence tests and mental hygiene. Beyond showing a lively interest in the idea of social control—a subject to which I shall return several times— historians in recent years have devoted much effort to attempting to spell out specifically the cultural importance of the intelligence tests and mental hygiene components of the new psychology.

Much of this interest grows out of presentist concern about mental health care delivery and the social consequences of IQ testing.* Beyond such literature, a number of real scholarly contributions have appeared. Hamilton Cravens, for example, has put the increasing emphasis on cultural factors among intelligence researchers into the historical context of the United States after the mid-1920's. Sol Cohen has traced the impact of the mental hygiene campaign on education, identifying it as a major source of many educationists' emphasis upon the personality of the school child—in the age of progressive education when emphasizing the child's social and emotional development was a major influence in educational institutions and efforts. Fred Matthews, in his major interpretive essay on mental hygiene, attempts to steer historical discussion back to the intellectual and social impact of mental hygiene, which acted as a social ideology that reinforced other values already present in American culture, particularly those found in the social gospel.†

---

* One obvious exception is Norman Dain, *Clifford W. Beers: Advocate for the Insane* (Pittsburgh: University of Pittsburgh Press, 1980), and another is Michael M. Sokal, "The Origin of the Psychological Corporation," *Journal of the History of the Behavioral Sciences*, 17 (1981), 54–67.

† Hamilton Cravens, "The Wandering IQ: American Culture and Mental Testing," *Human Development*, 28 (1985), 113–130. Sol Cohen, "The Mental Hygiene Movement: The Development of Personality and the School: The Medicalization of American Education," *History of Education Quarterly*, 23 (1983), 123–148. Fred Matthews, "In Defense of Common Sense: Mental Hygiene as Ideology and Mentality in Twentieth-Century America," *Prospects*, 4 (1979), 459–516. The two standard works I have already alluded to: Merle Curti, *Human Nature in American Thought: A History* (Madison: University of Wisconsin Press, 1980), and Hamilton Cravens, *The Triumph of Evolution: American Scientists and the*

The next paper (given as an overview for a series of lectures on psychoanalysis in America) builds on the insights and information from the foregoing chapter's close look at all of the new psychology in the 1920's and alludes to it. But now I refocus my inquiry by (1) extending it to all of the first three-quarters of the twentieth century and (2) at the same time narrowing the subject to psychoanalysis alone. My intention is to show the extent of the influence as well as to trace the changes that occurred as a core group of pioneers evolved into the world center of psychoanalytic thinking and enthusiasm.

Heredity-Environment Controversy 1900–1941 (Philadelphia: University of Pennsylvania Press, 1978). One broad and authoritative historical survey is Raymond E. Fancher, *The Intelligence Men: Makers of the IQ Controversy* (New York: W. W. Norton and Company, 1985). Recent scholarship is in Michael M. Sokal, ed., *Psychological Testing and American Society, 1890–1930* (New Brunswick: Rutgers University Press, 1987).

The Influence of Psychoanalysis upon American Culture

Late in the 1960's an era ended when, in both medicine and American culture in general, psychoanalysis increasingly came under attack. Competent eyewitnesses were agreeing that, as California psychiatrist Judd Marmor put it, "the prestige of psychoanalysis in this country appears to have dropped significantly in academic and scientific circles." Substantial numbers of psychiatrists hastened to dissociate themselves from a strictly analytic stance, and the analyst was no longer so often the ideal of youngsters in the profession. Other intellectuals felt free to portray Freud's work as an undesirable holdover from the past. The shifting opinions of medical and cultural leaders may well have reflected merely the total victory of psychoanalytic thinking, a point in time beyond which attack was not a real threat to those in and near psychoanalysis. Or a real change, to something new, may have occurred. Not enough time has passed yet to reveal which. But in either case, the historical turning point affords some perspective on the impact of psychoanalysis upon American culture.[1]

Freud's work came upon Americans in two different waves. The first wave coincided with Progressive reform, psychotherapy, and new ideas about the place of children and sexuality in American society. The second wave came with the bureaucratic society that developed in the 1930's and after, especially following World War II, when the numbers of people increased so

"The Influence of Psychoanalysis upon American Culture" is reprinted from Jacques M. Quen and Eric T. Carlson, eds., *American Psychoanalysis: Origins and Development* (New York: Brunner/Mazel, Inc., 1978), pp. 52–72, with the kind permission of Eric T. Carlson and Jacques M. Quen.

as to move American society to a new scale and when new groups with new values became dominant.

In both periods, the primary carriers and disseminators of Freud's teachings were the physicians; increasingly, as the years went on, those who practiced psychoanalysis.[2]

Well before World War I the followers of Freud clustered together in a few cities, reinforcing each other and attempting to convert others to the psychoanalytic viewpoint. Fifty years later the conversion experience and ways of holding beliefs among Freudians still suggested religious institutionalization and commitment. Members of analytic groups, usually later formalized into psychoanalytic societies and institutes, performed two important functions. First, they acted as apostles who could persuade others to join the ranks, for, as in all other major innovations in science, true belief and conversion almost invariably required personal explication before a potential believer made a commitment to new views. Second, they presented relatively undistorted versions of what Freud taught.[3]

The influence of psychoanalysis was of course not limited to propagation of orthodox Freudianism by the best-qualified analysts and their immediate lay adherents. Far more often Freud's influence was partial and piecemeal, carried by cultural agents who had little or no comprehension of the total work of Freud, its internal consistency, or its significance. Nevertheless, the analytic groups represent initial influence and provide indications of the general direction of the flow of events. And it would be as much a mistake to underestimate the analysts' influence as to overestimate it.

The two phases of psychoanalysis in America are in fact most easily delineated by internal changes in both content and personnel in the analytic movement. During the 1920's the initial propagators of psychoanalysis lost much of their effectiveness. The most prestigious Freudian, J. J. Putnam of Boston, died in 1918. The most loyal and vigorous disciple, A. A. Brill of New York, went through a period of bad personal relations with Freud. Illness incapacitated Horace W. Frink, the most promising of the Yankees. Trigant Burrow developed his own ideas. Many others tended to retreat into more general psychiatry, particularly in the guise of mental hygiene.

By the end of the 1920's, the analytically sophisticated understood that Freud had turned aside from his earlier emphasis on instinctual drive and repression as such. Within a decade or two, most of Freud's close adherents were building on his new structural scheme of id, ego, and superego to work within what was called ego psychology, in practice emphasizing the strengths and competences of the psychical apparatus. These new ideas were often carried by distinguished refugees who came to dominate American psychoanalysis, ably seconded by a new group of Americans who had studied directly with Freud or some other European in the twenties and early thirties. The combination of new versions of analysis and new person-

nel represented essentially a fresh departure and furnished a burst of energy that pushed the second wave so fast and so far as to overshadow completely the substantial continuity from the initial group of Americans who took up Freud's ideas.[4]

By 1940, in fact, as people at that time recognized, the center of world psychoanalysis had shifted to the United States. The refugee analysts were self-confident and extraordinarily able. The ease with which they moved into the analytic community, moreover, reflected the substantial success of the psychoanalytic movement in maintaining an international character. This transit of endeavor, ideas, and personnel was facilitated markedly by a new and particular receptivity of American culture to international viewpoints.[5]

Since the discontinuity within organized psychoanalysis coincided with major shifts in American culture, the impact of the analysts has to be viewed in terms of rapid changes in social groups. The formerly dominant cultural groups, both Progressive and conservative, consisted mostly of persons narrowly American, often dominated by New England consciences. By 1940, however, the nation's cultural life was dominated by a new elite, a Jewish and WASP group in revolt against ethnic provincialism—the WASP against "100 per cent Americanism" and all that it stood for, the Jews against the village culture of the ghetto. The new ideal was a cosmopolitan culture, and the rise of Hitlerism made this American aggregation feel like the inheritors of Western civilization and humaneness, a feeling intensified as European emigrants joined the group.[6]

The new liberal intelligentsia played the essential role in popularizing psychoanalysis and broadening the influence of Freud's teachings. Relatively direct evidence exists in the form of known personal contacts and, perhaps even more important, personal analyses. A similar, and in part identical, group dominated the mass media, especially those originating in New York and Los Angeles, and these leaders exerted a similar influence on a lower level of American culture. Many major figures in the entertainment world were in fact psychoanalyzed. Brill held back from writing an autobiography for fear that it might turn out to be something of an exposé involving many well-known members of the art and literary world.[7] So close were the contacts between the analysts and the new arbiters of culture that it was more than coincidence that the end of dominance of the liberal intelligentsia in the 1960's came at the same time as troubled questioning among the analysts.

Within this very concrete and specific social context of direct influence, it is possible to suggest how powerful the impact of psychoanalysis was and to go on and suggest that, in fact, changes that occurred could represent actual influence. In the context of the intelligentsia as the embodiment of Western civilization, for example, the importance of the analyst's image as cultured cosmopolitan emerges. Many intellectuals saw discussions of literary interpretation in analytic scientific literature as lamentable demonstrations of analysts' soft-headedness, or at least tender-mindedness (read: "unscien-

tific"). But to the liberal intelligentsia, the analysts represented scientists who were sensitive to the values of other intellectuals who shared the intellectuals' concern with preserving Western civilization and at the same time with denying those traditional standards that were merely ethnocentric and self-serving. Franz Alexander sensed the core belief when he wrote in 1956, "Psychoanalysis is a true product of that phase of Western civilization which had deep respect for individual differences that people actually have in our complex free societies."[8]

Examination of the second phase of the penetration of Freud's influence into the United States is particularly important because there already exist competent historical accounts of much of the first phase.[9] In that first phase, psychoanalysis was carried primarily within two successive, more general movements, psychotherapy and mental hygiene, and popularization was confounded with both general intellectual rebellion and a myriad of books and articles for "the nervous." The second phase of psychoanalysis is complicated by the fact that intellectual *avant-gardism*, books for the nervous, and mental hygiene persisted for many decades even though no longer as significant, or at least only percolating down to those Americans subject to cultural lag. Despite such obscurity and uncertainty, contributed by the continual alterations of the social matrix, it still appears that first-phase knowledge did not necessarily contribute to or even facilitate second-phase psychoanalysis. Rather, persistence and lag merely added another, contemporaneous version of influence—and distortion.

The core group from whom influence in American culture emanated, the analysts, never numbered more than several hundred. In the heyday of analysis, the 1950's, the various institutes were turning out fewer than a hundred new analysts a year (and the institutes were turning down, and often embittering against psychoanalysis, many times that number of psychiatrists who sought admission).[10] The pressures on the lives of those few hundred were very great. Many agreed with Karl Menninger of Topeka, who asserted in 1944 that there was need in the world for "psychiatric counseling" and that psychoanalysts had important insights they "can and should give to the world." Yet most analysts in fact resisted pressures to involve themselves in various outside causes and reforms. An analyst mostly, as Lawrence S. Kubie lamented in 1950, "practices analysis all day and teaches analysis all night." Such an analyst also worked to maintain skepticism and detachment rather than dedication and belief—except, of course, belief in psychoanalysis.[11] The number of the core group, even very late, then, who were active in influencing American life was very small indeed. The more is the wonder that their impact was so great. Magnification occurred not only because of their effects upon elites, especially the WASP-Jewish cultural leaders, but because of two further factors: the institutional setting and the general cultural readiness for Freud's teachings.

The analysts were first of all psychiatrists. Earlier in the twentieth cen-

tury they had also been neurologists or, more generally, nervous and mental disease specialists. After World War I, the profession of "neuropsychiatry"— soon generally shortened to the conventional "psychiatry"—developed, with half of the psychiatrists no longer in hospital practice by 1930 and the specialty of psychiatry no longer necessarily identified with psychotic patients. Although still under the domination of hospital psychiatrists until World War II, increasingly the profession took on a public aspect of possessing both wisdom and omnipotence, particularly as preventive mental hygiene moved into many public arenas, including business and education, in the 1920's. The image of the psychiatrist in the 1930's was augmented by widespread publicity given to physiological determinants of behavior, such as endocrine activity, and to new medical procedures, such as electroencephalography and shock therapies.[12]

Despite the physical orientation of most psychiatrists, it was the psychotherapy and psychological manipulation advocated by conspicuous specialists, including the analysts, that caught the imagination of the public and, eventually, of the specialty itself. The critical event was World War II. By the late 1940's, the by then familiar figure of the psychiatrist was very frequently identified as an analyst, complete with couch and, to the distress of the analysts, a note pad. This was the cartoon stereotype, and despite the ambivalence he represented, he embodied an astonishing popular belief in his knowledge and power.[13]

It is only fair to observe that this idealization of the psychiatrist as analyst was in part based upon the attitudes of the psychiatrists themselves. The bulk of American psychiatrists in the post–World War II years often utilized approaches based upon psychoanalytic formulations, the strategy generally referred to as dynamic psychiatry. The extreme in this direction was the analyst, and he increasingly was functioning as an ideal as well as, to a diminishing minority, a devil. And while the ranks of analysts were limited to a few hundred, psychiatrists increased in number to tens of thousands by the 1960's. For years, many of the best students in medical school were becoming interested in psychiatry, and in turn the best residents in psychiatry tended to go on into analytic training.[14]

What happened in World War II therefore had two aspects. First, psychiatry gained immense importance in the eyes of both physicians and the general public. Second, everyone, both within and without psychoanalysis, traced to psychoanalysis the content that made such an impression. While a good deal can be shown of the way in which the war experience left a popular impact, exactly what happened to open the door to dynamic, or psychoanalytic, interpretations in medicine and popular thinking remains obscure. One basic fact, with innumerable instances applicable to both medical practice and public awareness, was the personal contact of physicians and service personnel with psychiatric disabilities and psychiatric treatment. While similar experience with so-called shell shock in World War I had led to substan-

tial popularizing of mental hygiene and neuropsychiatry, the scale and conspicuousness of psychiatry in the World War II experience had much more far-reaching effects. Conventional wisdom of the day, both lay and medical, remarked about the large number of cases of "battle fatigue" and the excessive proportion of exclusions and discharges for psychiatric reasons. The great influx of psychoanalytic thinking came, presumably, in explaining to officers, physicians, public, and patients *why* the mental disability occurred and was to be taken seriously.[15]

It was in this situation that the analysts, despite their small numbers, clearly gave the most satisfying answers. And they had the chance. At the beginning of the war, the screening instructions for recruits had their origins with Harry Stack Sullivan, who had his own version of dynamic psychiatry. By the end of the war, the man in charge of Army psychiatry and most effective in selling it was William C. Menninger, a member of the Topeka Psychoanalytic Society. John M. Murray, of the Boston Psychoanalytic Society, headed up the Army Air Force psychiatric service. Many a physician or layman who saw the results of psychotherapy or group psychotherapy or especially narcoanalysis, in which the abreaction effects were strikingly like those reported by Freud in his earliest period, decided that there was validity in dynamic explanations of inexplicable behavior and even of some physical problems. The demand for psychiatric treatment and consultation far outran supply, and the hard core of hospital psychiatrists was swamped and passed by.[16]

While institutional factors in the 1930's and after account for the propagation of dynamic ideas that were fundamentally Freudian in origin, the readiness of Americans to take up those dynamic explanations is not so easy to explain. Menninger himself noted that the time was ripe for what he was fostering. In May 1945 he reported that "psychiatry, for better or for worse, is receiving a tremendously increased interest. This is manifest on all sides by articles in magazines, in the newspapers, frequent references to psychiatry and psychiatric problems on the radio and in the movies. It is reliably reported that at least six pictures currently being made in Hollywood have a psychiatric tone or overtone. This interest is widely manifest in government agencies, and . . . we have had inquiries and requests for help from a wide variety of such agencies and also from civilian groups".[17]

Despite persistent publicity in the 1930's, pre-war America offered no adequate foundation for a mass movement in favor of psychoanalysis or even psychiatry such as Menninger reported in 1945. The dominant hospital physicians of the late thirties were conservative and tended to view even mental hygiene suspiciously.[18] Indeed, in 1945 a number of progressive specialists felt constrained to form the Group for the Advancement of Psychiatry in order to get around the still powerful conservatives in the profession. During the 1930's, psychoanalysis itself was not conspicuous in the mass media, however sophisticated the liberal intelligentsia was in the use

of analytic terms, and in the early war years popularization ebbed further, if the *Reader's Guide* is an accurate index. Yet by 1948 psychoanalytic and other varieties of popularization of psychological dynamics caused Frederic Wertham to write in the *New Republic* that "the tremendous amount of popular reading in psychopathology is an important social phenomenon." He himself thought that it distracted people from pressing world problems to what he termed a "cult of personal contentment."[19] By 1950 the frequent appearance of couch situation jokes not just in the *New Yorker* but even in cheap cartoon magazines was the best indicator that the man in the street, even he who was not quite up to illustrated magazines, was expected to know the psychiatrist/psychoanalyst.

For those who not only looked at the pictures in *Life Magazine* but read the articles, there was an official—and well informed—article in 1947 in that weekly:

A boom has overtaken the once obscure and much maligned profession of psychoanalysis. It is part of the larger boom which simultaneously has engulfed the whole science of psychiatry, in which psychoanalysis is a special therapeutic technique, and which has made the 4,011 accredited psychiatrists about the most sought-after members of the entire medical profession. From the horde of outright psychotics who now occupy more than half of all the hospital beds in the country to the simple-minded folk who seek guidance and solace from the phony tea-leaf "psychiatrists" in Los Angeles and elsewhere, the story is the same—a mass demand for psychiatric help which has swamped facilities and practitioners alike. And of all psychiatrists, the comparative handful of analysts—there are only about 300—seem to be the most heavily besieged.

In part this reflects the alarming prevalence of mental and emotional disorders in the population today; in part, it merely reflects the increase in popular knowledge and acceptance of psychiatry, and especially psychoanalysis, as a cure. During the war millions of service personnel had direct contact with psychiatry for the first time and large numbers of them received more or less elaborate psychiatric treatment. Meantime, a whole new literary genre became popular, with the learned Freudian and the analytic couch as its symbols. Novels about mental illness (*Private Worlds, The Crack-Up, Brainstorm, Snake Pit,* etc.) were frequent. Hollywood quickly followed suit, and numbers of "big" pictures of late have had psychiatric overtones. Indeed it is rare to find a Hollywood musical these days without some sort of pseudo-Freudian "dream sequence," a convention dating from the huge success of Moss Hart's *Lady in the Dark*, which concerned the efforts of a mixed-up editor of a fashion magazine to solve her difficulties through psychoanalysis.

All this has happened quite suddenly. Several decades ago, to be sure, a few psychoanalytical terms—notably *ego* and *libido*—were part of the vocabulary of the country-club set, and moralists were complaining that the loose conduct of the times was due to Sigmund Freud's engaging theory that sex makes the world go 'round and that it might be dangerous to harbor repressions in this sphere. As far as the average man was concerned, however, psychoanalysis remained dark science, with no apparent usefulness except to the neurotic idle rich.[20]

Similar evidence of the widespread popularization of psychoanalysis continued in the following decades. By the 1960's, there were at least three *children's* books alone devoted entirely to Freud. In the 1940's, mental hospital reform flourished in many states and the federal government began heavy subsidies of mental health research and personnel training. By 1963, before a whole new federal program was undertaken, the budget of the National Institute for Mental Health was almost seventy million dollars. Part of the public support for these massive efforts grew out of sympathy for the mentally ill; but a more significant segment involved American hopes for the overall benefits psychiatry might bring.[21]

To explain this acceptance, conventional wisdom of that day and since suggested that the psychiatrist had become the priest or authority figure in American culture within a new secularism. But the development of a new authority figure did not take place in a vacuum, nor did World War II destroy religion. A better explanation is that the enthusiasts of dynamic psychiatry and psychoanalysis, like the Menninger brothers, were asserting that they and their colleagues could contribute to a better world because they knew the causes of human unhappiness. Later a conservative cult of contentment—as Wertham suggested—may have been important, but for the decades coinciding with the high tide of psychoanalytic influence in America, the analysts, the deviant analysts, and many of their psychiatric and lay followers persisted in describing the benefits of psychoanalytic treatment and applied psychoanalytic psychology in terms of glowing promises. The public acceptance of psychoanalysis/psychiatry mushroomed in that brief moment of expansive optimism of the 1940's when many Americans really did believe that they could make the postwar social environment a significantly better place in which to live. In 1947 members of the New York Psychoanalytic Institute predicted that 20,000 psychiatrists would be needed for preventive work alone.[22] The members of a number of analytic splinter groups were particularly devoted to social reform and wrote eloquently on the subject, drawing substantial public attention. But more than just psychiatry was involved.

Beyond psychiatry, the analysts were involved in medicine and science, and in the image of each one. The rise of psychoanalysis coincided almost exactly with the spectacular transformation of medicine, and the care that Americans took to keep formal psychoanalysis within medicine helped shape

the direct influence. Increasingly, descriptions of the functions of medicine in society included not only curing the ill but bringing happiness by means of both physical and mental manipulation. "It is increasingly evident," reported the Rockefeller Foundation as early as 1934, "that physicians generally are being looked to for knowledge that will help in interpreting as well as in guiding the behavior of man."[23] The idea that physicians could work miracles with surgery and pharmacology carried over to the psychiatric realm, and once again the analyst was portrayed as the ultimate wise man and manipulator. One sign of medical acceptance was the number of physicians and members of their families who were analyzed; in the 1950's over half the analytic patients in Los Angeles, for example, fell into this category.[24]

But in fact the increasing prestige of science, especially after the advent of atomic energy, endowed anyone who wore a white lab coat with a special kind of authority. And within medicine and science, the second wave of psychoanalysis had a particular claim to prestige: Freud's work, and psychoanalytic literature in general, emphasized the theoretical—far more than comparable medical, scientific, or psychological publications. In another day the theoretical content of Freudian literature had alienated many Americans who preferred that their science be highly empirical. The most damaging criticism of psychoanalysis had always been that it was unscientific. Analysts were deeply offended, for example, when the 1925 president of the American Association for the Advancement of Science, psychologist J. McKeen Cattell, asserted: "Psychoanalysis is not so much a question of science as a matter of taste, Dr. Freud being an artist who lives in the fairyland of dreams among the ogres of perverted sex."[25] To combat the unscientific image, American proponents of Freud in fact showed an extreme readiness to work with psychological testing, with psychosomatic medicine, and with neurology to try to connect Freudian theory with the concrete, the material, the statistical, and the replicable. But as theoretical science became more and more prestigious in the United States, the situation reversed, and the analysts shared in that prestige and were called upon to join, and offer insights and theory to aid the work of, organismic holists and other very "respectable" scientists.

Despite the analysts' attempts to keep their subspecialty within medicine, another discipline, psychology, became almost as important in disseminating knowledge about the work of Freud and his successors. The profession had two rather separate aspects, both of which involved members in spreading the influence of psychoanalysis. The first was as teachers of, ultimately, hundreds of thousands of college students who took elementary courses in the subject each year. As early as 1916 a general textbook had mentioned Freud's ideas, and various teachers, most importantly Edwin B. Holt at Harvard, had even earlier discussed psychoanalytic ideas in lectures. Yet by and large most psychology teachers remained hostile, in general emphasizing their methodological objections and agreeing with Madison Bentley, an experimentalist, who in 1921 commented on the Freudian unconscious

that "this confusion of hypothesis with observed and verifiable fact is extremely common within psychology today . . . an illegitimate substitution of forces and faculties for the empirical existence of mind."[26] But the relentless urge of the academic psychologists to gain students and influence led to a steadily increasing inclusion of psychoanalytic ideas in even elementary instruction. Once again, World War II seemed to bring a critical transformation. Textbooks changed to meet what one set of authors described frankly as an alteration in point of view, associated with the war, so as to require material on "problems of personal adjustment." The only obvious event that might have been a cause for any of these new attitudes, beyond the psychological testing of all service personnel, was the production of an extremely widely distributed popular paperback book, *Psychology for the Fighting Man* (1943)—"What you should know about yourself and others." As that book engendered new images and expectations, so increasingly in elementary expositions postwar psychologists concerned themselves with motivation, emotion, abnormality, and personal problem solving with increasingly frequent discussions of psychological therapy and allusions to psychoanalysis. Over the years, as psychology classes proliferated, a substantial fragment of the population had had at least some exposure to material and vocabulary that had its origin with the Freudians.[27]

Even more spectacular in growth was the second aspect of psychology, clinical psychology. After World War II, for every new psychiatrist added to the ranks, two clinical psychologists sprang up, with about the same effectiveness in spreading some knowledge of psychoanalysis. Although many clinical psychologists were attached to school programs, many more were undertaking psychotherapy and sometimes psychoanalysis, in spite of the analysts' attempts to restrict their own numbers to M.D.'s only. Even many relatively well educated people did not discern much difference between a psychiatrist, a psychologist, and a psychoanalyst—and very often there wasn't much, in terms of actual functioning.[28] In fact popular interest—again as reflected in the *Reader's Guide*—increased in the postwar decades in the psychology headings far more than in those for psychoanalysis. Such psychologist psychotherapists as Carl Rogers were portrayed in texts and popularizations as equal and competitive with Freud. And unhappy as the Freudians were about it, all psychotherapy brought knowledge of Freud's work, however partial and distorted, from 1905 to the 1970's.[29]

The expanding role of psychologists in using and spreading Freud's ideas came to be based increasingly on the changing content and theory of psychology itself. The influence of behaviorism had been to inhibit attention to intrapsychic events but to encourage both adaptive and genetic viewpoints. Because Freud's psychology helped so much in conceptualizing emotion and motivation, however, psychoanalysis was not far from the interests of many psychologists. By the forties and fifties, the learning theorists, who represented the most prestigious element in the discipline, were finding

that their concerns, problems, and formulations were startlingly like those of the ego psychologists within psychoanalysis who had inherited the mantle of theoretical orthodoxy among the Freudians—each emphasizing the way a person adjusted to both internal and external reality, and developed competence.[30] Much of this change represented Freud's influence on the psychologists. By persistently standing for an ideal or extreme position—as with the psychiatrists—the Freudians helped to give courage to hard-headed experimentalists in dealing with difficult problems such as contexts of perceptions, or motivation and drive. Curiously, the influence in psychology grew on itself: The selfsame group of psychologists who joined Clark Hull's seminars on psychoanalysis and learning at Yale in the 1930's (initiated by Neal Miller, an analysand) were the leaders in the movement to establish and expand clinical psychology after World War II—using government money and existing, usually experimental, departments of psychology for training the new personnel.[31]

All of this specific activity by the analysts, the psychiatrists, and the psychologists provides a set of social structures through which Freud's influence can be traced in definite ways as it came into the United States. The reaction of the dominant WASP-Jewish intelligentsia further shows how receptive were cultural institutions, formal and informal, especially just before, during, and after World War II. Indeed, the confluence of signs of influence in the early 1940's raises the question of what psychoanalysis had to offer Americans at that time, for the phenomena were too striking to represent merely general cultural compatibility.

The obvious need that was met was described by psychiatrist Henri Ellenberger after a visit to the United States in 1952: "In Europe," he observed, "people go to the psychiatrist because of a *symptom*, in America because of a *problem*." The European patient wishes to be restored, Ellenberger continued, while the American wants to have a problem solved, and the psychiatrist therefore becomes a person "who solves problems." And in the United States, Ellenberger observed, the ideal treatment for such patients was psychoanalysis, "acknowledged in America as the therapeutic method par excellence." For whatever reasons, social or personal, post–World War II Americans were willing to spend large amounts of money themselves and through their government in the pursuit of a happiness that consisted of solved problems.[32]

The cartoonists' ambivalent portrait of the omnipotent analyst, the enthusiasm for social control, first noted in the Progressive era and then surfacing again in the 1940's, and the anti-mental health campaign of the McCarthy period and after—all suggested the power of psychiatry, and especially psychoanalysis, to give people hope that problems could be solved, indeed that people should be happier.[33] Advocates—and opponents—of psychoanalysis were all well aware of the possibilities in Freud's teachings. He had himself explored some of them as they affected social processes as well

as individual concerns. Freudians were among the leaders in questioning pressures to conform, in suggesting that non-conformists could be happy and well adjusted (although, of course, within analysis there was a vigorous debate on this and kindred issues). The promise of happiness and normality, as philosopher Walter Kaufmann of Princeton pointed out in 1960, was based on the leveling tradition inherited from Freud: "Like no man before him, he lent substance to the notion that all men are brothers. Criminals and madmen are not devils in disguise, but men and women who have problems [the common heritage] similar to our own; and there, but for one experience or another, go you and I."[34]

Focusing on personal problems and solving them, as a number of observers pointed out, was a particularly effective tactic employed by managers of the increasingly bureaucratic American society, a tactic to head off, indeed, deny, the existence of social discontent.[35] The most brilliant of the post-Freudian theorists, Erik Erikson, showed that every culture developed more or less adequate social institutions to accommodate every developmental stage and drive in the life cycle of human beings—all of whom, in every culture, shared life cycles that embodied the universal human so vital in the assumptions of the liberal intelligentsia. Erikson's teachings were easily corrupted into the conservative assumption that any changes that needed to be made were on a one-by-one, individual basis—as in psychoanalytic psychotherapy—and in that individual, not in the culture.[36] Similarly, the stress of the ego psychologists on competent, non-disruptive functioning fit precisely into the needs of the bureaucratic society for citizens who were function-oriented and played their assigned social roles in the complex machinery of production, distribution, and gratification. Indeed, the idea that Freud's teachings were merely the agencies of social forces raises directly the possibility that psychoanalysis was a symptom of historical change rather than a cause of it. Surely the distortions of Freud's ideas in the United States, in the direction of making them both more medical and more social than in Europe, suggests the powerlessness of ideas to mold rather than to be used by presumably deeper historical currents.

One sensible way of testing the impact of psychoanalysis on American culture is to examine very specific areas where the influence can be demonstrated, most notably the learned disciplines. In psychiatry the impact was fundamental, and in psychology also. In anthropology and sociology, from William I. Thomas's four wishes to recent social psychological theory, again competent studies suggest basic influence.[37] Other students have demonstrated impressive use of the ideas of Freud and his followers in literature and art and religion.[38] In short, such evidence covers all of what is conventionally known as culture, both high and, as noted earlier, popular culture. The positive evidence that psychoanalytic ideas affected those who embodied both cultures is profound and impressive.[39]

But in order to assess possible negative evidence—the changes at-

tributed to psychoanalytic thinking that can be accounted for as well or better by other historical forces—a different approach is appropriate. A brief test of two alleged influences, which can be called, respectively, hidden motives and sex, suggests much use of the name and vocabulary of psychoanalysis to cover the effects of other forces—and at the same time much real influence.[40]

Americans learned about the hidden motives of men from many sources in Western culture besides Freud. The most concrete and contemporary was Marxism. Bohemians and intellectuals who began uncovering hidden motives, presumably in the Freudian mode (in fact usually crudely sexual in the early days), had before that learned the technique of analyzing economic motives hidden behind common, socially accepted rationalizations. Yet the mechanisms of motive conversion that Americans did learn from Freud made analysis of hidden motives more systematic and more convincing.[41]

The discussion and to a lesser extent the acceptance of sexual feelings and behavior presumably so characteristic of twentieth-century America have often been attributed, for good or ill, to Freud. In this case the social hygiene movement was clearly antecedent in time and was in part—because Freud was one of the few authors available in English who had touched on the subject—the agency through which Freud's ideas were popularized. Certainly during the first wave of psychoanalysis Freud was the rationale, not the cause of events. As Waldo Frank recalled, girls who came to Greenwich Village wanting to be seduced would have given in just as easily to persuasion couched in terms of social liberation as they did to warnings about the dangers of being inhibited. Like those young ladies, writers favoring or opposing what they imagined to be changes in American sexual attitudes and actions blamed and praised Freud. In later years it was common to overlook the analysts' emphasis on the intrapsychic functioning of sexuality and rather—and inaccurately—to connect the analysts with perceived behavior and with the stress on undifferentiated "outlets" found in the works of Alfred Kinsey and his successors.[42]

If, then, these examples are expanded to a systematic evaluation of the influences of psychoanalysis on the United States, account must be taken not only of multifarious levels and types of influences but of possible concurrent cultural changes in which Freud's work was merely incidental. What can be made, for instance, of the fact that Freud was stressing intrapsychic conflict just when the writers of novels were shifting their focus from external actions and social relationships to inner feelings and psychological development? Or, again, if Freud's ideas of the unconscious and instinctual drives were utilized to verbalize a new theory of evil in the world, that is, to provide a way of articulating an awareness of irrationality in human affairs, how much influence does that mere use of a psychoanalytic vocabulary signify? Contrary instances, in which concepts are used without vocabulary, are equally complicating. The most important is the evidence of A. Michael Sulman that the influence of psychoanalysis was profound indeed in the work of Benjamin

Spock and other child-rearing advisers who utilized many psychoanalytic ideas without the terminology, including concepts previously absent from child-rearing literature, such as penis envy and sibling rivalry.[43]

When all of the filtering of the complications is completed, the evidence reveals a number of modes in which psychoanalysis affected American culture—even discounting the ability of Americans to read Freud as they read the Bible, namely, picking out parts and interpreting the text so as to be able to cite passages in defense of almost any position at all.[44]

In many areas, such as changes in sexual attitudes or the need to have problems solved, larger forces than psychoanalysis *were* determining the general direction of change. What psychoanalytic ideas contributed was some of the form that the changes took. The causes of apparently inexplicable behavior, for example, were often found in instinctual drives and defense mechanisms rather than the devil or economic man. On quite a different level, the patient-analyst relationship became an important model for social interaction and for suggesting human relationships in the process of overcoming difficulties (most conspicuously and formally in the pastoral counseling movement). While Freud's work was not the cause of much social change as such in many areas, he and his followers did influence the ways in which historical forces worked themselves out in American society.[45]

As in both psychiatry and psychology, one fundamentally important function of psychoanalysis in American life was that of representing an extreme position. Political historians have long since pointed out the role of extremists in social processes in the United States. An extremist to either left or right makes a substantial shift in position toward the extreme appear to be "moderate," and moderate, middle-of-the-road positions are those that command the consensus necessary for Americans to take action. So psychoanalysis, a well-thought-out, generally consistent position, enabled basically conservative people in many fields to move at least some distance toward Freud's position—and to take it seriously. Such partial acceptance may represent distortion—but it does also represent influence.[46]

This role of psychoanalysis as extreme or ideal was particularly important in helping the dominant cultural group maintain important values—those encapsulated in the Western civilization conception. The perceptive Chicago analyst, Maxwell Gitelson, who chose to speak for the most orthodox Freudians in 1955, believed with considerable justification that in practice his work and that of his colleagues created "a bastion of creative individualism."[47]

Freud was influential in the culture because he made sense within that Western tradition. People have been puzzled to understand the force that caused many important and central literary people and scientists alike to repeat in print elementary formulations of psychoanalysis as if trying to convey some of Freud's basic ideas to the reader. So often the id, ego, and superego, or the list of so-called mental mechanisms, were entirely alien to previous—

and successive—work of such thinkers. Some of the interest of course can be written off in ad hominem terms as merely the attempt of a person to solve his own personal problems, or perhaps an aberration, like a temporary interest in Marilyn Monroe or genealogy. But the list of such cultural leaders, including those who were not analyzed, was over the years far too long to be dealt with on an individual level. In the mass, interest in even the detailed structure of the Freudian schema was a cultural phenomenon, symptomatic not necessarily of cultural attraction so much as of the awesome power of the intellect of Sigmund Freud. Good minds recognized that power, and in that recognition they translated it into a historical force. Such a major thinker who was widely read could influence any civilization in which surpassing intellectual achievement commanded respect.

Attempts at overarching assessment such as the foregoing are rare, despite the amount of material published on the historical impact of psychoanalysis. This interpretation raises the question of evidence and yet is designed to show that substantial amounts of specific evidence of the impact of psychoanalysis are available, certainly enough to mute skepticism about the cultural impact of Freud's teachings and his institutional legacy. But even specific cases show that historical and social forces acted in concert with an identifiable specific, psychoanalysis.*

Examinations of the place of psychoanalysis in American society and culture have continued to appear, some of which build on the foregoing work.† In another place I also tried a further conceptualization of the process of the penetration, acceptance, and use of Freud's teachings. When, especially before World War II, there was an intellectual *avant-garde* in the United States, Freud's work gained attention as part of advanced thinking in both medicine and culture. One unhappy critic of 1914 listed psychoanalysis along with "occultism, symbolism . . . cubism, futurism, modernism . . . the problem play" as an imposition on the civilization that he knew. Many advocates of the *avant-garde* who believed that it furnished sure signs of the direction as well as the fact of progress portrayed Freudianism as the orthodoxy of the future: The psychoanalytic physician, wrote Florence Kiper Frank in 1916, was "the modern medicine man . . . the priest of the new order!" Later, when the idea of the *avant-garde* was disappearing from the culture, psychoanalysis became just another medical specialty in a bureaucratic society built around specialization, at best merely representative of the general psychological-mindedness of the mid– to late twentieth century.‡

In the next section, I explore a very specific area in which psychoanalysis and the other neurosciences interfaced with other,

---

* Considerable light is thrown upon the impact on the United States by comparisons with other countries; see especially the collection of papers in *Comparative Studies in Society and History*, 24 (1982), 531–610.

† For example, John Gach, "Culture and Complex: On the Early History of Psychoanalysis in America," in Edwin R. Wallace IV and Lucius C. Pressley, eds., *Essays in the History of Psychiatry* (Columbia: Wm. S. Hall Psychiatric Institute of the South Carolina Department of Mental Health, 1980), pp. 135–160.

‡ John C. Burnham, "From Avant-Garde to Specialism: Psychoanalysis in America," *Journal of the History of the Behavioral Sciences*, 15 (1979), 128–134.

and very important, elements in social history—elements that involved the continuing controversies over the place of sex, self-control, and social control in America. While my emphasis will be on social context, ties between the far-ranging subjects of psychological assumptions, medicine, and the neurosciences as well as moral standards as such are a reminder of the unity of culture that appeared as American society evolved.

PART III

American Moral Standards

My work in the field of moral standards grew, curiously enough, directly out of my research into the history of psychoanalysis and the medical, especially psychiatric, background of the reception of Freud's work in the United States. As observations in chapters in the previous section suggest, Americans associated psycho-analysis with sex and, more specifically, with openness about sex and new attitudes toward sex.* I was astonished to discover that even before Freud's teachings arrived, Americans found them-selves trying to cope with powerful forces that made for changes in the realm of attitudes and behavior in the sexual sphere. As a responsible historian, then, I attempted to find the social forces other than psychoanalysis that accounted for early movements for sex education and what many people believed was more en-lightened sexual behavior. In this way I early became one of the few scholars doing any systematic investigation into the history of sexuality per se.

The following chapter was a report on the state of scholarship just when other historians were beginning to recognize the im-portance and legitimacy of this type of question. A version of the chapter was, in fact, presented in 1970 at the very first session of the American Historical Association annual meetings ever de-voted to the history of sex. Nowadays it appears to be a survey of what many historians would consider largely the pioneer stage in the development of the field, at a time when women's history, in particular, had not yet come into its own. But this chapter is also more than a survey, for the evidence cited in it shows that the history of sex has always been, however slight, an element in social and cultural history, and an element with ties to many aspects of the culture. Moreover, the terms of analysis suggested an approach to the subject.

* A recent further historical investigation of this question is Leslie Fishbein's "Freud and the Radicals: The Sexual Revolution Comes to Greenwich Village," *Canadian Review of American Studies*, 12 (1981), which describes how even rad-icals drew back from the radical implications of Freudianism and merely used it as a rationale for tame experimentation that had origins elsewhere.

American Historians
and the Subject of Sex

Historians often claim that their discipline has an intimate relation to that of literature. Romantics and realists in fiction have had their counterparts among those portraying the actual past, and essayists of various eras and persuasions have on occasion produced both history and literature maintaining a particular preoccupation such as proletarian, regional, or psychological. But the tendency of many creative writers of our times to deal with themes of sex has elicited very few imitators among historians. Especially have chroniclers of American culture appeared to avoid what would in another day have been called delicate subjects. Only just recently have a handful of researchers ventured inquiries topically parallel to those of the literateurs.

I

So far no one has attempted to make a bibliographical survey of discussions of sex in American historical writing.[1] And, in candor, the amount of labor involved would give the task a most forbidding aspect. Of the immense bulk of written history covering the various civilizations of the world, only a tiny proportion contains discussions of sexual matters of any kind. In American history the proportion is probably smaller than in any other, and the job of locating it, therefore, commensurately harder.

American history, moreover, presents one special difficulty not found, for example, in much of the history of sex in European history: sexual

"American Historians and the Subject of Sex" is reprinted from *Societas*, 2 (1972), 307–316, with the kind permission of Societas, Inc.

material is not grouped or organized, but rather scattered here and there throughout the body of all American history. One general book does exist, *Marriage, Morals and Sex in America*, by Sidney Ditzion.[2] His work is essentially a somewhat selective history of ideas and attitudes. All other Americanists' contributions are fragmentary and specialized, insofar as they exist. Sex comes in only as part of a larger subject, or it shows up in a parallel, as, for instance, the comparison of public morals with private morals in the Gilded Age.

It is a comment on male chauvinism in the profession that most of this work on sex, including Ditzion's book, centers upon the history of women and women's status in America. This generalization applies even to the most sophisticated writers, including the literary critic William Wasserstrom's discussion of female sexuality in American Victorian fiction and James R. McGovern's recent article moving the Jazz Age revolution in manners and morals back to the 1910's.[3] Compared to American research on the subject, Europeans have very meagre offerings in the history of women, while we are relatively well endowed with historians of our womenfolk. One is tempted to suggest that it is a sign of American virility that we think that sex and women go together. While the association no doubt contributes to the mental health of half the population, yet the question must be raised whether subsuming the one subject under the other is necessarily advantageous for history. It may be time that American historians discover that men have sex, too.

II

Within limits, then, there have been a number of at least partial studies of sexual attitudes, institutions, and activities in America. These works tend to vary from one period of time to another. Modern social historians dealing with the colonial period, having a limited population and often fairly good records, have contributed the most to our information about actual sexual behavior. As Henry Bamford Parkes observed as early as 1932, "Puritan-baiters have taken obvious delight in the suggestion that standards of conduct [in early New England] were lower than was once supposed." Much good history has grown out of this continuing movement to show that the Puritans did not meet Victorian standards of conduct.[4] One of the best recent works, for example, by Emil Oberholzer, Jr., is ingeniously based upon church records and descriptively entitled, *Delinquent Saints*. Even historians free from this particular iconoclastic bias such as Edmund Morgan tend nevertheless to follow in the anti-Puritan tradition.[5]

Historians of the nineteenth century have in their reticence, by and large, reflected the age about which they wrote. Having to do research on a large and growing population, they have avoided statistical studies reflecting sexual behavior, studies such as have become very exciting in European

history. Instead, their demography is unrevealing of its ultimate genesis, and discussions of sexuality are based upon impressionistic evidence. Indeed, historical information about sexual activity in America's Victorian Age is largely non-existent. Most historians touching on the subject of sex have specifically avoided referring to actual behavior and have brought the subject up only indirectly. The largest part of what we know is to be found in works focused on institutions such as the family, or on general reform movements such as temperance and (inevitably) women's rights. Treatises on the family such as Arthur W. Calhoun's classic volumes are the most valuable sources of information.[6] Sex in its scandalous aspects does occasionally creep in through incidental discussions of divorce and prostitution, and recently black historians have revived in detail the charges of the abolitionists that slavery exercised a corrupting influence upon both black and white sexuality.[7] The most eloquent comment on the history of sex in the United States in the nineteenth century, however, is that the fullest and highest quality work in the field comes in accounts of attempts to suppress it! Included under such headings, for example, would be Paul S. Boyer's recent history of book censorship and other authors' studies of Comstockery.[8]

Many sources for the history of sex in America since about 1800 remain largely untapped. Not only are there statistical materials similar to those that the colonialists have utilized but medical journals and the whole corpus of nineteenth-century newspapers, an amazingly rich source, are all for the most part still unexplored.[9] In the twentieth century a new source was added: open discussions of the sexual scene, which ranged from fiction to essays to social science. So far, however, much of this material has been neglected by historians who, like everyone else, remain deluded about the history of sex in their own culture and century. Few of them—or of those who should be learning from them—are aware of the fact that there was more sex education in many schools in the 1910's than in recent years or that the 1950's represented a period of regression and repression as far as openness of sexual discussion is concerned. There are but few happy exceptions to this depressing picture of historical works about the twentieth century, the most outstanding of which is William L. O'Neill's many-faceted analysis, *Divorce in the Progressive Era*.[10] Even sex research itself has so far engendered but one serious history, although a study by James H. Jones of the Institute for Sex Research in its full cultural setting is now under way.[11]

III

The fact that sexuality has been incidental in American history has had an interesting consequence: General historians have often been aware of what exists of it. They certainly have discussed Morton's Maypole at Merrymount, miscegenation, the Eaton affair, Maria Monk, the Mormons, Lincoln's jokes,

bachelor Cleveland's dependent child, and much more. Recently, one historian was even so ungentlemanly as to allude in print to the historically momentous love-life of a leading American statesman of the last few decades. (The conservative Republican bosses apparently let the statesman know that if he tried to gain the presidential nomination, they would publicize his deviation from the conventions of the day.)

American social historians, especially, those who should have been concerned with the subject, have kept sex closely intertwined with other historical topics, and, while in a way hiding it, have not totally neglected it. All of the relevant material in the old standard *History of American Life* series, edited by Arthur M. Schlesinger and Dixon R. Fox, would, if laid end to end, make a highly variable but not narrow account of many aspects of sex in America. Carl Russell Fish, for example, in his account of *The Rise of the Common Man, 1830–1850*, observed that while standards of propriety were very strict, "the most conspicuous advertisements of the newspapers related to sex functions with a directness and completeness which would disgust if not shock even the present generation." Contraceptive devices and prostitution particularly, he noted, were well-known to the public.[12]

In short, although American history has been kept relatively chaste, many of its practitioners have discussed sex incidentally. What is lacking is systematic work to parallel existing research on the family, Ditzion's work on attitudes, and such surveys as Nelson M. Blake's book on divorce in the United States.[13] Americans have, for example, not even the stodgiest general history of prostitution in the United States, although a number of works written years ago cover that phenomenon in Europe.[14] Indeed, by neglecting such areas historians have permitted, perhaps compelled, other kinds of scholars to write history. Already the sociologists have been working on the history of the family since historians have failed to do so; John Sirjamaki, for example, produced the Library of Congress series volume on *The American Family in the Twentieth Century.*[15]

IV

But it is not enough simply to note the shortage and unavailability of sound work. Perhaps this superficial survey of the state of sex in American history can permit us to raise a question. What do we want of sex in history? What specifically is this topic about which there has been so much difficulty? What place does sex have, for example, in biography, in so far as biography is contained in history? What place does the subject have in the history of various institutions—religious, political, social? What place in general histories of American culture? Are Herbert Marcuse and Norman O. Brown correct in maintaining that our modern civilization, a bureaucratic society

that Robert Wiebe traces back in America to the late nineteenth century, should be interpreted primarily in terms of sexual desire and behavior?[16]

Historians need not be interested in sex—whatever it is—because it is arresting, fun, and absorbing in and of itself. They need to be interested in it only because it is important, and they need to say *why* it is important. To this end they ought to be introducing distinctions and categories that further historical analysis. Some historians of other cultures are already using distinctions such as that between expressive and instrumental sexuality or between compulsive and impulsive behavior. We need more history based on this type and level of analysis.[17]

In some ways our ability to make such distinctions and to define sexuality meaningfully has been diminished in recent times. In another day and age, people who spoke about sexual phenomena had a fairly concrete idea of what was involved—the sex act, marriage, divorce, courting, adultery, pornography, prostitution and perversions, child-bearing, and to some extent male-female social relations, child rearing, and the like. Through the ages, many observers of their fellow men were aware that sexual interests had important relationships with cultural phenomena such as artistic expression and violence and power, but lacking systematic ways of describing these relationships, our ancestors restricted their understanding of sex to its obvious and biological aspects.

Today we have some knowledge of psychological functions that have some connection with sexual drives, and we often label attitudes and behavior sexual in the absence of conscious and overt genital activity. This very great expansion of the sexual realm requires us to recognize that historians, who are children of their own times, will have to deal with sex in its psychological as well as biological aspects.

V

It is possible to deprive sexuality of any meaning by interpreting all human phenomena in sexual terms, by translating all mental and social functioning into sexual equivalents. Black history especially has suffered from this type of illogical shifting of the level of discourse in which the most literal sexual exploitation has been confused with other types of human relationships. Earl E. Thorpe has recently protested against this tendency, questioning, for example, the idea that castration is really and accurately equivalent to depriving a black man of economic independence.[18] Punning has its functions, no doubt, but in serious intellectual endeavors it is out of place because it is misleading. Winthrop Jordan's well-known book on early racial relationships, for instance, in its very title, *White over Black*, suggests how easy it is to fall into ambiguity when dealing with human interrelationships.[19]

The extreme of generalizing sex into meaninglessness is to be found in the works of writers such as Herbert Marcuse and Norman O. Brown who interpret the history of a whole culture in sexual terms. Both of them utilize primarily infantile sexual modes in their reconstructions. They must, in order to be sufficiently general. History, however, concerns adults in their adult roles almost exclusively, and in adulthood, infantile trends, while present, nevertheless take an adult form. Many of the mature social expressions of the infantile are not immediately convertible into actual regressive sex. Without qualifications and distinctions such loose use of the concept of sexuality as Marcuse's and Brown's simply dissipates the meaning of the term "sexual." Such radical psychosexualizing of sex is objectionable because it causes a loss in precision of meaning. More specifically, extreme sexualizing of history does not permit basic distinctions that ought to be made about sex itself. Three of these are (1) sex as biological activity; (2) sex as social or institutional activity, as in marriage and the family; (3) sex as a facet of psychological existence—the momentous experience alluded to by modern romantics, for example. Such distinctions are endlessly useful in historical discussions. Surely, it is foolish to discuss the changing psychology of love making without taking into account the biological ability of people to carry out the sex act, an ability that has varied in the most elemental way with changing standards of living—diet, disease, and working conditions—throughout history.

It is precisely such discriminations as these that enable historians to use modern social sciences constructively. In turn, those disciplines have greatly enhanced our ability to maintain meaningful distinctions among psychological, biological, and cultural-institutional aspects of sex. Sigmund Freud, drawing on classical European *Sexualwissenschaft*, set up a series of such distinctions to elucidate the operations of the biological force of the sexual drive within the psychological realm. He distinguished between the functioning of the physical source of stimulation, the psychological force or energy, the object of the drive, and the aim of the drive (typically discharge in orgasm). The independence of aim and object is particularly crucial to our modern understanding of sexuality. Recent social science material, also, such as that analyzing the differences between styles of love making of the various social groups in American society, can illuminate our understanding of by-gone eras even while attempting to answer the recurrent question as to how we can literally apply modern models to the past.

Historians must approach sex imaginatively in order to bring their work on the subject up to the standard normally expected in the profession. When Oberholzer, for example, wished to organize his record of the peccadillos of the Puritans, he followed the conventional classification of behavior that was set up by nineteenth-century German sexologists. His work unintentionally shows that Richard von Krafft-Ebing simply is not a suitable model for the historian. When he got that far down on the standard list, for example, Oberholzer could produce among the erring saints only one case of bestiality.

While, then, we suggest that American historians have been negligent in incorporating the subject matter of sex into history, we must stipulate that the quality of any such work needs to be upgraded drastically. Historians cannot be limited to learning about this vital aspect of existence from legal sources embodying legal attitudes or from people preoccupied with suffrage rights.[20] The historian has much to teach behavioral and social scientists, whose historical knowledge is scandalously lacking, but a study of the modes and types of analysis found in those disciplines can at least indicate what kinds of questions historians ought to be raising about sex.

VI

Within American history, there are already a few examples of what appears to be a new generation of informed analytic histories of human sexuality. The most notable is O'Neill's book on divorce, mentioned above. Much of this new work either has not been published, or has been published only in part. Among doctoral dissertations there is a most rewarding discussion by Stephen Nissenbaum of mid-nineteenth-century attitudes. Innovative approaches include investigation of the scientific study of sex,[21] homosexuality,[22] and masculinity/femininity.[23] Others are finding value in fresh approaches to traditional lines of research: feminism,[24] censorship,[25] and prostitution.[26] Altogether such contemporary scholarship promises to do much to bring sex into proper repute as a significant and essential area of historical inquiry.

We can hope that the Americanists of this new generation will continue to maintain the tradition of incorporating sex into the general history of the culture and bringing the general historical context into treatments of sex. In the past, incidental treatment has been a means of suppressing embarrassing content. In our age, such synthesis can be a strength by illuminating and sophisticating good historical craftsmanship. Since historians can no longer ignore sex, biological, psychological, or social, they ought at least to incorporate it into history in a meaningful way.

One recent piece of research should serve as an object lesson to them. In his book, *Purity Crusade*, David Pivar shows how the mainstream of the American reform impulse after the Civil War went into the crusade against prostitution and social impurity of all sorts. He documents specifically the continuity between the old abolitionists and the new abolitionism that was aimed at ending white slavery and kindred evils. American historians for decades have been looking elsewhere (albeit ingeniously), especially in politics, for American reform between the Civil War and the Progressive movement. Some have said that it disappeared. Others have tried to make of civil service the strategic retreat of reform. By and large these historians have been so afraid of sex that they have neglected not only the anti-prostitution movement but other movements closely associated with it, such as temper-

ance. By focusing on the concern of Americans of the Gilded Age with their sexual institutions and particularly the double standard, Pivar has provided the missing link in the evolution of American reform.[27] Let his achievement warn other American historians: They neglect the topic of sex at their own professional peril.

My program for conceptual clarity in dealing with sexuality in history I think went nowhere. Rather than psychological, biological, and social categories, what historians mostly turned to were ideological approaches and antiquarianism, except for some continued work within the social category. Yet my work was symptomatic of a rapidly growing interest among historians who were finding many topics in social history to be of the greatest interest. The problem continued to be to show that they were significant as well.

In 1976, on the occasion of a symposium dedicated to the memory of Sidney Ditzion, I had another chance to survey the work of American historians on the subject of sexuality. Ditzion was the author of the pioneer book mentioned in Chapter 7, and I was abashed to have to recognize that historians, as the title of Chapter 8 indicates, had chosen his approach to the subject, not mine. I have revised this chapter to reflect and include writings from the past ten years, which have continued to prove the soundness of Ditzion's approach as well as the ambivalence and unsteadiness of historians when they try to handle the subject.

How Recent Historiography Vindicates Ditzion's Approach to the History of Sex

Several years ago I wrote a paper surveying and commenting on the ways in which American historians had dealt with the subject of sex, meaning erotic sexuality.[1] Naturally the first book that I mentioned was Sidney Ditzion's monumental volume. Since writing my paper, I have of course had numerous second thoughts, often inspired by publications that have appeared since I tried to open the subject up further. I would like to pass on some of these afterthoughts and explain why it appears to me that Ditzion's book is still the starting point and exemplar for American historians of sex and sexuality.

Quantitative Patterns

I restrict myself to second thoughts because much of what was true several years ago is still true. One big change is of course the number of relevant scholarly productions that have been appearing each year, including an increasing number of doctoral dissertations. Although articles are still concentrated in the *American Quarterly* and the *Journal of Social History* and such specialized journals as *Feminist Studies* and *Population Studies*, for some years relevant papers have also been showing up occasionally in such outlets as the *Journal of American History*.[2] Where scholars in other disciplines can contribute, they, too, have been adding to the volume of publication; a good example is the field of pornography and obscenity, to which both literary and legal historians have added significantly.[3]

Yet I have qualifications to add to these signs of apparent success, or at least prosperity. In the first place, I have the impression that there is a

disparity between the number of doctoral dissertations dealing with sexual subjects and the corresponding number of publications. Remarkably few dissertations have in fact appeared even in article form, much less as books—in contrast to the situation in other fields of history with which I am acquainted. It may be that this disparity derives from the fact that the quality of the research is, on the whole, not up to standard; at the best, the material is often presented in a narrow, limited, or provincial way (and I shall return to this problem shortly). And it may be also that editors and publishers still shy away from material that is in some sense "unconventional."

My second reservation is again based on impressions gained from searching bibliographies and obvious sources: The number of historical works on sexuality did indeed increase up to the late 1970's, but at that point, works explicitly devoted to sexual subjects stopped increasing in the historical literature and have since actually declined in both absolute and relative numbers. Whether or not that trend will continue in the future is of course uncertain at this time, nor is it possible to say whether or not incidental—as opposed to explicit—discussions of sexuality have stopped increasing in a parallel way.[4]

Limiting the Subject

The place of merely incidental history of sexuality, which for so long was the basic mode in which sexual material appeared, has been made more elusive because of another major change that occurred, namely, that a whole new body of research was published that was no longer hidden in treatises on other subjects. Ditzion was almost unique before the mid-1970's in writing explicitly on the subject of sex and not merely tucking it into work on some other subject. In this respect alone, then, recent work is following Ditzion's lead dramatically and obscuring any material that may be appearing incidentally.

One other change has come into recent writings on the history of sexuality: The definition seems to be narrowing somewhat as the field develops. When I wrote some years ago, I attempted to combine both the traditional elements and the commonsensical ones that would be included under the heading of sex. Vern Bullough, writing in 1979 on teaching the general history of sexuality, likewise followed a very traditional definition in deciding what he would include in the course, focusing really upon the genital and institutional and the immediate social context.[5] But as the history of the family and the history of demography have grown, they have tended to become independent fields and are not easily subsumed any more under the heading of sexuality, as articles in the *Journal of Family History* (founded in 1976), for example, demonstrate graphically.[6]

Yet Ditzion insisted that "man's economic, political, intellectual, and

social activities are inextricably enmeshed with his sexual activities." Ditzion's approach to sexuality was therefore very broad, emphasizing the social-cultural matrix at the same time that he labeled the subject sex. He has consequently, except for family and demography specialization, been something of a prophet for recent writers because he started with sexuality and related it to society. I really had thought the glorification of sensuality expressed in writings of the most extreme elements in the so-called sexual revolution of the late 1960's and after might have inspired historians to focus much more on sexual activity as such. Moreover I did and do deplore the neglect of the sex act itself in all three of its major aspects: biological, social, and psychological.

Emphasizing Social Context

But historiography in general continues in the tradition of Ditzion, keeping sex in sociocultural context, and in so doing shedding light on both the sexuality and the culture of the past. Ronald G. Walters in 1976 indeed suggested that the proper categories of analysis (categories that contrast with my biological, social, and psychological) are values, norms, and behavior. His categories are all sociocultural, and they keep even erotic sexuality decidedly within American societal structures, events, and forces. Thomas L. Altherr in 1983 ingeniously used a social concept, "sexual attitudes," to tie together a collection of sources on the history of sex in America.[7]

Perhaps the best example to make my point that historians have emphasized the social is found in work on what would appear to be the least social of sexual acts, masturbation. Vern Bullough and Martha Voght pointed out (using a substantial proportion of American sources) that for a long time solitary sexual acts—the secret vice as it was called—were confused with homosexual and other stigmatized activities. Only in the late nineteenth century in both Europe and America did the idea of homoerotic and other perversions develop as entities distinct from masturbation.[8] Arthur Gilbert, in another article based on both American and European materials, related concern about masturbation to the increasing valuation of children in the nineteenth century. The decline of concern, he continues, then reflected the ability of physicians to account for childhood malfunctioning with explanations other than the so-called sin of onanism.[9] H. Tristram Engelhardt, Jr., in a third article on the general subject, considered the disease entity around masturbation in terms of perceptions of normality, values, and illness, that is, social and attitudinal dimensions of behavior and medical theory.[10]

As I indicated, what is remarkable is that in all of these discussions of this most unsocial act, the authors continued to concentrate on the cultural determinants and milieu. They did not talk about changes in technique or focus on individual psychological realities.[11] And as with masturbation, so

with other, more interpersonal aspects of sexuality, historians have persistently related Americans' sexual attitudes and activities to other aspects of American social existence.

American Culture

The scholars who have written about sexuality emphasizing the sociocultural have involved their work in a number of prevailing conventions and traditions, not to mention assumptions. Only in the context of an explicit unity of the culture, for example, have historians been able to maintain their nationalistic category of "American history." It is a category that might well be questioned in discussing the history of sexuality. Ditzion himself slipped very easily from considering Americans as colonials, essentially Europeans, to considering Americans in terms of a mostly insulated culture by the mid–nineteenth century. Much recent writing reflects the continuing assumption that the United States constitutes a viable unit in social history just as in political history. While European influences receive recognition, it is the uniquely American context that shapes most of the work of American historians.

One problem with nationalism in the history of sex is that if a writer gets too far from the realm of culture, the paucity of purely provincial materials tempts him or her to introduce better-known or more accessible European materials to flesh out a narrative. No doubt the widespread influence of European, and especially English, intellectuals upon literate Americans justifies this cultural mixing to some extent. But a number of recent writers have not followed carefully the example that Ditzion set years ago explicitly to distinguish the colonial from the indigenous.

In a curious reversal of this process, more general historians have increasingly used American materials. In addition to the works on masturbation that I mentioned, two notable examples of New World materials in Western or world history are Stephen Kern's history of the human body, which deals very largely with sexuality and utilizes many American materials, and Vern Bullough's *Sexual Variance in Society and History*, in which American culture is the subject of a substantial fraction of the book. And when Paul Robinson undertook to write comprehensively about *The Modernization of Sex*, two of his three examples were American.[12] Whereas at one time almost all historical work on sexuality except Ditzion's was to be found in more general but still specifically American social history, now important discussions of sex in America have also to be sought in works encompassing all of Western civilization.

Despite the importance and usefulness of such general works, I, for one, am uneasy with the possibility of losing the context of a distinctly American culture. Even with all of the class, ethnic, and geographical divisions in

the United States, travelers throughout the nineteenth and twentieth centuries sensed substantial cultural differences between the Americans and the Europeans, with a particular sense that relations between the sexes in particular differed very greatly. Gordon S. Haight in 1971, for example, pointed out the striking evidence that American nineteenth-century upper and upper-middle classes, at the very least, were remarkably more proper in their demeanor and took advantage of the double standard much less frequently than did their European counterparts.[13] This evidence tallies with that in other studies,[14] all of which suggest that, nationalism or no, cultural units more restricted than Western civilization in general are appropriate units for the history of sexuality. Historians of sexuality are in fact far from having tested fully Ditzion's contention that the entire nation constitutes an appropriate cultural unit.[15]

The Impact of Women's History

The most notable sociocultural context for the history of sexuality, however, has been women's history, and it is in this subfield that much research appears, both in a clearly labeled form and mixed in with other historical analysis.[16] Indeed, in this case at times another context, the particular writer's point of view, obscures both the historical matrix and the actual empirical findings when the point of view is mistaken for historical context, sometimes by the readers and often by the writers themselves. Not every author in this tradition is as careful as Linda Gordon was to explain that her "history" of birth control was "both a historical and a political work," which in practice meant not only that the carefully footnoted sections should be read differently from the unfootnoted analysis and opinion but that the whole was presented from an explicit point of view.[17]

By the 1980's, not only insights from but disagreements among women's historians, reflecting differences among feminists in general, affected the work of many historians who worked within the area of human sexuality. Feminists argued about the extent to which the subject of women's history was a history of a subculture—or the now central culture—or a part of the whole culture. In either case, however, sexuality of course had a cultural context. Another theme also persists in all of this work: Women in America individually used sexuality to increase their personal autonomy. A series of disagreements therefore developed around questions of actual behavior, on the one hand, and, on the other, the extent to which women consciously and in the social sphere also tried to use attitudes toward sexuality and sexual norms to advance feminist aims and women's autonomy.[18]

Even a sampling, therefore, shows at once that women's historians, like other historians, have included sex only in a much broader context, indeed, that in the Ditzion tradition they subordinate sex as such to social dynamics on one level or another. Ditzion himself emphasized social reform, in the

direction of equality between the sexes, holding that sexual reform and social reform necessarily went together. Practitioners of women's history have in addition very effectively traced the self-awareness of women as mothers, as part of sisterhood, as particular kinds of reformers. Women's perceptions of the sex act, as Carroll Smith-Rosenberg points out, was only part of the whole experience of being a woman in a specific cultural context.[19]

One of the most important subjects that the women's movement shepherded into historical discussion was sex roles. While the identity of women gained the most attention initially, in fact the whole question of male-female sexual differentiation has been opened up. An ambitious effort, for example, is a book by Peter G. Filene dealing with both men's and women's identifications. Filene contributes the idea that changes occurred by generations, but he restricts himself to the upper classes (as opposed to the lower classes).[20] And in fact the social class elements of sexual identification (accessible, for example, in a half-century's social science research dealing with masculine and feminine polarities) have yet to find a historian. Why, for example, was masculine identified with lower class, feminine with upper class? And what is the significance of the shift of upper-class Americans toward the masculine since World War II?

The literature on the history of sex roles has grown in such a way as to constitute an independent field, like family history no longer necessarily encompassed within the history of sexuality. Rosalind Rosenberg, Diana Long Hall, and others have opened up the general subject of science and social science as transmitters and determinants of sexual roles.[21] Neither women's historians, who have done most of the research, nor other scholars have answered Smith-Rosenberg's challenge to show in detail just how relevant role was to sexuality in the narrow sense in the past—in part because women's becoming more "active" is so multi-layered and ambiguous an idea.[22]

The History of Prostitution

Feminist historians have taken a special, almost possessive, interest in one subject, prostitution, but even among feminist scholars, ideological divisions have deeply affected writing on this topic. These divisions have been intensified because the large volume of research on prostitution has grown out of scholars' interest in these women as ideal subjects for the history of common and oppressed people. Prostitutes had the right social attributes, since they were workers scorned by society in their own day, largely inarticulate, and clearly exploited. In addition, numerous records remain because prostitutes, unlike other workers, were constantly caught up in legal processes. Many prostitutes now appear in the historical literature, therefore, as victims but at the same time as autonomous people who controlled their own destinies. Historians are still arguing whether or not prostituting one's body was a voluntary or involuntary act, and in what sense—thus rehashing

the white slavery debate of the pre–World War I era. Ruth Rosen, for example, in her history of early-twentieth-century prostitution, says that "It may
be safely assumed . . . that white slavery, though it did exist, was probably
experienced by less than 10 percent of the prostitute population," by her
phrasing showing her bias against admitting the implications of the fact that
a significant number of prostitutes were held in bondage by overt force. In
playing down the outrageous circumstances of all kinds that caused women to
enter "the life," some historians try to give more dignity to those women who
were exploited and less to those who effectively worked to end the exploitation, but the equally viable opposite viewpoint also shows up in historical
reconstructions.[23]

This emphasis on the ways in which prostitutes and their opponents
contributed to feminist history has led scholars to miss some of the most interesting aspects of prostitution. Many have missed the fact that prostitution
changed as society changed; the institution of the mid–nineteenth century
was hardly the same institution as that of a hundred years later, when different profiles of the social class of customers existed and when the emphasis
on what was expected had also changed. In the nineteenth century all social
relationships rested upon a cash nexus; many decades later social interactions followed other models. Observers in different eras, for example, have
noted that in their terms paying for a sexual act turned it into a perversion;
this important viewpoint that prostitution involved a variety of motives did
not carry the same meaning in 1890 and 1960. Business arrangements, too,
varied over time; the international trade that depended on transportation and
accessibility developed and changed—again with consequences that have not
been explored adequately by modern scholars.[24]

At least some work on the history of prostitution does integrate into
more general history, and it is now possible through the new scholarship
to show that prostitutes can be subjected to ordinary social analysis, like
other people, and that more than sex was involved. Anne M. Butler, for
example, describes vividly the lower-class status of prostitutes in the West
in the nineteenth century. She details their opportunism as workers as well
as the system that both supported and exploited them. And another, heavily
iconoclastic example, is provided by Claudia D. Johnson, who has shown
that the involvement of prostitution in the theater fundamentally affected the
economic and social nature of that institution. The subsequent elimination of
prostitutes from the gallery therefore transformed the whole institution in a
way that standard historians either suppressed or did not know.[25]

Gay and Lesbian History

A substantial volume of historical writing has been published on both
so-called gays and lesbians. Gay and lesbian history fits well into Ditzion's

approach, for while in fact a sexual-orientation interest group supports most of the scholarship, in fact identifiable historical figures and relevant activities have been mostly political and cultural, not sexual. The most recent outstanding piece of scholarship on American subjects, John D'Emilio's *Sexual Politics, Sexual Communities*, is both political in subject matter and studiously placed in historical context.[26]

Despite the great efforts that have gone into expanding this subject matter and viewpoint, scholars in the field operate under a number of handicaps, not the least of which is the fact that they do focus only on social phenomena, not restricted patterns of behavior (as in fetishes) or even secret sexual orientation (the biological and psychological levels that I continue to think have potential in all fields of the history of sexuality). There is a special publication, the *Lesbian/Gay History Researchers Network Newsletter*, and there are at least three major substantive special archives serving gay and lesbian history, plus any number of special local projects devoted to documenting evidences of homoerotic sexual orientation and social activity. Indeed, one well-known general work on gay/lesbian history in America is a collection of documents. The explicit motive of most of these scholars is to legitimate current sexual-orientation groups by showing that they have a long history as part of American culture. Current debates, parallel to some of those in the women's movement, argue the different consequences for history if sexual orientation is culturally formed in an individual or is in some other way a free choice or foreordained.[27]

Handicaps of Advocacy

Despite their many substantive contributions, scholars who use the history of sexuality for advocacy—women's historians, gay/lesbian historians, liberationist historians, and any other activists—in the end tend to undermine scholarly standards and discredit the subject. Sometimes such writers permit standards of propaganda to prevail; at other times they merely isolate their work from mainstream discussions. It seems odd that such good scholars confuse their attempts to correct and balance the historical record with taking a social stance; "The question now," writes one advocate, "is whether the new history of sexuality will be feminist defined or male dominated," as if there were no other choices.[28] But what is most unfortunate is that when focused on special groups, these historians have often manifested the same antiquarian and filiopietistic tendency found in inferior local chroniclers, but in this case conditioned by another kind of parochial interest.

In the field of the history of sexuality, moreover, both ideological interest and efforts to legitimate social groups involve special hazards. The urgency to establish either the presence of a particular kind of sexual activity or the fact that society oppressed some citizens on the basis of sexual

orientation has led some scholars to think that additional documentation of activity and/or oppression constitutes a real contribution to history. In fact, unless some fresh point is raised, or an important question addressed in a refreshing way, mere rehashing of detail in the history of sex can go beyond antiquarianism and border on soft-core pornography, whereas in fact the intention may have been mere consciousness-raising—as opposed to historical exploration.[29]

Advocates writing in the field of the history of sexuality have also developed another—and quite unnecessary—handicap: They tend to isolate their work from other historical discussions. Failure to build on and cite the findings of other historians simply removes a writer from the community within which historical discussion takes place, and the fact that the subject matter is sexual should not be cause for making an exception, especially now that so much good history is available. This flaw has been especially conspicuous in the work of some self-defined radical scholars, and in so far as they suffer from this kind of scholarly deprivation, so in proportion do they influence less the mainstream discussions that they affect to scorn. Some feminists suffer from this disability, as do some of the more traditional radicals, who not only fail to integrate their findings into other research but fail to cite it. Scholars who have to discover everything anew for themselves in their own terms cannot expect well-read colleagues to give much attention to an exposition involving already familiar materials, especially when the writer seems to believe he or she has made a new discovery.

Finally, it should be observed that the first wave of allegedly liberated history has often consisted chiefly of tendentious and/or Whiggish accounts of America's sexual past. Historians have portrayed men, and particularly physicians, who set or embodied standards and transmitted or fostered attitudes, as outrageous characters who were determined to suppress both women and sexual enjoyment.[30] Heroes and heroines have been, conversely, those who found ways for women and men to fulfill themselves both personally and sexually. The repression—or imagined repression—of the past has, in short, been used to justify the frantic search for orgasm in the age of *Playboy*, swingers' liberation, and non-procreative sex in general. Such a tone pervades much, if not most, of the literature, even that on subjects of obviously substantial social significance such as the history of birth control.[31] It is very difficult to get away from the impression that even "the politics of sexuality" argument is implicitly an argument for indiscriminate and unrestrained sexual acting out. This unfortunate and often ahistorical aspect of the work by scholars affected by the advocates of the supposed sexual revolution is, of course, not the *necessary* product of new attitudes. Yet in the confusion engendered by disturbing ideas—and, it is only fair to add, the discovery of rich, unexploited source materials—the temporary letdown of customary historical standards should probably have been expected.

Such are the distinctive qualities of a substantial proportion of the work

in this essentially fresh field, the history of sexuality. Despite the quantity of publications and intrinsically interesting ideas, special problems diminish the impact of the scholarship. Even good historians have found themselves so distracted by the subject that they have neglected to apply the usual standards or have feared to speak up for fear that their motives will be mistaken. Ironically, fears of disease that appear to have changed sexual attitudes in the mid-eighties—presumably irrelevantly—may be being paralleled by better historical work, although neither trend is clearly more than transient at this point.

Sexuality is a very difficult subject at best, and attempting to understand it in the setting of past times complicates the difficulties. Especially in a romantic period like the present, when subjective feelings are highly valued, discussions of romantic love of course confuse it with both sexual passion and also with social institutions and movements.[32] As more Americans increasingly disconnect sex from reproduction and emphasize subjective feelings, understanding the past will be proportionately more difficult. Finally, it should be noted that even when emphasizing the feelings, the concept of romantic love and other things that appear to be common sense can be misleading in historical work in the realm of sex. Historians would have benefitted from bearing in mind that sexual feelings involve many elements, not only those that are social in a simplistic way but those representing many elements of culture and psychology. Commenting on the extreme reactions—feelings—of a fetishist going "absolutely 'ape' over a pair of galoshes," more than in ordinary sexual activity, Richard C. Robertiello observes that sexuality "has a lot more going for it than sex"—a statement worthy of Ditzion's broad approach but one that can remind historians of the powerful forces that operated in the past and need as careful dissection and understanding as possible.[33]

New Types of Contributions

Despite the difficulties and distortions, the fact remains that much of the recent research is significant and even arresting. Some is frankly revisionist, such as the evidence of Joseph A. McFalls, Jr., and George S. Masnick that the black birth rate varied at the turn of the twentieth century largely because of contraceptive activities, especially the use of condoms. Other research re-emphasizes insights that are not yet well established, such as Sheldon S. Cohen's demonstration of how little privacy couples had in love making in an eighteenth-century community.[34]

In addition, various historians have emphasized other facets of sexuality, beyond those that I have already noted. The relationship of physicians to sexual advice and behavior has expanded further in a number of ways, including physicians' involvement in treating women, in abortion, and in birth

control.[35] Historians have taken a special interest in the sexual practices of utopian or communitarian groups, using them as mirrors for society more generally.[36] Sex radicals have likewise become the object of serious historical investigation—with the inevitable demystifying finding that they, like the communitarians, reflected and defined the values of American society.[37]

All of this writing and research about sexual relationships once again embodies Ditzion's emphasis upon institutions and attitudes, the areas in which biological sexuality was transformed by sociocultural processes. Indeed, William Simon and John H. Gagnon, among other analysts, suggest that as a biological phenomenon, sex may well turn out to be relatively insignificant and that, in fact, the importance of the subject has all along been strictly culturally determined—again essentially more vindication of Ditzion's decision to attach discussion of sexuality to both marriage and morals as well as general social history.[38]

One result of recent shifts in attitude—again in justification of the sociocultural emphasis symbolized by Ditzion's work—is that normative and prescriptive materials from the past have been enjoying a little renaissance in the field as scholars understand better how to interpret and use them in historical context. In part, historians have sensibly suggested that norms reflect reality and in turn affect behavior—as, in the nineteenth century, romantic love replaced more formal rules governing the relations between the sexes. Even in her stunning reconstruction of middle-class American courting practices, for example, Ellen Rothman utilized normative materials to give shape and meaning to evidence of behavior.[39] Norms, too, have furnished the beginning of attempts to understand the very recent past, particularly as scholars have grappled with events of the 1960's. John Modell, for example, used attitudinal materials effectively to pinpoint 1968 as the year in which anti-natalism became effective among Americans generally and reproduction became less valued in the society.[40]

The often futile attempt to discover actual sexual behavior in the past continues to attract historians' attention. It is the more urgent because many advocates have made naive assumptions concerning actual sexual behavior in times gone by. In fact, findings in recent years do not justify any new conclusions about what Americans in the past actually did. Most of such information continues to come from legal documents and is subject to great disagreement as to validity and meaning.[41] The most exciting finding was a survey of forty-five late Victorian women's sexual attitudes and behavior that seemed at odds with the normative literature of that time. These women, contrary to at least some historical myth, tended to enjoy and look forward to making love with their husbands, although of course there was a wide range of action and attitude. This evidence sparked a renewed debate over the role of sexuality in Victorian society, which mostly came down to concluding that there were indeed wide variations in sexual expectations and performances among our forebears.[42]

In a parallel finding, Martin Duberman uncovered a pair of letters showing that two young men of the upper class in South Carolina at the beginning of the nineteenth century had engaged in sex play with each other in a flippant and animal way—behavior without any evident consequences to men who became pillars of society.[43] These letters are remarkable not for the universality of the animality they displayed but because the evidence is so unique. The most that these letters, the Mosher survey of Victorian wives, court records of early Massachusetts, and other fragments about behavior in the past will allow later historians to conclude is still that human beings in the past have shown a wide range of behaviors and attitudes, without any necessary connection between the two. Types of behavior seem to have been constant; what varied was the culture in which the behavior took place—and what it meant in that culture.

The Sociocultural Matrix of Sexuality

The possibilities afforded in the idea that sexuality is a social artifact have, as I have indicated, begun to find some realization in historical writing. Some works are frankly corrective, particularly those suggesting the complexities of Victorian-era attitudes, institutions, and relationships.[44] Those and other recent essays that suggest a new ability to discuss sexuality and open up new perspectives can also free historical discussion from present-mindedness. Carroll Smith-Rosenberg in particular has tried to move much of the discussion of the nineteenth century to an entirely fresh level in which historians ask what people at that time meant when they spoke of passion and love. She places the question of meaning in a context of gender, class, and geography and also extends sociocultural discussion by turning to the analysis of symbol and language.[45]

Charles Rosenberg in a landmark paper condemning present-mindedness in historians of sexuality points out that sexually repressive aspects of American society in the nineteenth century could be viewed as adaptive, that is, functional for that society. Like Ditzion, Rosenberg insists on integrating sexuality into other aspects of the culture, and he suggests that it was precisely because the elements of the culture were synchronized that the culture made sense.[46]

Even if writings about the history of sexuality continue to diminish, as now seems likely, they will not disappear, for the subject has established a place for itself, especially among American historians who are sensitive to the importance of social history. Some scholars have produced evidence that sexual social institutions had an important determinism and integrity of their own. The car, as David L. Lewis shows, was an instrument, not a conditioner of sexual activity; sexual patterns were independent even of economics, as Lee A. Gladwin shows from eighteenth-century Virginia.[47] Such tantalizing

evidence, combined with recent sophisticated analysis, suggests the promise of a broadgauged and deeply contextualized history of sexuality.

Ditzion therefore continues to stand as an inspiration and guide in the way in which he approached his materials. Working in this tradition, for example, Peter Gardella in a profoundly challenging work has traced to nineteenth-century religious attitudes modern values based on sexual pleasure.[48] Even if sexuality should turn out not to be biologically trivial, Ditzion's scholarship and that of others who have worked with attitudes, institutions, and groups will still remain significant and helpful in understanding the past. His efforts may also provide guidance to historians who try to work with sources and problems of all highly charged subjects, whether those already in sight, like the social-class aspects of sexuality,[49] or subjects such as sadomasochism, which are not yet within the purview of the historian or even, perhaps, the social scientist.

With the background provided by the past two chapters, I turn now to some of my own contributions to the history of sexual standards and moral standards in general. How this interest grew out of my research into the history of psychiatry will become more obvious now.

In searching for the roots of the purity and social hygiene movements that—even before psychoanalysis—brought sex before the American public, I found that the medical profession was continuously involved. Discussions frequently mentioned the St. Louis experiment in the medical inspection of prostitutes, an experiment that came to symbolize many of the forces in the anti-prostitution campaigns out of which the purity movement grew. Chapter 9 assesses this important incident in American public life.

The field of morals, I also found, has often been the area in which social "experiments" have been carried out. In Chapter 9 the idea of the social experiment appears, and the concept and use of the label will appear again in Chapter 11. That there could be an experiment in St. Louis in 1870 showed that people at that time believed that they could arrange social institutions so as to make significant improvements in their society and their lives. In such social experiments the idea of controlling events gave evidence of both modernization and the reform impulse. The problem in St. Louis, as the members of the medical profession showed clearly in their divided loyalties, was that exactly what constituted reform in this case was not clear.

CHAPTER NINE

Medical Inspection of Prostitutes in America in the Nineteenth Century

The St. Louis Experiment and Its Sequel

The story of the official physicians who inspected prostitutes in continental Europe during the nineteenth century does not constitute one of the more inspiring chapters in the history of medicine. Despite the opportunities of the medical examiners, few of them made any contribution to knowledge about any aspect of venereal diseases. Except for some government statistics, the validity and meaning of which were debated for generations among physicians and public health officials, not even epidemiology profited from this great opportunity for research.[1]

Yet the systematic attempts begun in the time of Napoleon to control venereal diseases are of the greatest interest.[2] Syphilis, with which the medical inspection of public women was concerned primarily, had been known since the sixteenth century to be contagious and venereal in nature (giving rise, for example, to the old maxim, "One night with Venus and a lifetime with mercury"). The system of compulsory medical inspection of prostitutes, or reglementation, as it came to be called in English, involved the not unfamiliar practice of segregation and quarantine of the ill. As George Rosen has pointed out, such an arrangement was suitable for countries with a strong cameralist tradition in which the population was accustomed to medical police regulation of everyday life.[3] With the growth of cities and a commensurate increase in numbers of women of the night, the hazard of disease seemed to demand some such control.

"Medical Inspection of Prostitutes in America in the Nineteenth Century: The St. Louis Experiment and Its Sequel" is reprinted from the *Bulletin of the History of Medicine*, 45 (1971), 203–218, with the kind permission of the Johns Hopkins University Press.

138

In England and America, however, systems of medical inspection of prostitutes did not flourish.[4] In the middle and late nineteenth century, when the public health movement was well under way in those countries, there were attempts to institute the Continental system as one of a number of public health measures. Ultimately these endeavors were defeated.[5] Reglementation, one might perhaps conclude, did not thrive where liberal traditions against controls over personal life prevailed (the liberal traditions including attitudes of laissez faire and caveat emptor). Or one can conclude that moral standards in the Victorian Anglo-American community impinged directly upon medical questions. Such was certainly the belief of American physicians of that day. In 1899 a New Orleans physician, Sigmund Lustgarten, reviewed the debate on the issue and concluded, "The United States will, I feel, still stand by and watch the experiments made abroad, before adopting measures foreign to the spirit of its people, and its laws."[6]

The history of government-enforced inspection of prostitutes in the United States sheds light particularly upon this latter question, the influence of community standards and values upon the practice of medicine. Owsei Temkin has pointed out that the ancient question of the moral significance of syphilis changed when physicians accumulated additional information about the disease in the nineteenth century.[7] Even the new knowledge, however, did not affect appreciably the status of reglementation as a standard public health measure in Europe, where officials continued to believe that the chief source of contagion was prostitutes. Many Americans in the medical fraternity shared these European attitudes. Before 1870, however, few of these men were willing to speak up concerning either prostitution—the social evil, as they called it—or its connection with disease.

Just before the Civil War, in 1858, William Sanger, a prominent New York physician, published a comprehensive study of prostitution in New York City and advocated strongly the adoption of the Parisian system of compulsory medical inspection of prostitutes, under a special medical department of the police. Sanger argued that in Paris "the number of cases of disease and the virulence of its form have materially abated."[8] His monumental volume, however, was almost unique as an American contribution to the medical and social literature on prostitution. Most subsequent advocates of reglementation in the United States cited Sanger but relied primarily on the more extensive English medical literature for evidence and authority. That literature originated in 1857, when an eminent London venereologist and student of Ricord, William J. Acton, published a painstaking review of prostitution and made the same strong recommendation as that of Sanger, for compulsory medical inspection.[9] In the years following, British government and military officials published medical opinions confirming the need for examining public women. The few American advocates of medical inspection who spoke up in the decade after Sanger published drew on this British material. Such, for example, was the editor of the *California Medical Gazette*, who in 1869

expressed the hope that San Francisco would "be the first city in our broad Union to adopt the French police system of examination of prostitutes."[10] He was destined to be disappointed, for it turned out, in fact, to be St. Louis, in 1870.

For some time much of the discussion of reglementation in the United States centered on the so-called St. Louis experiement. From 1870 to 1874 that city set up a system of government inspection of prostitutes and quarantine of those women found diseased. After the Civil War, many American cities had created boards of public health, usually following the example of New York, with a physician as health officer. The major concern of such boards was anything that offended the senses: the dirty, the smelly, the foul.[11] St. Louis had such a board, which was trying to clean up food establishments, abate odoriferous tanneries, and run the hospitals (essentially charitable institutions). Somewhat surprisingly, the city health officer, Dr. William L. Barrett, in his third annual report, in 1870, made a strong plea for medical regulation of "the social evil," as he called it. "It is," he wrote, "destroying the health and vigor of a large portion of our inhabitants, and tainting their blood with an ineradicable poison." (At that time venereal contagion was believed by many to be effected by some self-perpetuating poison operating on and through mucous tissue.) Citing Sanger's work, Barrett asserted that prostitution could not be suppressed and therefore ought to be rendered as harmless to the community as possible.[12]

Taking advantage of a city charter provision (included by state legislators with this end in mind) permitting St. Louis "to regulate or suppress" prostitution, the City Council on July 5, 1870, passed the so-called "Social Evil Ordinance." Under the ordinance, six physicians were appointed by the Board of Health to inspect the registered public women in each of six districts in the city. Those women found afflicted with venereal disease were committed to a special Social Evil Hospital until certified cured. The Social Evil Hospital was to be financed by fees levied on licensed houses and individual prostitutes.[13] Although amended several times, the Social Evil Ordinance remained in effect until 1874, when it was nullified by the Missouri state legislature. For several years after nullification of the law, some medical inspection and the Social Evil Hospital operated on a voluntary basis and then faded away.[14]

It is extremely difficult to discover just who in St. Louis, before Health Officer Barrett's report, favored setting up medical inspection. The newspapers referred to a group of public-spirited citizens, led by Colonel Ferdinand Meyer of the Board of Police Commissioners, who obtained the enabling legislation from the state. The Mayor, Joseph Brown,[15] and many city councilmen seemed to believe in the sanitary efficaciousness of the ordinance when the subject came up. Except for Barrett, physicians of the city did not appear to be the major movers behind this important public health legislation.[16]

The members of the St. Louis Medical Society provide a good sam-

ple of contemporary medical opinion. In the late 1860's, Missouri physicians had been involved in controversy and agitation to get regular physicians licensed and thus established against their competition. In 1870, therefore, the St. Louis Society was largely preoccupied with the question of professional standards.[17] Nevertheless, in May of that year, S. F. Newman, one of the leading practitioners of the city, offered a resolution in support of "any wise measures on the part of the Honorable Board of health which look to the proper regulation of houses of prostitution." The reasons spelled out in the proposal were both moral—regulation would reduce temptations to youth by curbing harlotry—and medical, the latter including the observation that "the public welfare demands that means be devised to restrict and regulate this vice, so as to strip it as far as possible of its awful consequences." A number of the Society members immediately objected to the resolution on moral grounds, and it therefore eventually was laid on the table.[18]

About a year later, after the ordinance had been enacted anyway, the Society did pass a resolution concerning it. Characteristically, the physicians' concern expressed in this 1871 resolution centered upon the specific medical inspectors who had been appointed, at least some of whom Society members did not consider fully qualified. Only incidentally did the resolution endorse the ordinance. According to the wording of the resolution, the working of the ordinance had confirmed "the salutary and beneficial results which have for a long time obtained in Europe," and those results promised to increase if better-qualified physicians were appointed.[19]

As in the Medical Society, so in the larger community of St. Louis initial and continuing opposition to reglementation was mounted on moral grounds. The purity leaders were largely Protestant clergymen, and one of them, William Greenleaf Eliot, took credit for agitation that eventually led to nullification.[20] Since proponents, both medical and lay, constantly confused moral and hygienic arguments, opposition on moral grounds was entirely relevant and in order in the dialogue that developed around and following the St. Louis experiment. In 1873, in his plea for a chance to continue the experiment, for example, Health Officer Barrett produced widely quoted figures showing a decrease in not only venereal cases but in the number of prostitutes in the city. While the diminution of the number of public women could have been considered strictly a sanitary matter, neither Barrett nor his colleagues so restricted themselves. Two years before, for instance, Barrett had claimed that the law had already "lessened disease, suffering and death; reclaimed fallen women, and restored them to society, friends and home, and prevented them from becoming abandoned and profligate." Given this argument that reglementation led to moral improvement, it was not inappropriate, then, that the experiment was ended in the name of public morality rather than on the basis of its sanitary efficaciousness or lack thereof.[21]

The St. Louis experiment did nevertheless open the door in 1870 to a national discussion of the hygienic value of government-enforced medical in-

spection of prostitutes. Within a few days after the ordinance was passed, for instance, the editors of the *Medical Gazette*, of New York, were congratulating St. Louis on taking the first step in an inevitable national movement. The social evil, said the editors, "will always exist, and we can do little toward limiting it; but we can do something towards limiting the spread of syphilis, and it is high time that we should direct our energies to that task."[22] For a number of years various influential American physicians spoke up in a similar vein. Chicago, Cincinnati, and San Francisco, for example, all harbored strong reglementation movements in the early 1870's, inspired explicitly by the St. Louis experiment. As a Cincinnati medical editor explained: "As we advocate quarantine, Boards of Health, the collection of statistical data, and spread of science generally, so we also devote the *Lancet* to the advocacy of social evil laws, to the end that we may have less venereal disease and better facilities for studying the little we may have."[23]

The fact that these movements got started before the results from St. Louis were in—that is, immediately after passage of the Social Evil Ordinance—suggests that there existed already the basis for medical agitation for inspection of prostitutes, and in fact a more comprehensive movement soon overshadowed the St. Louis experiment. This movement had determinants far more profound than mere reaction to the St. Louis ordinance. Even before 1870 similar legislation had been proposed in other cities, and Cincinnati, for example, came close to being the experimental city.[24] Prostitutes had been strictly inspected and regulated in some areas during the Civil War, it turned out, and in New York, for years after Sanger's book was published, influential citizens advocated medical inspection of public women. In 1867, for instance, the grand jury there spoke out specifically on the issue.[25]

The political defeat of the St. Louis experiment for some reason tended to discredit it, but the discussion of reglementation nevertheless continued among physicians.[26] A number of eminent practitioners boldly advocated inspection. In the mid-1870's the renowned Philadelphia surgeon, Samuel D. Gross, spoke out in favor of some legal measures similar to the British Contagious Diseases Acts. In addressing the American Medical Association in 1874, he observed:

> We send missionaries among the heathen in foreign lands, but neglect this fearful plague-spot at our own doors and at our own fireside. . . . We permit our own brother to contract a loathsome disease . . . taint and infect his offspring unto the third or even unto the fourth generation. The only remedy for this evil is the licensing of prostitution.[27]

Gross's efforts to initiate national discussion of an inspection program were seconded in 1876 by J. Marion Sims, father of American gynecology, in his presidential address to the American Medical Association. Formerly,

said Sims, syphilis had been an exclusively medical matter, a disease to be treated. With the new knowledge at hand, he continued,

> it is no longer a question for the therapeutist, but one for the sanitarian, the philanthropist, the legislator, the statesman. . . . Shall it be said that we, the representatives of the medical profession of a great nation, the custodians of the health of forty millions of people, cognizant of all these facts, will longer let the people remain in ignorance of the dangers that surround them? . . . We must sound the alarm.

Sims shrewdly perceived that the physician as reglementarian had to enter the public arena. The growing public health movement had already forced the doctors into playing a quasi-political role, and practitioners such as Sims were prepared to take medical knowledge, even about venereal diseases, to the public, or at least to local boards of health, for action.[28]

Characteristically, the Association ordered 10,000 copies of Sims's address distributed but nevertheless did not respond to Gross's eloquent plea to give reglementation official Association endorsement. As in the St. Louis Medical Society, members of the AMA in a heated debate divided between advocates and opponents of compulsory medical inspection of prostitutes, and the issue was never resolved in that organization.[29]

In general, then, members of the medical profession reacted to the suggestion of a system of reglementation in one of three ways: They favored any sensible public health measure to curb venereal diseases, especially syphilis, or they doubted the efficacy of medical inspection of prostitutes although sympathizing with the sanitary aims of the program, or they shared the moral outrage of those who opposed what they characterized as legalizing and licensing vice. Each of these reactions requires a little exploration.

The public health campaign for reglementation, from Sanger's brave effort before the Civil War down to the twentieth century, was essentially constant. Physicians continued to believe that prostitutes were the main carriers of venereal poison and that medical inspection would cut down on disease and, incidentally, provide pressure and opportunity for the women to reform themselves. Two medical advances gave urgency to this public health program. In the mid–nineteenth century, physicians discovered the so-called syphilis of the innocent, for by that time the evidence was clear that wives, children, wet nurses, and others become infected through no fault of their own,[30] and the common view that venereal diseases were punishment for moral transgressions was open to question. Indeed, so well was the epidemiology of venereal illnesses developed that the germ theory of disease had nothing fundamental to add to it.

In the 1890's the campaign for public prophylaxis took on a new stridency after a number of venereologists had worked out the full clinical effects of syphilis and gonorrhea. By the 1880's, long before the discovery of the

spirochete, Fournier and Erb and others had assembled widely accepted evidence showing that many afflictions, including paresis, locomotor ataxia, and some arthritic affections, were of luetic origin. Paresis, or general paralysis, as it was known, was the object of particular fear and loathing among both physicians and laymen. Often euphemistically referred to as "softening of the brain," the disease spread terror among late Victorian Americans, a terror that was compounded by the proof that it grew out of syphilis contracted many years before. Contemporaneously Noeggerath and Neisser and their colleagues were demonstrating that gonorrhea was a serious disease not easily amenable to treatment and responsible for blindness and sterility and other gynecological disorders. Many physicians at the end of the century were frankly horrified by these new findings and urged some kind of action. Eventually there was action, but it did not come in the form of reglementation.[31]

The international medical congresses of the nineteenth century, particularly those dealing with quarantine and contagion, helped to inspire all of the public health movement, including that part of it devoted to venereal diseases, and many Americans cited international meetings as the initial source of their concern rather than, say, the St. Louis experiment. A recommendation made at an international medical congress in Paris in 1867 was particularly important in inspiring agitation for medical inspection.[32] But the international movement for reglementation did not find a broad enough basis of support to work effectively through the public health movement in America.

A dramatic confrontation at the Indianapolis meetings of the American Public Health Association in 1882 summarizes succinctly what happened in the movement in general. Albert L. Gihon, Medical Director of the U.S. Navy, presented a report from the committee on venereal diseases urging each state to enact a law that would make venereal diseases and other contagious illnesses subject to compulsory reporting and treatment. One clause was understood, perhaps incorrectly, perhaps not, as opening the door for local governmental medical inspection and quarantine of prostitutes. John Shaw Billings, the famous medical administrator and librarian, moved to lay the entire subject upon the table, arguing that even discussing the topic had already brought the religious pressure groups upon the Association. Public health advocates, he declared, would damage their own political effectiveness by endorsing the measure. It would, he said, embarrass them "in obtaining power to deal with things which lie next to our hand,—getting sewerage in the villages, doing away with polluted well-water, etc." The members present, by a vote of thirty-eight to twenty, followed Billings's advice. Afterwards Gihon said that he regretted Billings's remarks and thought that had he been in practice and seen more cases he would not have made them, but Gihon promised not to trouble the Association again with the subject. Then he added:

I have for seven years worked on this matter, and I do not intend to give it up. As long as I remember the one good woman who is now in my mind,—a woman pure and good and virtuous beyond expression; a wife who died a miserable, wretched agonizing death, through contact with her husband, who diseased her,—as long as I remember that woman I pledge myself to work on in this field.[33]

The contentions of well-meaning advocates of medical inspection of prostitutes were often rejected because many physicians doubted that such measures were really effective. The skeptics believed that venereal diseases were spread largely by women who, for one reason or another, were not registered and probably could not be, and who were therefore not going to be inspected. Such doubts eventually discredited, for example, even the Parisian inspection system.[34]

The other basis for skepticism was that the inspection process itself was not efficient enough to be justified. Health Officer Barrett of St. Louis, for example, in 1871 took pains to explain that the number of syphilitics who did not manifest a discoverable lesion was statistically very small, not enough to impair the efficacy of the inspection system.[35] But other physicians did not agree with assessments such as Barrett's, and their arguments were at the very least disquieting to advocates of reglementation. In 1871 the editors of the *Medical Record* reprinted from the prestigious British *Medical Times and Gazette* a comprehensive survey of the world literature on the subject, casting serious doubts upon the ability of the most skilled physician to detect syphilis in women by inspection. Until well after 1900 the method of inspection was essentially visual. The Wassermann test for syphilis was announced only in 1906, and not until several years after that were it and other laboratory methods of diagnosis in general use in American medicine. Although Neisser had identified the gonococcus in 1879, use of the microscope in the diagnosis of gonorrhea was not common before the 1900's except for purposes of confirmation and differential diagnosis, in cases in which pus or other symptoms had already been found by visual methods. Even very late in the nineteenth century, then, skeptics could show in detail how faulty the inspection process was because of technical inadequacies alone.[36]

An excellent example of the late-nineteenth-century skeptic was Edmund Andrews, professor of principles and practice of surgery in the Chicago Medical College, who in 1875 spoke effectively at the American Medical Association meetings in opposition to Gross's advocacy of a public health program against venereal diseases.[37] In 1867, after a trip to Europe, Andrews had reported and documented his skepticism of reglementation.[38] When news of the St. Louis experiment caused some prominent citizens to initiate a move to bring the system to Chicago in 1871, Andrews in a widely quoted article and pamphlet denounced the measure as ineffectual. After reciting

the evidence that reglementation was not preventing the spread of syphilis, Andrews remarked that

> it is a matter of utter astonishment, that any surgeon, or even any man of uneducated common sense, should suppose that a medical examination can give the least security to cohabitation with prostitutes. . . . There would be no possibility of checking the disease by such methods, unless the men as well as the women were examined, and all prostitution prevented, except where both parties were proved to be healthy. Now, I submit the question, whether it is advisable for the community to adopt a costly system, which, while it affects no diminution of general disease, acts as a delusive advertisement to lead men to suppose that the chambers of prostitution have at last become almost safe resorts.

All that Andrews could advocate instead, however, was voluntary treatment and toleration of prostitution as it existed.[39]

It is amazing that in the face of the problems raised by skeptics such as Andrews, the medical advocates of inspection did not back down in the late nineteenth century. But the newly discovered extreme dangers of the diseases led many conscientious physicians to advocate any action whatsoever on the chance that it might lead to at least a little amelioration. Typically, such physicians were those who continued to believe that prostitution was an incradicable human phenomenon and who, at the same time, were deeply alarmed by the new clinical and pathological evidence of the ravages of the diseases.[40] Ironically, such counsels of desperation eventually carried a large number of physicians into the camp of the moralists. The converts found it more bearable to believe that prostitution could be eliminated than to believe that the diseases would have to be tolerated as an essential of the human condition.

Those who opposed compulsory medical inspection of prostitutes on the moral grounds that it constituted recognizing or legalizing sin were at first not necessarily optimistic about eliminating prostitution, but they at least hoped to hold it in check. Unwittingly they got themselves involved in a number of social changes that around the turn of the twentieth century metamorphosed the essentially medical public health campaign to control venereal diseases.

The new moralists of the late nineteenth century were already far removed in attitude from those who held venereal disease to be a punishment for sin. The initial systematic opposition to governmental licensing and inspection of public women arose among laymen. The chief organizer of an international movement to that end was an Englishwoman, Mrs. Josephine Butler, who was inspired to action by her uplift work among women affected by the notorious British Contagious Diseases Acts that created a limited sys-

tem of reglementation. A number of British clergymen and public-spirited Victorians joined Mrs. Butler and her female collaborators in reform, and by 1869, before the St. Louis experiment was initiated, the British purity forces had organized—indeed, in time for involvement of their propaganda and personal aid in the successful fight to nullify the St. Louis Social Evil Ordinance.[41]

Following old lines of trans-Atlantic communication among reformers, especially Quakers, the British group quickly established formal American outposts on the East Coast.[42] As David Pivar has shown, the same personnel and channels were involved as in the pre–Civil War abolitionist crusade, and the reformers of the 1870's came to be known as the new abolitionists, this time working for the abolition of prostitution rather than of slavery. The new abolitionists early included in their ranks a number of physicians, who, as in St. Louis in 1870, reacted spontaneously to the call of morality. Unlike many of their colleagues, they believed that the social evil might actually be destroyed. In America the movement to abolish prostitution gradually grew into a movement to purify all of society, not only by abolishing various evil institutions such as the brothel and saloon, but by bringing children up to live clean lives. This upper-middle-class movement for purity of mind and body attracted an increasingly large number of physicians. They argued, among other things, that venereal diseases could best be controlled by destroying prostitution and immorality. Some British physicians were abolitionists from the beginning, and they and other opponents of medical inspection tried hard to recruit American medical men into the anti-prostitution movement. By 1900, as Pivar points out, both of the leading purity organizations were headed by M.D.'s.[43]

Many, perhaps most, physicians, however, continued to believe that prostitution and immorality were ineradicable and beyond the proper province of medicine anyway. Then, in the early years of the twentieth century, a group of basically conservative American venereal specialists, led by the formidable Prince A. Morrow of New York, decided that the consequences of syphilis and gonorrhea were so horrible that many traditional attitudes and institutions, not just the red light district, had to be changed. These physicians entered into public life and launched the social hygiene movement. They united with the purity forces and, by the time of World War I, had achieved new standards of sexual behavior, for the middle classes at least, and the destruction of prostitution in its traditional form in America.[44]

By the twentieth century, then, the medical inspection of prostitutes, whatever its actual sanitary effectiveness, was no longer a socially viable alternative for controlling venereal diseases in the United States. Ironically, the modern method of control, improved morality plus individual treatment, grew out of the efforts of the abolitionists who had opposed public health advocates of an earlier day on moral grounds. Some physicians had tried

to remove moral considerations from their advocacy of medical preventive measures, but Americans in St. Louis and elsewhere seemed unable to keep moral arguments out of their public health campaigns. Then, in the twentieth century, prophylaxis improved greatly, in large part because physicians followed to a logical conclusion the bringing of moral considerations into the area of professional responsibility.

The St. Louis experiment did help inspire a later experiment in San Francisco, as Neil Larry Shumsky has shown, an experiment that was, however, based on rules of the city board of health, not legislation. In the case of the San Francisco experiment, which began in 1911, a highly organized clinic reflected the advance of medicine as well as the bureaucratization that was typical of social endeavors in the early twentieth century. But the efforts of proponents of medical inspection in San Francisco ran afoul of the same forces that the St. Louis experiment galvanized and that are the subject of the next chapter.*

The St. Louis experiment itself has been examined by another scholar, James Wunsch, in a comparative study of late-nineteenth-century prostitution. Wunsch found that the impetus for inspection came from police officials and that members of the medical community only went along with the program of municipal officials who were attempting to introduce the first stage of bureaucratization, order.†

The connection between medical personnel and American moral standards, particularly in the area of sexual behavior, has been the subject of a number of commentators whose works were noted in Chapter 8.‡ The most critical incident, however, came in the Progressive era, as was foreshadowed at the end of Chapter 9 and is explained in detail in Chapter 10, which continues the narrative.

---

* Neil Larry Shumsky, "The Municipal Clinic of San Francisco: A Study in Medical Structure," *Bulletin of the History of Medicine*, 52 (1978), 542–559.

† James L. Wunsch, "Prostitution and Public Policy: From Regulation to Suppression, 1858–1920" (doctoral dissertation, University of Chicago, 1976). Wunsch's work puts in perspective my own local history of the incident, "The Social Evil Ordinance—A Social Experiment in Nineteenth Century St. Louis," *Bulletin of the Missouri Historical Society*, 27 (1971), 203–217.

‡ The most conspicuous recent effort is Allan M. Brandt, *No Magic Bullet: A Social History of Venereal Disease in the United States Since 1880* (New York: Oxford University Press, 1985).

CHAPTER TEN

The Progressive Era Revolution in American Attitudes Toward Sex

In the optimistic and melioristic Progressive atmosphere of the early twentieth century, many reform movements flourished. The supporters of each one attempted in some specific way to alter institutions and beliefs characteristic of their culture in that period. Of all Progressive reform movements, the most extraordinary was the social hygiene movement, a campaign to change American attitudes toward sex. As a typical reform movement it illustrates how people of the Progressive generation attempted by manipulating the social environment, especially through the use of education, to change attitudes and behavior. The unusual quality of the movement derives from both the ambitious nature of the goal and the extent to which the reformers succeeded. The so-called revolution in morals became one of the lasting legacies of Progressivism to American life.[1]

Reformers directed their campaign against two fundamentals of Victorian morality, the conspiracy of silence[2] and the double standard.[3] In 1914 William T. Foster, president of Reed College, described what he and others had been combating:

Throughout the nineteenth century the taboo prevailed. Certain subjects were rarely mentioned in public, and then only in euphemistic terms. The home, the church, the school, and the press joined in the conspiracy. Supposedly, they were keeping the young in a blessed state of innocence. . . .[But] an abundance of distressing evidence showed

"The Progressive Era Revolution in American Attitudes Toward Sex" is reprinted from the *Journal of American History*, 59 (1973), 885–908, with the kind permission of the *Journal of American History*.

that nearly all children gained information concerning sex and reproduction from foul sources,—from misinformed playmates, degenerates,
obscene pictures, booklets, and advertisements of quack doctors. At the
same time the social evil and its train of tragic consequences showed
no abatement. The policy of silence, after many generations of trial,
proved a failure.[4]

Foster's appraisal was accurate, at least for the middle classes. There were
important exceptions to the rule of euphemism and silence, the most notable
of which were seduction themes in literature and scandal stories and advertisements of quack doctors that appeared in the newspapers.[5] But, on the
whole, social prohibitions against any open discussion of sex-related matters
were surprisingly well observed. As late as 1899, when Denslow Lewis, a
distinguished Chicago physician, attempted to discuss "the hygiene of the
sexual act" at the meetings of the American Medical Association, the famous
Baltimore gynecologist, Howard Kelly, objected: "The discussion of the subject is attended with filth and we besmirch ourselves by discussing it in
public." Most physicians were not as prudish in medical matters as Kelly, but
the association refused to publish Lewis's paper.[6]

Like the conspiracy of silence, the double standard of conduct—for
women, strictest purity, and for men, considerable freedom to indulge their
"inherent bestiality" before and outside of marriage—was subject to reserva-
tions and exceptions as a general social standard. Many members of evangeli-
cal churches or otherwise well-bred young men did not use prostitutes, but
hewed to a higher standard. Perhaps the best-known example was Theodore
Roosevelt, who confided to his diary at the time of his engagement, "Thank
heaven I am absolutely pure."[7] Such behavior was exceptional, however, for
it was a common, if ancient, belief, held and taught even by physicians, that
sustained continence is injurious to a man's health. Advocates of the double
standard could cite the most venerable opinion, including that of Augustine:
"Suppress prostitution, and capricious lusts will overthrow society."[8]

By 1900 pressure was mounting against the social stability embodied in
the conspiracy of silence and the double standard. One set of forces, acting
through a purity movement, undermined the double standard. Another set
of forces, working through sophisticates and rebellious intellectuals, tended
to break the conspiracy of silence. In the Progressive era the opponents of
the double standard and the conspiracy of silence were fused and absorbed
into the social hygiene reform movement as it acted to initiate the revolution
in sexual standards.

Many factors contributed to the movement to purify American life. The
most central was the small-town religious idealism that shaped the aspirations and even behavior of many Americans.[9] Women often took seriously
their claim to moral superiority, and many of them, along with male uplift
leaders, joined the international campaign to keep governments from legally

sanctioning prostitution.[10] Anti-prostitution efforts created the white slavery scare that expressed itself in a sensational literature as well as the Mann Act of 1911.[11] But another and more significant result of the battle against "commercialized vice" was a general social movement dedicated to purifying American life, particularly by means of rearing children of both sexes to lead pure lives. By 1895 these "purity groups" had created a well-defined and identifiable movement. They endorsed not only personal purity and public stands against immorality but also rescue work to save "fallen women" and their patrons. Moreover, the advocates of purity backed feminism; a limited kind of moral sex education to protect children from vice and disease; and vigorous local and specific campaigns against prostitution, pornography, and suggestive literature. The purity reformers were remarkably successful, particularly in the suppression of "impure" publications and discussions. They sustained and guarded the conspiracy of silence.[12]

By the early twentieth century, the anti-prostitution campaigns were more sophisticated and inclusive. Yet the Progressive reformers retained the same concern for home training as a meliorative measure. The idea of a totally purified society, too, was common to both the religiously inspired reformers before 1900 and their secular counterparts after 1900. The Progressives, however, recognized that the problem was not with the individual prostitute or pimp, but with the large-scale business that exploited public women. The reformers of the new century also connected the elimination of the red light district with social efficiency and municipal reform. The bordello was only one among many noxious social institutions fought by the Progressives— temperance, housing, wages, and many other reforms were inseparable parts of the promise of American life.[13]

At the turn of the century the very conspiracy of silence that constituted a bulwark of purity was also being attacked, often by persons who were interested in making a better society. Both feminists and literary craftsmen were raising the particular question of fulfillment—fulfillment in life in general and in marriage in particular.[14] The first evidence of a new standard of morality for the twentieth century appeared in discussions of divorce, one of the troublesome questions that fulfillment raised.[15] Divorce, and remarriage, especially, required modifications in the Victorian image of the sexless woman protected by a double standard. The well-publicized "revolution in morals" of the 1910's and 1920's involved primarily changes in the nature of acceptable and expectable female behavior.[16] Throughout the previous century American writers had recognized that in addition to embodying purity and idealism, the American girl had impulses that could "electrify" both herself and her male counterpart. By 1900 authors of fiction and drama with increasing frequency were suggesting that a woman has a sexual existence in addition to her spiritualizing and uplifting role.[17]

A number of intellectual rebels in the United States went further than conventional literati who dealt with family, romantic love, divorce, and fulfill-

ment. To confirm the right of women to sexual as well as economic, political, and social equality, they appealed to European propagandists and exemplars of frankness. To late Victorians, Henrik Ibsen, George Bernard Shaw, Émile Zola, and other literary innovators appeared bold and iconoclastic.[18] By the early 1900's the writings of Edward Carpenter and Ellen Key were available, and, at the same time, a number of reputable social scientists of the era questioned the universality and, implicitly, desirability of such hallowed customs as monogamy. For the educated, therefore, an impressive array of both radical and more respectable writers had suggested thinking about "the sexually unthinkable."[19]

Except for the feminists, the radicals and others who overtly or covertly sought for many years to deal with sex more openly were not in any way operating in American society to end the double standard. Their conception of a sexual revolution was incomplete. Where literary people and agitators pioneered in public discussion of sexual matters, they did not advocate more than just breaking the conspiracy of silence. Two characters in a story in the leading naughty-but-nice publication, *Smart Set*, for example, had this conversation: "Women cannot boldly defy all the conventions and expect to be received." "And men?" "Oh, they were always privileged." Advanced litterateurs could openly discuss and condemn untranslatable French songs, cheap novels, and other underground materials that sophisticates knew existed, or even Ibsen and Zola. But however worldly, such American writers dared not question conventional morality and immorality; they left the double standard unchallenged, even while archly or romantically suggesting that women as well as men have sexual natures.[20]

By the opening years of the twentieth century, social changes embodied largely in advances by both purity and anti-purity forces foreshadowed innovations in American attitudes toward sex, particularly the conspiracy of silence and the double standard. But the revolution in the ways that middle-class Americans coped with sex grew out of an independent reform movement that a group of conservative medical specialists created.

The physicians who founded the social hygiene movement were impelled to their crusade not so much by the general sentiments that usually energize reform movements but rather by new scientific discoveries about venereal diseases. Syphilis had long been known as a dangerous disease. Generally those afflicted knew that they had it and took treatment until the obvious symptoms disappeared. The other major venereal disease, gonorrhea, was regarded as little dangerous as a bad cold. Both maladies were considered by early Victorians to be the result of immorality, and there was widespread opinion that God utilized these diseases to punish sin. As a result, sympathy for those affected was rare.

During the course of the nineteenth century, medical technology brought to light horrifying facts about these illnesses. Syphilis had complications that no one had suspected; it lay behind major diseases of every organ

of the body, even, for example, types of arthritis, degenerative nervous disorders, and paresis, a peculiarly grisly form of mental illness that caused "almost mortal terror" among physicians, in the words of a Providence psychiatrist of the day.[21] Gonorrhea also turned out to be a dangerous and deadly infection, the cause of diseases, especially women's diseases, the nature of which medical authorities had theretofore not guessed. Moreover, the known prevalence of venereal illnesses increased, and a huge fraction of the population appeared to be infected. Most terrifying of all was the fact that the obvious symptoms proved no safe guide as to the presence or absence of the versatile microorganisms responsible for the illnesses. In some cases the victims reaped an appalling harvest of wild oats twenty or twenty-five years after infection.[22]

Physicians dealing with syphilis and gonorrhea became particularly disturbed when they discovered that many victims of these sad afflictions were not men who took advantage of the double standard but women and children whose purity was beyond question. The doctors spoke therefore of "syphilis of the innocent." The innocent were wives whose husbands had infected them. There were children, too, who had so to speak "inherited" the disease from their parents at birth, if, indeed, they were not stillborn. The innocent included people of all ages whose infections were not associated with sex at all but with a chaste kiss, a wet nurse, a common towel. The diseases appeared to threaten not only the family but also the individual, sexless person. In many areas squeamish citizens cooperated with medical personnel who campaigned to secure legislation to outlaw the ubiquitous common drinking cup.[23]

By the turn of the twentieth century, what had only a few decades earlier seemed just one of many public health problems, emerged as an intolerable menace to society. Physicians, especially specialists, expressed their concern through articles in professional journals and papers presented at professional meetings. On February 25, 1901, for instance, while doctors in New York heard an important paper on the urgency of preventing venereal diseases, the Physicians' Club of Chicago convened an evening discussion of "Ravages of Venereal Diseases." By 1903 the American Medical Association had a committee on the prevention of venereal maladies. By and large the various medical commentators advocated, as steps toward prevention, the education of the public and/or compulsory medical inspection of prostitutes in the Continental fashion. Both ideas were controversial, indeed, unpopular, and the physicians kept the discussion almost entirely within the profession. Because of popular prejudice some hospitals refused to admit venereal disease patients. The doctors therefore made treatment of the ill a third aspect of the program, but again they found that they were dealing with general social attitudes, not just medical practice.[24]

The physicians were stymied primarily by the advocates of purity. On only one occasion had inspection of public women been tried in the

United States. St. Louis passed an inspection ordinance in 1870, but in 1874 the forces of righteousness succeeded in nullifying it. Furthermore, as anti-prostitution writers pointed out, it was not clear that inspection was effective.[25]

The extreme concern of medical leaders, however, made a number of them so desperate that they were willing to fight the purity groups and their own doubts, and they advocated inspection measures that they hoped would pass for public health legislation.[26] The major reason that the doctors could not produce change was the conspiracy of silence; they were afraid to disclose publicly what they knew. The whole profession was placed in the tragic situation of being unable to warn potential victims of the dangers they faced. The man who discovered that physicians need not stand helpless in this predicament was a dignified and most eminent specialist, Prince A. Morrow of New York.

Morrow had been born in Mt. Vernon, Kentucky, in 1846. After graduating from Princeton College, a small institution in Kentucky, he studied medicine at New York University and took advanced training in Paris and other European medical centers. Not long after entering practice in 1874 he gained distinction as a specialist in dermatology, which at that time included venereal diseases.[27]

Morrow had given few indications of his potential as a social reformer. As a youth he had financed his education by teaching school, but so had many Americans who were not reformers.[28] The only clear symptom was his work in 1880, at the age of thirty-four, in translating a book, *Syphilis and Marriage*, by the world renowned French syphiligrapher, Jean-Alfred Fournier. Fournier described in frightening detail the tragic consequences that follow when a person infected with syphilis marries. Fournier believed that physicians should persuade such persons to postpone marriage until after the most rigorous treatment. Morrow in the introduction to the translation remarked on the importance of Fournier's book to "family and society." But otherwise there is very little evidence of Morrow's opinions in those years.[29] In 1885 his remarks in a manual on venereal diseases showed him to be pessimistic about preventing those afflictions. In the light of the St. Louis experience, he dismissed inspection of prostitutes as "practically a failure" in this country. For prophylaxis he offered only the common-sense observation that chances of infection were diminished if a prostitute were visited early in the evening before she had much business. In the same book, however, his description of a newborn syphilitic baby, although objective, left no doubt that he harbored strong feelings about what he saw in his practice.[30]

In 1893 Morrow edited a collective work on syphilis written by a number of specialists. He was especially impressed by an article in that book by another New York doctor, Samuel Treat Armstrong, who wrote about the public health aspects of syphilis. Armstrong had set about gathering statistics and information about infection rates, intending to show that legislation

requiring the medical inspection of public women would control the spread of syphilis. He was surprised to discover that the body of medical opinion, including his own, was mistaken; nowhere had inspection controlled the disease over a period of time. The only suggestion that Armstrong was able to make then—the one picked up by Morrow—was that society expedite the treatment of every infected person, particularly by opening hospitals to venereal cases.[31]

A few years after this work appeared, Morrow in 1899 attended, at his own expense, the first of two international conferences held in Brussels to consider the public health aspects of venereal diseases. Many of the physicians and public health officials attending the Brussels meeting concluded that venereal diseases were more prevalent than was generally believed and that inspection of prostitutes was not effective. The resolutions of the conference aimed at improving inspection systems and educating the public concerning the dangers of venereal infection.[32]

In the wake of this meeting Morrow began his career as a social reformer by presenting a powerful address to the New York County Medical Society. He declared that the principal sufferers from syphilis and gonorrhea were either innocent women and children or unwitting youngsters who had no idea of the dangers to which they exposed themselves. Morrow despaired of wiping out prostitution, but urged improving social conditions and the wages of women and prosecuting the merchants of flesh who made money off the social evil. Again he suggested prophylaxis by the direct means of treating all of those afflicted. He also thought that young men ought to be warned about the dangers of the diseases. After hearing Morrow the society appointed a committee to investigate the subject further, and Morrow was named chairman. The committee gathered some statistics about the high incidence of venereal diseases, and, presumably under Morrow's guidance, stressed in their report education and treatment—and not inspection of prostitutes—as the best means of preventing venereal diseases.[33]

Morrow and his committee asserted that they were not utopians and that they accepted the inevitability of commercial immorality. "Prostitution," they wrote, "is inherent in the human race; it cannot be annihilated, it is a necessary evil in our social system." But Morrow was now unmistakably committed to agitation for social reform. The only clue as to why after so many years as a medical specialist he was at last ready to speak out against the established order was his emphasis on the complications of gonorrhea. Knowledge about them and their ominous nature was relatively new. Again, the victims were usually women and children. "To-day," he declared in 1901, "we recognize it [gonorrhea] not only as the most widespread but also as one of the most serious of infective diseases; it has risen to the dignity of a public peril."[34]

Morrow was active in organizing the second Brussels conference, which met in 1902. The delegates there heard reports by members of a French

group, the French Society of Sanitary and Moral Prophylaxis, founded in 1900 by Fournier, who had successfully undertaken an educational campaign to warn youth against venereal diseases and to urge infected persons to seek treatment.[35] After the meetings Morrow was asked to found such an organization in the United States.[36] At the time he was busy writing *Social Diseases and Marriage*, which emphasized "moral and educational influences," as the most efficient means of preventing disease,[37] and it was not until May 1904 that he made a public plea for an American organization.

Morrow proposed that the organization include not only medical men but also prominent laymen, leaders of opinion especially, for the problem was moral as well as medical. "It is the consensus . . . among those who have studied this subject," he emphasized, "that a general diffusion of knowledge respecting the dangers, individual and social, of venereal diseases, their modes of communication, direct and indirect, would constitute the most efficient means of prophylaxis." Morrow attacked directly the tendency of society to conceal and ignore this "Social Peril," as he styled it, and he proposed an organization to educate the public.[38]

Morrow later spoke of the indifference and prejudice that he fought in those early days. He talked to innumerable people and wrote letters endlessly. It was almost another year, February 8, 1905, before he called an organizational meeting. Only twenty-five people responded to his call to meet at the New York Academy of Medicine, and the group adjourned to a smaller room adjoining the meeting hall so as not to feel so dispirited at the unimpressive turnout. In his address to the group, Morrow advocated a program of action that involved new ideas. He proposed that the society be the source of a forceful propaganda campaign to expose and publicize the dangers of venereal diseases and to eradicate prostitution.[39]

Morrow's proposal to end prostitution was especially startling, since only a few years before, he had helped to draft a committee report that had characterized the abolition of prostitution as utopian. Now, however, Morrow denounced even inspection of public women and asked the new organization to eliminate commercial venery by means of changing moral standards, specifically by destroying the double standard of conduct. Morrow was not yet allied with the purity movement, but he thought that the propaganda of his new organization should appeal to the public concern about preserving the family, a concern that, he pointed out, had been aroused by publicity about the divorce problem. Although his listeners may have been "halfhearted," they nevertheless constituted themselves the American Society of Sanitary and Moral Prophylaxis. "The object of the Society," declared its founders, "is to limit the spread of diseases which have their origin in the Social Evil."[40]

In spite of Morrow's hope to include lay leaders, five-sixths of the organizers and a similar proportion of the 120 charter members were physicians; and the movement remained primarily medical in membership and support

for some years. Quickly a number of affiliated organizations appeared all over the country—most of them organized under the auspices of local medical societies.[41] In general the response of individual physicians in every region was beyond any reasonable expectation. Lewis claimed the honor of being the first member of the Society in Chicago. In January, 1907, to cite another example, a Rochester specialist, E. Wood Ruggles, took note of Morrow's leadership. "Although not yet a member of this society," Ruggles wrote, "I am heartily in accord with its principles and aims and have undertaken to prepare this paper with the idea that a branch of the society might be established here also."[42] A large number of eminent physicians were sympathetic to what became Morrow's program, but they did not take the action that he did. Once he spoke up, however, they were willing to follow him into the treacherous areas of education and morals.

The ambitions of these reformers stand as a monument to the power of the Progressive reform impulse. Morrow and other leaders of the early social hygiene movement—almost all of them leading physicians—could hardly be characterized as other than conservative in their attitudes. None, certainly, was an extremist. Yet these doctors were aware that they were undertaking to bring about fundamental changes in prevailing opinion and attempting to alter, as Morrow said, "deep-rooted customs and habits of thought." They sought to break the conspiracy of silence, to eradicate incorrect folk beliefs concerning venereal diseases, and to convince the entire manhood of the nation that continence was entirely compatible with health. Most radical of all, they were bent on improving morals—something that centuries of religious training had failed to achieve.[43]

What drew the doctors to support Morrow was his emphasis on education as a preventive measure in fighting venereal diseases.[44] He and his colleagues and supporters therefore set about propagandizing both other physicians and the general public. So successful was Morrow's publicity campaign that the social hygienists soon began to influence the purity movement.

As early as 1904, O. Edward Janney, president of the American Purity Alliance, and himself a physician, said that while he hoped that eventually moral influences and reforms such as improving economic conditions would bring about purity, these forces acted only slowly. "The one method of relief, at once correct in theory and prompt in bringing about an improvement," he asserted, "is Education." Later that same year a writer in the official Purity Alliance journal, the *Philanthropist*, observed that the work of Morrow and others indicated that the leaders of the medical profession were at last giving up their campaign to have prostitutes inspected.[45]

By 1906 the editor of the *Philanthropist* not only took note of the early social hygiene societies but also urged that they be supported. Within a year this journal, although still stressing immorality and white slavery, was now increasingly emphasizing education and citing the work of Morrow and his allies. Early in 1908 the American Purity Alliance announced a new

objective. To the usual "devoted to the Promotion of Social Purity, the Better Protection of the Young by Prevention of Vice and the Prevention of its Regulation by the State" were added the significant words: "Its Work is Educational and Preventive."[46] By 1911, the successor magazine, *Vigilance*, was predominantly devoted to education. The other leading purity journal, the *Light*, showed a slower but parallel commitment to sex education.

In the years before World War I institutional amalgamations paralleled convergence of programs. In 1911 two of the major purity organizations, the American Purity Alliance and the American Vigilance Committee, elected the same officers, and the next year the two consolidated to form the American Vigilance Association, which was dedicated to fighting prostitution and educating the young about dangers of immorality. Many of the medically oriented groups that had followed Morrow's lead met in 1910 and elected him president of a new national organization, the American Federation for Sex Hygiene. After Morrow's death in 1913, the two forces, medical and purity, merged formally and symbolically, in 1913–1914, to form the American Social Hygiene Association. Since several of the chief financial supporters of both medical and moral reformers were the same, such as Grace H. Dodge, the change came more easily than had there been independent funding, but even so the process of amalgamation was a long and difficult one.[47]

The coalition of moral and sanitary reformers marked the purity leaders' surrender of the conspiracy of silence. It is important to spell out exactly what was surrendered. Purity leaders had long advocated providing children with moral training and a modicum of sexual instruction so as to prepare them for life's dangers and temptations. As early as the 1890's many of them were stressing that "innocence is not ignorance." In that decade a large number of sex education books appeared.[48]

Purity people, however, and Morrow's social hygienists interpreted differently the meaning of sexual enlightenment. The former believed primarily in using the home as the agency of education; they did not wish to disturb the prohibition on public discussion of sexual matters. Morrow and other physicians wanted to use all possible social institutions, including schools and the press, for education and propaganda aimed at both adults and children. Medical men were particularly eager to get the ill to take treatment; purity groups were never comfortable with using blunt propaganda such as that which the social hygienists soon had posted in many public rest rooms.

The tone of the writings of the two groups also tended to differ. Purity materials were usually pious and positive; their authors believed that "the physiological facts of reproduction may be clothed in delicate language and surrounded by an atmosphere of sacredness and self-reverence that will render the knowledge thus obtained a guarantee of right conduct."[49] Examples were often from nature—bees and flowers—and the rhetoric had a religious flavor, emphasizing the beauty of God's creation and the vague dreadfulness and guilts of uncleanliness of mind and weakness of will. Because purity writ-

ers maintained that bad thoughts lead to bad deeds, they warned against the former more vigorously than the latter.

Many tracts from the American Society of Sanitary and Moral Pro- phylaxis groups took over rhetoric and reading lists intact from the well- established purity literature for children, but Morrow's medical groups also showed a tendency to accept clean, respectful, and monogamous sexual in- tercourse in fairly straightforward terms and to emphasize the hazards of actions rather than thoughts. This set of attitudes turned out to be compati- ble with advocating sexual fulfillment, as later liberated writers who adopted social hygiene ideas showed. Purity people were apt to put a great deal of emotional content into discussions of the dangers of masturbation. Morrow and his group, in part because they were more open in their discussions, painted frankly what fate awaited those who actually had sexual intercourse. In an official pamphlet of the American Society of Sanitary and Moral Pro- phylaxis, *The Young Man's Problem*, for example, Morrow opened with a discussion of continence, masturbation, and use of prostitutes. In comment- ing elsewhere on the purity type of sex education, he observed:

> While too much credit cannot be given the high motives which actu- ate this teaching, it may be questioned whether the method employed is the wisest and best. The inculcation of purity as abstract principle without an understanding of the bodily conditions to which it relates, often fails in its effects. Unfortunately, in these exhortations to purity the impression is often given that the whole question of sex is un- clean, something shameful and even sinful; further, that punishment for sexual sin is reserved for the hereafter. Unfortunately the penalty is not sufficiently proximate to act as a deterrent.[50]

Both the venereologists and the purity people were, like other Progres- sives, attempting to impose middle-class standards on the total population by means of education. The purity people were aiming chiefly at a clientele susceptible to religious-moral appeals, those who were largely middle class in attitude. Morrow and his compatriots, by contrast, were greatly concerned about the working as well as the middle classes, and a significant part of their propaganda, including a number of graphic "exhibits," was aimed at fright- ening people with bad thoughts and wicked tendencies into refraining from sexual activity—to surrender something now in the hope of greater rewards in kind later. Purity people accepted this kind of "education" only slowly and reluctantly.[51]

When the American Federation for Sex Hygiene resolved to join in with the purity groups, the majority in the governing council represented only a minority of Morrow's forces. The Federation, however, as an anonymous observer wrote at the time, had "lost its real leader and spirit." The official statement of one constituent society reflected the new emphasis: "The actual

dealing with disease has gradually sunk more and more into the background of our Society's activities." Instead the social hygiene groups were emphasizing moral rather than sanitary prophylaxis. The purity people were always suspicious of the medical interest in preventing and treating diseases among the immoral. When World War I mobilization raised urgent and immediate public health questions, the doctors once again tended to overshadow the purity forces. A deep split occurred, for example, over the question whether or not Army medical authorities should furnish soldiers with prophylactic devices that would make immoral conduct safe.[52]

The impact of Morrow's work cannot be measured merely in terms of formal organization. As already noted, before 1905 powerful forces were at work preparing for change in the realms of public moral standards and public discussion. The fact remains that the first revolution in American attitudes toward sex came only after Morrow stepped forth to lead the new campaign against both the conspiracy of silence and the double standard. Physicians and purity workers found themselves drawn together under his leadership.[53] The medical groups that originally joined him in societies for "sanitary and moral prophylaxis" crystallized much opinion, and it was only after the doctors began their campaign that others joined. A number of educators, for example, who had been giving sex education talks covertly now spoke openly.[54] Of those anxious for reform Morrow alone had the courage to speak out, and his actions had momentous effects.

Morrow's challenge to the double standard is still affecting American life. In his own day the forces that he mobilized compelled the ancient institution of prostitution to retreat in the realm of morals and the domain of law enforcement. Reformer Jane Addams of Chicago proclaimed that Americans had developed a new conscience sensitive to the ancient evil, and the success of the anti-prostitution and social hygiene physicians in convincing their colleagues and the public that continence was compatible with health signified a remarkable change in middle-class attitudes.[55] The whole effort, of course, hinged on the promise that with proper sex education marriage would bring sexual fulfillment. Undoubtedly the most striking tangible alteration in American social life in the Progressive era was the decline of the traditional red light or segregated district in American cities.

In city after city so-called "vice commissions" of citizens investigated and recommended that the universal system of toleration give way to repression. The spontaneity with which the segregated districts disappeared in the years around 1910 is truly remarkable.[56] Beyond the roles of municipal reform, feminist agitation, the purity crusade, and the white slavery scare, social hygiene propaganda was the vital factor in the demise of the old order. Not only were the publications of the various social hygiene societies and leaders available but also local medical reform groups often assisted vice commission personnel. Morrow's name appeared conspicuously in almost all of the commission reports, and typically they advocated the program of the

social hygiene movement: suppression of vice, treatment of the ill, and, above all, education and propaganda. Because action followed the reports, Morrow and his followers were well aware that they were playing an important part in Progressive reformism.[57]

However striking was the diminution of old-fashioned prostitution (which had often involved middle-class men), Morrow's work in breaking the conspiracy of silence was even more dramatic. As early as 1906, for example, Edward Bok, editor of the conservative and religious *Ladies' Home Journal*, published editorials and articles advocating that the young should be enlightened regarding the facts of life.[58] Foster of Reed, an eyewitness of the changes that took place before World War I, in 1914 summarized what had happened to the conspiracy of silence:

> Subjects formerly tabooed are now thrust before the public. The plain-spoken publications of social hygiene societies are distributed by hundreds of thousands. Public exhibits, setting forth the horrors of venereal diseases, are sent from place to place. Motion-picture films portray white slavers, prostitutes, and restricted districts, and show exactly how an innocent girl may be seduced, betrayed, and sold. The stage finds it profitable to offer problem plays concerned with illicit love, with prostitution, and even with the results of venereal contagion.

He went on to tell of details that were printed in newspapers and in novels on the bestseller list. "Generations of silence," he concluded, "enforced by the powerful influence of social custom, have been suddenly followed by a campaign of pitiless publicity, sanctioned by eminent men and women." Printed records of those years provide ample evidence of the accuracy of Foster's observation about the new freedom of discussion.[59]

The most dramatic breach in the conspiracy of silence was the exposure of children to sex education outside the home. Many of the purity people never surrendered their beliefs that parents should enlighten their own children.[60] The bulk of the purity groups, however, finally joined the social hygienists in advocating that public agencies, particularly schools, carry on a general program of sex education. In 1912, and only after having avoided the subject before, the National Education Association resolved: "We believe that the time has arrived when normal schools and teachers' colleges should give adequate courses of instruction in sex hygiene, with the view ultimately, of the introduction of similar instruction into the courses of study in public schools."[61]

Implementing sex education stirred up more controversy than advocating it. The physicians who had initiated the movement insisted that the subject of venereal diseases be included, and others wanted the psychology of sex in addition. That biology, physiology, and reproduction should be a part of the curriculum seemed generally acceptable among those who favored the idea at all, although many advocates wanted various types of material taught

earlier or later. There was no agreement on how much frankness should be included, and reactions to sex education therefore varied largely according to the understanding of how much would be taught and by whom and when.[62]

In the rush to equip teachers, clergymen, physicians, and parents with information suitable for the children, large numbers of books, pamphlets, and articles appeared, along with bibliographies of suggested readings.[63] The quantity of such material was striking, but even more striking was the variety. In a typical reading list, for example, the most pious and unsubstantial purity pamphlet might stand next to detailed medical works on sexual perversion by Richard von Krafft-Ebing and Venyamin Tarnowsky. Such confusion and carelessness of course played into the hands of forces working to maintain the conspiracy of silence and keep sex education out of the schools lest the educators engage in "Teaching Vice to Little Children," as a Philadelphia newspaper headline put it in 1913.[64]

School instruction in sexual matters did engender much opposition. The *Nation*, for example, represented a certain type of liberal opinion appalled by the thought of a school teacher's imparting sexual knowledge. Conservatives, such as John A. Sheppard, a clergyman of Jersey City, declared, "Just at present our ears are dinned with the fad of sex hygiene. Its introduction into the schools is discussed throughout the country. If ever there was a system diabolically devised to injure our youth, and to make them voluptuaries, this is by far the most effective." Still others saw sex education as only one aspect of the general breaking of the conspiracy of silence and denounced it along with other public recognitions of the existence of sexuality.[65]

Such conservatives were not altogether unrealistic in their appraisal of what was happening. As soon as the physicians had convinced a number of prominent Americans that for the sake of health and morals sexual subjects ought to have public exposure, social rebels took advantage of the social hygiene crusade to sanction as educational whatever might be written. In the *Masses*, for example, writers repeatedly discussed sex for the sake of defiantly discussing sex. Such liberated persons created a great demand for material on the subject, and the intellectual *avant-garde* therefore came to know and talk about certain standard types of writings that just happened to be available, regardless of content. The authors cited consisted mostly of Europeans who for one reason or another had published on the subject: Key, Auguste Forel, Havelock Ellis, Sigmund Freud and the psychoanalysts.[66] Another obvious source of writings about sex was the social hygiene literature itself, and the works of Morrow and others showed up conspicuously in the comments of the liberated. H. L. Mencken's description of the sophisticated flapper, for example, contains a large percentage of material from the physicians' movement:

Life, indeed, is almost empty of surprises, mysteries, horrors to this Flapper of 1915. . . . She knows exactly what the Wassermann reaction

is, and has made up her mind that she will never marry a man who can't show an unmistakable negative. . . . She has read Christabel Pankhurst and Ellen Key, and is inclined to think that there must be something in this new doctrine of free motherhood. She is opposed to the double standard of morality, and favors a law prohibiting it.[67]

Those who wished to bring matters sexual into the public arena and did so in the wake of the social hygiene movement paid a price for their new freedom of discussion: Moral idealism had to accompany the discussion. The Progressive generation was more than friendly to combining idealization with sex, particularly in advocating romantic love. Walter Lippmann, who often voiced the aspirations of many younger Progressives, wrote in 1914:

So too, the day is passing when the child is taught to regard the body as a filthy thing. We train quite frankly for parenthood, not for the ecstasies of the celibate. Our interest in sex is no longer to annihilate it, but to educate it. . . . And there is an increasing number of people who judge sexual conduct by its results in the quality of human life. They don't think that marriage justifies licentiousness, nor will they say that every unconventional union is necessarily evil.[68]

Lippmann and others were clearly opposed to the double standard as well as the conspiracy of silence.

The extent of the impact of the social reformer physicians upon many aspects of American civilization is illustrated best by their venture into drama. Eugène Brieux, the famous French playwright, had written a play, *Les Avariés*, to show the tragic consequences that follow when a man ill with venereal disease marries. Fournier had helped Brieux so that the play was accurate in medical matters, and the French Society of Sanitary and Moral Prophylaxis had used the drama as propaganda. After it was translated into English and published under the title, *Damaged Goods*, Thomas N. Hepburn, a Hartford physician and one of Morrow's lieutenants, in 1912 obtained permission to order 10,000 copies of the play to be used for propaganda purposes in the United States.[69] Not content with that, Hepburn worked with the famous actor and manager, Richard Bennett, to produce the play on Broadway in 1913, with Bennett in the leading role. At first performed before a private matinee audience, *Damaged Goods* then was shifted to a night bill and became a notable commercial success. Late in September the play moved to the Blackstone Theater in Chicago, where it was sponsored by the local social hygiene society in conjunction with the local anti-prostitution organization.[70] It also played in Washington. Even with such respectable backing the play met criticism as well as much praise for its frankness. Brieux's drama was meant to be educational, but its presentation had a consequence not directly intended by the sponsors: It helped break taboos in the theater.

The financial success of *Damaged Goods*, according to drama critic W. H. Denny, led to "a rush on the part of managers and authorities to provide the public with plays on kindred subjects, called vice plays." That such plays—often European in origin—were available was a symptom of the presence of forces besides the social hygiene movement at work inimical to the taboos.[71]

The intense reaction to *Damaged Goods* and the other dramas that followed in its wake showed that all the purity forces were far from reconciled to the program of "education" envisaged by the medically oriented social hygienists. A writer in the New York *Herald* traced the opposition to those who were uncomfortable that the new "white slavery" plays "are showing up the connection of the politicians and office-holders and so-called respectable men with these disorderly houses." More fundamentally the conservatives objected that all of the plays, in the words of Roman Catholic poet and journalist Joyce Kilmer, "take the responsibility of sin from the individual and place it upon society."[72] Many purity people simply doubted that the plays and the moving pictures that followed them were educational. The audiences came for sensational purposes, according to New York journalist Hans von Kaltenborn: "They found what entertainment they could, and ignored the rest." The fact that the popular magazines as well as the stage were treating sexual matters more openly than in previous years intensified the discomfort of conservative purity people.[73]

The social hygiene reformers were not always pleased by the Pandora's box of sexual discussion that they had opened. The doctor who was president of the original New York organization in 1914, E. L. Keyes, Jr., declared, "As the primitive centre for discussion of sex in this country, we must assume at least some of the blame for, and be the first to protest against, the flood of 'Sexology' amidst which we struggle for breath today." He made it clear, however, that he and his group had no regrets if they had coincidentally encouraged rebellious intellectuals and other free souls who advocated that everyone read Ellis. First of all, he said, the social hygiene movement at its most medical stood for high morality, not free love, and certainly not prostitution. Second, he continued, bringing sex into the open was a relatively superficial change, despite the emotion that the subject engendered.[74]

Like other Progressives, the social hygiene reformers were fundamentally conservative. Compared to preserving the nation's health and guarding the home and the sacred institution of the family, upholding the conspiracy of silence and the double standard seemed of secondary importance. As Morrow observed after reviewing what he himself had seen in medical practice to be a result of venereal diseases, no system of morals that fostered such evils could possibly be right.[75]

The physicians' campaign to break the conspiracy of silence and eliminate the double standard of morality stands as a classic example of a Progressive reform movement. Like other Progressive reformers, Morrow and his group were inspired by moral fervor and sought to impose social change

from above. They were if not patrician reformers upper-middle-class reformers. The impact of science in inspiring them was particularly striking. New
knowledge about the cause of a large amount of human misery suggested
that it might be obliterated if only social conditions permitted. The doctors
never gave up the idea that a large part of prevention consisted simply of
treating the ill.[76] The Progressive mood contributed the idea that it was no
longer necessary to endure and ignore evil, not prostitution and certainly not
disease.[77]

In Part IV I shall return to the theme that social hygiene reformers represented Progressive reform, and at that point I shall emphasize their contributions to Progressive efforts more than I did in Chapter 10. But within the present section, on morals, Chapter 10 raises other issues besides the palpable and profound effects of a change in norms for sexual behavior, although the fact remains, as I suggested in Chapters 8 and 9, that prescriptive writings from the past can be very revealing.

As I noted in Chapters 8 and 9, the debate over the significance of standards of sexual behavior continues. The revolution in attitudes that I have described for the Progressive era was, despite the momentousness of the consequences, limited largely to the upper and middle classes and other groups that they could influence. The question of whether or not actual sexual behavior also changed continues to rest on answers derived from uncertain evidence, although the Kinsey interviews suggested that those who grew up in the Progressive years did in fact behave differently from their parents in the realm of premarital sexual activity. As Howard I. Kushner, particularly, points out, my findings do not address the questions of sexual activity in or outside of marriage or the standards and behavior of the lower classes, and he recasts my findings to state that the Progressives attempted "to institutionalize the very goal of the nineteenth-century social reformers: a uniformly shared sexual consciousness" of a "repressive" type.*

The momentous part of the revolution, however, was in fact the positive program of the social hygienists: Fulfillment was possible, indeed, desirable and socially necessary, within monogamous marriage. The impact of norms, although only one aspect of the history of sexuality, appeared not only in the diminution of prostitution and the impact of the breaking of the conspiracy of silence but in the actual functioning of the institution of mar-

---

* Howard I. Kushner, "Nineteenth-Century Sexuality and the 'Sexual Revolution' of the Progressive Era," *Canadian Review of American Studies*, 9 (1978), 34–49. Kushner uses as a point of departure the literature described in Chapter 8 casting doubt on the puritanical and "repressed" behavior of Victorian-era women. Another direction of development from my description of the change in standards is the way in which middle-class people reacted to lower-class behavior; see Stephen Slossman and Stephanie Wallach, "The Crime of Precocious Sexuality: Female Juvenile Delinquency in the Progressive Era," *Harvard Educational Review*, 48 (1978), 65–94.

riage. Elaine Tyler May has found vivid evidence of the shift in attitudes in divorce records that show clearly the new role that expectations of satisfaction within marriage played in the early twentieth century—as opposed to the concerns about duty and the protection that the institution afforded in the 1880's.[†]

The restrictive aspects of the social hygiene campaign have also attracted scholars, historians who have confirmed the widespread social impact of the reformers' efforts, particularly during World War I, a story that I refer to only by allusion. The tension between purity and efficiency in efforts at social control continued, but traditional institutionalized prostitution in the United States receded farther into the past during the mobilization and after.[‡]

In terms of norms, the expectation that women as well as men should find marriage satisfying was indeed a shift, in spite of the forerunners I noted from the 1890's. Both men's and women's attitudes toward women as well as matrimony changed, with great portent for the future. By the late twentieth century, however, as Barbara Epstein has shown in putting my narrative into a more extended context, the ideal of fulfilling marriages, which was serviceable for decades, was not surviving intact in a much changed world. In recent decades, new roles for middle-class women became realistic possibilities and the work place and family changed the context for marriage. Then, too, especially in the 1960's, supposedly new ideas from both Right and Left challenged what Americans believed they were doing in setting up—and avoiding —domestic arrangements. All of these recent notions, of course, were in turn rendered obsolete in the 1980's, just as at the turn of the century, by a new venereal disease scare. That sexually satisfying monogamy was still very much an immediate and widely acceptable answer to Americans' fear of disease suggests again the fundamental nature of the Progressive era revolution.[§]

[†] Elaine Tyler May, *Great Expectations: Marriage and Divorce in Post-Victorian America* (Chicago: University of Chicago Press, 1980).

[‡] Fred D. Baldwin, "The Invisible Armor," *American Quarterly*, 16 (1964), 432–444; Donald Smythe, "Venereal Disease: The AEF's Experience," *Prologue*, 9 (1977), 64–74; David Jay Pivar, "Cleansing the Nation: The War on Prostitution, 1917–21," *Prologue*, 12 (1980), 28–40; Allan M. Brandt, *No Magic Bullet: A Social History of Venereal Disease in the United States Since 1880* (New York: Oxford University Press, 1985), chaps. 2–3. Neil Larry Shumsky, "Vice Responds to Reform: San Francisco, 1910–1914," *Journal of Urban History*, 7 (1980), 31–47, describes how in one instance representatives of vice attempted to co-opt the social hygiene concern and fend off suppression.

[§] Among the new scholarship is Ellen Kay Trimberger, "Feminism, Men, and Modern Love: Greenwich Village, 1900–1925," in Ann Snitow, Christine

Still another reform central to Progressivism was prohibition. The next chapter therefore returns to the theme of social experiments and reform, but in this case the use of the idea of "experiment" eventually was utilized to undermine meliorism. Where the history of standards of sexual behavior is filled with surprises, the history of Americans' attempts to prescribe norms and control institutions concerned with the consumption of alcoholic beverages is marked by misrepresentation and misleading characterization.

Stansell, and Sharon Thompson, eds., *Powers of Desire: The Politics of Sexuality* (New York: Monthly Review Press, 1983), pp. 131–151. Barbara Epstein, "Family, Sexual Morality, and Popular Movements in Turn-of-the-Century America," in Snitow, Stansell, and Thompson, *Powers of Desire*, pp. 117–130. A number of historians have commented on the irony that the so-called AIDS crisis was having consequences that paralleled the social hygiene story told in Chapter 10; see especially Brandt, *No Magic Bullet*.

New Perspectives
on the
Prohibition "Experiment"
of the 1920's

Recently a number of historians have shown that the temperance movement that culminated in national prohibition was central to the American reform tradition. Such writers as James H. Timberlake have demonstrated in detail how the Eighteenth Amendment was an integral part of the reforms of the Progressive movement.[1] Yet we commonly refer to the "prohibition experiment" rather than the "prohibition reform." This characterization deserves some exploration. The question can be raised, for example, why we do not refer to the "workmen's compensation law experiment."

One explanation may be that of all of the major reforms enacted into law in the Progressive period, only prohibition was decisively and deliberately repealed. The Sixteenth and Seventeenth Amendments are still on the books; the Eighteenth is not. For historians who emphasize the theme of reform, referring to prohibition as an experiment gives them the option of suggesting that its repeal involved no loss to society. To characterize the repeal of prohibition as a major reversal of social reform would seriously impair the view that most of us have of the cumulative nature of social legislation in the twentieth century.[2]

We have been comfortable for many decades now with the idea that prohibition was a great social experiment. The image of prohibition as an experiment has even been used to draw lessons from history: to argue, for example, that certain types of laws—especially those restricting or forbidding

"New Perspectives on the Prohibition 'Experiment' of the 1920's" is reprinted from the *Journal of Social History*, 2 (1968), 51–68, with the kind permission of the *Journal of Social History*.

An earlier version of this paper was read at the Organization of American Historians meetings, Kansas City, April, 1965.

the use of liquor and narcotics—are futile and probably pernicious. Recently, however, some new literature has appeared on prohibition, whose total effect is to demand a re-examination of our customary view.[3]

The idea that prohibition was an experiment may not survive this renaissance of scholarship in which the reform and especially Progressive elements in the temperance movement are emphasized. But it is profitable, at least for the purposes of this article, to maintain the image of an experiment, for the perspectives available now permit a fresh evaluation of the experiment's outcome.

Specifically, the prohibition experiment, as the evidence stands today, can more easily be considered a success than a failure. While far from clearcut, the balance of scholarly evidence has shifted the burden of proof to those who would characterize the experiment a failure. It is now becoming clear, moreover, how the myth of failure developed and why it flourished.

In order to understand how prohibition came to be a Progressive reform measure, it is necessary to take into account turn-of-the-century class structure among Americans, their drinking habits, and particularly their liquor-by-the-drink retailing institution, the saloon. At that time, typical middle-class[4] Americans did not drink, except sometimes wine. Respectable men were careful about being seen in or about a saloon. The saloon was for the most part a noxious institution, in fact inextricably bound up with prostitution, gambling, police corruption, and crime. The image of the respectable, old-fashioned saloon with its free lunch and manly conviviality was to a surprising extent the product of sentimental reminiscing. There were, it is true, many such delightful neighborhood institutions, but most saloons were disreputable places.[5]

Although connected with social evils, the saloon did serve social needs of the working class, especially the first generation immigrants.[6] The fact that the unfortunate and exploited were also the victims of the perniciousness associated with the saloon did not make them hate it, and when middle-class reformers took it away from them, the deprived opposed the reform. Wet voting strength, however, lay principally in highly localized parts of urban areas and was therefore ineffective.[7]

The Progressive movement represented an alliance of upper- and middle-class reformers with two different groups. Many reforms, such as workmen's compensation laws, were achieved by a combination of urban labor elements and the reformers. Other reforms, of which prohibition was the prototype, were achieved by the reformers only with the active aid of a part of the business community in its business capacity.[8] For the progressives, prohibition, with its elements of moralism, social desirability, meliorism, and scientifically demonstrated need, provided a perfect vehicle for reform. Here was a means by which they could use law to change the personal habits of Americans in general in such a way that both the nation and the individual would profit.[9] The viewpoint of the business elements was not so altruistic,

but it was equally convincing. They believed that a sober, temperate worker was a more productive, a more stable, and a happier worker.

One of the sources of the concern of businessmen was the increasing use of machinery in industry. The intemperate worker, once merely inefficient, now became a veritable menace. For safety reasons, many industrial concerns did not employ problem drinkers. The best example of industrial prohibition was "Rule G" of the American Railway Association, which called for the dismissal of operating employees who drank on duty or even frequented saloons. In the years before World War I some railroads enforced even stricter regulations. A number of other businesses followed suit, and there was widespread belief that sobriety and industrial safety were inseparable.

Employer groups were the sources of various opinions about the way in which both employee and employer benefited from enforced sobriety.[10] Not least striking was the argument that the money spent on liquor might well go to pay for other consumer goods. While large segments of business, including industries economically dependent upon the liquor industry, opposed prohibition or anything like it as government interference with business, a wealthy segment of the business community was committed, with the Progressives, to temperance reform. The brewers' blacklist of April, 1915, for example, contained, in some cases without justification, the names of the Pennsylvania Railroad, United States Steel Corporation, John Wanamaker's, Pittsburgh Coal Company, Goodyear Rubber Company, and S. S. Kresge Company.[11]

The American prohibition experiment grew out of the transformation that the combination of Progressive reformers and businessmen wrought in the temperance movement.[12] Beginning in 1907 a large number of state and local governments enacted laws or adopted constitutional provisions that dried up—as far as alcoholic beverages were concerned—a substantial part of the United States. The success of the anti-liquor forces, led by the Anti-Saloon League, was so impressive that they were prepared to strike for a national prohibition constitutional amendment. This issue was decided in the 1916 Congressional elections, although the Amendment itself was not passed by Congress until December 22, 1917.[13] A sufficient number of states ratified it by January 16, 1919, and it took effect on January 16, 1920.

In actuality, however, prohibition began well before January, 1920. In addition to the widespread local prohibition laws, federal laws greatly restricted the production and sale of alcoholic beverages, mostly, beginning in 1917, in the guise of war legislation. The manufacture of distilled spirits beverages, for example, had been forbidden for more than three months when Congress passed the Eighteenth Amendment late in 1917. The Volstead Act of 1919, passed to implement the Amendment, provided by law that wartime prohibition would remain in effect until the Amendment came into force.

The Eighteenth Amendment prohibited the manufacturing, selling, importing, or transporting of "intoxicating liquors." It was designed to kill off

the liquor business in general and the saloon in particular; but at the same time the Amendment was not designed to prohibit either the possession or drinking of alcoholic beverages. At a later time the courts held even the act of buying liquor to be legal and not part of a conspiracy. Most of the local and state prohibition laws were similar in their provisions and intent. The very limited nature of the prohibition experiment must, therefore, be understood from the beginning.

At the time, a number of union leaders and social critics pointed out that the Eighteenth Amendment constituted class legislation; that is, the political strength of the drys lay among middle-class Progressives who wanted, essentially, to remove the saloon from American life. The Amendment permitted those who had enough money to lay in all the liquor they pleased, but the impecunious workingman was to be deprived of his day-to-day or week-to-week liquor supply.[14] The class aspect of prohibition later turned out to have great importance. Most of the recent revisionist writers have concentrated upon the interplay between prohibition and social role and status.

The primary difficulty that has stood in the way of properly assessing the prohibition experiment has been methods of generalization. Evidence gathered from different sections of the country varies so radically as to make weighing of evidence difficult. In addition, there has been a great deal of confusion about time: When did prohibition begin? What period of its operation should be the basis for judgment? The difficulties of time and place are particularly relevant to the fundamental question of enforcement.

As the country looked forward to prohibition after the elections of 1916, widespread public support, outside of a few urban areas, was expected to make prohibition a success both initially and later on. It was reasonable to expect that enforcement would be strict and that society both institutionally and informally would deal severely with any actions tending to revive the liquor trade. These expectations were realistic through the years of the war, when prohibition and patriotism were closely connected in the public mind. Only some years after the passage of the Volstead Act did hopes for unquestionably effective enforcement fade away. In these early years, when public opinion generally supported enforcement, the various public officials responsible for enforcement were the ones who most contributed to its breakdown. This breakdown in many areas in turn led to the evaporation of much public support in the country as a whole.

Successive Congresses refused to appropriate enough money to enforce the laws. Through its influence in Congress the Anti-Saloon League helped to perpetuate the starvation of the Prohibition Bureau and its predecessors in the name of political expediency. Huge sums spent on prohibition, the drys feared, would alienate many voters—and fearful Congressmen—more or less indifferent to prohibition. The prohibitionists therefore made the claim that prohibition was effective so that they would not have to admit the necessity

of large appropriations for enforcement. A second act of irresponsibility of the Congresses was acquiescing in exempting the enforcement officers from Civil Service and so making the Prohibition Bureau part of the political spoils system. League officials who had written this provision into the Volstead Act hoped by using their political power to dictate friendly appointments, but the record shows that politics, not the League, dominated federal enforcement efforts. Not until 1927 did the Prohibition Bureau finally come under Civil Service.[15]

The men charged with enforcement, the Presidents of the 1920's, were, until Hoover, indifferent to prohibition except as it affected politics. Wilson, although not a wet, vetoed the Volstead Act, and it was passed over his veto. Harding and Coolidge were notoriously uninterested in enforcing prohibition.[16] When Hoover took office in 1929 he reorganized the administration of enforcement, and his effectiveness in cutting down well-established channels of supply helped give final impetus to the movement for a re-evaluation of prohibition.

In some areas prosecutors and even judges were so unsympathetic that enforcement was impossible. Elsewhere local juries refused to convict in bootlegging cases. These local factors contributed greatly to the notable disparities in the effectiveness of prohibition from place to place.[17]

By a unique concurrent enforcement provision of the Eighteenth Amendment, state and local officials were as responsible for enforcement as federal authorities. The Anti-Saloon League, because of its power in the states, expected to use existing law enforcement agencies and avoid huge federal appropriations for enforcement. Contrary to the expectations of the League, local officials were the weakest point in enforcement.[18] Most of the states—but not all—enacted "little Volstead" acts; yet in 1927 only eighteen of the forty-eight states were appropriating money for the enforcement of such acts.[19] Local enforcement in many Southern and Western areas was both severe and effective; in other areas local enforcement was even more unlikely than federal enforcement. For years the entire government of New Jersey openly defied the Eighteenth Amendment, and it was clear that the governor was not troubled a bit about his oath of office. Some states that had enforced their own prohibition laws before 1919 afterward made no attempt to continue enforcement.

With such extreme variations in the enforcement of prohibition over the United States, judging the overall success of the experiment on the basis of enforcement records is hazardous. Bootlegging in New York, Chicago, and San Francisco clearly was not necessarily representative of the intervening territory, and vice versa.

An easier basis for generalizing about the effectiveness of enforcement is the impact that prohibition had on consumption of alcohol. Here the second major complication mentioned crops up: The availability of liquor varied greatly from time to time and specifically from an initial period of effec-

tiveness in 1919–1922 to a later period of widespread violation of the law, typically 1925–1927.

In the early years of national prohibition, liquor was very difficult to obtain. In the later years when the laws were being defied by well-organized bootleggers operating through established channels, the supply increased.[20] By the late 1920's, for example, the domestic supply of hard liquor in northern California was so great that the price fell below the point at which it was profitable to run beverages in from Canada by ship.[21] In the last years of prohibition it became very easy—at least in some areas with large populations— to obtain relatively good liquor. Many people, relying on their memories, have generalized from this later period, after about 1925, to all of the prohibition years and have come, falsely, to the conclusion that enforcement was neither real nor practical. Overall one can say that considering the relatively slight amount of effort put into it, enforcement was surprisingly effective in many places, and particularly in the early years.

Both so-called wet and dry sources agree that the amount of liquor consumed per capita decreased substantially because of prohibition. The best figures available show that the gallons of pure alcohol ingested per person varied widely over four different periods. In the period 1911–1914, the amount was 1.69 gallons. Under the wartime restrictions, 1918–1919, the amount decreased to .97. In the early years of national prohibition, 1921–1922, there was still further decrease to .73 gallons. In the later years of prohibition, 1927–1930, the amount rose to 1.14 gallons.[22]

These figures suggest that great care must be used in making comparisons between "before" prohibition and "after." Statistics and memories that use 1920 as the beginning of prohibition are misleading, since not only were federal laws in force before then but there was also extensive state prohibition. The peak of absolute consumption of beer, for example, was reached in the years 1911–1914, not 1916–1918, much less 1919.[23] The real "before" was sometime around 1910.

The best independent evidence of the impact of prohibition can be found in the available figures for certain direct and measurable social effects of alcohol consumption. The decrease from about 1915 to 1920–1922 in arrests for drunkenness, in hospitalization for alcoholism, and in the incidence of other diseases, such as cirrhosis of the liver, specifically related to drinking was remarkable. The low point of these indexes came in 1918–1921, and then they climbed again until the late 1920's. Because of confusion about when prohibition began, the significance of these well-known statistics has seldom been appreciated: There is clear evidence that in the early years of prohibition not only did the use of alcohol decrease but American society enjoyed some of the direct benefits promised by proponents of prohibition.[24]

Undoubtedly the most convincing evidence of the success of prohibition is to be found in the mental hospital admission rates. There is no question of a sudden change in physicians' diagnoses, and the people who

had to deal with alcohol-related mental diseases were obviously impressed by what they saw. After reviewing recent hospital admission rates for alcoholic psychoses, James V. May, one of the most eminent American psychiatrists, wrote in 1922: "With the advent of prohibition the alcoholic psychoses as far as this country is concerned have become a matter of little more than historical interest. The admission rate in the New York state hospitals for 1920 was only 1.9 percent [as compared with ten percent in 1909–1912]." [25] For many years articles on alcoholism literally disappeared from American medical literature. [26]

In other words, after World War I and until sometime in the early 1920's, say, 1922 or 1923, when enforcement was clearly breaking down, prohibition was generally a success. Certainly there is no basis for the conclusion that prohibition was inherently doomed to failure. The emasculation of enforcement grew out of specific factors that were not organically related to the Eighteenth Amendment.

Nor is most of this analysis either new or controversial. Indeed, most of the criticism of prohibition has centered on assertions not so much that the experiment failed but that it had two more or less unexpected consequences that clearly show it to have been undesirable. The critics claim, first, that the Eighteenth Amendment caused dangerous criminal behavior; and, second, that in spite of prohibition more people drank alcohol than before. If a candid examination fails to confirm these commonly accepted allegations, the interpretation of prohibition as a failure loses most of its validity. Such is precisely the case.

During the 1920's there was almost universal public belief that a "crime wave" existed in the United States. In spite of the literary output on the subject, dealing largely with a local situation in Chicago, there is no firm evidence of this supposed upsurge in lawlessness. Two criminologists, Edwin H. Sutherland and C. H. Gehlke, at the end of the decade reviewed the available crime statistics, and the most that they could conclude was, "There is no evidence here of a 'crime wave,' but only of a slowly rising level." These admittedly inadequate statistics emphasized large urban areas and were, it should be emphasized, *not* corrected to reflect the increase in population. [27] Actually no statistics from this period dealing with crime are of any value whatsoever in generalizing about crime rates. [28] Apparently what happened was that in the 1920's the long existent "underworld" first became publicized and romanticized. The crime wave, in other words, was the invention of enterprising journalists feeding on some sensational crimes and situations and catering to a public to whom the newly discovered "racketeer" was a covert folk hero.

Even though there was no crime wave, there was a connection between crime and prohibition, as Frederick Lewis Allen suggested in his alliterative coupling of "Alcohol and Al Capone." [29] Because of the large profits involved in bootlegging and the inability of the producers and customers to obtain

police protection, criminal elements organized and exploited the liquor business just as they did all other illegal activities. It would be a serious distortion
even of racketeering, however, to emphasize bootlegging at the expense of
the central criminal-directed activity, gambling.[30] Since liquor-related activities were not recognized as essentially criminal in nature by substantial parts
of the population, it is difficult to argue that widespread violation of the Volstead Act constituted a true increase of crime. Nevertheless, concern over
growing federal "crime" statistics, that is, bootlegging cases, along with fears
based on hysterical journalism, helped to bring about repeal.

We are left, then, with the question of whether national prohibition
led to more drinking than before. It should first be pointed out not only
that the use of 1920 as the beginning of prohibition is misleading but that
much of the drinking during the 1920's was not relevant to the prohibition of
the Eighteenth Amendment and Volstead Act. Private drinking was perfectly
legal all of the time, and possession of liquor that had been accumulated
by the foresighted before prohibition was entirely lawful. The continued
production of cider and wine at home was specifically provided for also.
Indeed, the demand for wine grapes was so great that many grape growers
who in 1919 faced ruin made a fortune selling their grapes in the first years
of the Amendment.[31] Ironically, many an old lady who made her own wine
believed that she was defying prohibition when in fact the law protected her.

We still face the problem of reconciling the statistics quoted above that
show that alcohol consumption was substantially reduced, at one point to
about half of the pre-prohibition consumption, with the common observation
of the 1920's that as many or more people were drinking than before.

What happened, one can say with hindsight, was predictable. When
liquor became unavailable except at some risk and considerable cost, it became a luxury item, that is, a symbol of affluence and, eventually, status.
Where before men of good families tended not to drink and women certainly
did not, during the 1920's it was precisely the sons and daughters of the
"nice" people who were patronizing the bootleggers and speakeasies, neither
of which for some years was very effectively available to the lower classes.
This utilization of drinking as conspicuous consumption was accompanied by
the so-called revolution in manners and morals that began among the rebellious intellectuals around 1912 and reached a high point of popularization in
the 1920's when the adults of the business class began adopting the "lower"
social standards of their children.[32]

We can now understand why the fact was universally reported by journalists of the era that "everyone drank, including many who never did before." Drinking, and often new drinking, was common among the upper
classes, especially among the types of people likely to consort with the writers of the day. The journalists and other observers did indeed report honestly
that they saw "everyone" drinking. They seldom saw the lower classes and
almost never knew about the previous drinking habits of the masses. The

situation was summed up by an unusually well qualified witness, Whiting Williams, testifying before the Wickersham Commission. A vice-president of a Cleveland steel company, he had for many years gone in disguise among the working people of several areas in connection with handling labor problems. He concluded:

> Very much of the misconception with respect to the liquor problem comes from the fact that most of the people who are writing and talking most actively about the prohibition problem are people who, in the nature of things, have never had any contact with the liquor problem in its earlier pre-prohibition form and who are, therefore, unduly impressed with the changes with respect to drinking that they see on their own level; their own level, however, representing an extremely small proportion of the population.
>
> The great mass who, I think, are enormously more involved in the whole problem, of course, in the nature of things are not articulate and are not writing in the newspapers.[33]

The important point is that the "everyone" who was reported to be drinking did not include working-class families, that is, the preponderant part of the population. Clark Warburton, in a study initiated with the help of the Association Against the Prohibition Amendment, is explicit on this point: "The working class is consuming not more than half as much alcohol per capita as formerly."[34] The classic study is Martha Bensley Bruère's. She surveyed social workers across the country, and the overwhelming impression (even taking account of urban immigrant areas where prohibition laws were flouted) was that working people drank very much less than before and further, as predicted, that prohibition had, on the balance, substantially improved conditions among low-income Americans.[35]

Even in its last years the law, with all of its leaks, was still effective in cutting down drinking among the workers, which was one of the primary aims of prohibition. Here, then, is more evidence of the success of the prohibition experiment. Certainly the Anti-Saloon League did succeed in destroying the old-fashioned saloon, the explicit target of its campaign.

Taking together all of this evidence of the success of prohibition, especially in its class differential aspects, we are still left with the question of why the law was repealed.

The story of repeal is contained largely in the growth of the idea that prohibition was a failure. From the beginning, a number of contemporary observers (particularly in the largest cities) saw many violations of the law and concluded that prohibition was not working. These observers were in the minority, and for a long time most people believed that by and large prohibition was effective. Even for those who did not, the question of repeal—once appeals to the Supreme Court had been settled—simply never arose.

Bartlett C. Jones has observed, "A peculiarity of the Prohibition debate was the fact that repeal, called an absolute impossibility for much of the period, became irresistibly popular in 1932 and 1933."[36] Not even enemies of prohibition considered absolute repeal as an alternative until quite late, although they upheld through all of these years their side of the vigorous public debate about the effectiveness and desirability of the prohibition laws.[37]

In the early days of prohibition, the predominant attitudes toward the experiment manifested in the chief magazines and newspapers of the country were either ambivalent acceptance or, more rarely, impotent hostility. In 1923–1924 a major shift in the attitudes of the mass circulation information media occurred so that acceptance was replaced by nearly universal outright criticism accompanied by a demand for modification of the Volstead Act.[38] The criticism was based on the assumption that Volsteadism, at least, was a failure. The suggested solution was legalizing light wines and beers.

The effectiveness of the shift of "public opinion" is reflected in the vigorous counterattack launched by the dry forces who too often denied real evils and asserted that prohibition was effective and was benefiting the nation. By claiming too much, especially in the late 1920's, the drys discredited that which was really true, and the literate public apparently discounted all statements that might show that prohibition was at least a partial success, partly on the rigidly idealistic basis that if it was a partial failure, it was a total failure.

Great impetus was given to sentiment hostile to prohibition by the concern of respectable people about the "crime wave." They argued, plausibly enough given the assumptions that there was a crime wave and that prohibition was a failure, that universal disregard for the Eighteenth Amendment was damaging to general respect for law. If the most respectable elements of society, so the argument went, openly showed contempt for the Constitution, how could anyone be expected to honor a mere statute? Much of the leadership of the "anti's" soon came from the bar associations rather than the bar patrons.[39]

Coincident with this shift in opinion came the beginning of one of the most effective publicity campaigns of modern times, led by the Association Against the Prohibition Amendment. At first largely independent of liquor money, in the last years of prohibition the AAPA used all it could command. By providing journalists with reliable information, the AAPA developed a virtual monopoly on liquor and prohibition press coverage.[40] In the late 1920's and early 1930's it was unusual to find a story about prohibition in small local papers that did not have its origin—free of charge, of course—with the AAPA.

The AAPA had as its announced goal the modification of the Volstead Act to legalize light wines and beers. The organization also headed up campaigns to repeal the "little Volstead" acts most states had enacted. By the late 1920's the AAPA beat the Anti-Saloon League at its own game, chipping

away at the state level. State after state, often by popular vote, did away with the concurrent enforcement acts. Both the wets and the drys viewed state repeals and any modification of the Volstead Act as only steps toward full repeal.[41] Perhaps they were correct; but another possibility does need examination.

Andrew Sinclair, in the most recent and thorough examination of the question, contends that modification of the Volstead Act to legalize light wines and beers would have saved the rest of the prohibition experiment. It is difficult to differ with Sinclair's contention that complete repeal of the Eighteenth Amendment was unprovoked and undesirable.[42]

When President Hoover appointed the Wickersham Commission, public opinion was almost unanimous in expecting that the solution to the prohibition problem would be modification. The Commission's report strengthened the expectation. Not even the Association Against the Prohibition Amendment hoped for more than that, much less repeal. But suddenly an overwhelming surge of public sentiment brought about the Twenty-First Amendment denouement.

The cause of this second sudden shift in opinion was the Great Depression that began about 1929. Jones has shown convincingly that every argument used to bring about repeal in 1932–1933 had been well known since the beginning of prohibition. The class aspect of the legislation, which had been so callously accepted in 1920, was suddenly undesirable. The main depression-related argument, that legalization of liquor manufacture would produce a badly needed additional tax revenue, was well known in the 1910's and even earlier. These rationalizations of repeal were masks for the fact that the general public, baffled by the economic catastrophe, found a convenient scapegoat: prohibition. (The drys had, after all, tried to credit prohibition for the prosperity of the 1920's.)[43] The groundswell of public feeling was irresistible and the entire "experiment, noble in motive and far-reaching in purpose," was not modified but thrown out with Volsteadism, bathwater, baby, and all.

Because the AAPA won, its explanations of what happened were accepted at face value. One of the lasting results of prohibition, therefore, was perpetuation of the stereotypes of the wet propaganda of the 1920's and the myth that the American experiment in prohibition (usually misunderstood to have outlawed personal drinking as well as the liquor business) was a failure. Blanketed together here indiscriminately were all of the years from 1918 to 1933.

More than thirty years have passed since the repeal of the Eighteenth Amendment. Surely the AAPA has now had its full measure of victory and it is no longer necessary for historians to perpetuate a myth that grew up in another era. For decades there has been no realistic possibility of a resurgence of prohibition in its Progressive form—or probably any other form.

The concern now is not so much the destruction of myth, however; the concern is that our acceptance of the myth of the failure of prohibition has prevented us from exploring in depth social and especially sociological aspects of the prohibition experiment. Recent scholarship, by treating prohibition more as a reform than an experiment, has shown that we have been missing one of the most interesting incidents of twentieth-century history.

As I indicated earlier, I came onto the prohibition question in the course of looking at the history of psychiatry, specifically the decline of alcoholism as a psychiatric problem during prohibition and the involvement of many psychiatrists in anti-alcohol campaigns in their attempts to solve a medical problem through social means. Historians still have not filled in many of the elements in medical history that pertain to prohibition, including the abrupt disappearance of the special hospitals for treating alcoholics.

Confirmation of the idea that prohibition was surprisingly successful, regardless of wet propaganda to the contrary (propaganda still being repeated down to the present day, as it turns out), came initially from the works, cited previously, of Norman Clark on prohibition in the state of Washington and Andrew Sinclair, the English writer who concluded that outright repeal of the Eighteenth Amendment was a mistake. Since these early writings, historians have been able to take a fresh look at prohibition, and Clark, in his classic work, *Deliver Us from Evil* (1976), expands and extends the points made in the foregoing chapter. Comparisons with other Western countries, he points out, show that the American experience was not unique in either revulsion from liquor or the middle-class and mass-media developments that brought it back. But the stereotypes of anti-prohibition propaganda that I challenged in the last chapter probably will not survive—in history, at least—in the flood of good scholarship and broad social interpretation, which Clark heralded and which has developed spectacularly since.* In fact the level of per capita alcohol consumption in the United States that inspired prohibition in the pre–World War I era was not reached again until the early 1970's—a remarkable evidence of the lasting importance and effectiveness of the noble "experiment."†

* Norman H. Clark, *The Dry Years: Prohibition and Social Change in Washington* (Seattle: University of Washington Press, 1965). Andrew Sinclair, *Prohibition: The Era of Excess* (Boston: Little, Brown and Company, 1962). Norman H. Clark, *Deliver Us from Evil: An Interpretation of American Prohibition* (New York: W. W. Norton and Company, 1976). The new scholarship can be followed in large part in the *Social History of Alcohol Review* and its antecedents. See especially Paul Aaron and David Musto, "Temperance and Prohibition in America: A Historical Overview," in Mark H. Moore and Dean R. Gerstein, eds., *Alcohol and Public Policy: Beyond the Shadow of Prohibition* (Washington, DC: National Academy Press, 1981), pp. 127–181, an article that effectively refutes the inept subtitle of the book.

The most substantial challenge to my findings lies in historians' explorations of the still intriguing question, Why was the Eighteenth Amendment repealed? The suggestion that there was a mysterious entity, public opinion, that materialized without the mass media and propaganda, much less organization, I find untenable. In addition, K. Austin Kerr, in his recent innovative history of the Anti-Saloon League, shows not only how the League reflected the new politics of the organizational society but how the leadership was unable to adapt to conditions after the Volstead Act. Indeed, Kerr, using documents only recently available, shows that the ASL had little financial support in the 1920's and that substantial organized opposition to repeal—an opposition the power of which everyone took for granted—did not exist, in large part because of organizational failure.[‡]

One fact that recent literature on the subject of temperance and prohibition has consistently confirmed has been that prohibition was in the tradition of American reforms. Kerr, in particular, has shown that the Eighteenth Amendment was decidedly a reform as such, regardless of the fact that later historians, succumbing to "Whiggish" presentistic interpretation, suggested that the means of enactment—a pressure group—denied reform status to the measure. Moreover, prohibition was an integral part of what emerged as the program of Progressive reform, and it becomes clearer every day that the label of "experiment" was and is inappropriate.[§] Prohibition was, in fact, one more piece of evidence that led me to emphasize the non-political dynamics of Progressivism.

[†] See, for example, Mark Edward Lender and James Kirby Martin, *Drinking in America: A History* (New York: Free Press, 1982), which in specifics reflects the influence of my foregoing chapter.

[‡] David Kyvig, *Repealing National Prohibition* (Chicago: University of Chicago Press, 1979). K. Austin Kerr, *Organized for Prohibition: A New History of the Anti-Saloon League* (New Haven, CT: Yale University Press, 1985).

[§] Ibid. The basic work of James H. Timberlake, *Prohibition and the Progressive Movement, 1900–1920* (Cambridge, MA: Harvard University Press, 1963), still has not had adequate recognition. I shall comment later on this problem of understanding prohibition as a reform and particularly as a Progressive reform. The problem of denying the link probably lies not so much in scholarship on prohibition as in a contorted view of Progressivism; see, for example, H. Roger Grant, review of Kerr, *Organized for Prohibition*, in *Social History of Alcohol Review*, Spring, 1986, p. 20.

PART IV

Progressivism

My focus is now shifting yet one more time, but my argument continues that no part of the culture changed unless other parts also changed in a synchronized way. The way in which inter-meshing occurred was particularly obvious early in the twentieth century. At that one point in time, the history of moral standards and the history of science and medicine paralleled each other and converged in a particular way that suggested that all aspects of American life were aiming in the same direction, and such concrete reinforcement provides my specific histories significance beyond that of topical investigations.

Chapter 12, in which I go back to the neurosciences and use the interest in social control in modern America (already alluded to previously, especially in Chapters 3 and 5) as a point of depar-ture, suggests specific evidence that might carry Progressivism beyond the traditional and narrow. This step is the more neces-sary as a number of historians have expressed doubts that Pro-gressivism existed in any meaningful way.* These historians' mis-givings have grown out of trying to interpret Progressivism in politics; I find the doubts bemusing in light of the fact that not only many later historians but so many articulate observers from the early twentieth century knew and said that something un-usual and distinctive was taking place. Chapter 12 may still show some of the surprise that I felt when I first discovered strongly reformist statements and formulations in strictly technical publi-cations of the Progressive era. This was before social historians of medicine and the social sciences had done much concrete explo-ration of the affinity of scientists as well as other intellectuals with the dominant currents in the social thought of their times.

* For example, Peter Gabriel Filene, "An Obituary for 'The Progressive Move-ment,'" *American Quarterly*, 22 (1970), 20–34; Daniel T. Rodgers, "In Search of Progressivism," *Reviews in American History*, 10 (1982), 113–132; I return to this problem later, in the final chapters of this part.

Psychiatry, Psychology, and the Progressive Movement

Recent interpretations have made the Progressive movement of the pre-1917 era one of the most interesting topics in American history. Much of this new scholarship represents the search of modern liberals for their own political identity. Currently a more thoroughgoing reinterpretation is being undertaken by a group of historians who are studying *social control* as the Progressives visualized it and put it into action.[1] This latest research on Progressivism ranges far beyond what is essentially political history.

A study of the two professions dealing with the human psyche, psychiatry and psychology, before World War I, contributes to a broader view of Progressivism by suggesting the hypothesis that the Progressive movement was not limited to politics, economics, and social philosophy but pervaded all of the endeavors of middle-class Americans. If the physicians and scientists of the mind were prototypical, an examination of the rest of national life—as it is ordinarily subdivided—will also show that early-twentieth-century Americans in their occupations and other social capacities operated on "Progressive" assumptions or at least were aware of the relevance of their activities to "Progressive" ends.[2] The basis for the hypothesis is the striking fact that reformers in psychiatry and psychology shared with reformers in politics and economics a set of social assumptions that identified them all as Progressives.

From the more traditional research on the subject we already know the suppositions of Progressivism. The essence of the movement was the "firm belief that to a considerable degree man could make and remake his own

"Psychiatry, Psychology, and the Progressive Movement" is reprinted from the *American Quarterly*, 12 (1960), 457–465, with the kind permission of the American Studies Association. Copyright 1960, American Studies Association.

world."[3] Although the Progressives did not all believe that man is inherently good, they agreed at least that the human being is malleable. The responsibility for the ills of the world rested, therefore, largely or entirely upon the social environment in which the individual lived.[4] Although modern environmentalism grew out of Darwinian thinking, the Progressives believed that man could change his own environment and so reconstruct both societies and individuals.[5]

The most elusive element in the basic social thinking of the Progressives was—Who should tamper with the environment and so foreordain the fates of his fellow men? It turned out, inevitably, that the Progressives themselves were to be the self-appointed arbiters of man's destiny. They were able, literate, and largely professional groups, accustomed to the role of leadership and, like Theodore Roosevelt, unafraid of it.[6]

The Progressives were consciously motivated by altruism. Direction was to come from the Man of Good Will who had transcended his own interests; he governed by right of his moral superiority.[7] The Calvinistic background of many Progressives indicated a direct relationship as well as an analogy between Progressive leadership and the stewardship of the elect. Social responsibility inspired in many Progressives a feeling of guilt for all of the evil that a faulty society had caused, and the sophisticated with New England consciences equated righteousness with social reform.[8]

These, then, were the elements of Progressivism—optimism, environmentalism, moral fervor, and leadership by an enlightened elite. None of them was new in American thought, but at the time they took on a special meaning because of the frequency with which they appeared and because of their application to social control. Although most obvious in political and social thinking, they also characterized, first, the psychotherapy movement in the psychiatry of that day and, second, the revolt of the behaviorists in contemporaneous psychology. In each case it turned out that an autonomous historical development within a science contained the same elements as a new political and social movement.

Psychiatry (which at that time included neurology) provides a nice example. In the late nineteenth century, physicians who dealt with the mentally ill usually were "organicists" who adhered strictly to scientific materialism. They believed that behavior and thinking were but the expression of the functioning of the nervous system and that physical defects or diseases were at the bottom of all mental diseases. The organicists performed autopsies on the brains of deceased mental patients, searching for evidence of lesions or brain damage. The work of this group was vindicated by the discovery that a common type of insanity was caused by syphilis. Yet nothing is quite as depressing as the literature of psychiatry-neurology around the turn of the century—endless reports of post-mortem examinations of demented brains and discussions of the problems of keeping and managing the insane. The psychiatrist was expected to do little more than deliver a prognosis of the

melancholy course of the disease and then supervise the housing, feeding, and restraining of the patient.[9] Well into the twentieth century the three main causes of insanity were thought to be heredity, alcohol, and syphilis.[10]

By the 1890's a great deal of discussion of hysteria (disease symptoms occurring in the absence of physical disease), hypnotism, and faith healing, plus a rebellion against the dreary routine of prognosis and commitment, led to a revival of attention to so-called "moral treatment." Every experienced physician knew the importance of the patient's state of mind for the treatment of illness, and early in the first decade of the century, following developments in continental Europe, American medical practitioners took up the fad of psychotherapy. In large part the psychotherapy movement was a formal recognition of the medical value of a constructive intellectual and emotional environment, especially in the treatment of what we would now call neurotic diseases.[11]

Strict organicists who believed that insanity was caused by heredity, alcohol, and syphilis were not necessarily outside of the Progressive movement. There were reform groups dedicated to the elimination of the baneful effects of all three. The eugenics movement, advocating the sterilization of insane, defective, and criminal persons in order to improve the race, represented the Progressive attempt to deal with that part of man which was not malleable.[12] Many psychiatrists supported the efforts of the prohibitionists to remove from commerce what they regarded as social poison. And one of the lasting reforms of Progressivism was effected by the crusaders (many of them physicians) who opposed both prostitution and promiscuity with the powerful argument that only prevention could control venereal diseases.[13] These were typical Progressive reform movements, but Progressive psychiatrists fought their finest—and most fundamental—battles in the name of psychotherapy.

Basically the physicians who employed or advocated psychotherapy in any of its many forms were unwilling to accept the pessimistic attitude of current psychiatry and neurology. Under the competitive pressure of Christian Science and other faith cures that were demonstrably effective, these physicians ignored materialism and undertook to cure patients by whatever method worked. Effective psychotherapy required hope—indeed, faith—in the patient's ability to cure himself. C. P. Oberndorf, one of the first psychoanalytic psychotherapists in the United States, later attributed his early successes in treatment to his enthusiasm and to his confidence in the new tools with which he worked. Others using quite different methods of psychotherapy likewise showed an optimism that set them apart from conservatives in the psychiatric profession.[14]

The basis for the new hope was the conviction that an individual's behavior was determined—to a large extent—by his environment. A Boston physician in 1909 defined psychoneurotics "as people who, for one reason or another, are not well adapted to their environment." The conclusion was obvious; as one psychiatrist observed in 1911, "If the mental habits and the

surroundings of an individual are largely responsible for the onset of a psychosis, we can look forward to accomplishments which may rival the success achieved in the crusade against tuberculosis."[15]

The psychotherapists' primary objective became, then, to re-educate the patient so that he adapted himself to his environment, adjusted himself to the reality that surrounded him. Thoughtful physicians quickly perceived that the largest part of the environment that required the patient to change his conduct was the society in which he lived, including his family. A New York asylum superintendent reported in 1913, "The patient is no longer regarded simply as a separate individual, but also as a social unit, whose cure cannot be considered complete until he has been restored to social adaptability and efficiency."[16] At the same time physicians saw the possibility of altering not just the patient but also his environment. Since the important environment was social, the forward-looking psychiatrists found themselves committed to social meliorism, and therefore were Progressives indeed.[17]

The environment of children was especially a target for the social-reformer psychiatrists. Under the influence of early Freudian ideas, they asserted that childhood experiences were of overwhelming importance in later life. The most influential of these psychiatrists was William Healy, a conventionally trained specialist in nervous and mental diseases, who gave up his practice (at considerable sacrifice) in 1909 to work with juvenile delinquents in Chicago. Through his own experience with the motivations of youthful lawbreakers, Healy came to a strongly psychoanalytic point of view. His works (richly illustrated with interesting case histories) persuaded untold numbers of persons that favorable changes in the social environments of youngsters could prevent delinquency and promote not only mental health but social progress.[18]

The presumptuousness of psychiatrists in deciding how the world should be run was not different from that of other Progressives. Like Dr. George Van Ness Dearborn of Boston, physicians appealed to "the sound principle of *noblesse oblige*." Moreover, as doctors they dealt with matters of life and death, and as psychotherapists in daily practice they undertook to interfere in and change the attitudes and ways of life of their patients. They were, therefore, accustomed to the responsibilities of leadership. As early as 1907 E. W. Taylor of Boston pointed out that the role of the physician was expanding and that he had to look after the social as well as the physical welfare of his patients. He was becoming, said Lewellys Barker of Johns Hopkins, the "moral director" of his patients.[19]

A number of theories were used by the psychotherapists in rationalizing their attempts to recast the world. A New York neurologist who advocated a type of psychotherapy called suggestion proposed in 1912 that physicians combat the psychic infections of civilization—noxious suggestion—with psychotherapy, that is, with suggestion that would foster what he believed to be the better cultural elements (surely an ambiguous goal for social con-

trol).[20] Most Americans were not strong on systematics, and hope sufficed to nourish many of their opinions; only those who used the most radical of the psychotherapies, psychoanalysis, invoked a fairly consistent theory to justify their reformism.[21]

The psychoanalysts, whose alleged commitment to a so-called "sexual" view of the world was notorious, illustrated most strikingly the intense moralism of the Progressive psychiatrists. By means of sublimation man's evil would be turned into good, they asserted; even the grossest sexual perversions would become artistic creations and love for fellow man. James Jackson Putnam, scion of the Puritans, married to a Cabot, and professor of neurology at Harvard, wrote: "It may well be urged that psychoanalysis does not take the cultivation of social ideals as an end for which it should directly strive. Technically, this is true. But psychoanalysts know well the evils that attend the over-assertion of personal desires, cultivated too exclusively in and for themselves, and the importance of the opposite course follows by inference." In their long, conventional textbook on nervous and mental diseases, two of the leading psychiatrists of the country, Smith Ely Jelliffe and William A. White, reminded their readers of the "socially useful ends" of psychotherapy. As sophisticated about right and wrong as the most advanced intellectual rebels of the time, Progressive psychiatrists found altruism medically justifiable.[22]

Some of the psychotherapists were psychologists who had abandoned strictly experimental psychology. Like the psychiatrists, these men tended to be lay preachers who sought to reform the world by means of re-education and retraining. The scholarly psychologist of Boston, L. E. Emerson, for example, repeatedly pointed out the ethical and reform possibilities of Freudianism. More orthodox psychologists were likewise led, when dealing with matters outside of experimental psychology, to dilate on the possibilities of fostering the "higher aspirations" of men through psychotherapy and psychoanalysis.[23] The best example of the foregoing is the famous book of E. B. Holt of Harvard on *The Freudian Wish and Its Place in Ethics*.[24] Holt asserted that Freudian psychology justified the ancient belief that knowledge is virtue, with the implication that evil need not be always with us. Holt saw man as an individual interacting with his environment and, significantly, utilized not only psychoanalytic psychology but also behaviorism. For within orthodox experimental psychology the Progressives were those who adhered to behaviorism.[25]

For years psychologists had been aware of ferment and discontent in their profession. Most of the criticism centered on the fact that dry, descriptive academic psychology was not useful. Then John B. Watson took leadership of the revolt of the behavioristic psychologists. They dispensed with consciousness and introspective methods and studied the human organism in its environment, using the methods of animal psychology. Watson began his behaviorist manifesto in 1913 by making the purpose of the revolt clear:

"Psychology as the behaviorist views it is a purely objective experimental branch of natural science. Its theoretical goal is the *prediction and control of behavior.*"[26] Here was usefulness with a vengeance.

The behaviorists had observed that animals' innate patterns of action could be modified by training, and the young Turks soon tended to embrace a radical environmentalism. Most psychologists more or less covertly subscribed to an instinct psychology such as that of William James or William McDougall. Now out of the laboratory itself came a challenge to essentially conservative nativism.[27] One would misunderstand behaviorism if he overlooked the explicit meliorism involved in the movement. Watson himself took pains to clarify the relation of behaviorism to social control, and the more alert members of the profession also realized what was involved.[28] The goal of behaviorism was, after all, merely a restatement of the classical purpose of any science including psychology: to predict. And prediction, to the Progressive behaviorists as to other scientists, involved control.[29]

The elements of Progressivism thus appeared as conspicuous features of reform movements within psychology and psychiatry. The mass of material in both sciences remained, as before, primarily descriptive. But the social attitudes of some of the practitioners of the two disciplines led to profound changes in the very nature of psychiatry and psychology, just as Progressivism left its mark on American political and social institutions.

Progressive psychiatry and Progressive psychology were uniquely American phenomena. The European professional literature was devoid of the optimistic social reformism of the New World versions of these disciplines. Psychologist Carl Rahn shrewdly epitomized the situation in his observation about psychoanalysis: "Where the European follower of Freud emphasizes the point that the formulation of the symbol is indicative of a 'renunciation of reality,'" wrote Rahn, "the American disciple sees it as a 'carrier of energy' exquisitely fitted for increasing man's control over his environment."[30]

One can easily account for the rise of psychotherapy and the rise of behaviorism in terms of the internal histories of psychiatry and psychology. But the fact that these movements coincided in time with the Progressive social reform movement, and the fact that social control was an aim of reformers in both politics and science, can be accounted for only by treating the developments in psychiatry and psychology and in all other middle-class endeavors as part and parcel of the Progressive movement itself.[31] The historian will discover the full dynamics of Progressivism only when he examines not just politics, economics, and social philosophy but all aspects of American life.[32]

In recent years, historians have understood better that mental health efforts, if not also academic psychology, have been central to Americans' understandings of major streams in American culture. Not least of these streams has been reform. Mental hygiene meant a great deal more than the humane treatment of the mentally ill, and in arguments paralleling my contentions, Fred Matthews in particular has asserted that mental health worked out so as to stand for civilized and reasonable behavior as well as therapy.[*]

In a similar way, historians of Progressivism have extended the ideas that (1) reformers of that era held in common important assumptions such as environmentalism and optimism and (2) Progressives attempted to establish a degree of social control in order to make a better world. The most enlightening extension has been to show how professionals and professionalism combined idealism and social control and served as models for meliorists of that period.[†] The next chapter in part summarizes and gives a reprise of the previous chapters that describe the place of mental hygiene

[*] Examples include Barbara Sicherman, *The Quest for Mental Health in America, 1880–1917* (New York: Ayer, 1979); Norman Dain, *Clifford W. Beers: Advocate for the Insane* (Pittsburgh: University of Pittsburgh Press, 1980), especially pp. 110–115; and quite specifically for this chapter, E. Bruce Tucker, "James Jackson Putnam: An American Perspective on the Social Uses of Psychoanalysis, 1895–1918," *New England Quarterly*, 51 (1978), 527–546. Fred Matthews, "In Defense of Common Sense: Mental Hygiene as Ideology and Mentality in Twentieth-Century America," *Prospects*, 4 (1979), 459–516.

[†] There is a rapidly proliferating literature on the professions and their place in the evolution of American society; a collection touching on much recent work is Thomas L. Haskell, ed., *The Authority of Experts* (Bloomington: Indiana University Press, 1984). One point of view is represented by Burton J. Bledstein, *The Culture of Professionalism: The Middle Class and the Development of Higher Education in America* (New York: W. W. Norton and Company, 1976), and Bledstein argues for historical context in "Discussing Terms: Professions, Professionals, Professionalism," *Prospects*, 10 (1985), 1–15. Eliot Freidson, *Professional Powers: A Study of the Institutionalization of Formal Knowledge* (Chicago: University of Chicago Press, 1986), offers a concrete analysis of professionals' functioning in part to refute the loose assertions that historians of the Progressive era have made about the role of professionals in American society. The social control interpretation was later carried to untenable extremes; see, for example, the dissection by William A. Muraskin, "The Social-Control Theory in American History: A Critique," *Journal of Social History*, 19 (1976), 559–569.

and social hygiene in Progressivism, but now it is possible to set the social control theme in a context not only of the specialized organizational society but specifically of the paradigmatic profession, medicine.

Medical Specialists and Movements Toward Social Control in the Progressive Era

Three Examples

Medicine provides an excellent example of how in the Progressive era American society functioned through well-defined groups devoted to systematic and specific social changes. At all times a numerous and important segment of the culture, physicians by the turn of the century were already specialists who deferred to and depended upon each other. The best men—the leaders—were usually those who limited the range of their practices. Physicians often had to take account of the nature of the society in which their patients functioned. Medicine, particularly in its preventive activities, frequently led doctors to take explicitly social roles. Sometimes the exciting scientific discoveries of the period inspired the public stance of a physician. Sometimes he simply acted according to social values. In either case he tended to see the physician's values as those that ought to guide the behavior of his fellow Americans in both their collective and individual capacities. Repeatedly the leaders of American medicine sought to impose such values upon others, that is, to exercise social control.

Physicians involved themselves in many reform movements of the Progressive era. They were conspicuous among the advocates of eugenics and prohibition and in groups working for the protection of children; in addition, they took a prominent part in public health campaigns of a very specifically medical nature, such as the crusade to end hookworm disease in the

"Medical Specialists and Movements Toward Social Control in the Progressive Era: Three Examples," is reprinted from Jerry Israel, ed., *Building the Organizational Society: Essays on Associational Activities in Modern America* (New York: Free Press, 1972), pp. 19–30, 249–251, with the kind permission of the Free Press. In its first form, this essay had no notes, and those that are now reprinted were added at the time of original publication as a minimum to conform to a changed format.

South. Within American medicine itself, one of the great reforms of the period took place: the dramatic improvement of medical education following the Flexner Report of 1910. But the work of physicians in actually leading reforms that were based only partially in medicine provides the most illuminating instances of the pervasiveness and similarity of reform movements of the Progressive years.

Three versions of this medical reformism, the anti-tuberculosis, the social hygiene, and the psychotherapy movements, show how upper-/middle-class Americans became involved in both the ideology and practice of social reform. The first two of these movements resulted in the formation of organizations within the private sector that affected American society in substantial ways; the third, although fathering the mental hygiene societies, was important chiefly for its general implications for social control by a reformist elite.[1]

The anti-tuberculosis crusade was the model for a number of other organized reform movements. Physicians and social workers provided a skilled, dedicated, and persistent leadership. They were inspired by the combination of promise and frustration that confronted them in both the scientific and social spheres.

During the nineteenth century, medical researchers had learned much about tuberculosis: the forms that the disease took, its pathology, and even the identity of the tuberculosis bacillus. The mortality rate from the white plague, as it became known, was extremely high: In 1900 almost 200 a year for each 100,000 population. The malady was one of the major concerns of turn-of-the-century physicians. Since the doctors understood the cause and course of the disease, they were hopeful that society could eradicate "the great destroyer" (another sobriquet).[2]

Rising rates of mortality in the United States confirmed the widespread belief that, as one New York physician put it in 1904, "tuberculosis is a disease of civilization, of housing, and of confinement."[3] As the cities grew, the white plague thrived in crowded and unhealthy areas, and tuberculosis became pre-eminently the disease of the urban poor and especially of the young. The sentimental prose of the day, describing the heartbreak in "The Lung Block" where tuberculosis flourished in the tenement district, probably came as close as words can to conveying the terrible burden imposed by the disease upon the most helpless members of society.[4]

In that day there were many truly public-spirited citizens—and they were among the upper and middle classes—who furnished both support and leadership to a reform aimed at this dread malady. Among them were a number of physicians and a significant segment of social workers. Reformers with such backgrounds appealed for improvement of housing conditions, treatment for the ill, and, indeed, any changes that might interrupt the vicious cycle that made poverty cause tubercular affliction and the disease in turn re-

sult in further poverty. From the beginning concerned reformers recognized that measures against tuberculosis had to be both medical and social.[5]

Because members of the same families tended to become infected, doctors, and others, had for many years made the reasonable clinical inference that tuberculosis was a hereditary disease. When, late in the nineteenth century, it was demonstrated to be a communicable illness, the entire attitude of responsible medical and social leaders changed. As noted in the opening statement of an article distributed in 1903 by one of the earliest state anti-tuberculosis societies, "To know that it is *not* an inherited disease should bring hope and gladness to thousands of tuberculous parents, and to the children of such parents."[6]

Seldom has there appeared so clear a connection as existed in the anti-tuberculosis campaign between the development of belief in environmentalism and the development of a reform movement. The improvements involved had to take place on a large scale over a long period. Unlike diphtheria, for example, tuberculosis presented a problem. It did not lend itself to the quick technological fix: No immune serum could be devised, and no drug therapy could be developed that would permit treatment without major modification of existing institutions. Hence both the physicians and social workers were frustrated. They believed that tuberculosis could be wiped out—but only through a massive campaign involving very large parts of the population.

A purely empirical cure for consumption (tuberculosis of the lungs, the form of the disease considered of major importance then) had been utilized for a long time: sanitarium treatment. This method served the dual functions of curing the ill and of isolating potential carriers from the susceptible population. But the treatment was expensive and took a very long time.[7] Indeed, merely the economic difficulties of diverting resources on a large scale to treating all of the ill seemed insurmountable, and only the enthusiasm of the reformers made the idea even conceivable.

Still another grave difficulty existed to frustrate efforts to restrict and eliminate the tuberculosis cycle: No one would admit having the disease. If it was inherited, the family line was tainted, one's self and one's children unmarriageable. Then after the idea of infection became known popularly, the unfortunate "lungers," as they were pejoratively called, were dismissed from their work and hounded from their housing lest they infect their associates. In either case, before or after, social taboos against discussing, much less admitting to having, tuberculosis were almost unbelievable—among the lower classes much stronger than Victorian resistances against sex.[8]

The men and women who began the anti-tuberculosis campaigns, in short, were brave people launching an unpopular work of incredible magnitude. A large number of physicians and most of the public continued to be hostile toward any effort to pinpoint the disease or even talk about it. The reformers had to keep reminding themselves, as a Boston physician, E. O.

Otis, told the American Invalid Aid Society in 1901, "To stamp out consumption is not an iridescent dream, but a sober possibility, even a probability."[9]

What these courageous reformers set out to do was twofold: to educate the public to accept and demand treatment and public health measures, and to see to it that every consumptive was treated. Obviously if every carrier was cured, the disease would disappear. (In New York City alone the cost of a ten-year program of universal treatment was estimated in 1911 to be fifty million dollars—utopian but also really possible, as its promoter pointed out.)[10] The use of education as a reform device has been well understood and may be traditionally American. But use of social coercion to bring about a widespread social change, individual by ill individual, in the name of science, was typical and indicative of the ambitiousness of the reformers.

The organizations that developed to channel the anti-tuberculosis campaign usually were the creations of forward-looking public health physicians. During the 1890's, for example, many public health officials—despite the vigorous opposition of conservative physicians who believed tuberculosis to be hereditary—began distributing educational pamphlets and, in New York City, registering cases of tuberculosis just as other infectious diseases were registered. In Philadelphia, for example, Dr. Lawrence F. Flick found physicians who refused to accept the evidence of contagion in control of the local medical profession. In 1892 Flick therefore turned to lay people to support a Pennsylvania Society for the Prevention of Tuberculosis. This group carried out an educational program, tried to get treatment for the ill, and lobbied for government support for all aspects of the campaign. By the early 1900's, when medical opposition to the idea of contagion had disappeared, physicians in other parts of the country organized various groups to effect some action to stop "the people's disease." A few laymen also took up this campaign. Not least was the work of the Charity Organization Society of the City of New York. It alone almost ensured that social workers would be included in any anti-tuberculosis efforts. In Europe a large number of organized efforts to expand treatment, pool medical knowledge, and educate the public had already been undertaken. By 1904 in America it became clear that some analogous national organization would evolve to lead the campaign.

Several groups vied for the honor. Many physicians favored a purely medical society. The issue of excluding laymen was resolved, largely under the leadership of a group of doctors from the Johns Hopkins medical school, with the formation in 1904 of the United States Society for the Study of Tuberculosis, later the National Tuberculosis Association. This organization, like Flick's, admitted both laymen and physicians. Nevertheless, an impressive roster of well-known medical men played leading roles in the Association. The Association devoted itself to educating physicians and the public, to fostering meetings and congresses, to developing local societies where none existed, and to securing legislative support for sanitary measures, education, and treatment.[11]

Measured in terms of visible works, the efforts of the NTA were sensationally successful. When attempts to obtain state legislation were only partially effective, the crusade leaders turned to local and county governments to support sanitaria. Anti-spitting ordinances across the land made a moderate change in public manners. But above all, organization and education flourished. As early as 1909, for example, there were 350 (mostly local) anti-tuberculosis societies in the United States, and that same year someone figured that the press carried each week a half-mile of column space devoted to tuberculosis. By 1911 the campaign had shifted somewhat away from mere treatment and more toward prevention by means of educational efforts.[12]

Whether or not this frantic activity actually diminished the white plague is another question. In the fifteen years from 1904 to 1919, the tuberculosis mortality rate declined by about 30 per cent. It is true that the rate had already been declining rapidly because of rising standards of living, but it seems likely that the efforts of workers in the anti-tuberculosis campaign accelerated the social-biological process to some extent.[13]

The pioneers in the anti-tuberculosis movement generated such faith in the efficacy of their exertions that Americans concerned with other diseases quickly emulated them. Undoubtedly the bravest and most foolhardy were the physicians who founded the social hygiene movement to control and eradicate venereal diseases. In the 1890's public mention of any sexual subject was tabooed, and even medical societies were not always friendly to discussions of sexual activities and venereal diseases. At the same time, a double standard of morals prevailed. Men sowed their wild oats or for imagined "reasons of health" used the services of the red light district available in every city or town, all without fear of serious social repercussions. Women, by contrast, were expected to be pure and innocent (unless they by chance fell into the class of unspeakable but apparently desirable "fallen women").[14]

Under these circumstances, venereal diseases flourished because they were spread, as everyone knew, chiefly by prostitutes. By the late nineteenth century a number of European medical experts realized that syphilis and its cousins were also carried by the patrons of the prostitutes, that is, respectable family men who infected their wives. Mothers who were too guileless to know the nature of their shameful illness in turn infected their children (and even hardened physicians of that day were unlikely to forget the sight of a newborn baby deformed by syphilis).[15]

In addition to this clinical discovery of "syphilis of the innocent," physicians of the late Victorian period became aware of the implications of new medical knowledge. Sophisticated people who learned about bacterial infection came to fear that they would become contaminated with venereal diseases through contact with neutral objects, such as the omnipresent common drinking cup. Moreover, as research continued, the forms and hazards of venereal diseases seemed to expand endlessly. General paralysis of the insane, for example, one of the major (and most horrible) mental illnesses,

was shown by the 1890's to be a form of syphilis of the brain. Even gonorrhea, previously thought to be about as serious as a cold, was shown to have crippling and even fatal consequences, including dangerous gynecological disorders and blindness. To the even slightly alert physician, venereal diseases appeared to be far more widespread and serious than anyone had dreamed.[16]

Beginning in 1901, the leading French syphiligrapher, Jean-Alfred Fournier, led a movement to organize physicians and laymen together into societies to propagandize the dangers of venereal diseases and the advisability of continence. In France, and elsewhere, his efforts generated only meager results, but in the United States the social hygiene movement, under the leadership of a pre-eminent and awesomely austere and conservative New York medical specialist, Prince A. Morrow, flowered in a most unpredictable way.[17]

There already existed in the United States a vigorous purity movement, aimed primarily at preventing the legalization of prostitution and at improving personal moral standards. Although the purity leaders advocated that parents provide in the home a vague and circumspect sex education for their children, purity forces were also responsible for much of the effectiveness of the formal and informal censorship that prevented public discussion of sex-related subjects.[18] By and large the purity leaders were for many years on the defensive and unable effectively to attack prostitution as a social institution.

There also existed an increasingly effective rebellion of intellectuals and others, represented in an extreme form by Greenwich Village advocates of freedom of expression. These rebels were inspired mostly by foreign movements of which the symbols were Shaw and Zola.[19] But whatever their agitation for openness, the literati and their hangers-on in general did not challenge the double standard.[20] Feminists, allied with the purity groups, were among the first to see both idealization and prostitution of women as barriers to equality.[21]

Morrow, who achieved what none of his noisier contemporaries could or would, began speaking publicly about the dangers of venereal disease in 1901. The next year he attended in Brussels an international congress on the public hygiene of syphilis, and at that time Fournier asked him to found in the United States a reform society similar to the French model. Not until 1905, however, was Morrow able to gather a small group together to form the American Society of Sanitary and Moral Prophylaxis (later the American Social Hygiene Association). It was largely a New York organization, but Morrow hoped to develop local branches elsewhere. The membership at first was heavily medical, but almost immediately a few influential lay reformers, such as Grace Dodge, the leading financial angel of the purity movement, gave Morrow monetary and moral support.[22]

The aspirations of Morrow and his fellow do-gooders were, in all truth, presumptuous. These men were bent on destroying the conspiracy of si-

lence and substituting for it sex education and "pitiless publicity." They were likewise devoted to wiping out the double standard of morals and changing ancient beliefs such as the idea that continence is detrimental to a man's health. Essentially social conservatives, the social hygienists knew that they were setting out to alter, as Morrow put it, "deep-rooted customs and habits of thought." They became reformers simply because they thought, as Morrow observed, that no system that fostered such evils as the doctors were seeing in their practice could possibly be right.[23]

As soon as Morrow and his group started their campaign of publicity, they crystallized support from two different groups: the physicians and the purity workers. Many American medical practitioners like Morrow and his first followers had become alarmed by the ravages of venereal diseases. When he appeared with an organization, a program, and the courage to speak out, they joined in, founding local societies and contributing publicity and propaganda aimed at getting the infected to seek treatment and the young to avoid infection. The purity forces were slower to join. They first had to give up their opposition to public discussion and education. This sacrifice took a little time, but by 1911 they had come into the social hygiene movement almost completely and given it a strong anti-prostitution flavor. This stance tied in with the aspirations of municipal reformers to rid the cities of their obnoxious "regulated districts" and all of the political corruption associated therewith.[24]

The social changes that actually resulted from Morrow's campaign were even more surprising than the boldness of his goals. The movement achieved large amounts of organizational success. Activities varied from the distribution of hundreds of thousands of pamphlets, warning the young against indulgence and disease, to the passage of the Mann Act in 1911 (once it was possible through publicity to spread the white slavery scare among the public at large). Morrow's work was cited by virtually all of the vice commissions of that era which, cumulatively, almost destroyed the institution of prostitution in the form in which it had been known. But the two most enduring and dramatic achievements of the movement that Morrow and the physicians had pioneered were essentially their original strategic goals. First, the conspiracy of silence was dead by the 1910's, and the forces of purity, like it or no, were committed to Morrow's "pitiless publicity" to cleanse public morals.[25] Second, sexual standards changed, and the double standard of morals to a surprising extent became typical of only older or lower-class Americans.

While the social hygiene movement drew support from the forces of reform, purity, feminism, and social ferment imported from abroad, it would be a mistake to play down how much Morrow and his collaborators actually achieved. For instance, they financed and sponsored a propaganda play, translated especially for them, Brieux's *Damaged Goods*. The presentation of that drama opened the New York stage to a flood of so-called "vice plays," starting a trend toward "frankness" that has not yet been reversed.[26] The

social hygienists' marketing of sex education materials likewise had lasting effects and opened the door to other changes in American attitudes, most especially (and contrary to myth) the strengthening of monogamous marriage.[27] And that was, after all, the institution that Morrow and his colleagues set out to protect from disease.

The anti-tuberculosis campaign involved two levels of action: on the one hand providing direct medical treatment of the ill, on the other hand improving general public health and living conditions. The anti–venereal disease campaigners were even more dedicated to altering popular attitudes, but they, too, were basically committed to urging the ill to seek treatment so as not to carry contagion any further. The third of the examples of Progressive era reform in medicine, psychotherapy, involved specific campaigns against disease and certain substantial changes in medical theory and practice that had profound implications for all reformers. Psychotherapy did contribute to the organized mental hygiene movement, but it was primarily important for what it did to the reformers' imaginations. Walter Lippmann, one of the intellectual spokesmen for political Progressivism, for example, incorporated ideas from psychotherapy theory into his prescriptive writings such as his 1914 book, *Drift and Mastery.*

Where the anti–venereal disease campaign initially involved dermatologists (who in that day treated those diseases), the psychotherapy movement was peculiar to the neurologists and, later and secondarily, their congeners, the hospital psychiatrists. The neurologists dealt with organic diseases of the brain and nervous system, but since their practice consisted largely of outpatients, they also treated sufferers from neuroses and other mental illnesses who did not have to be hospitalized. Both the large number of persons applying to physicians for relief and a flood of popular and semi-popular books on "nervousness" were symptoms at the time that a large part of the population felt themselves afflicted by "nerves." Not unnaturally, considering their training and their exposure to the tendency toward scientific materialism in physiology in the late nineteenth century, neurologists tended to view minor neuroses in terms of organic, physical disorder, using disease classifications such as neurasthenia (literally, physical exhaustion of the nervous system). The view that mental illnesses, major and minor, were organic and physiological was strengthened by the proof that general paralysis of the insane was a syphilitic affliction, suggesting that similar physical causes such as bacterial infection were also behind other forms of mental disorder.[28]

In the age of serums and chemotherapy, however, the neurologists offered very little in the way of effective therapy for their "nervous" patients. Furthermore, the best physicians were forced to admit that in many such cases verifiable cures were produced by certain competitors of the medical profession, namely, the faith healers. When, then, a number of European physicians suggested that certain psychological measures had an ameliorating, and even curative, effect on neurotic disorders, many American doctors

turned to such psychotherapy because it promised immediate help for patients whose maladies were, as a class, resistant to the rest, travel, hydrotherapy, and palliatives then generally prescribed. The physicians presumed that their psychological ministrations, although perhaps close to the practice of the faith healers, were medical and therefore safe, ethical, and scientific.[29]

The psychotherapy fad came into American medicine suddenly, in 1905–1906. By 1907 George C. Smith, a Rhode Island physician, was speaking explicitly of the "psychic fad," adding that "in Boston at present it [is] almost a monomania." This enthusiasm was explained as early as 1906 by an editorial writer in the *Interstate Medical Journal*, who said it resulted from a need "felt by every earnest worker in the field of the psycho-neurosis" for a new type of medical therapeutics.[30] Very quickly psychotherapy in medicine developed popular counterparts. The advice to the nervous in books and magazines increased greatly, and two organized movements spun off from the medical fad. The first was the Emmanuel movement in religion, that is, the use of psychotherapy in a revival of the healing mission of the churches.[31] The second was the mental hygiene movement.

The mental hygiene movement originated at first as a reform effort devoted to improving the lot of mental patients, chiefly in hospitals. Mental hygiene was broadened, however, by both the successful example of the anti-tuberculosis crusade and by the implications of psychotherapy. As early as 1907 the physicians of the New York Psychiatric Society sponsored some public lectures, and, as one journal editor observed, "with a view to the organization of a movement toward prophylaxis and the development of sound interests," that is, healthy mental habits, a movement aimed therefore at reforming many social institutions, not just hospitals. Nothing happened immediately, but when two years later ex-patient Clifford Beers stirred up interest in changing hospital practice, he found himself involved at once with neurologists and even psychiatrists who were thinking in terms of an organization more broadly than Beers had conceived. And as in the cases of the groups fighting tuberculosis and venereal diseases, the mental hygienists enrolled both lay and medical personnel, however domineering the latter were.[32]

The mental hygiene movement was only one reflection of the hope and enthusiasm engendered by psychotherapy that represented scientific evidence that the reformers' faith in education was justified. One mentality could influence another regardless of heredity; even a severely diseased mind could be reformed. As in the case of tuberculosis, the discovery that very specific environmental manipulation might change the fate of men led to programs to implement the changes.[33] An eminent New York psychiatrist, James V. May, in 1911 summarized the feelings of the reformers: "If the mental habits and surroundings of an individual are largely responsible for the onset of a psychosis, we can look forward to accomplishments which may rival the success achieved in the crusade against tuberculosis."[34]

Environmentalists among the nervous and mental disease specialists

quickly saw the social implications of psychotherapy.[35] Not only did the neu-rologist now have to deal with the social as well as the physical welfare of his patients but mass psychotherapy could obviously be used to reform the whole society. Not all Progressive era physician reformers shared this aspira-tion, but many did urge that various institutions, and especially hospitals and schools, be used to spread altruism and mental health, seen as two sides of the same coin. Two eminent specialists, for example, in a widely used 1917 textbook remarked that psychoanalytic psychotherapy, in curing neurotics, would make available "psychic energy which is bound up in infantile ways of pleasure-seeking and set it free for socially useful ends."[36]

The three reforms in medicine, the anti-tuberculosis, social hygiene, and psychotherapy crusades together provide insights into the nature and dynamics of reform in the Progressive era. The three were cut from the same cloth. They functioned in modes similar each to the other, and the latter two were explicitly modeled on the first.[37] Moreover, the personnel, both medical and philanthropic, overlapped. The internist, Lewellys F. Barker of Johns Hopkins, for example, was a prime mover in both the anti-tuberculosis and psychotherapy movements. His colleague in neuropsychiatry at Hopkins, Adolf Meyer, was deeply involved in both mental hygiene and social hygiene. Meyer headed a psychiatric clinic sponsored by Philadelphia industrialist Henry Phipps, who was also helping finance the anti-tuberculosis campaign. Such commonality in persons and organizations existed among reformers all across the country.

This overlap makes it more understandable that very similar ideas and circumstances gave rise to each of the movements. All three movements were inspired by the knowledge that environmental changes could bring about major and dramatic improvements in health and happiness. In each case the newly discovered power of science to change the destiny of man in concrete ways was also an inspiration, but neither tuberculosis, mental illness, nor even, for some time, venereal disease was amenable to easy cure on any level. Furthermore, in each instance major social factors were believed to be involved in the epidemiology and treatment of the disease. The special-ists were concerned about unfavorable public attitudes and a social system that created mental distress, and the slums and taboos that fostered tuber-culosis and venereal diseases. Reformers dealing with each type of disease had therefore to re-educate large parts of the American public before any substantial improvement could be effected.

These reformers, therefore, adopted two concurrent approaches to any given program. The first was to create a mass movement, by education or propaganda to change the actions of masses of people. The second was to treat individuals in order to eradicate contagion and evil. It was this latter ef-fort that made these three movements in medicine in the Progressive period so breathtaking, the conception that it was possible to reach on an individual

basis by concerted, organized effort each of the millions of atoms composing American society.

The institutional means set up to conduct this dual style reformism was both typically American and typically Progressive. In the United States voluntary health reform groups were a well-established institution, from the Physiological Reform Societies of the 1840's to the Sanitary Commissions of the Civil War.[38] The public health movement had accelerated the growth of such groups. The anti-tuberculosis societies resembled these earlier organizations, especially in that both physicians and laymen were invited to join. What gave the turn-of-the-century anti-tuberculosis campaigners an advantage over their predecessors was their ability to exploit not the promise of science but the demonstrated powers of science that were clearly changing the world.[39] The result was that the Progressive era health reform organizations each quickly developed substantial popular followings that on occasion could be invoked as mass support. In the first five years of the National Tuberculosis Association, for example, the percentage of lay membership increased from 15 to over 50.[40] The membership of the social hygiene and mental hygiene groups showed a similar pattern.

The fact that the anti-tuberculosis crusade set the tone for Progressive reformism in medicine reveals still more about what was involved. The effects of organization on the tuberculosis disease and death rates at best were not extremely dramatic and in any event were unknown when the other crusades were launched. Of course in both Europe and America anti-tuberculosis groups, whether justified or not, took credit for any diminution of the disease. But what appealed to them was not results in hand but the promise of results in the future through the creation of an organization that could in one way or another, by law or education, coerce and persuade vital parts of the population to follow certain courses of action. The organizers of all of the movements boasted of results in terms of tangible effort more than measurable hygienic change—the numbers of pamphlets distributed, audiences reached, laws passed. In the Progressive period, physicians and their followers evidently believed that concrete changes in health and happiness inhered in organization and education, as long as both lay under their direction. Accustomed to deciding matters of life and death, doctors easily accepted responsibility for shaping the fates of their fellow men. These health crusades did in fact contribute, in one way or another, to making substantial changes in American life. Seldom in history have events appeared so well to justify feelings of omnipotence in men who set out to manipulate the world.

After the foregoing recitation of the tangible effects of reform, I now turn to Progressivism as such, and themes of many of the previous chapters appear in the general context of American history in the early twentieth century. My efforts fit in with the work of other historians in which they make very specific connections between the professions and reform* and more general approaches to the significance of Progressivism.†

For this book, Chapter 14 therefore serves in large part as a summary, illustrating how the history of the neurosciences, medicine, and morals provides access to the dynamics of at least one major movement in the evolution of modern American society as well as of the thought of that society. Conventional historians continue to get lost in traditional avenues of understanding this one aspect of American reform. Daniel T. Rodgers, for example, in a recent survey concedes that something significant was going on early in the twentieth century, but he notes that historians preoccupied with political phenomena and ideology have made no progress in finding a general and understandable configuration in Progressive phenomena. Rodgers by insisting himself on staying with political history therefore is left with the suggestion that reality in those years inhered in the detail of events and that no pattern existed in "Progressivism."‡

Chapter 14 asserts otherwise. It was part of a symposium in which Robert Crunden focused on the religious impulse in turn-of-the-century reformers without stipulating a social pattern and John Buenker argued that Progressivism consisted of shift-

---

* Mary O. Furner, *Advocacy and Objectivity: A Crisis in the Professionalization of American Social Science, 1865–1905* (Lexington: University Press of Kentucky, 1975). A specific example involving the medical profession is Alan I. Marcus, "Professional Revolution and Reform in the Progressive Era: Cincinnati Physicians and the City Elections of 1897 and 1900," *Journal of Urban History*, 5 (1979), 183–207.

† Examples include Paul S. Boyer, *Urban Masses and Moral Order in America, 1820–1920* (Cambridge, MA: Harvard University Press, 1978); and Robert M. Crunden, *Ministers of Reform: The Progressives' Achievement in American Civilization, 1889–1920* (New York: Basic Books, Inc., 1982).

‡ Daniel T. Rodgers, "In Search of Progressivism," *Reviews in American History*, 10 (1982), 113–132. Rodgers's survey of the literature is sufficiently complete that it need not be repeated here. Michael Roe, *Nine Australian Progressives: Vitalism in Bourgeois Social Thought, 1890–1960* (Brisbane: University of Queensland Press, 1984), provides essential international comparison.

ing coalitions in American politics. In that symposium, all of the participants at least agreed that something of moment was going on. Critics of the idea of a Progressive movement, as I shall note, have, among other errors, forced the idea of a historical movement into the rigid pattern that they conceptualized after the form of a later "Movement," the Communist Party, U.S.A. Such a narrow conception of the term "movement" might conceivably fit components of the Progressive movement, such as the industrial safety movement or the simplified spelling movement. But a coherent social movement in the broader sociological literature is very different from a 1930's idea of "the Movement"; my use instead is not only technically correct, as I state in a note in Chapter 14, but commonsensical. The broader but precise definition in fact fits the Progressive movement. Moreover, it permits a meaningful chronological definition, with conditioning factors before and results afterward. Using that definition, lasting results of Progressivism also become obvious—obviating the argument that Progressive reform was not significant. The changes that occurred in fact show otherwise.

The Cultural Interpretation
of the
Progressive Movement

For two generations many of America's best historians struggled to portray the Progressive era of the early twentieth century in a meaningful way. Their analyses were revealing and stimulated much research. Yet none of these writings left historians, generally, with a sense of closure. By 1970 one of their younger colleagues could write "An Obituary for 'The Progressive Movement,'" suggesting that, so far, accounts of the pre–World War I era had been merely a justification of politicians of another era, politicians who had claimed some sort of unique righteousness but whose claim their descendants would disallow.[1] The obituary was premature, however, for at almost that same time sufficient fresh scholarship became available so that a new understanding of the reality and significance of Progressivism was possible. Now, after even more research has appeared, a fresh perspective is imperative.

Reconstruction of the history of Progressivism, it should be stated candidly, is impossible without first examining the false turns that mark and mar the first fifty years or so of historical effort. The chief of these errors was a focus that was too narrow, for Progressivism wrought effects very broadly in American society. Nor have historians tended to view the Progressives in terms of what was real in those times rather than the actuality of later generations. The substantive achievements of the reformers are in fact instructive. So, too, is the structure of the movement. And essential to historical un-

"The Cultural Interpretation of the Progressive Movement" is reprinted from John D. Buenker, John C. Burnham, and Robert M. Crunden, *Progressivism* (Cambridge, MA: Schenkman Publishing Company, 1977), pp. 3–29, with the kind permission of Schenkman Books, Inc.

derstanding are the qualities that distinguished Progressivism from earlier reform movements.

The historians who failed to master Progressivism made two types of errors. First, they focused on political history. Progressivism was in fact not fully comprehensible within the old Presidential synthesis of American history. The records of Theodore Roosevelt and Woodrow Wilson did not explain or even illustrate what people at the time considered a major reform movement. Even state histories of Progressivism tended to degenerate into mere political narrative, although many events there suggest some of the ferment. And despite rich source materials, investigators of Progressivism in the cities found the phenomenon confusing, because municipal reform was well under way in the late nineteenth century, before the Progressive label existed, and that same municipal reform was still a force long after World War I. All of this attempted political interpretation in later historical writing is understandable, for the political ideas, ideology, and unsystematic sentiments of many Progressive era writers were particularly appealing to subsequent generations of intellectuals. The older historians did in fact provide a good intellectual history of political thinking of that period, and from one point of view verbalizations of reform sentiment and programs constituted a most substantial legacy of Progressivism. The writings of Herbert Croly, Walter Lippmann, and even Roosevelt and Wilson have persistent significance and appeal. But the better political historians insisted that, to be viable, Progressivism had to be based on actual political behavior.[2] Many scholars found themselves turning, therefore, to specific local history, in much of which reform was surprisingly conspicuous,[3] but they, like other writers, ended up refining Progressivism out of existence because there seemed to be no clear beginning or end of local reform. Honoring the tradition that history is past politics, it never occurred to them that developments in politics could be mere epiphenomena of more basic forces and changes.

The error of emphasizing the political face of Progressive reform had more causes than simply the traditions of the historical craft alone. Writers of the early twentieth century who articulated the "Progressive" point of view spoke in terms of political power and legal and legislative redress of wrong and prevention of evil. Many of the Progressives—perhaps most—believed that politics was of overwhelming importance. The most reformist journals led off with and focused on everyday—and usually national—politics. Because reformers conceptualized events of their own times in this conventional mode, they diverted later students from the sources and arenas of the most dramatic and effective campaigns to bring about change in America.

Beyond a mistaken emphasis on politics, historians were plagued by casting all Progressive reforms in the pattern of the New Deal (or an idealized New Deal). The result was to portray the Progressives as Americans who wanted to extend the power of government, and particularly of the federal government, over the lives of the citizens. No one should blame post-1930

writers for being children of their own times. But what is disturbing is that the model persisted for more than one generation and that Progressivism seemed to constitute a subject largely immune to professional self-criticism. When Arthur M. Schlesinger, Jr., attempted to remake Jacksonian democracy in the image of Franklin Roosevelt's political coalitions, he was soon called to account.[4] But even when faced with substantial evidence that what passed for reform in the early twentieth century differed from that of the 1930's, historians did not face up to the fact that Progressivism had importance and coherence above and beyond the relevance of Progressivism to the New Deal.[5]

A whole new perspective on the meaning and significance of Progressivism is therefore long overdue. Recent research suggests two ways of conceptualizing what happened. The first is that a number of streams in American reform coalesced for a few years, reinforcing each other so as to cumulate in what contemporaries recognized as Progressivism. This model has the particular advantage of explaining how many reform efforts, such as those in the cities, existed before and after the critical prewar decade, and how at the same time Progressivism was meaningful in terms of a special ferment that people at the time recognized as important in effecting changes in American life and institutions. Some of the dynamics of this coalescence are discussed below.

The second way to conceptualize Progressivism is to focus on the changes that actually did occur in those years, and on how those changes came about. Clyde Griffen has made a good start in describing a "progressive ethos," an idealism marked by "the juxtaposition of a practical piece-meal approach to reform with a religious or quasi-religious vision of democracy." Even conservatives, Griffen points out, were confused by the moralism and idealism and evangelism that welled up together, affecting and marking a generation.[6] That the coincidence of directions of historical development also coincided with the ethos is what gives substance to the existence of Progressivism.

Because long extant reform movements became a part of Progressivism, various writers tried to set the date of the exact beginnings of Progressivism all the way from the 1880's to several years into the twentieth century. In fact, the movement crystallized sometime around 1907. What happened just then showed up in both public mood and in the pace and quality of change. Maxwell Bloomfield has shown that the popular magazines of the day changed in tone suddenly in 1907–1908, from defensive, sometimes muckraking criticisms, to discussions of a positive nature about the promise of American life. The age of the negative exposé gave way to an age of positive reform—Progressivism.[7]

Institutional and organizational developments paralleled the development of the new mood. Dewey W. Grantham, Jr., in tracing the genesis of

Progressives' political crusades to the expansion of local activities, cites 1906 as the year when activity boiled up to the state level. In the private sphere, it was about 1908 that philanthropic fund raising was transformed both in organization and in public appeal.[8] Many other signs compel the conclusion that for about a decade before the entry of the United States into World War I, there was a direction of change sufficiently coherent to constitute the Progressive movement—recognizable by the confluence of specific reform streams and by a general ethos.

So powerful was the ethos that for years large parts of the population believed that they were involved in a social movement and that the times somehow demanded certain reforms in American life. Robert Wiebe has shown, for instance, how self-interested economic groups in business and labor allied themselves from time to time with a central reform coalition so as to obtain specific legislation.[9] With all of the different streams coming together at once, Progressivism of course took on many different appearances to various different people. But sensitive bellwethers of American opinion, even such as Calvin Coolidge, who had a brief "Progressive" period, all pointed the same general direction in the years before the war. In 1912 Thomas A. Edison wrote his old friend, Henry Ford:

> This is a pretty raw, crude civilization of ours—pretty wasteful, pretty cruel, which often comes to the same thing, doesn't it? And in a lot of respects we Americans are the rawest and crudest of all. Our production, our factory laws, our charities, our relations between capital and labor, our distribution—all wrong, out of gear. We've stumbled along for a while, trying to run a new civilization in old ways, but we've got to start to make this world over.[10]

Those who defied prevailing pressures by pursuing selfish interests were careful to insist that their intentions were public spirited, and, indeed, who can know for certain the exact mix of motive? In 1913 Harry A. Wheeler, president of the Chamber of Commerce of the United States, asserted that the Chamber was "officered by the most virile life of the community, interested not only in the upbuilding of commerce but in the purification of civic life." Perhaps the political bosses did support welfare legislation because the growing masses of immigrants strained the system of welfare, patronage, and graft, and perhaps high tax rates did bring property owners into campaigns for honesty and efficiency.[11] Nevertheless a whole range of reform efforts in politics and in the private sector materialized in those days because there was substantial support for reform among many kinds of Americans.

Insistence on the public weal was what made Progressivism so distinctive. In the rhetoric of the day, "selfish" and "self-serving" were bad adjectives, "unselfish" and "public spirited" good. Herbert Croly in 1914

caught the spirit by contrasting "live and let live" with "live and help live."
Service in the public interest was an ideal that a surprisingly large number
of Americans took seriously.[12]

Because the Progressive movement was an aggregate of a great many
efforts to reform American life, another traditional historical approach, the
biographical, was not particularly profitable to scholars trying to understand
the whole movement. Many a participant in one of the constituent reform
efforts would in other aspects of his life be relatively inactive. Even very
conspicuous Progressives were often inconsistent, leading one specific reform movement while ignoring or opposing another. Prohibition and anti-
monopoly stances in particular created many well-known personal inconsistencies. John Braeman, working just with political figures, was able to spell
out the values of two types of apparent Progressives, the forward looking and
the backward looking, the latter those Theodore Roosevelt once labeled believers in "a kind of rural toryism."[13] Individual men and women were in life
inconsistent in many ways. That circumstance, however, should not obscure
the independent fact that such apparently idiosyncratic actions added up to
a social movement discernible both then and now.

Moreover, despite such specific differences of opinion, a fluid but identifiable set of leadership groups existed across the country that in the Progressive decade headed up reform efforts and shared general attitudes and
values. Research over the years has described this leadership within philanthropy and social work, within health and technical reform, and within many
other specific areas. The core group of Progressives had good informal com-
munications. Religious reformers in Chicago and Atlanta had direct ties with
the Boston elite involved in charities, and both groups had easy access to
intellectual radicals in New York and practical moral and health reformers in
the cities of the Pacific Coast. A surprisingly large percentage of the leaders
had ties of one kind or another to Harvard, and there were many signs of
New England background.[14] Each of the many specific reform efforts that
went into Progressivism called forth differing sets of supporters, but channels used for opposing child labor also tended to be used for prison, peace,
health, and religious reform—in each case varying according to differences
in mode of operation among the prime movers.[15]

Numerous studies of the Progressive political leaders and individual
biographies of other types of Progressives show that the leadership was almost invariably upper middle or upper class in background. So also, however, were most of the leaders who embodied resistance or opposition to
reform. The Progressives differed from the others only in that they were,
on the average, substantially younger than the non-Progressives.[16] Progressivism appears therefore to have been reform that was led and supported
primarily by one segment of the "better" people in America. What differentiated them besides youth—and started them off to carry out substantial and

rapid social changes? These identifiable leaders offer at least a partial answer to the question of the historical origins of the movement.

The actions and the convergence of ideals of the Progressives can be understood in part in terms of negative reactions to earlier events and in part in terms of positive forces that had been building up in the late nineteenth century. On the negative side, David Thelen suggests that in Wisconsin and, presumably, other areas, the depression of the 1890's shocked various elements of the state into an awareness that most members of the community were both consumers and taxpayers, and so attempts to shift power back to "the people" gradually came to replace home-and-morality reform efforts.[17] Other negative reactions to the acute hard times and violence of the 1890's persisted long after hard times had disappeared. In part this negativism metamorphosed itself into the "quest for community," the search for neighbors supportive of traditional values, that was so characteristic of the times. In part negative reactions intensified other aspects of the search for order and righteousness.[18]

The effectiveness of the well-known muckraker movement in the years just after the turn of the century testifies to a widespread discontent that made magazine readers particularly susceptible to believing that the country's businessmen and politicians were causing the most pressing social problems. The negative tone of the muckrakers removes them from the generally constructive spirit of the Progressives, and, in fact, as noted above, the demise of muckraking coincided with the rise of Progressivism proper. In the Progressive years even such a stalwart among the muckrakers as Lincoln Steffens reached a point where he felt the need of positive "solutions" instead of mere criticism.[19] Exposing the corruptions in American life was not a comprehensive part of the reformers' attempts at social reconstruction, but muckraking was nevertheless an important negative preliminary to reform.

Still another type of revulsion that set the stage for a new vision of American life was revulsion against the image of the city. Even within urban areas themselves large numbers of Americans were still seeking the virtues of rural communities that they had known as children. This contrast of the idyllic with the crowded and diseased city underlined the reaction of most Americans to the evils that festered in the slums, especially as the alien New Immigration increasingly became identified with the large metropolis. A number of Progressive reforms involved attempts to change both the character of the city and its inhabitants.

As Roy Lubove has emphasized, the uplifters did not reject the city itself, where specialization and cooperation could thrive.[20] The city image engendered negative feelings because of the indolent, indulgent, and degenerate aspect of civilization found there. Beginning with Theodore Roosevelt's advocacy of manliness and the strenuous life right down to the Boy Scout movement and Walter Lippmann's quest for "mastery," the Progressive lead-

ers seemed preoccupied by what James R. McGovern has called the "virility impulse," embodying a positive image of strength, character, personal force, and primitivism exalting the romantic view of the wilderness.[21] This type of thinking could easily be directed against convention or even gentility as well as urban degeneracy and was deeply involved in the upsurge in nationalism that marked the Progressives' visions. During the 1890's, in fact, great changes had taken place in both popular and genteel culture in America. The concern with health, exercise, activity, and vigor that showed up in the virility impulse coincided with the growth of romantic individualism. This new consciousness of self therefore became another element in the Progressive ethos. At first negative, and always subversive of traditional ways and forms, the activism of the new generation provided energy to reform before World War I.[22]

The Progressive ethos, however, could not have developed as a purely negative force. Neither the older moral and community reformers nor the muckrakers were able to galvanize Americans into the activities of Progressivism. Anger about the corruptions of city life, the trusts, the bosses, and "the system" did not suffice to develop post-1907 constructive efforts. The Panic of 1907, the only concrete event connected with the crystallizing of the movement, did move many businessmen to defensive positions as well as inspire others to ally with social workers to reduce the level of discontent in the community.[23] But the real history of Progressivism lies rather in the clearly delineated positive ethos and in the specific accomplishments of that generation.

The ethos has been described by historians already. In the decade before World War I, large numbers of Americans embraced many or all of a number of beliefs that facilitated change: optimism, leadership by an enlightened elite, environmentalism, romantic individualism, and cultural nationalism. That congeries is not equivalent to welfare statism nor what came to be the rationale for the New Deal. What was both real and truly effective was that Progressives, with all of their inconsistencies, were united in a general viewpoint, not in support of particular types of meliorism or agendas of reforms. In 1916 a former social worker, James Oppenheim, summed up the Progressive shift in a three-line poem:

> Understanding—not faith.
> Will—not hope.
> Service—not charity.[24]

The Progressives rightly understood that their sense of their own power to change the world was different from the pessimism of an earlier day, whether represented by thinkers convinced of the futility of disturbing a fragile social order during the 1890's or intellectuals who shared William

Graham Sumner's passive belief in automatic progress. As the young Walter Lippmann expressed the new sense of competence in his significant contrasting of *Drift and Mastery* (1914), actuality "is plastic, and ready to be moulded by him who understands it."[25]

The Progressives could be optimists because they were fundamentally environmental determinists. Most of the visions of the future, about which the reformers were so sanguine, depended upon changes in American society that would transform citizens and alter behavior. These leaders argued that human beings are to some extent malleable.[26] Their environmentalism ranged from attacking indirect causes of social problems—housing, recreation, sanitation, and alcohol—to a general advocacy of education, uplifting influences, and fresh air and open spaces. Even inherited defect, many Progressives believed, could be minimized in a society that motivated the practice of eugenics (especially positive eugenics). The many analyses by the social workers, social scientists, educators, and thinkers of the day who talked about achieving social control show that these environmentalists were for the most part sophisticated and hard-headed, however much they shared basic assumptions with enthusiastic reformers of the Enlightenment or pre–Civil War periods. "There is always present the danger of superficiality," wrote Southern reformer Edgar Gardner Murphy, "but the risk of making fools is of smaller import than the chance of making men." And social gospeller Walter Rauschenbusch admitted that "the world can be neither sinless nor painless. . . . If perfection were reached to-day, new adjustments would be demanded tomorrow." Yet he went on to insist on the possibility and urgency of "Christianizing the social order." "We shall demand perfection," he wrote, adding, "and never expect to get it."[27]

About the crucial question of precisely who should manipulate the environment and who should decide which manipulations were desirable, the Progressive leaders had no doubts or hesitations: They would. Deference to experts and technicians was an important theme in Progressive thinking. Intellectuals did talk about the difficulties of reconciling paternalism with "democracy," but usually the goal was an informed, self-reliant citizen who presumably would agree with the controlling elite.[28] In fact, many did, and the reformers often generated widespread public support.

The final ingredients that marked Progressives' outlooks, cultural nationalism and romantic individualism, are difficult to evoke for a cynical later generation. Idealization of the citizen who would be produced by meliorism was one aspect of the individualism. He would be, in the words of Jane Addams, imbued with the "social ethic." Another aspect of individualism was a widespread belief in the power of each person to remake his own life and his own culture (such beliefs often ignoring the social determinism inherent in environmentalism). Charles Brodie Patterson, an inspirationalist writing in 1910, urged Americans to do well but to recall that "individual

success must never be considered apart from its effect upon society." Still, such writers urged each man and woman to maximum effort to discover the potentialities within the self:

> The Will is God, the Will is Man
> The Will is power, loosed in thought. . . .
>   (Frank Channing Haddock, 1916.)[29]

In so far as these exhortations were directed to the leaders, the individualism was consistent with ideas of social control. The discovery of inner potential in both child and adult gave much of the flavor to both the leadership and the environmentalism that would free those forces.[30]

The fervent nationalism of the Progressives is perhaps even more difficult to re-create sympathetically than romantic self-discovery. Because the rhetoric later was used to justify both participation in World War I, and wartime and postwar suppression of dissent, Americans of another day mistakenly discounted the patriotic fervor that was involved in "the promise of American life." The Progressives' paradoxical attitudes toward imperialism, non-involvement, pacifism, and war dovetailed well together as versions of "national interest." "The American democracy," wrote Croly, "can . . . safely trust its genuine interests to the keeping of those who represent the national interest. . . . Only by faith in an efficient national organization and by an exclusive and aggressive devotion to the national welfare can the American democratic ideal be made good."[31]

It is entirely possible, as a number of historians have shown, to discover the internal inconsistencies in Progressive thinking and the differences between various leaders or intellectuals. While sometimes suggestive of the sources of tension in the Progressive movement, these studies fail to explain the perceptions of the people of that day that Progressives had a vital commonality that linked their efforts together. "One of the most inspiring movements in human history is now in progress," wrote political scientist Frederick A. Cleveland in 1913. Moreover, the general style that emphasized sometimes conflicting private organizations dedicated to the public interest was symptomatic of a more fundamental agreement that such groups could and should advance the public interest and especially temper the conflict between social demands and individualism.[32]

Just to have thought and felt as they did, and to have expressed themselves, would have made the Progressives significant in American history. But beyond that, they took action on the basis of their beliefs. Many of their endeavors, it is true, resulted in little accomplishment and were essentially bureaucratic exercises in an increasingly bureaucratic society. Other ventures, however, had profound effects upon the lives of many Americans, and on that basis the Progressives, their beliefs, and their accomplishments were and are of major importance.

The Progressives' record shows that those reforming Americans tended to have very broad and inclusive approaches to social problems. The historians' error of emphasizing political events has been particularly misleading by obscuring the diversity and heterogeneity of the Progressives' effective concerns. The Country Life Commission, for instance, was given a comprehensive charge and then went on to investigate homemaking, education, buying and selling, communication, organizations, land (tenancy and rent), farm labor, finance, public health, and social life—an imposingly non-political analysis of the constituents of Americans' existence.[33]

The agency through which the Progressives usually effected change was the traditional American voluntary organization. Just as economic development was based in large part upon private parties operating through private entities, so reformers utilized voluntary groups to mobilize both leadership and monetary support. Each of these organizations existed fundamentally to change the behavior of Americans in a certain limited area, usually by means of persuasion, so that educational programs were common to all of the efforts. Because of the Progressives' increasingly sophisticated views of the causes of particular evils, they often ventured far afield in attempts to overcome those evils. The confluence and cumulation of the programs, both old and new, that constituted the coherence of the movement therefore tended to appear in the form of comprehensive meliorism. The organizations, with their wide range of goals, were the cutting edge of reform, and the achievement of many of those goals the measure of Progressivism.

Typically, the earlier efforts, such as the peace and settlement house movements, all of which coalesced into Progressivism, continued with a vigor derived from social reinforcement.[34] Marginal groups such as the anti-tuberculosis societies found themselves suddenly in the mainstream. And some of the older groups rewrote their history to show that they were "Progressive" in an earlier period. Such were the health officers of New York City who had been collaborating with political bosses interested in patronage matters; when Progressivism became fashionable, the health officials cast off their involvement with compromising politics and pretended that they had always been the purest of reformers, in effect denying the impact of the spirit of the times upon them.[35]

New groups with new hopes flourished. The nationalization of reform, like the nationalization of business, involved a dramatic shift in scale and aspiration. "National," embodying both aspirations to aggrandizement and cultural nationalism, was the first word in the names of many of the most conspicuous reform organizations such as the National Civic Federation.[36] Indeed, the large, private corporation in many ways provided a model for the organizational society that blossomed in the Progressive years.[37]

Progressivism appeared in virtually every aspect of existence—even beyond the list of concerns of the Country Life Commission. Life itself and health were among the most pressing interests of reformers. The safety-in-

industry movement grew out of both industrialists' solicitude and a collaboration between social workers and businessmen.[38] Special campaigns against tuberculosis and venereal diseases combined the social workers with physicians.[39] Improvement of diet and "health habits" in general also represented a major task of the uplifters. Special campaigns, such as arranging supplies of pure milk to the cities, were especially effective.[40] Many general alterations of the physical environment, too, were undertaken in part for the sake of health.

Basic social institutions were another focus of the reformers. Both pro- and anti-divorce campaigners wanted to strengthen the family. General purity and anti–venereal disease campaigners came to foster sex education as the best way to make monogamy work. They saw satisfaction in marriage as not only the best preventive of both disease and impurity but the key as well to preservation of the family. Thus wiping out prostitution and preventing disease contributed to both health and marriage. Labor reformers of varying interests, too, invoked the sanctity of the family as an argument for one course of action or another.[41] The churches increasingly became involved in the social gospel in general and in social regeneration in particular. In 1912 the congress of the Men and Religion Forward Movement was told that "religious questions have become so closely related to ethical theories and moral issues that the line of demarcation between the secular and religious, as such, has been erased."[42] The schools, entrusted with a rapidly expanding clientele, served both as objects of reform, as professionalization increased, and as the means through which many of the Progressives hoped to uplift the nation permanently.[43] Through such agencies as settlement houses and the YMCA, adult education, too, expanded dramatically, often in the interest of reforming the way of life of the urban masses, although this generation witnessed also the effective establishment of the county extension agent and other rural education and improvement institutions. Basic charity institutions were organized, reorganized, and invigorated for the purpose of both caring for the unfortunate and, like the churches and schools, uplifting them.

Business was no more immune to reform than other institutions. "The new competition" represented efforts to set up rules of fair play and eliminate extreme competitive practices that benefited no one. Industrial democracy and industrial welfare took root in the United States before World War I. Workmen's compensation schemes and laws came from the efforts of reformers and businessmen together.[44] The gospel of efficiency and scientific management spread from the industrial plant and affected all of society. Nor was the pursuit of efficiency mere rhetoric. The standardization of parts and products that the engineering societies helped implement during World War I had already, a few years earlier, actually reduced production costs. "Rationalization" within business and industry worked out in many ways.[45]

Within the professions the Progressive impulse appeared in multifari-

ous guises. Reformers tried particularly to broaden the nature of professional functioning, most notably in education, social work, and engineering, and to refine the nature of professionalism and professional behavior in American society. The most dramatic example of this trend was the revolution in medical education following the Flexner Report of 1910.[46] The ideal of professional behavior itself was close to the dynamics of Progressivism.

Many of the reforms had to do with the quality of life in general. The conservation movement, for example, based on concern for both efficiency and environment, was one of the most significant legacies of the era. Attempts to adjust children to live rewarding lives in the twentieth century and to become socialized and cooperative were the concern of reformers in education. Housing reformers attempted to make the physical environment more conducive to both personal and social well-being. Each of such reform efforts, so easily listed, affected the lives of millions of Americans, often in most significant ways.[47]

The cumulative impact of all of this activity to upgrade conditions in America and reform American habits was immense. One English student of the American scene suggested in 1911 that the times were ripe for a new prophet to arise in the United States, and people at the time did not entirely discount the idea.[48] In many instances, as noted above, concrete achievements beyond membership lists, meetings, propaganda dissemination, and other formal organizational efforts are hard to demonstrate. But taken as a whole, the programs of the reformers constitute an awesome demonstration of the power of determined private citizens working together to effect social change on a large scale.

Any general textbook in American history lists the federal government policies and enactments that presumably represent Progressivism. Anti-trust efforts and attempts to rationalize competition in interstate commerce appear prominently in these lists, along with pro-labor or pro-labor union actions and incidental items such as the Mann Act and, in the better texts, prohibition. Sometimes imperialism is characterized as Progressive, sometimes not. Most text writers also mention achievements on the state and local levels: workmen's compensation insurance laws; the initiative, referendum, and recall; the city manager and commission systems.

Certainly this list of governmental reforms is impressive. But the fact remains that the Progressives were at best ambivalent about using government action. At times they did have high hopes that a reform executive, legislature, or judiciary, or some specific law, might bring about needed changes. Repeatedly, good government advocates built up their own expectations and those of others. The many attempts to get at the will of the people—presumably wise and public spirited, in contrast to "the interests"— are a tribute to the reformers' good will and optimism. But the overwhelming result of righteous persons' entering politics was an almost unbroken record

of ultimate defeat for virtue. It is no doubt symbolic that only after he was defeated for office did Seth Low, mayor of New York, turn to private channels to effect reform.[49]

Events of the late nineteenth century had caused so much distrust of government that few decent people wanted to get involved.[50] One precedent for a private alternative had been set by the purity movement, in which women who could not vote were attempting through the influence of their homes to strengthen basic social institutions. When governments failed even to enforce decency and to protect the family, the private reform groups of the purity crusade, including the Women's Christian Temperance Union and the mothers' movement, attempted to foster in each home and community a social environment that would cause the children to grow up to be pure, public spirited, and strong.[51] Throughout the Progressive years reformers continued to show their mistrust of government by placing primary reliance upon non-political agencies and institutions to make meliorism effective. The reformers did not, for the most part, shy away from organization or bureaucracy in the private sector; indeed, the principal agencies through which they worked, organized groups, were sometimes highly structured. And as Gerd Korman points out, one of the most important and effective agencies through which reformers imposed their ideas on other Americans was the private employer. Industrial firms, by providing a workable, effective alternative for the exercise of power, permitted Progressives to bypass political processes.[52] The Progressives' aversion to government was therefore based on experience, an experience that diminishes dramatically the importance and significance of the political history of that era.

Equating the extension of governmental power for social justice purposes, or what came to be called welfare statism, to the spirit of Progressivism is therefore an error. It is true that many Americans admired German cameralism and socialism. And many Americans did come to think that the neutral state would have to intervene more actively to maintain traditional liberty and freedom in society and so become a service state. But to portray the attitudes of Progressives toward political activity and power as anything beyond ambivalence is to distort the movement beyond recognition. "Our national ideal," wrote David Graham Phillips as early as 1905, "is not a powerful state, famed and feared for bluster and appetite . . . but manhood and womanhood, a citizenship ever wiser and stronger and more civilized—alert, enlightened, self-reliant, free."[53]

Reformers showed their aversion to government in two general strategies. The first was to avoid government involvement entirely, as in endeavors such as the community chest movement, the Boy Scouts, and many aspects of health reform. The reformers' second strategy to keep the private sector dominant was using government in a strictly secondary, derivative way to achieve their ends. A good example is provided by the campaign to wipe out hookworm in the South, the debilitating parasite that became known as "the

germ of laziness." Charles Wardell Stiles, a zoologist and public servant, led a persistent campaign that finally resulted in funding by the Rockefeller charities. From 1909 to 1914, using the Rockefeller money and support donated by the railroads, Stiles and his cohorts carried on a campaign to get people to wear shoes and employ sanitary privies. The campaign consisted partly of education, partly of enlisting the administrative powers of sometimes reluctant local health authorities. Stiles and his kind had no commitment to government but only to any means that appeared effective. In terms of economics and health alone, the impact of the hookworm crusade on the lives of millions of people was momentous.[54]

This aversion to government was in part an aversion to party politics, to the selfishness that the reformers saw in partisan loyalty and the working of the party and spoils system. The voluntary associations represented a counterforce to regular parties and sometimes, as in the cases of the purity and temperance movements, to the churches as well. Many of the political changes associated with Progressivism, such as the initiative and referendum, were intentionally subversive of partisan politics (although the innovations were sometimes turned back and used against the reformers themselves). Non-partisan elections and the model law and uniform state law were other tactics symptomatic of a general revulsion against inefficiency and self-serving partisans. It was no coincidence that the rhetoric of the day coupled together selfishness, parties, and inefficiency. Except for the Progressives' commitments to the family, the nation, and morals, they might be considered in effect anti-institutional.[55]

The apolitical or anti-political orientation of the activists was not what distinguished Progressivism from American reforms, whether pre–Civil War or New Deal, however. The Progressive movement differed from other reforms and the era differed from times before and after particularly because of the quality of the moral fervor of the reformers. Clyde Griffen has shown that both within the churches and within many of the individual movements that made up the whole, the ethos involved mass striving for a culture in which small-town virtues such as decency and brotherhood were worked out within a large-scale democratic and melioristic framework.[56]

The evangelistic framework also helps to explain the social basis for the hegemony, for a few years, of a Progressive generation—the young people whose leadership set them apart even in politics. They grew up in the late nineteenth century when there existed a powerful revivalism that separated sentiment and behavior from theological orthodoxy. To a remarkable extent a consensus idealism, worked out in practice in such forms as the purity and mothers' movements, pervaded the middle classes. Most of the Progressives came of age in the decades of intense religious feeling when the better families devoted themselves to decency, self-improvement, and altruism. Even young Henry Morgenthau, Sr., who was not in the Protestant mainstream, remembered being inspired by "a vision of a life of unselfish devotion to the

welfare of others." Benjamin Flower in 1901 recognized "a rapidly growing band of young men and women who are consecrating their lives to the service of man and the making of a higher, juster, and truer civilization." George W. Perkins, later of Progressive political fame, always made social service evangelism a part of his life, even when he was selling insurance.[57] In countless instances, late-nineteenth-century homes in which uplift was stressed can be shown to be the factor that produced a Progressive generation.

Gregory Singleton has suggested that the practical evangelism of late-Victorian Americans was an attempt of the white Anglo-Saxon Protestants and those identified with them to form an ethnic group in response to the development of the Irish ethnic group of the mid-century period. The success of the WASPs in imposing standards upon their own group led them consequently to attempt to impose those standards upon the entire culture. Likewise, numerous commentators have described American imperialism and interventionism as a drive to extend WASP culture to the whole world.[58] Progressivism can be understood, therefore, as the culmination of a general cultural movement that agitated the entire society before World War I.

The moral idealism of the reform generation coincided with other general social developments of the new century. In an increasingly complex and interdependent society, bureaucratic organization and control flourished in all areas of American life at least as much as in uplift groups. As Americans more and more worked out their own specializations of function in society, they tended to view their roles in that society in terms of the function. The ideal functionary could negate self-interest and other interests and view his functioning as a service to society. In innumerable instances appointees who were supposed to represent an interest found themselves playing instead a bureaucratic role and advocating courses of action growing out of role function rather than special interest, courses of action that answered to general rather than selfish needs.[59] The growth of the bureaucratic way of life and of the ideal of unselfish service therefore complemented each other.

Within the constituent reform efforts of Progressivism the professionals were most easily identifiable because of both numbers and contributions. As professionals, they embodied the idea of unselfish service. Physicians, clergymen, educators, and social workers—the men and women of the helping professions—were particularly conspicuous. The Progressive movement in turn accelerated the general trend toward professionalization in all of American life by popularizing the goal of disinterested service and coupling it with social approbation, most dramatically in social work and engineering. The ideal of a vocation as a "profession" found its way into many areas of American existence and carried with it at least some of the service ideal, even, for example, in advertising.[60] Sensitive to moral requirements of the culture, "professionals" were quick to claim moral benefits of their activities. Although affected by Progressivism, the social changes involved in bureaucratization

and professionalization in their turn helped to reinforce the idealism and enthusiasm of reformers.

The practical result of all of this moral fervor was that the Progressive movement embodied an immediacy that distinguished the prewar phenomenon from any comparable reform ferment. Contemporary English reformers, for example, although they spoke as fervently as the Americans, were unable to take action effectively on a broad social front. Their reform proved to be merely rhetorical. American reform, by contrast, was marked by not only enthusiasm but also frantic activity.[61] It is easy enough to laugh at the energy of Theodore Roosevelt, recalling the wit who thought him a combination of St. Paul and St. Vitus, but a whole generation of reformers did show their commitment in effort and active organization.

Such immediacy and commitment to reform suggests that the Progressives possessed an unusual confidence in their ability to change the world. And they were confident. Moreover, their optimism was the essential force behind both aspiration and achievement—so much so as to demand explanation.

Despite their sometimes simplistic rhetoric, the Progressives were not naive. Nor was their optimism naive. They did not attempt, for example, so much to get rid of prostitution as to take the profit motive out of it.[62] Likewise they did not attempt so much to do away with the drinking of alcoholic beverages as to get at the profiteers in human misery. Rather than evangelize the lazy Southerners, the Progressives tried to get rid of the physical burdens that disadvantaged so many people. The reformers were as willing to attack hereditary liabilities through the eugenics movement as to try to improve the environment by means of a host of other reforms. The literature as well as the activity of the reformers repeatedly showed that the leaders, at least, were often aware of the complexities of man, of society, and of history. They tried to concentrate on prevention of ills rather than correcting results, and the leaders' conceptions of causation moved their programs toward the long range—hence their attention to the upbringing and environment of children even more than of misguided adults already set in their ways. It is particularly in the light of the Progressives' sophistication that their optimism demands explanation.

The inspiration for reform was science, broadly understood to embrace also technology and medicine. And the inspiration was not theoretical but very real to those people. The contrast with earlier reform movements underlines the practicality of Progressives. Where the vegetarians of the 1840's, whatever stimulation they may have received from technological innovation, had promised long life and female suffrage, men of 1900 saw both old and young rescued from the grave by new surgical techniques. Where there was in an earlier day promise of governmental reform, in 1903 the Wright brothers' flight had actually taken place. Electricity entered into everyday life,

far more eloquent than visions of a republican utopia. What for years had been promise—largely the promise of political institutions—became, in the twentieth century, performance in non-political areas. The performance was not casual or expectable. The ability of physicians suddenly to arrest diphtheria and permit a dying child to breathe once more and recover was a miracle comparable with those described in the Bible. Science had justified both extravagant hopes and men's beliefs in their own power to change the world. Moreover, the changes often involved the details of existence and gave personal meaning to optimism about transforming American life.[63]

Science in the Progressive era had many public aspects. By themselves the material achievements of the generation before 1906 provided concrete evidence of the almost unlimited possibilities of change. But the scientific attitude was abstracted and translated into two strategies that were applied to non-technical areas of endeavor: the cult of efficiency and the use of the expert. In fact the wonders of pure science were not generally a part of the usual conception of science held by the educated public, except when external signs of prestige such as Nobel prizes and research endowments suggested esteem for science on the part of men of affairs.[64]

Efficiency embodied a number of attributes that added up to hardworking, profitable, competent, and socially harmonious individuals and groups. As in the scientific management movement, Progressives conceived of efficiency as the rational maximization of result for effort and organization—and planning and rational control to that end constituted "science." This objective use of intelligence was the nexus between science and the popular conceptions of science, particularly technology and the results of technology.[65]

In so far as the reformers held in common any ideal of technique, the most striking allegiance they showed was to the expert in the service of uplift or democracy (the latter sometimes known as the "Wisconsin idea"). Herbert Croly, in his eloquent verbalization, *The Promise of American Life* (1909), set up the scientists' way of proceeding as the model for citizenship. "No scientist as such has anything to gain by the use of inferior methods or by the production of inferior work. There is only one standard for all scientific investigators—the highest standard."[66] By using experts in all aspects of American life, the Progressives expected to bring the generalized benefits of disinterested science to the entire society. The socialist William English Walling in 1911 looked with approval upon the direction that Progressive reform was tending: "Science is becoming more consciously pragmatic, more consciously concerned with the service of man. . . . And this is the science which now has the unqualified support and respect of the most able and advanced scientists of the time."[67]

The objectivity of the scientist was embodied in the tendency of members of professions, as noted above, to avow their dedication to unselfish service and technical objectivity. As professionals foreswore personal gain, their expertise could serve a democratic society without the self-interest that

would otherwise corrupt and discredit such an elite. For this rapidly growing, extremely influential segment of society, the ideals of unselfish service and efficiency served to validate both personal and social goals. And in organizations they tended to reinforce the process of bureaucratization.

Later generations who believed that interest groups and big government constituted the one true model for reform did draw inspiration from the Progressives, but only in some of the rhetoric and some of the tactics and vision of their predecessors. The voluntary organizations could be viewed as pressure groups—but only if each group was turned into a selfish interest group.[68] Voluntary organizations pursuing altruistic ends are decidedly different from interest groups representing the self-serving demands of the New Deal and post–New Deal broker state. Chambers of commerce and trade associations, which also flourished early in the twentieth century, were not of the same category as the Urban League or Mental Hygiene Society. "If by some magic," wrote social gospeller Walter Rauschenbusch in 1914, "business life . . . could be plucked out of our total social life in all its raw selfishness, and isolated on an island, unmitigated by any other factors of our life, that island would immediately become the object of a great foreign mission crusade for all Christendom."[69]

The cultural nationalism of the early twentieth century easily translated into identifying with an enhanced federal government, as was indicated by the common ground often noted between the New Nationalism and the New Deal. Likewise cultural nationalism contributed to the growing eclipse of local and regional non-conformity, another process hastened and blessed by WASP reformers.

Perhaps most intriguing of the Progressive legacies was the vision that for every ill of every person there was or should be a specialist to do away with that ill. Not content with general measures, such as those embodied in laws and public campaigns, the Progressives saw the possibility of reaching every member of society to educate, to uplift, and to care. The anti-tuberculosis and anti–venereal disease campaigns were both based upon treating every infected person, that is, every carrier of disease, regardless of the numbers of persons and the costs involved. This technique of providing special protections and services for each and every citizen was at the heart of the later welfare state strategy and at the same time constituted the major controlling device of the bureaucratic society that came to dominate mid–twentieth century America.[70] Particularly the health and social work contingents among Progressives pioneered individual care and control. But they worked primarily through voluntary organizations operating for altruistic purposes, as opposed to the welfare state style that came to emphasize personal need and want—that is, selfishness.

The experience of World War I intensified the Progressives' already ambivalent attitudes toward government. The actions of both state and local bodies estranged many, who typically moved into either disillusioned advo-

cacy of purely private endeavor or the American Civil Liberties Union. Still another group saw in the wartime emergency a chance to bypass the usual political barriers to social reconstruction and to use the enhanced powers of the executive for reformist purposes. Such reformers typically lost faith in the power of an intelligent public but did not surrender the idea of leadership by an enlightened elite.[71] These various experiences with government in fact contributed to the disintegration of the reform consensus in the divisiveness and self-centeredness of the 1920's.

After World War I, the parallel reforms that had coalesced into Progressivism once more parted. Many wealthy patrons of uplift associations died. A number of important spokesmen for the movement withdrew into art for art's sake or some similarly pure attempt, often with Progressive roots, to strive for the ideal.[72] Muckrakers of the Jazz Age, as Richard H. Pells observes, aimed their criticisms at "stupidity, aimlessness, and vulgarity." Others suffered disillusionments of various kinds, with various consequences. Harold Stearns in 1919 summed up a common re-evaluation and reconceptualization of American reform in the years just past:

> We are becoming increasingly self-critical and dissatisfied with mere acquisition. Both our intellectuals and our creative literary men were emerging from their Transcendental towers of isolation. But American liberalism had two bad heritages to fight against . . . one the heritage of race-hatred psychology of the unacknowledged negro problem, making for intolerance; the other the heritage of perverted moralism or the attempt to use a native idealism for specific prohibitions, making in its turn for coercion. Such, in brief, seems to me the strength and the fragility of American liberalism as it met the challenge of 1914.[73]

This was the "liberal" view that was to become commonplace in another decade, one that ignored the positive achievements of the Progressives.

Yet in the postwar years much of the voluntary associationism of the Progressive era continued, and indeed the "association idea" was of central importance in the 1920's in general and in the career of Herbert Hoover in particular. Industrial welfare and business cooperation represented an enlightened continuation of ideas fostered in an earlier day.[74] When the New Deal came, coercion and centralization grew as an addition onto the core legacy. The tradition of caring and experiment continued, but the essentials of an earlier day, extreme reliance on voluntary groups and aversion to selfishness, diminished significantly.[75]

A number of historians who in later times criticized the Progressives in ahistorical contexts distracted attention from the strengths, accomplishments, and significances of the pre–World War I reformers. The Progressives were not lower class, and they did seek to impose a WASP style of life on other people. The voluntary association is a device that upper classes tra-

ditionally used to help control the lower classes.[76] But to suggest that the changes were good or bad simply because of the attitudes of agents who carried them out would be purely ad hominem argument. The intent of the Progressives was, by placing primary reliance on voluntary organizations, to change the living habits of most Americans. The organizations used education and persuasion and sometimes types of coercion to teach people to observe safety regulations and not to spit, and to coerce those who continued anti-social behavior in spite of explanations that would have convinced a prudent, educated WASP. That the Progressives had somewhat less respect for cultural variation than sentimental later generations is hardly relevant to the causes and consequences of a major reform program.

Likewise, later critics, impatient of change in their own times, thought the Progressives worthy of scorn because they were essentially conservative. Perhaps the young intellectuals of the prewar period, who with Randolph Bourne thought of themselves as "radicals," misled later readers. In fact the reformers were interested in morals and in basic institutions, like any conservatives. And the Progressives, whatever their dedication to justice, did not envisage any overturn of the general social hierarchy, although the term uplift involved increased well-being as well as social harmony. No doubt many believed, implicitly as well as explicitly, that reform was necessary for preservation, with emphasis upon the preservation.

Still another line of criticism is advanced by those who argue that the Progressives did not make enough changes, that they failed to achieve completely all of their own goals.[77] The proper historical question is not whether changes matched the avowed aims but, first, how the goals moved people to action, and, second, what actual changes, intended or not, occurred.

And the fact remains that the reformers advocated and carried out many changes in a short time, and, to save some institutions, they attacked others. To save and strengthen the family and traditional morals, the reformers were willing to break taboos and undermine the double standard. To preserve private ownership of business and a traditional labor system, the business Progressives were willing to set limits to competition, to organize together, and to begin systems of welfare capitalism. To protect an open society, the Progressives subverted political parties. These and a myriad of other changes suggest that, in that generation, conservatism may not have been a major force unless defined very flexibly. Probably it is more useful to follow Richard Hofstadter and Samuel P. Hays and characterize the reformers as people with guilty consciences who would not stand idly by when they saw social wrongs.[78]

Since the Progressives tried so hard to be unselfish, latter-day critics belittled them by showing that public-spirited actions were really self-serving—that comfortably well-off people would profit from social stability, that the managers of organizations would benefit from increasing bureaucratization, that businesses would make more money in an efficient society.

Progressives have been portrayed as downwardly mobile people who were exalting experts in order to reverse social processes, and also as businessmen bent on greater monopoly. And of course they were damned in particular for not invariably advocating central government and/or cultural pluralistic solutions to all social problems, which fact in itself engenders suspicion on the part of anti-business "liberal" historians that "interests" were at work.

For all of these doubters and ahistorical critics, two facts are enough answer. First, Progressivism involved many aspects of American life, including every major social institution—except, in some respects, perhaps, government. And, second, the Progressives left behind them a substantial number of specific accomplishments. All of them were products of both human aspiration and complex historical forces.

What is left of Progressivism now is the memory of a moment in time, perhaps ten years, when an altruism that was based on WASP ethnic group values united with hard facts of scientific and technological change. "It is this union of the idealistic and the efficient," wrote intellectual Randolph Bourne in 1913, "that gives the movement its hold on the disinterested and serious youth of to-day."[79] The result of the combination was as pure an unselfishness as has been seen in history, operating through voluntary associations to bring about widespread and significant changes in American life.

Conclusion

Historians who are conventionally cynical and carry skepticism about human motives into their reconstructions of the past can by their debunking become as removed from reality as those who concentrate on people's aspirations and constructive achievements. Common wisdom shows that humans contain in themselves a mix of motives individually; no evidence suggests that this same mix does not exist on the social level as well. I have provided evidence that demonstrates how assumptions and idealism in the Progressive era led to an important common social orientation among a critical number of Americans, including major social leaders in all areas of life.[1] Through their work, the ideals and the ideas had consequences.

Chapter 14 therefore suggests that Americans in the early twentieth century—and also importantly to some extent before and after—had goals other than power for the sake of power, regardless of what the unrealistic cynics have suggested. Historians who concentrate on power, either in politics or in economics and other areas, work under the same disadvantage as many of those working in the history of sex: In either case the obscene detail obscures events in the larger culture that were truly momentous and that gave the sexual act or push for power real social significance. Despite the technical excellence of many such maladroitly focused accounts, I have persisted in attempting to find and call attention to another approach to understanding events in American culture.

Generations who are familiar with psychological thinking should be comfortable with recognizing that psychological assumptions were important in forming ideals and in suggesting ways of achieving all human ends. As the unitary moral agent that was also the thinking agent fragmented in the nineteenth century, that breakup reflected and reinforced the conflicting social

and cultural trends, along with Americans' needs to decide which trends to follow and which forces to respond to. As the sciences of both body and mind advanced, the new knowledge helped give leaders in various areas and on various levels the confidence that reformers could affect both individual and social destiny. Later generations cannot understand the early twentieth century without following the confidence of belief that let reformers think that they knew the causes of social and even personal problems, indeed, that discoverable instinctual drives and the ways in which they expressed themselves gave insight into evil and how to combat it. The model of seeking out causes both personal and social that showed up in the campaign to destroy prostitution is but the most obvious example with which I have been concerned in this book.

Nor was the tactic of seeking to eliminate the causes of evil rather than the direct manifestations of evil unique to the Progressive era; there were many precedents, especially after the Enlightenment. The place of the rationalists of the American Social Science Association in nineteenth-century uplift has been the subject of important historical work, but another, older paradigm was the temperance movement. Early in the nineteenth century Americans recognized that specific desirable indirect social effects might follow the diminution of alcohol consumption in any community.[2]

In so far as non-cultural historians have been concerned with social control, they have come some distance with the rest of us. They have used the concept of social control—itself articulated during the Progressive years—to describe the exercise of power and attempts to exercise power in many areas besides politics. By suggesting that economic interests were pursued through eleemosynary institutions, for example, such historians have made the case for cynicism, but they have also thereby acknowledged that charitable efforts and even voluntarism were important in American life and helped shape it.

It is not my intention here to rehearse the arguments over the place of ideology or even whether or not ideology, used in the strictly instrumental sense, is a useful explanatory concept in history. I simply offer my evidence that the neurosciences and psychiatry evolved in harmony and synchrony with the rest of American culture, including medicine and moral standards, as both cause and effect, whether on the specific level of Progressive uplift and reform or the more global recognition of manipulatable narcissism.

As I noted in Chapter 14, however, uplift in the United States came to signify seeking individual well-being in addition to social harmony. Where, for example, David Thelen years ago suggested the importance of the growth of consumer consciousness as a part of the struggle for power in American politics, numerous other historians have pursued in individual terms the idea of well-being and the social impact that masses of self-seekers have had. Christopher Lasch, focusing on the "me generation" of the 1970's, took up his own by-the-way insight that psychological adjustment could turn into

social control and used the same term that I applied to the 1920's to talk about a whole *Culture of Narcissism*.[3]

I have remarked in numerous places in this book on the fit between the bureaucratic society based on industrialism and the work of professionals, particularly in medicine and the neurosciences. In large organizations, managers found it useful to concentrate on meeting individual wants of individual members of the organization, and in the larger society, professionals found that they could do good and increase obvious happiness by addressing individual adjustments—solving problems rather than relieving symptoms—as well as effecting general social changes that would intervene in the connection between cause and result. Mental health, social hygiene, and prohibition campaigns therefore worked in parallel, all based on ideas that led many Americans to believe that reductionistic explanations promised actual ability to control fates. It was in such a schema that instinct theory, for example, was entirely compatible with the functioning of the bureaucratic society.

In recent years a number of historians have added a whole new dimension to industrial/post-industrial organizational society by tracing the origins of the consumer culture. They have gone beyond the economic and political self-consciousness that Thelen discovered and now talk about leisure and affluence and subjective feelings of comfort and well-being—the concrete basis for a culture of narcissism. These historians are in fact looking for the historical basis for the type of impact that television had in the last half of the twentieth century. Their search has, unsurprisingly, led them to urban elites and professionals.[4]

In this fresh and insightful literature on the historical dynamics of post-industrial culture, scholars focus on the new internal realities that developed along with industrial and intellectual change. Investigators are finding as a determinant of American existence not so much the exercise of power as the manipulation of subjective realms of existence that were significant because they were widely shared, particularly in the media and more particularly in advertising.

The historians of consumer culture have focused increasingly on public spaces, and particularly the department store that in cities furnished an exciting, tempting, and colorful world into which individuals were invited to enter in their capacities as consumers. This view of late-nineteenth-century America has taken on even greater urgency as women's historians discover that the consumer role was quintessentially a female role, particularly that of the women who were socialized into being shoppers (as was obvious in, for example, Edward Bellamy's *Looking Backward* and many other novels of a less reformist nature).[5]

The history of the neurosciences and medicine, not to mention morals and pleasure seeking, intersected continually with the development of consumer culture at all levels of description. Prohibitionists were specifically

concerned about the misuse of public space in the saloon, and the role of social hygienists in bringing on and responding to the ethic of self-indulgence by promising fulfillment in marriage is a subject currently under debate.[6] As part of inner reality, prescriptive literature (such as I have used for the early twentieth century) has taken on new meaning, especially when tied to measurable changes in the theater, which now appears even more central as an American institution in the consumer culture.

The technical history of psychology in advertising also has attracted the attention of historians even beyond John B. Watson's work in the J. Walter Thompson agency. But even more important, general ideas about human beings' mental and emotional functioning interacted with the new worlds of fantasy that came with the consumer culture. Elaine S. Abelson, for instance, has connected the rise of the disease label, kleptomania, with the interaction of middle-class women with the new merchandising of the late nineteenth century. And Roland Marchand, to cite another example, in his new cultural history of advertising utilizes the paper that appears herein as Chapter 5 to talk about the ways in which advertisers simplified and personalized a complex, mass society.[7]

As the essays in this book show, then, the history of both the neurosciences and moral standards are useful in understanding the evolution of the United States as an organizational society and as a consumer culture, to say nothing of as a civilization. Neuroscience and morals are useful because they provide fresh and different perspectives—in part precisely because psychology, psychiatry, sexuality, temperance, and medicine all have their own histories, each of which had internal momentum as well as cultural determinants.

Those areas, moreover, were extremely sensitive, even threatening, and therefore were areas in which scientific objectivity, as I have shown, came with the greatest difficulty. Yet thinkers were able to develop reductionism, even the very complex reductionism of physiological and psychological atomistic thinking, that could demystify and still serve as a basis for cybernetic and computer-based modeling of mind and emotion. The confidence that science gave helped bring about behavioral and institutional and imaginative changes. Whether in revealing patterns or in causing historical shifts, the cultural elements meshed with each other inexorably in the evolution of American civilization.

Civilization, as I have indicated, included more than just the complexity of a culture with elements in synchrony. The scientists and physicians who worked to achieve intellectual precision contributed to civilization. So, too, did reformers. Vision from the one arena informed efforts in the other. The enduring achievement of that civilization therefore did not consist of the ephemeral exercise of power within a society but rather the vision that in people attuned to human possibilities, intellectual and moral aspirations can work together—and at one extended point in time did.

Notes and Index

Notes

Introduction

1. David A. Hollinger, "Ethnic Diversity, Cosmopolitanism and the Emergence of the American Liberal Intelligentsia," *American Quarterly*, 27 (1975), 133–151.
2. Gilbert Allardyce et al., "The Rise and Fall of the Western Civilization Course," *American Historical Review*, 87 (1982), 695–743. The recent critics of the civilization tradition not only focus on instruction at Harvard, where historians never did succeed in establishing the tradition in the classroom, but bring in irrelevant and even political considerations; this was pointed out gently by Evelyn Edson, "Reflections on the History of Western Civilization: An Unblushing Apology, or Perhaps a Love Letter," *AHA Perspectives*, February, 1984, pp. 16–17. The same political preoccupations that undercut the civilization concept in college curriculums appear in the research work of historians who reject the idea of civilization.
3. Later I give special attention to the place of Freudian thinking in this constellation.
4. This idea was popularized in a musical show, "Camelot," written by Alan Jay Lerner and Frederick Loewe and based upon T. H. White, *The Once and Future King* (New York: Dell Publishing Company, Inc., 1960 [1958]). Compare the gloomy conclusion in Lewis Perry, *Intellectual Life in America: A History* (New York: Franklin Watts, 1984), pp. 451–454.
5. A general latter-day discussion of these issues is John Higham and Paul K. Conkin, eds., *New Directions in American Intellectual History* (Baltimore: Johns Hopkins University Press, 1979), in which Paul Conkin in the afterword, pp. 227–234, especially notes the persistence of the new history tradition, which is spelled out in detail in Robert Allen Skotheim, *American Intellectual Histories and Historians* (Princeton, NJ: Princeton University Press, 1966).

6. A summary of discussions of the fads in cultural history is Robert Darnton, "Intellectual and Cultural History," in Michael Kammen, ed., *The Past Before Us: Contemporary Historical Writing in the United States* (Ithaca, NY: Cornell University Press, 1980), pp. 327–354. See especially Warren I. Susman, *Culture as History: The Transformation of American Society in the Twentieth Century* (New York: Pantheon Books, 1984).

7. Richard M. Weaver, *Ideas Have Consequences* (Chicago: University of Chicago Press, 1948).

Chapter 1

1. B. Horowitz, "The Ultra-Scientific School," *Popular Science Monthly*, 85 (1914), 463.

2. Merle Curti, *Human Nature in American Thought: A History* (Madison: University of Wisconsin Press, 1980).

3. A recent discussion of the concept, in which analysis and complexity are distinguished, is Keith Stewart Thomson, "Reductionism and Other Isms in Biology," *American Scientist*, 72 (1984), 388–390.

4. Perhaps the most cogent of the surveys of the concept are L. D. Arnett, *The Soul—A Study of Past and Present Beliefs* (Worcester, MA: Clark University, 1904); and H. B. Alexander, "The Conception of 'Soul,'" *Journal of Philosophy, Psychology and Scientific Methods*, 9 (1912), 421–430.

5. See the philosophical context of this emphasis in Stephan Strasser, *The Soul in Metaphysical and Empirical Psychology*, trans. by Henry J. Koren (Pittsburgh: Duquesne University, 1957), especially p. 9. One rather different Continental stream, vitalism, which was not central in American thought, is traced in Sergio Moravia, "The Capture of the Invisible. For a (Pre)history of Psychology in Eighteenth-Century France," *Journal of the History of the Behavioral Sciences*, 19 (1983), 370–378.

6. George Bush, *The Soul; Or, an Inquiry into Scriptural Psychology, as Developed by the Use of the Terms, Soul, Spirit, Life, etc., Viewed in Its Bearings in the Doctrines of the Resurrection* (New York: J. S. Redfield, 1845), p. 4.

7. Lyman Abbott, *A Study in Human Nature* (New York: Chautauqua Press, 1887 [c. 1885]), p. 15.

8. Standard reference works and histories of philosophical psychology detail the development of European ideas; American versions as they developed are described in Jay Wharton Fay, *American Psychology Before William James* (New Brunswick, NJ: Rutgers University Press, 1939).

9. George Moore, *The Power of the Soul over the Body, Considered in Relation to Health and Morals* (New York: Harper and Brothers, 1847), p. 7.

10. Thomas C. Upham, *Elements of Mental Philosophy, Embracing the Two Departments of the Intellect and the Sensibilities*, 2 vols. (New York: Harper and Brothers, 1840), I, 47.

11. Joseph Haven, *Mental Philosophy, Including the Intellect, Sensibilities, and Will* (Boston: Gould and Lincoln, 1859 [c. 1857]), p. 29. Fay, *American Psychology*, summarizes the literature lucidly.

12. See especially John O. Lyons, *The Invention of the Self: The Hinge of Con-

sciousness in the Eighteenth Century (Carbondale: Southern Illinois University Press, 1978); and Morse Peckham, *Beyond the Tragic Vision: The Quest for Identity in the Nineteenth Century* (New York: George Braziller, 1962); Koenraad W. Swart, "'Individualism' in the Mid–Nineteenth Century," *Journal of the History of Ideas*, 23 (1962), 77–90; and Nathaniel Southgate Shaler, *The Individual: A Study of Life and Death* (New York: D. Appleton and Company, 1901), p. 71.

13. Richard S. Storrs, Jr., *The Constitution of the Human Soul: Six Lectures Delivered at the Brooklyn Institute, Brooklyn, N.Y.* (New York: Robert Carter and Brothers, 1856), p. 35.

14. Particularly pertinent is the discussion of "decomposition" in Robert Rogers, *A Psychoanalytic Study of the Double in Literature* (Detroit: Wayne State University Press, 1970), especially pp. 11–13. There is substantial writing on the "double" in literature, most notoriously Dr. Jekyll and Mr. Hyde, and a cogent summary of this approach to dissociation in fiction is the editorial comment in Morris Beja, *Psychological Fiction* (Glenview, IL: Scott, Foresman and Company, 1971), pp. 276–280. See also Masao Miyoshi, *The Divided Self: A Perspective on the Literature of the Victorians* (New York: New York University Press, 1969), especially p. xv. To Victorians in general, what Matthew Arnold called "the dialogue of the mind with itself" therefore took on increasing significance as doubt opened the way to making choices. Matthew Arnold, *The Poems of Matthew Arnold, 1840–1867* (London: Oxford University Press, 1926), p. 1; and, in general, Walter E. Houghton, *The Victorian Frame of Mind, 1830–1870* (New Haven, CT: Yale University Press, 1957).

15. Fay, *American Psychology*. D. B. Klein, *The History of Scientific Psychology: Its Origin and Philosophical Backgrounds* (New York: Basic Books, Inc., 1970), pp. 394–396.

16. See especially John D. Davies, *Phrenology, Fad and Science: A Nineteenth-Century American Crusade* (New Haven, CT: Yale University Press, 1955); and Madeleine B. Stern, *Heads and Headlines: The Phrenological Fowlers* (Norman: University of Oklahoma Press, 1971).

17. See previous note and David de Giustino, *Conquest of Mind, Phrenology and Victorian Social Thought* (London: Croom Helm, 1975).

18. [Charles Caldwell], "Moral Aspects of Phrenology," *Christian Examiner*, 17 (1834), 254; and N. L. Rice, *Phrenology Examined, and Shown to Be Inconsistent with the Principles of Phisiology, Mental and Moral Science, and the Doctrines of Christianity: Also an Examination of the Claims of Mesmerism* (New York: Robert Carter and Brothers, 1848), pp. 90–91, 142.

19. James P. Morgan, "The First Reported Case of Electrical Stimulation of the Human Brain," *Journal of the History of Medicine and Allied Sciences*, 37 (1982), 51–64; E. F. Brush, "The Faculty of Speech," *Popular Science Monthly*, 24 (1884), 793–794; Edward M. Brown, "Neurology and Spiritualism in the 1870s," *Bulletin of the History of Medicine*, 57 (1983), 573–575. Basic background and distinctions are in Frederick Gregory, *Scientific Materialism in Nineteenth Century Germany* (Dordrecht, Netherlands: D. Reidel Publishing Company, 1977), especially pp. x–xi.

20. Oliver Wendell Holmes, *Mechanism in Thought and Morals: An Address Delivered Before the Phi Beta Kappa Society of Harvard University, June 29, 1870.*

With Notes and Afterthoughts (Boston: J. R. Osgood and Company, 1871); Morton Prince, *The Nature of Mind and Human Automatism* (Philadelphia: J. B. Lippincott Company, 1885), especially pp. 102, 133–142.

21.   Charles E. Rosenberg, *No Other Gods: On Science and American Social Thought* (Baltimore: Johns Hopkins University Press, 1976), p. 4; and T. H. Huxley et al., *Half-Hours with Modern Scientists: Lectures and Essays* (New Haven, CT: C. C. Chatfield and Company, 1872), pp. 60–61.

22.   A modern perspective on these origins is George L. Engel, "The Need for a New Medical Model: A Challenge for Biomedicine," *Science*, 196 (1977), 129–136.

23.   Philip J. Pauly, "The Appearance of Academic Biology in Late Nineteenth-Century America," *Journal of the History of Biology*, 17 (1984), 369–397. See, for example, Frances Emily White, "Protoplasm," *Popular Science Monthly*, 21 (1882), 361–370; Frederick G. Kilgour, "Scientific Ideas of Atomicity in the Nineteenth Century," *Proceedings of the Tenth International Congress of the History of Science*, 2 vols. (Paris: Hermann, 1964), I, 329–331; Garland E. Allen, *Life Science in the Twentieth Century* (New York: John Wiley and Sons, 1975).

24.   L. L. Langley, ed., *Homeostasis: Origins of the Concept* (Stroudsburg, PA: Dowden, Hutchinson and Ross, Inc., 1973).

25.   See, for example, Ernest Borek, *The Atoms Within Us* (New York: Columbia University Press, 1961).

26.   Charles F. Cox, *Protoplasm and Life: Two Biological Essays* (New York: N. D. C. Hodges, 1890), especially pp. 5, 29–37. C. H. May and Smith Ely Jelliffe, *May's Anatomy, Physiology, and Hygiene: For Use in Primary and Intermediate Schools*, 4th ed. (New York: William Wood and Company, 1899), p. 17.

27.   See, for example, Andrew McClary, "Germs Are Everywhere: The Germ Threat as Seen in Magazine Articles 1890–1920," *Journal of American Culture*, 3 (1980), 33–46.

28.   J. J. R. MacLeod, "Vitalism and the New Physiology," *Journal of Laboratory and Clinical Medicine*, 2 (1916), 209–212. It should no doubt be noted that ecological thinking was evolving in other areas of biology at this same time. Even more to the point was the rise of general biology at the turn of the century.

29.   Robert E. Kohler, Jr., "The Enzyme Theory and the Origin of Biochemistry," *Isis*, 64 (1973), 181–196.

30.   Allen, *Life Science*. Albert P. Mathews, "The Chemistry of Life," *Science News-Letter*, May 5, 1928, p. 280. Shepherd Ivory Franz, "New Phrenology," *Science*, 35 (1912), 321–328.

31.   Stephen Y. Wilkerson, "James Jackson Putnam and the Impact of Neurology in Psychotherapy in Late Nineteenth-Century America" (doctoral dissertation, Duke University, 1970). Nor are genetic or developmental assumptions discussed here.

32.   Elwood Worcester, Samuel McComb, and Isador H. Coriat, *Religion and Medicine: The Moral Control of Nervous Disorders* (New York: Moffat, Yard and Company, 1908), pp. 24–25, 86–87.

33.   James Rowland Angell, *Psychology: An Introductory Study of the Structure and Function of Human Consciousness*, 4th ed. (New York: Henry Holt and

Company, 1908), p. 2. Some of the flavor of the contemporary debate around the change can be found in such writings as James T. Bixby, "Is the Soul a Baseless Hypothesis?" *Bibliotheca Sacra*, 47 (1890), 191–215.

34. Boris Sidis and Simon P. Goodhart, *Multiple Personality: An Experimental Investigation into the Nature of Human Individuality* (New York: D. Appleton and Company, 1904), especially pp. 32, 356–360.

35. The standard work is of course Hamilton Cravens, *The Triumph of Evolution: American Scientists and the Heredity-Environment Controversy 1900–1941* (Philadelphia: University of Pennsylvania Press, 1978).

36. See, for example, John C. Burnham, "The New Psychology: From Narcissism to Social Control" (reprinted herein as Chapter 5), in John Braeman, Robert H. Bremner, and David Brody, eds., *Change and Continuity in Twentieth-Century America: The 1920's* (Columbus: Ohio State University Press, 1968) pp. 351–398.

37. Frank Marshall White, "The Soul Machine," *Harper's Weekly*, December 19, 1908, pp. 12–13, 32. See, for example, G. T. W. Patrick, "The Search for the Soul in Contemporary Thought," *Popular Science Monthly*, 78 (1911), 460–468.

38. Maurice Mandelbaum, *History, Man, and Reason: A Study in Nineteenth-Century Thought* (Baltimore: Johns Hopkins University Press, 1971), pp. 365, 367; Gordon W. Allport, *Personality: A Psychological Interpretation* (New York: Henry Holt and Company, 1937), especially p. 48; and John C. Burnham, "Historical Background for the Study of Personality," in Edgar F. Borgatta and William W. Lambert, eds., *Handbook of Personality Theory and Research* (Chicago: Rand McNally and Company, 1968), especially p. 73.

39. William James, *A Pluralistic Universe: Hibbert Lectures at Manchester College on the Present Situation in Philosophy* (London: Longmans, Green, and Company, 1909), p. 210.

Chapter 2

1. P. K. Feyerabend and Grover Maxwell, eds., *Mind, Matter, and Method: Essays in Philosophy and Science in Honor of Herbert Feigl* (Minneapolis: University of Minnesota Press, 1966). Seymour M. Farber and Roger H. L. Wilson, eds., *Man and Civilization: Control of the Mind* (New York: McGraw-Hill Book Company, 1961). Ludwig von Bertalanffy, "The Mind-Body Problem: A New View," *Psychosomatic Medicine*, 26 (1964), 29–45. J. R. Smythies, *Brain and Mind: Modern Concepts of the Nature of Minds* (New York: Humanities Press, 1965). Robert Efron, "Biology Without Consciousness—And Its Consequences," *Perspectives in Biology and Medicine*, 11 (1967), 9–36.

2. Albert G. A. Balz, "The Sixteenth Annual Meeting of the American Philosophical Association," *Journal of Philosophy, Psychology and Scientific Methods*, 14 (1917), 200–217, especially pp. 215–217.

3. For example, Oskar Vogt, "Psychologie, Neurophysiologie und Neuroanatomie," *Journal für Psychologie und Neurologie*, 1 (1902), 1.

4. See, for example, the summary in James Bissett Pratt, *Naturalism* (New Haven, CT: Yale University Press, 1939), pp. 94–142.

5. William McDougall, *Body and Mind: A History and Defense of Animism* (London: Methuen, 1911).

6. A. Earl Walker, "The Development of the Concept of Cerebral Localization in the Nineteenth Century," *Bulletin of the History of Medicine*, 31 (1957), 99–121.

7. See Chandler McC. Brooks, "Current Developments in Thought and the Past Evolution of Ideas Concerning Integrative Function," in F. N. L. Poynter, ed., *The History and Philosophy of Knowledge of the Brain and Its Functions* (Oxford: Blackwell Scientific Publications, Ltd., 1958), pp. 235–252, especially p. 238.

8. C. D. Broad, *The Mind and Its Place in Nature* (London: Kegan Paul, Trench, Trubner and Company, 1925), p. 111.

9. L. Edinger and A. Wallenberg, *Bericht über die Leistungen auf dem Gebiete der Anatomie des Centralnervensystems, 1905–1906* (Leipzig, Germany: Hirzel, 1907), pp. 1–2.

10. R. J. A. Berry, *Brain and Mind: Or the Nervous System of Man* (New York: Macmillan Company, 1928).

11. C. S. Sherrington, *The Integrative Action of the Nervous System* (New Haven, CT: Yale University Press, 1906); the quote is from pp. 3–4.

12. K. Brodmann, "Beiträge zur histologischen Lokalisation der Grosshirnrinde," *Journal für Psychologie und Neurologie*, 2 (1903), 79; 10 (1908), 231–246.

13. Shepherd Ivory Franz, "The Functions of the Cerebrum," *Psychological Bulletin*, 11 (1914), 131–140, especially p. 131.

14. Karl S. Lashley, *Brain Mechanisms and Intelligence: A Quantitative Study of Injuries to the Brain* (Chicago: University of Chicago Press, 1929), p. 173. See also R. M. Brickner, *Research Publications of the Association for Research in Nervous and Mental Diseases*, 13 (1934), 259.

15. Robert M. Young, *Mind, Brain and Adaptation in the Nineteenth Century: Cerebral Localization and Its Biological Context from Gall to Ferrier* (Oxford: Clarendon Press, 1970).

16. Shepherd Ivory Franz, "New Phrenology," *Science*, 35 (1912), 321–328, especially p. 328.

17. For example, Kurt Goldstein, *Human Nature in the Light of Psychopathology* (Cambridge, MA: Harvard University Press, 1940).

18. J. R. Kantor, "The Nervous System, Psychological Fact or Fiction?" *Journal of Philosophy*, 19 (1922), 38–49, especially p. 40.

19. E. Stanley Abbot, "The Biological Point of View in Psychology and Psychiatry," *Psychological Review*, 23 (1916), 117–128, especially p. 125.

20. For example, John Broadus Watson, *Psychology from the Standpoint of a Behaviorist* (Philadelphia: J. B. Lippincott, 1919), and G. V. Hamilton, *An Introduction to Objective Psychopathology* (St. Louis: C. V. Mosby Company, 1925).

21. John Broadus Watson, "The Place of the Conditioned-Reflex in Psychology," *Psychological Review*, 23 (1916), 89–116.

22. Watson, *Psychology from the Standpoint of a Behaviorist*.

23. Hamilton Cravens and John C. Burnham, "Psychology and Evolutionary Naturalism in American Thought, 1890–1940," *American Quarterly*, 23 (1971), 635–657.

24. William McDougall, *An Introduction to Social Psychology*, 11th ed. (Boston: John W. Luce and Company, 1916).

25. See John C. Burnham, "The Medical Origins and Cultural Use of Freud's Instinctual Drive Theory" (reprinted herein as Chapter 4), *Psychoanalytic Quarterly*, 43 (1974), 193–217.

26. Peter Amacher, *Freud's Neurological Education and Its Influence on Psychoanalytic Theory* (New York: International Universities Press, 1965).

27. Watson, *Psychology from the Standpoint of a Behaviorist*, p. 195n.

28. This history is detailed in Arthur Beidl, *The Internal Secretory Organs: Their Physiology and Pathology*, trans. by Linda Forster (New York: William Wood and Company, 1913), and H. D. Rolleston, *The Endocrine Organs in Health and Disease: With an Historical Review* (Oxford: Oxford University Press, 1936).

29. Harvey Cushing, "Psychic Disturbances Associated with Disorders of the Ductless Glands," *American Journal of Insanity*, 69 (1913), 965–990.

30. S. W. Bandler, *The Endocrines* (Philadelphia: W. B. Saunders Company, 1920), p. 2.

31. Walter Timme, *Proceedings of the Association for Research in Nervous and Mental Diseases*, 14 (1933), 91.

32. A contemporary summary can be found in Jien Rikimaru, "Emotion and Endocrine Activities," *Psychological Bulletin*, 22 (1925), 205–258.

33. R. G. Hoskins, "Endocrine Factors in Vigor," *Endocrinology*, 11 (1927), 97–105.

34. Albert Kuntz, *The Autonomic Nervous System*, 2d ed. (Philadelphia: Lea and Febiger, 1935), pp. 13–17, 41.

35. Erwin H. Ackerknecht, "The History of the Discovery of the Vegetative (Autonomic) Nervous System," *Medical History*, 18 (1974), 1–8.

36. Walter B. Cannon, *Bodily Changes in Pain, Hunger, Fear and Rage* (New York: D. Appleton and Company, 1915).

37. George W. Crile, *The Origin and Nature of the Emotions* (Philadelphia: W. B. Saunders Company, 1915).

38. See L. L. Langley and Jeanne L. Brand, "The Mind-Body Issue in Early Twentieth-Century American Medicine," *Bulletin of the History of Medicine*, 46 (1972), 171–179.

39. Eugen Bleuler, *Affectivity, Suggestibility, Paranoia*, trans. by Charles Ricksher (Utica, NY: State Hospitals Press, 1912).

40. J. S. Haldane, *Mechanism, Life and Personality: An Examination of the Mechanistic Theory of Life and Mind*, 2d ed. (London: J. Murray, 1913), pp. 11–12.

41. Walter B. Cannon, "The Autonomic Nervous System: An Interpretation," *Lancet*, 218 (1930), 1109–1115.

42. Frederick G. Kilgour, "Scientific Ideas of Atomicity in the Nineteenth Century," *Proceedings of the Tenth International Congress of the History of Science*, 2 vols. (Paris: Hermann, 1964), I, 329–331.

43. Garland E. Allen, *Life Science in the Twentieth Century* (New York: John Wiley and Sons, 1975).

44. Diana Long Hall, "Endocrinology and Sexuality: The First Fifty Years," paper read at the History of Science Society meetings, San Francisco, 1973.

45. John C. Burnham, "Historical Background for the Study of Personality," in Edgar F. Borgatta and William W. Lambert, eds., *Handbook of Personality Theory and Research* (Chicago: Rand McNally and Company, 1968), pp. 3–81.

Chapter 3

Acknowledgments: Some of the research leading to this paper was carried out while the author was postdoctoral fellow of the Foundations' Fund for Research in Psychiatry. Additional research was supported by a grant from the Ohio State University, and typing was generously furnished by the Department of History, University of Melbourne, while the author was Fulbright lecturer there.

1.   Gustav Bergmann, "The Contribution of John B. Watson," *Psychological Review*, 63 (1956), 265–276; Albert E. Goss, "Early Behaviorism and Verbal Mediating Responses," *American Psychologist*, 16 (1961), 285–298.

2.   Thomas S. Kuhn, *The Structure of Scientific Revolutions* (Chicago: University of Chicago Press, 1962).

3.   Edwin G. Boring, *A History of Experimental Psychology*, 2d ed. (New York: Appleton-Century-Crofts Company, Inc., 1950), especially pp. 641, 643. John Broadus Watson, "Psychology as the Behaviorist Views It," *Psychological Review*, 20 (1913), 158–177.

4.   Ibid.

5.   Gardner Murphy, *Historical Introduction to Modern Psychology*, 2d ed. (New York: Harcourt, Brace and Company, 1949), p. 260; Paul Hanly Furfey, "After Psychoanalysis—What?" *Catholic World*, 127 (1928), 681. Watson was at Yale in November, 1908, but there seems to be no contemporary record of the content of his lecture or lectures; see, for example, *Yale Daily News*.

6.   John Broadus Watson, in Carl Murchison, ed., *A History of Psychology in Autobiography* (Worcester, MA: Clark University Press, 1936), III, 276.

7.   For example, Willard Harrell and Ross Harrison, "The Rise and Fall of Behaviorism," *Journal of General Psychology*, 18 (1938), 367–421.

8.   E. B. Titchener, "On 'Psychology as the Behaviorist Views It,'" *Proceedings of the American Philosophical Society*, 53 (1914), 1–17.

9.   André Tilquin, *Le Behaviorisme: Origine et Developpement de la Psychologie de Reaction en Amerique* (Paris: Librairie Philosophique J. Vrin, 1950), pp. 29–43.

10.   A. A. Roback, *Behaviorism and Psychology* (Cambridge, MA: Sci-Art, 1923); Robert S. Woodworth, *Contemporary Schools of Psychology* (New York: Ronald Press Company, 1931), pp. 43–92.

11.   William James, *The Principles of Psychology*, 2 vols. (New York: Henry Holt and Company, 1890); William James, "Does 'Consciousness' Exist?" *Journal of Philosophy, Psychology and Scientific Methods*, 1 (1904), 477–491.

12.   James McKeen Cattell, "The Conceptions and Methods of Psychology," in Howard J. Rogers, ed., *Congress of Arts and Science, Universal Exposition, St. Louis, 1904*, 8 vols. (Boston: Houghton Mifflin Company, 1906), V, 593–604.

13.   Herbert S. Jennings, *Behavior of the Lower Organisms* (New York: Columbia University Press, 1906).

14.   Max Meyer, *The Fundamental Laws of Human Behavior* (Boston: R. G. Badger Company, 1911).

15.   William McDougall, *Physiological Psychology* (London: J. M. Dent, 1905), pp. 1–2; William McDougall, *Psychology: The Study of Behavior* (New York: Henry Holt and Company, 1912). After C. Lloyd Morgan published his *Animal Be-

haviour (London: E. Arnold, 1900), comparative psychologists not infrequently used the term, "animal behavior." Watson, as a comparative psychologist, of course acknowledged Morgan as one of his intellectual fathers, but Morgan's well-known views had very little in common with what became Watsonian behaviorism.

16. Since Watson later utilized the concept of conditioned responses, Pavlov has also been counted as one of the fathers of behaviorism. Although Pavlov's work was well known in America, it was understood to concern glandular reflexes primarily; it was only later that the idea became known that the work might have a more general applicability to the commoner associative processes. See, for example, Robert M. Yerkes and Sergius Morgulis, "The Method of Pawlow in Animal Psychology," *Psychological Bulletin*, 6 (1909), 257–273, in an issue edited by Watson; John Broadus Watson, "The Origin and Growth of Behaviorism," *Archiv fuer systematische Philosophie und Sociologie*, 30 (1927), 248–249. Pavlov himself remained an orthodox neuromechanist and reductionist; see Y. P. Frolov, *Pavlov and His School: The Theory of Conditioned Reflexes*, trans. by C. P. Dutt (London: Kegan Paul, Trench, Trubner and Company, 1937), especially pp. 13–14.

17. Donald D. Jensen, "Foreword to the 1962 Edition," in Herbert S. Jennings, *Behavior of the Lower Organisms* (Bloomington: Indiana University Press, 1962), pp. ix–xvi.

18. John Broadus Watson, review of Jennings in *Psychological Bulletin*, 4 (1907), 288–291. See, for example, John Broadus Watson to Robert M. Yerkes, November 2, 1905, December 12, 1906, Robert M. Yerkes Papers, Yale Medical Library, New Haven, CT.

19. See Herbert S. Jennings, "Diverse Ideals and Divergent Conclusions in the Study of Behavior in Lower Organisms," *American Journal of Psychology*, 21 (1910), 349–370. See also the interesting letter avowing his belief in consciousness but adding that "the man that denies it all the way through is tolerably safe from overthrow," Herbert S. Jennings to Robert M. Yerkes, November 19, 1904, Yerkes Papers. John Broadus Watson, *Psychology from the Standpoint of a Behaviorist* (Philadelphia: J. B. Lippincott Company, 1919), p. vii, commented directly on this confusion: "Those so-called objectivists, so far as concerns their human psychology,—and this is true of Bechterew as well,—are perfectly orthodox parallelists." Watson was far more at home in philosophy than he let on or than his critics would admit.

20. See Donald Fleming, "Introduction," in Jacques Loeb, *The Mechanistic Conception of Life* (Cambridge, MA: Harvard University Press, 1964), pp. vii–xli.

21. John Broadus Watson to Jacques Loeb, January 2, 1914, Jacques Loeb Papers, Library of Congress, Washington, DC.

22. For example, John Broadus Watson to Robert M. Yerkes, October 29, 1909, Yerkes Papers. John Broadus Watson, review of Jacques Loeb, in *Psychological Bulletin*, 4 (1907), 291–293.

23. Watson, in Murchison, *A History of Psychology in Autobiography*, III, 276. Meyer actually did not arrive in Baltimore until some time after Watson.

24. Knight Dunlap, in Carl Murchison, ed., *A History of Psychology in Autobiography* (Worcester, MA: Clark University Press, 1932), II, 44–46; Watson, in

Murchison, *A History of Psychology in Autobiography*, III, 277. See, for example, Knight Dunlap, "Dr. Yerkes' View of Psychical Causation," *Psychological Bulletin*, 8 (1911), 400–403; even Knight Dunlap's "The Case Against Introspection," *Psychological Review*, 19 (1912), 404–413 was irrelevant to behaviorism, and Knight Dunlap's "Muscular Activity and Thought Processes," *Scientific American Supplement*, 78 (1914), 322–323, which appeared after Watson's paper, had an emphasis completely foreign to Watson's way of thinking.

25. Watson, in *A History of Psychology in Autobiography*, III, 276.

26. Watson, *Psychology from the Standpoint of a Behaviorist*, p. vii.

27. Cattell, "The Conceptions and Methods."

28. John Broadus Watson, "The Need of an Experimental Station for the Study of Certain Problems in Animal Behavior," *Psychological Bulletin*, 3 (1906), 151.

29. Watson, review of Jennings; Watson, review of Loeb.

30. See John Broadus Watson to Robert M. Yerkes, October 2, 1907, December 12, 1907, January 3, 1908, Yerkes Papers. John Broadus Watson, "A Point of View in Comparative Psychology," abstract in *Psychological Bulletin*, 6 (1909), 57–58.

31. Ibid. Since Watson had been at Johns Hopkins only a few weeks when this paper was presented, it is at most problematical that either Dunlap or Jennings had any influence on it, especially since there is evidence that this paper or a similar one was presented elsewhere earlier (see previous discussion in this chapter). As late as September 29, for example, Watson and Jennings had met only once (John Broadus Watson to Robert M. Yerkes, September 29, 1908, Yerkes Papers).

32. John Broadus Watson, *Behaviorism*, 2d ed., 1930 (reprinted, Chicago: University of Chicago Press, 1958?), p. v.

33. John Broadus Watson, "The New Science of Animal Behavior," *Harper's Monthly Magazine*, 120 (1910), 346–353.

34. John Broadus Watson to Robert M. Yerkes, March 12, 1913, Yerkes Papers.

35. F. L. Wells, "Dynamic Psychology," *Psychological Bulletin*, 10 (1913), 434.

36. Watson, "The Origin and Growth," p. 248.

37. Kuhn, *The Structure of Scientific Revolutions*.

38. The psychological profession was manifesting an unmistakable sensitivity to a behavioral approach. A very restrained and eclectic textbook by W. B. Pillsbury of Michigan in 1911, for example, was already causing Titchener concern over the current trend (E. B. Titchener to Robert M. Yerkes, July 13, 1911, Yerkes Papers). Watson recorded his reaction to Pillsbury's book in "Psychology as the Behaviorist Views It," pp. 165–166.

39. Titchener, "On 'Psychology as the Behaviorist Views It,'" pp. 14–15. Titchener had the advantage of at least being acquainted with Watson; see Cedric A. Larson and John J. Sullivan, "Watson's Relation to Titchener," *Journal of the History of the Behavioral Sciences*, 1 (1965), 338–354.

40. See John C. Burnham, "Psychiatry, Psychology and the Progressive Movement" (reprinted herein as Chapter 12), *American Quarterly*, 12 (1960), 457–465. For a complementary discussion of the relationship of behaviorism to American culture, see David Bakan, "Behaviorism and American Urbanization," *Journal of the History of the Behavioral Sciences*, 2 (1966), 5–28, especially pp. 12–13, where social control receives a most interesting treatment. Another approach

to the relationship between behaviorism and American culture is to be found in Lucille Terese Birnbaum, "Behaviorism: John Broadus Watson and American Social Thought, 1913–1933" (doctoral dissertation, University of California, Berkeley, 1964).

Chapter 4

Acknowledgment: The author is grateful to Dr. Robert R. Holt for his helpful suggestions.

1. In 1924 Sigmund Freud, *Three Essays on the Theory of Sexuality*, in *Standard Edition of the Complete Psychological Works of Sigmund Freud* (hereinafter cited as *Standard Edition*), VII, 168n, added a footnote: "The theory of the instincts is the most important but at the same time the least complete portion of psychoanalytic theory."

2. For general material on the development of Freud's theories, see Ernest Jones, *The Life and Work of Sigmund Freud*, 3 vols. (New York: Basic Books, Inc., 1953–1957); O. Andersson, *Studies in the Prehistory of Psychoanalysis: The Etiology of Psychoneuroses and Some Related Themes in Sigmund Freud's Scientific Writings and Letters, 1886–1896* (Stockholm: Svenska Bokförlaget/ Norstedts, 1962); and the editorial notes throughout the *Standard Edition*.

3. For example, Sigmund Freud, *The Origins of Psycho-Analysis: Letters to Wilhelm Fliess, Drafts and Notes, 1887–1902*, Marie Bonaparte, Anna Freud, and Ernst Kris, eds. (London: Imago, 1954); Sigmund Freud, "Sexuality in the Aetiology of the Neuroses," *Standard Edition*, III; Walter Stewart, *Psychoanalysis: The First Ten Years, 1888–1898* (New York: Macmillan Company, 1967).

4. Sigmund Freud, "On the Grounds for Detaching a Particular Syndrome from Neurasthenia Under the Description 'Anxiety Neurosis,'" *Standard Edition*, III. Cf., James Strachey, "Editor's Introduction," in Sigmund Freud, "Project for a Scientific Psychology," *Standard Edition*, I, 291.

5. Sigmund Freud, *The Interpretation of Dreams*, *Standard Edition*, IV–V. Freud, *Three Essays*.

6. Peter Amacher, *Freud's Neurological Education and Its Influence on Psychoanalytic Theory* (New York: International Universities Press, 1965). L. B. Ritvo, "Darwin as the Source of Freud's Neo-Lamarckianism," *Journal of the American Psychoanalytic Association*, 13 (1965), 499–517.

7. The best general discussion of the various models of instinct up to the early twentieth century is in L. L. Bernard, *Instinct: A Study in Social Psychology* (New York: Henry Holt and Company, 1924).

8. Herbert Spencer, *The Principles of Psychology*, 2 vols., 3rd ed. (New York: D. Appleton and Company, 1880), I, 432. E. G. T. Liddell, *The Discovery of Reflexes* (Oxford: Clarendon Press, 1960).

9. Sigmund Freud, "Project for a Scientific Psychology," *Standard Edition*, I. R. R. Holt, "A Review of Some of Freud's Biological Assumptions and Their Influence on His Theories," in N. S. Greenfield and W. C. Lewis, eds., *Psychoanalysis and Current Biological Thought* (Madison: University of Wisconsin Press, 1965), pp. 93–124.

10. Alexander Bain, *Mental and Moral Science: A Compendium of Psychology and*

Ethics (London: Longmans, Green, and Company, 1884). Cf., J. A. Cardno, "Instinct: Some Pre-Experimental Landmarks," *Australian Journal of Psychology*, 10 (1958), 329–340; Strachey, "Editor's Introduction," in Freud, "Project for a Scientific Psychology, " pp. 291–292.

11. Cf., for example, the well-known work of Théodule Ribot, *Heredity: A Psychological Study of Its Phenomena, Laws, Causes, and Consequences* (London: Henry S. King, 1875). As late as 1910, for example, Charles Debierre, in a respectable French academic treatise, "L'hérédité normale et pathologique," *L'Oeuvre médico-chirurgical*, 58 (1910), 1–51, included as a major source Prosper Lucas's 1849 classic on heredity.

12. A. O. Lovejoy, *Reflections on Human Nature* (Baltimore: Johns Hopkins Press, 1961).

13. James Strachey, "Editor's Note," in Sigmund Freud, "Instincts and Their Vicissitudes," *Standard Edition*, XIV, 111–116. At one point Freud, *Three Essays*, p. 195, spoke of "inherited mental formations . . . in the human being—something analogous to instinct [*Instinkt*] in animals." Clearly he was thinking of highly patterned specific responses of the reflex variety as opposed to more general impulse and drive (*Trieb*).

14. E. C. Wilm, *Theories of Instinct: A Study in the History of Psychology* (New Haven, CT: Yale University Press, 1925). R. R. Holt, "Freud's Mechanistic and Humanistic Images of Man," *Psychoanalysis and Contemporary Science*, 1 (1972), 3–24, has pointed out the extent of inconsistency in Freud's writings, and especially the way in which scientism often gave way in his thinking to humanism, and vice versa, without logical reconciliation. While such dilemmas are to be found in Freud's own work, his followers were not sensitive to the difficulties. It was they who particularly read into Freud's teaching logical consistency and saw in his writings the "purely psychological" level of discourse. Those born later than Freud were more at ease than he with "fictions" (Freud, *Interpretation of Dreams*, p. 598), that is, hypothetical models, the scientific constructs familiar in twentieth-century scientific work. (See, for example, S. G. Margolin, "Freud's Concept of Constitution in Psychoanalysis," in Greenfield and Lewis, *Psychoanalysis and Current Biological Thought*, pp. 135–136.) Thus Freud's *effort* to maintain a purely psychological level of discourse was more important than his actual performance in doing so.

15. W. T. Preyer, *Die Seele des Kindes: Beobachtungen über die geistige Entwicklung des Menschen in den ersten Lebensjahren*, 2d ed. (Leipzig, Germany: Th. Greiben's Verlag, 1884). Freud, *Origins of Psycho-Analysis*, p. 75. Amacher, *Freud's Neurological Education*, p. 51.

16. For example, Sigmund Freud, "A Difficulty in the Path of Psycho-Analysis," *Standard Edition*, XVII, 140–141. For a brief systematic discussion of recapitulation in psychoanalysis, see S. W. Jackson, "The History of Freud's Concepts of Repression," *Journal of the American Psychoanalytic Association*, 17 (1969), 760–761.

17. Hamilton Cravens, "American Scientists and the Heredity-Environment Controversy, 1883–1940" (doctoral dissertation, University of Iowa, 1969). Cf., A. H. Sturtevant, *A History of Genetics* (New York: Harper and Row Publishers, Inc., 1965). F. B. Churchill, "August Weismann and a Break from Tradition," *Journal of the History of Biology*, 1 (1968), 214–225.

18. Cf., Cravens, "American Scientists." Hamilton Cravens and John C. Burnham, "Psychology and Evolutionary Naturalism in American Thought, 1890–1940," *American Quarterly*, 23 (1971), 635–657. G. W. Stocking, Jr., "Lamarckianism in American Social Science, 1890–1915," *Journal of the History of Ideas*, 23 (1962), 239–256. Karl Pearson, *The Grammar of Science* (London: A. and C. Black, 1892), p. 28.

19. C. Lloyd Morgan, *Habit and Instinct* (London: E. Arnold, 1896). James Mark Baldwin, "Physical and Social Heredity," *American Naturalist*, 30 (1896), 422–428.

20. William McDougall, *An Introduction to Social Psychology* (Boston: John W. Luce and Company, 1909). Bernard, *Instinct*. D. L. Krantz and D. Allen, "The Rise and Fall of McDougall's Instinct Doctrine," *Journal of the History of the Behavioral Sciences*, 3 (1967), 326–338. Cravens, "American Scientists." Cravens and Burnham, "Psychology and Evolutionary Naturalism." Karl S. Lashley, "Experimental Analysis of Instinctive Behavior," *Psychological Review*, 45 (1938), 445–472, asserts that the anti-instinct campaign was aimed primarily at the positing of imaginary forces that were supposed to explain behavior. In the course of the battle, genetic acquisitions of all mental determinants got destroyed too. Freud obviously escaped better than most theorists the onus of postulating imaginary forces because his theorizing was thought to be internally relatively consistent and because his basic model was familiar and accepted.

21. Ritvo, "Darwin as the Source."

22. Cf., H. Nunberg and E. Federn, eds., *Minutes of the Vienna Psychoanalytic Society*, 2 vols. (New York: International Universities Press, 1962–1967), II, 93. Ritvo, "Darwin as the Source." In 1913, Sigmund Freud, "The Claims of Psycho-Analysis to Scientific Interest," *Standard Edition*, XIII, 182, spoke of the biological "conception of an immortal [*unsterblichen*] germ plasm" and added: "It is only this conception which enables us rightly to understand the part played by the sexual instinctual forces in physiology and psychology." He was arguing the importance of sexual instinctual drives in life by suggesting their biological importance as well as by showing their many facets and transmutations. Since the statement was contemporary with his expressions of strongly Lamarckian views, it seems likely that he had in his mind somehow reconciled the germ plasm idea with the idea of inherited traits that could nevertheless be changed from generation to generation.

23. Karl Groos, *Die Spiele der Thiere* (Jena, Germany: Gustav Fischer, 1896). Karl Groos, *The Play of Man*, trans. by Elizabeth L. Baldwin (New York: D. Appleton and Company, 1901). For details about the relationship between Weismannism and instinct theory in German language science, where the issues were connected with the vitalism controversy, see John C. Burnham, "Instinct Theory and the German Reaction to Weismannism," *Journal of the History of Biology*, 5 (1972), 321–326.

24. Sigmund Freud, *Jokes and Their Relation to the Unconscious*, in *Standard Edition*, VIII, 128.

25. Sigmund Freud, "From the History of an Infantile Neurosis," in *Standard Edition*, XVII, 97. Sigmund Freud, "Fragment of an Analysis of a Case of Hysteria," in *Standard Edition*, VII, 112–114. Cf., Ritvo, "Darwin as the Source."

26. Cf., for example, W. Lauder, "Heredity in Relation to Disease," in *Health Lectures Delivered in Manchester, 1886–1887, Tenth Series* (London: John Heywood, 1887).

27. For a typical example, see A. Dietrich, *Die Bedeutung der Vererbung für die Pathologie* (Tübingen, Germany: Franz Pietzcker, 1902). For an annotated bibliography of this literature, see K. Brodmann, "Die Erblichkeitsfrage in der Neuropathologie, Kritische Literaturübersicht," *Zeitschrift für Hypnotismus, Psychotherapie sowie andere psychophysiologische und psychopathologische Forschungen*, 5–6 (1896–1897), 329–427, etc.

28. For example, Freud, "Fragment of an Analysis," p. 113.

29. As Preyer, *Die Seele des Kindes*, p. 202, and others recognized, in any individual the truly instinctual is very hard to separate from life history, except for sexual behavior. The conventional medical view of instinct in the abstract was no different from or better than that in biology (see M. P. E. Littré, *Dictionnaire encyclopédique des sciences médicales, de chirurgie, de pharmacie* [Paris: J. B. Baillièrc, 1878], pp. 817–818).

30. E. Bibring, "The Development and Problems of the Theory of Instincts," *International Journal of Psycho-Analysis*, 22 (1941), 102–131, and Richard Sterba, *Introduction to the Psychoanalytic Theory of the Libido* (New York: Nervous and Mental Disease Monographs, 1942), recognized the importance of this model to Freud's thinking, and as early as 1913 Freud, "The Claims of Psycho-Analysis," pp. 179–182, spelled out why sex had to be so important. See also, Heinz Hartmann, Ernst Kris, and R. M. Loewenstein, "Notes on the Theory of Aggression," *Psychoanalytic Study of the Child*, 3–4 (1949), 9–36.

31. Freud, *Three Essays*, p. 135n.

32. Freud, "Instincts and Their Vicissitudes." The present paper does not include a discussion of the economic viewpoint of instinctual drive theory; such exposition would in any case serve merely to confirm the points presently under discussion. See, for example, James Strachey, "Editor's Introduction," in *Standard Edition*, I, 394–397, and Hartmann, Kris, and Loewenstein, "Notes on the Theory." According to B. B. Rubinstein, "Psychoanalytic Theory and the Mind-Body Problem," in Greenfield and Lewis, *Psychoanalysis and Current Biological Thought*, especially pp. 44, 49, "Sexual excitation and its discharge through coitus are paradigmatic for the economic viewpoint." Somatic and psychical models or levels of discussion became confused, particularly in the concept of psychical energy, and recent thinkers have suggested abandoning the energic construct in psychoanalysis (cf., Lawrence S. Kubie, "The Fallacious Use of Quantitative Concepts in Dynamic Psychology," *Psychoanalytic Quarterly*, 16 (1947), 507–518.

33. Freud, *Origins of Psycho-Analysis*, p. 234.

34. Richard von Krafft-Ebing, *Lehrbuch der Psychiatrie auf klinischer Grundlage* (Stuttgart, Germany: Ferdinand Enke, 1883 [1879]), chap. 4, especially p. 77.

35. Richard von Krafft-Ebing, *Psychopathia Sexualis: With Special Reference to Contrary Sexual Instinct; A Medico-Legal Study*, trans. by Charles G. Chaddock (Philadelphia: F. A. Davis Company, 1892).

36. Emil Kraepelin, *Psychiatrie*, 6th ed., 4 vols. (Leipzig, Germany: Barth, 1899), I, 227.

37. Cf., for example, T. S. Clouston, *Clinical Lectures on Mental Diseases* (Philadelphia: Henry C. Lea's Sons, 1884); T. Kirchhoff, *Lehrbuch der Psychiatrie für Studierende und Aerzte* (Leipzig, Germany: Franz Deuticke, 1892); Amacher, *Freud's Neurological Education*, chaps. 2–3, the discussion of Freud's own immediate teachers. Hunger was dealt with often in a parallel way, and perversions of it were taken up systematically but not as extensively and clearly as in the case of sex. Freud himself opened the *Three Essays* (p. 135) by observing: "The fact of the existence of sexual needs in human beings and animals is expressed in biology by the assumption of a 'sexual instinct,' on the analogy of the instinct of nutrition, that is of hunger." The fact remains that psychiatric writers who tried to discuss the instinct of hunger did so in terms of the model of the aims, objects, and perversions that had already been worked out for sex. Freud (cf., Nunberg and Federn, *Minutes of the Vienna Psychoanalytic Society*, I, 86) in 1907 recognized this fact in a discussion of the Vienna Psychoanalytic Society when he asserted, "The comparison of hunger and love will remain unproductive until we know more about the sexual instinct." The use of the hunger example for expository purposes (for example, Sigmund Freud, *Introductory Lectures on Psycho-Analysis*, in *Standard Edition*, XVI, 313) tends to obscure the fact that the original model was the sexual instinctual drive.

38. After a number of years, even Freud forgot how commonplace were the ideas that he was using and tended to remember single, outstanding sources of his concepts; for example, Sigmund Freud, "The Libido Theory," in *Standard Edition*, XVIII, 255, and editor's annotation.

39. H. F. Ellenberger, *The Discovery of the Unconscious: The History and Evolution of Dynamic Psychiatry* (New York: Basic Books, Inc., 1970), for example, pp. 291–303, 502–510. Cf., Stephen Kern, "Freud and the Emergence of Child Psychology, 1880–1910" (doctoral dissertation, Columbia University, 1970). Henry Maudsley, *The Physiology and Pathology of Mind*, 2d ed. (London: Macmillan and Company, 1868), pp. 324–325, for instance, described cases in which very young children had manifested sexual behavior—"the instinct of propagation"—but he denied to the instinct in those so young either aim or object.

40. Theodor Meynert, *Psychiatry: A Clinical Treatise on Diseases of the Fore-Brain, Based upon a Study of Its Structure, Functions, and Nutrition*, trans. by Bernard Sachs (New York: Hafner Publishing Company, 1968 [1884]), pp. 169–170.

41. Cf., Bibring, "The Development and Problems," pp. 102–131. Even after 1920, Freud continued to suggest that the instinctual drives existed within the entire being of the person, before the ego and id could be differentiated. Those latter structures, and also the superego, he pictured as both logically and chronologically subsequent to the existence of instinctual drives (Sigmund Freud, *The Ego and the Id*, in *Standard Edition*, XIX, especially p. 65). A practical summary of the later history is in Hartmann, Kris, and Loewenstein, "Notes on the Theory," pp. 30–35.

42. Cf., note 14, above.

43. *Partialtriebe*. See Freud, *Three Essays*, pp. 166, 168n; Sigmund Freud, "Character and Anal Erotism," in *Standard Edition*, IX, 170–171; Sigmund Freud,

" 'Civilized' Sexual Morality and Modern Nervous Illness," in *Standard Edition*, IX, 187–188.

44. An example is H. Dahl, "Psychoanalytic Theory of the Instinctual Drives in Relation to Recent Developments," *Journal of the American Psychoanalytic Association*, 16 (1968), 613–637. Cf., C. Brenner, "Some Problems in the Psychoanalytic Theory of the Instinctual Drives," in I. M. Marcus, ed., *Currents in Psychoanalysis* (New York: International Universities Press, 1971), pp. 216–230.

45. Again, quantitative and energic dimensions are being avoided here.

46. A. Wettley and W. Leibbrand, *Von der "Psychopathia Sexualis" zur Sexualwissenschaft* (Stuttgart, Germany: Ferdinand Enke, 1959), p. 79. See also Freud, *Three Essays*, p. 149n.

47. Albert Moll, *Untersuchenungen über die Libido sexualis* (Berlin: H. Kornfeld, 1898), p. 225. Cf., H. Hartmann, "Comments on the Psychoanalytic Theory of Instinctual Drives," *Psychoanalytic Quarterly*, 17 (1948), 368–388. Freud, "The Claims of Psycho-Analysis," pp. 179–182, spoke of his "efforts to prevent biological terminology and considerations from dominating psycho-analytic work," but he again characterized the instinctual drive (*Trieb*) as a phenomenon of "the frontier between the spheres of psychology and biology."

48. Freud, "From the History of an Infantile Neurosis," pp. 119–121.

49. H. E. Ziegler, *Der Begriff des Instinktes einst und jetzt* (Jena, Germany: Gustav Fischer, 1910), p. 48. H. E. Ziegler, "Ueber den Begriff des Instincts," *Verhandlungen der Deutschen zoologischen Gesellschaft*, 1 (1892), 134–135. Meynert, *Psychiatry*, p. viii. Auguste Forel, *Gehirn und Seele* (Bonn: Emil Strauss, 1899), p. 25n. Auguste Forel, *Out of My Life and Work*, trans. by Bernard Miall (New York: W. W. Norton and Company, 1937), p. 164. Groos, *Die Spiele*, p. 51, has a long list of eminent converts to Weismannism, notable for the large proportion who dealt with psychological and instinctual topics.

50. Moll, *Untersuchenungen über die Libido*, pp. 101–102, 214-225.

51. J. Orschansky, *Die Vererbung im Gesunden und Krankhaften Zustande und die Entstehung des Geschlects beim Menschen* (Stuttgart, Germany: Ferdinand Enke, 1903). Ibid. and J. Orschansky, "Étude sur l'hérédité normale et morbide," *Mémoires de l'académie imperiale des sciences de St.-Pétersbourg*, 7th ser., 42 (1894), no. 9, and J. Orschanksy, "L'hérédité dans les familles malades et theorie générale de l'hérédité," ibid., no. 8. Orschansky was preoccupied early by the problem of identifying traits and followed Weismann's teachings to try to solve the problem. He did not refine the concept of instinct as Freud did. For another example of the increasing compatibility of the sexual instinct model and Weismannism, see Groos, *Die Spiele*, p. xxii.

52. Once again, discussion of economic and energic points of view is being omitted.

53. David Rapaport, "Introduction," in Erik Erikson, *Identity and the Life Cycle: Selected Papers* (New York: International Universities Press, 1959), pp. 10–11.

54. Wilfrid Trotter, *Instincts of the Herd in Peace and War* (London: T. Fisher Unwin, 1919), pp. 6, 252.

55. The development of such a society is best worked out in specific historical material by Robert H. Wiebe, *The Search for Order, 1877–1920* (New York: Hill and Wang, 1967). The relationship of psychological ideas to such a society is described in John C. Burnham, "The New Psychology: From Narcissism to

Social Control" (reprinted herein as Chapter 5), in John Braeman, Robert H. Bremner, and David Brody, eds., *Change and Continuity in Twentieth-Century America: The 1920's* (Columbus: Ohio State University Press, 1968), pp. 351–398.

56. In the late 1960's, a number of thinkers attacked the validity of ideas of instinctual drives and other hereditary aspects of human personality. Such writers as Robert Jay Lifton (*Thought Reform and the Psychology of Totalism: A Study of "Brainwashing" in China* [New York: W. W. Norton and Company, 1961]) and R. J. Lifton ("Protean Man," *Partisan Review*, 35 [1968], 13–27) emphasized the changeable, "protean" nature of man and raised doubts as to whether or not libidinal instinctual drives or any other more or less specific inherited determinants could survive as fundamental concepts, even in a psychiatry that was supposed to be psychoanalytically oriented.

Chapter 5

Acknowledgment: Many thanks are due to colleagues in addition to the editors who generously offered suggestions for improving this essay: Paul C. Bowers, Hamilton Cravens, Roy Lubove, Gerald D. Nash, John C. Rule, and Jack Tager.

1. Frederick Lewis Allen, *Only Yesterday: An Informal History of the Nineteen-Twenties* (New York: Harper and Brothers, 1931).

2. Henry F. May, *The End of American Innocence: A Study of the First Years of Our Own Time, 1912–1917* (New York: Alfred A. Knopf, 1959); Henry F. May, "The Rebellion of the Intellectuals, 1912–1917," *American Quarterly*, 8 (1956), 114–126; Arthur S. Link, "What Happened to the Progressive Movement in the 1920's?" *American Historical Review*, 64 (1959), 833–851.

3. Hornell Hart, "Changing Social Attitudes and Interests," in President's Research Committee on Social Trends, *Recent Social Trends in the United States*, 2 vols. (New York: McGraw-Hill Book Company, 1933), I, 395. See also, for example, *Psychological Review* and *Journal of Nervous and Mental Disease* in the 1910's.

4. Abram Lipsky, *Man the Puppet: The Art of Controlling Minds* (New York: Frank-Maurice, Inc., 1925), p. 11.

5. A. G. Tansley, *The New Psychology and Its Relation to Life* (London: G. Allen and Unwin, 1920).

6. E. W. Scripture, *The New Psychology* (London: Walter Scott, 1897).

7. Tansley, *New Psychology*, p. 5.

8. See, for example, L. L. Thurstone, "Contributions of Freudism to Psychology," *Psychological Review*, 31 (1924), 175. Monroe A. Meyer, in *Mental Hygiene*, 8 (1924), 649–650, said that a bookseller told him that there were then in print about a hundred "psychoanalytic works of the more or less introductory type, designed for popular consumption."

9. See, for example, Frederick J. Hoffman, *The Twenties: American Writing in the Postwar Decade* (New York: Viking Press, 1955), and W. David Sievers, *Freud on Broadway: A History of Psychoanalysis and the American Drama* (New York: Hermitage House Press, 1955). "Psychoanalytic" (and likewise "Freudianism")

is, as noted herein, used here in the loosest sense, as it was in the new psychology. In literature, for example, Jung's thinking probably had more influence than did strictly Freudian psychoanalysis.

10. See, for example, John Broadus Watson, *Behaviorism* (New York: W. W. Norton and Company, 1925), pp. 239–240.

11. The history of the competent, specialized practice of psychoanalysis in the United States is a subject in itself and is not taken up in the present paper; see C. P. Oberndorf, *A History of Psychoanalysis in America* (New York: Grune and Stratton, 1953).

12. No attempt is being made in the present essay to explore the image of the new psychology in contrast to technical psychoanalysis as it existed and was distorted in the 1920's, nor to explore the reasons for the distortions.

13. For example, Louis Berman, *The Glands Regulating Personality: A Study of the Glands of Internal Secretion in Relation to the Types of Human Nature* (New York: Macmillan Company, 1921).

14. Edwin E. Slosson, "From Complexes to Glands," *Scientific Monthly*, 15 (1922), 189.

15. See, for example, Lewellys F. Barker, ed., *Endocrinology and Metabolism, Presented in Their Scientific and Practical Clinical Aspects* (New York: D. Appleton and Company, 1922), and the mental hygiene and education publications of the middle 1920's.

16. See David Bakan, "Behaviorism and American Urbanization," *Journal of the History of the Behavioral Sciences*, 2 (1966), 5–28. See, in general, Lucille Terese Birnbaum, "Behaviorism in the 1920's," *American Quarterly*, 7 (1955), 15–30, and Lucille Terese Birnbaum, "Behaviorism: John Broadus Watson and American Social Thought, 1913–1933" (doctoral dissertation, University of California, Berkeley, 1964), especially p. 291. See also the discussion herein. There were attempts to add other components to the new psychology. The most notable was made late in the twenties by advocates of Gestalt psychology, which aroused much interest among professional psychologists. Aside from a few explanatory publications and even a few attacks, however, this attempt failed. Gestalt, significantly, lacked the potential for practical application possessed by the other elements of the new psychology and in other ways failed to mesh with American society of the 1920's. See, for example, Louis Berman, *The Religion Called Behaviorism* (New York: Boni and Liveright, 1927), which was more an advocacy of Gestalt than an attack on Watsonianism (Berman was he of gland fame, incredibly enough); Edward S. Robinson, "A Little German Band: The Solemnities of Gestalt Psychology," *New Republic*, 61 (1929), 10–14.

17. See, for example, C. Harry Brooks, *The Practice of Auto-suggestion by the Method of Emile Coué* (New York: Dodd, Mead and Company, 1922); this volume inspired the quoted "Rhymed Review" by Arthur Guiterman, in *Life*, 80 (1922), 31, used by permission of H. T. Rockwell.

18. See, for example, Joseph Collins, "Couéism," *North American Review*, 216 (1922), 190–199; Harry N. Kerns, review of Satow, *Hypnotism and Suggestion*, in *Mental Hygiene*, 8 (1924), 414: "One wonders why the public is asked to read another book on this question."

19. Even the gland fad left behind a solid contribution on a technical physiological level. The lack of professional backing for Couéism sets it apart. A. Kardiner,

for example, in a review of Northridge, *Modern Theories of the Unconscious*, in *Mental Hygiene*, 9 (1925), 419, observed caustically, "Coué's views are given such space and dignity as to cast serious doubt upon the author's ability to criticize his material."

20. See the discussion herein.

21. John C. Burnham, "Psychiatry, Psychology and the Progressive Movement" (reprinted herein as Chapter 12), *American Quarterly*, 12 (1960), 457–465.

22. Oberndorf, *A History of Psychoanalysis in America*, pp. 135–136.

23. The literature on shell shock is immense; one convenient summary is Mabel Webster Brown and Frankwood E. Williams, *Neuropsychiatry and the War: A Bibliography with Abstracts* (New York: National Committee for Mental Hygiene, 1918). For examples of popular literature, see Frederick W. Parsons, "War Neuroses," *Atlantic Monthly*, 123 (1919), 335–338, and indicative of how late in the decade the idea was still filtering down, "Second Wind," *Saturday Evening Post*, May 8, 1926, p. 8ff.

24. The standard histories of this movement are not very revealing; see, for example, Albert Deutsch, "The History of Mental Hygiene," in J. K. Hall et al., eds., *One Hundred Years of American Psychiatry* (New York: Columbia University Press, 1944), pp. 325–365.

25. Norman Fenton, *Shell Shock and Its Aftermath* (St. Louis: C. V. Mosby Company, 1926), chap. 1; M. W. Ireland, ed., *The Medical Department of the United States Army in the World War* (Washington, DC: U.S. Government Printing Office, 1929), X, chap. 1, and pp. 489–491.

26. Ireland, *The Medical Department*, X, *passim*.

27. For example, Pearce Bailey, "Applicability of the Findings of the Neuropsychiatric Examinations in the Army to Civil Problems," *Mental Hygiene*, 4 (1920), 301–311.

28. The mental hygiene movement is best followed in appropriate volumes of *Mental Hygiene*. General treatments also appear in the standard bibliographical indexes of the day.

29. Lawson G. Lowrey and Victoria Sloane, eds., *Orthopsychiatry, 1923–1948* (New York: American Orthopsychiatric Association, 1948). Oral history interviews of William Healy and Augusta Bronner, conducted by John C. Burnham, 1960–1961 (copies deposited in the Harvard University Library, Cambridge, MA, and at the Judge Baker Guidance Center, Boston).

30. H. L. Levin, review of Yellowlees, *Manual of Psychotherapy*, in *Mental Hygiene*, 8 (1924), 1077.

31. The function of eclecticism in the science and therapy of mental illnesses—of which mental hygiene was a sophisticated and extremely clever example—is a large subject. Some account of it appears in John C. Burnham, *Psychoanalysis and American Medicine, 1894–1918: Medicine, Science, and Culture* (New York: International Universities Press, 1967).

32. Frankwood E. Williams, "A Selected List of Books on Mental Hygiene and Allied Subjects," *Mental Hygiene*, 8 (1924), 327.

33. See Alfred Lief, ed., *The Commonsense Psychiatry of Dr. Adolf Meyer: Fifty-Two Selected Papers* (New York: McGraw-Hill Book Company, 1948); Burnham, *Psychoanalysis and American Medicine*.

34. See the discussion herein.

35. See, for example, William B. Terhune, "Modern Trends in Juvenile Mental Hygiene," *Education*, 44 (1923), 65. Bernard Glueck, "Constructive Possibilities of a Mental Hygiene of Childhood," *Mental Hygiene*, 8 (1924), 651, connected child mental hygiene to an "unprecedented interest in child health, and child welfare generally." The incidence of articles indexed in the *Readers Guide* provides concrete confirmation of these impressions.

36. Sidney I. Schwab, "Influence of War Concepts of Mental Diseases and Neuroses," *Modern Medicine*, 2 (1920), 192–199.

37. Nothing could underline as subtly and surely as this latter source the presence of narcissism in the phenomenon under discussion.

38. Ernst Theodore Kreuger, "Autobiographical Documents and Personality" (doctoral dissertation, University of Chicago, 1925), pp. 16–17.

39. Ibid., p. 31.

40. Ibid., pp. 31, 39. Freud had early noticed and condemned those who read case histories as if they were novellas; Sigmund Freud, *Collected Papers* (New York: Basic Books, Inc., 1959), III, 15.

41. David Seabury, *Unmasking Our Minds* (New York: Boni and Liveright, 1924).

42. Chester T. Crowell, "Nutshell Novels," *New Republic*, 40 (1924), 44. The idea of the illusory nature of appearances was not only important but one of the fundamentals in the credo of the age. It represented an aspect of general disillusionment (see Christopher Lasch, *The New Radicalism in America [1889–1963]: The Intellectual as a Social Type* [New York: Alfred A. Knopf, 1965], pp. 254–255) as well as of the currents discussed in the present essay. The denunciations of insincerity and hypocrisy and the cult of frankness, both of which were conspicuous in the postwar world, were other aspects of the feeling that the obvious is not the real. Rationalization, one of the major conceptual contributions of the new psychology, was exciting because it showed specifically how people fooled themselves and why the traditional, rational explanations for human behavior were both convincing and erroneous. See, for example, James Harvey Robinson, *The Mind in the Making: The Relation of Intelligence to Social Reform* (New York: Harper and Brothers, 1921), pp. 40–48.

43. Sherwood Anderson, quoted in Hoffman, *The Twenties*, p. 206; Louis E. Bisch, *Your Inner Self* (Garden City, NY: Doubleday, Page and Company, 1922); Seabury, *Unmasking Our Minds*, p. x.

44. See, for example, Hoffman, *The Twenties*, pp. 204–205.

45. See, for example, Elsa Barker, *Fielding Sargent: A Novel* (New York: E. P. Dutton and Company, 1922), and Sievers, *Freud on Broadway*, pp. 80, 95–96. Sievers, ibid., p. 138, quotes the critic Alexander Woollcott, suggesting that the action in a supposedly psychoanalytic play in 1927 is a good example of putting very conventional drama in a faddish Freudian form: "If what ails the girl can be said to be hidden, then so is the Woolworth Building."

46. Jungian psychology was a variant of psychoanalysis, emphasizing the immediate causes of a neurotic illness (as opposed to life history) and such mystical concepts as a Lamarckian racial unconscious. In conformity to the usual American eclecticism, writers customarily did not distinguish Jung's work from Freud's but utilized them alternatively without regard for consistency.

47. James Oppenheim, *Your Hidden Powers* (New York: Alfred A. Knopf, 1923), pp. 5–6. This conception of the unrealized powers of the hidden self was usually

not Freudian or even broadly psychoanalytic but had its origin in the psychopathology of Janet, of which Coué represented a distortion.

48. Lasch, *The New Radicalism*, pp. 142–143.

49. See the discussion herein.

50. For example, John Broadus Watson, *The Ways of Behaviorism* (New York: Harper and Brothers, 1928), especially p. 120.

51. The argument might be made here, and will be made later, that like so much of the late 1920's, the behavioristic phase of the new psychology in its emphasis on external social control belongs with the 1930's, not the early 1920's. See Birnbaum, "Behaviorism: John Broadus Watson," p. 345 and *passim*.

52. Burnham, "Psychiatry, Psychology and the Progressive Movement." See, for example, James Jackson Putnam, *Human Motives* (Boston: Little, Brown and Company, 1915).

53. See, for example, the contemporaneous observations of Stanley P. Davies, "What Grown-ups Cry For: Has an Eager Public Been Oversold on Mental Hygiene?", *The Survey*, 67 (1931), 253–254, 280–281. Similarly, a quipster in *Life*, 81 (1923), 8, caught some of the underlying appeal of Couéism: "One thing about auto-suggestion: It is practically the only suggestion the average man will take."

54. John Howard Lawson, quoted in Sievers, *Freud on Broadway*, p. 143.

55. In the bargain Tridon passed on tips on the serving of food: André Tridon, *Psychoanalysis and Man's Unconscious Motives* (New York: Brentano's, 1924), chap. 5.

56. William J. Fielding, *The Caveman Within Us, His Peculiarities and Powers: How We Can Enlist His Aid for Health and Efficiency* (New York: E. P. Dutton and Company, 1922), pp. 264–269.

57. In combination with psychoanalytic explanations, the environment was believed to affect glandular functioning and so to account in organic terms for what had appeared to be an essentially psychological relationship of cause and effect. See, for example, the indefatigable André Tridon, *Psychoanalysis and Gland Personalities* (New York: Brentano's, 1923).

58. Howard W. Haggard, *'Tisn't What You Know But Are You Intelligent?* (New York: Harper and Brothers, 1927), especially pp. 5–7.

59. Ross L. Finney, "Behaviorism's Silence as to Human Values," in William P. King, ed., *Behaviorism: A Battle Line* (Nashville: Cokesbury Press, 1930), p. 177. A. A. Roback, "Intelligence and Behavior," *Psychological Review*, 29 (1922), 54–55, noted that intelligence testing made assumptions similar to those of behaviorism in that from both points of view intelligence is passive, that is, mechanical—the machinery, rather than active or a part of the drive itself. Both the IQ movement and behaviorism picture intelligence as a passive, automatic reaction to a stimulus.

60. Watson, *The Ways of Behaviorism*, p. 138; Birnbaum, "Behaviorism in the 1920's," pp. 21–22, discusses on one level the inconsistency in behaviorism. Compare in general Birnbaum, "Behaviorism: John Broadus Watson."

61. Birnbaum, "Behaviorism: John Broadus Watson," especially pp. 291ff., contains the interesting characterization of behaviorism as an "outsider's" psychology. See the observations of Paul Hanly Furfey, "After Psychoanalysis—What?", *Catholic World*, 127 (1928), 681–685.

62. See, for example, Horace Bidwell English, "Dynamic Psychology and the Problem of Motivation," *Psychological Review*, 28 (1921), 239–248; Karl S. Lashley, "The Behavioristic Interpretation of Consciousness," *Psychological Review*, 30 (1923), 348.

63. H. M. Kallen, "Is Minding Behaving?", *New Republic*, 29 (1922), 285–286.

64. Of course, this motivation was presented in a context of belief that "facing the truth," with subsequent rational action, would have beneficial effects on both the individual and society.

65. Every student of the period will have his own list of movements, of social background factors, and of influential thinkers. See, for example, Oscar Cargill, *Intellectual America: Ideas on the March* (New York: Macmillan Company, 1941).

66. George A. Coe, *The Motives of Men* (New York: Charles Scribner's Sons, 1928), p. 45. Ibid., chaps. 1–7, gives a good summary of the relationship of science, World War I, and industrial society to the cult of irrationality of the new psychology.

67. The standard treatment is L. L. Bernard, *Instinct: A Study of Social Psychology* (New York: Henry Holt and Company, 1924).

68. William McDougall, *An Introduction to Social Psychology*, 11th ed. (Boston: John W. Luce, 1916).

69. Robert E. Spiller et al., eds., *Literary History of the United States*, 2d ed. (New York: Macmillan Company, 1953), pp. 1201–1202; Theodore Dreiser, *An American Tragedy*, 2 vols. (New York: Boni and Liveright, 1935), II, 56.

70. Tridon, *Psychoanalysis and Man's Unconscious Motives*, p. 106.

71. See Richard Hofstadter, *Anti-Intellectualism in American Life* (New York: Vintage Books, 1966 [1963]), pp. 364–365, 368–369; Lasch, *The New Radicalism*, pp. 86–87; Birnbaum, "Behaviorism in the 1920's," pp. 26–30. *Life*, 83 (1924), 24, pictures a nurse in a modern nursery saying, "A penny for your complexes, Master John."

72. Very frequently when the hidden self expressed itself in neurotic ways, they were understood to represent inappropriate adaptations essentially infantile in nature. Indeed, "infantile" was used commonly as a synonym for "neurotic" when describing thought or behavior. There was, in other words, a distinction between the childish content or impulse in the hidden self and the choice between adult or infantile modes of expressing the content.

73. Harold Rugg and Ann Shumaker, quoted in Lawrence A. Cremin, *The Transformation of the School: Progressivism in American Education, 1876–1957* (New York: Alfred A. Knopf, 1961), p. 207, which should be seen in general.

74. See the discussion herein.

75. Samuel D. Schmalhausen, *Why We Misbehave* (Garden City, NY: Garden City Publishing Company, 1928), p. 104.

76. E. Boyd Barrett, "Psychology or Science," *New Republic*, 52 (1927), 343.

77. André Tridon, *Psychoanalysis and Love* (New York: Brentano's, 1922).

78. Samuel D. Schmalhausen, "Family Life: A Study in Pathology," in V. F. Calverton and Samuel D. Schmalhausen, eds., *The New Generation: The Intimate Problems of Modern Parents and Children* (New York: Macaulay Company, 1930), pp. 275–299.

79. The concept of normality and concern about it is of course a very large subject of which only this hint can be given here.

80. Arthur G. Lane, review of Green, *Mind in Action*, in *Mental Hygiene*, 8 (1924), 422.

81. See, for example, Ben B. Lindsey and Wainwright Evans, *The Revolt of Modern Youth* (New York: Boni and Liveright, 1924), especially pp. 66–67; May, *End of American Innocence*, especially pp. 340–347; John C. Burnham, "Psycho-analysis in American Civilization Before 1918" (doctoral dissertation, Stanford University, 1958), chap. 9.

82. Floyd Dell, *Love in the Machine Age: A Psychological Study of the Transition from Patriarchal Society* (New York: Farrar and Rinehart, 1930).

83. E. Boyd Barrett, *The New Psychology: How It Aids and Interests* (New York: J. Kenedy and Sons, 1925), p. 310.

84. Ben Hecht, *Fantazius Mallare: A Mysterious Oath* (Chicago: Covici-McGee, 1922), p. 13.

85. Elizabeth Benson, quoted in Hoffman, *The Twenties*, pp. 89–90. Rachel Crothers, *Expressing Willie, Nice People, 39 East: Three Plays* (New York: Brentano's, 1924), pp. 42–43.

86. For example, André Tridon, *Psychoanalysis: Its Theory and Practice* (New York: B. W. Huebsch, 1919), chap. 21. Although often invoking the idea of subli-mation and socially useful expressions of forbidden impulses, such writings as Tridon's lacked the moralistic flavor of prewar expositions of psychoanalysis. The question has often been raised whether sexual behavior did change in the Fitzgerald period or not, and if so, whether fear of repressions—learned from the new psychology—was a cause or just a symptom of or rationalization for the change. It was true that adventure-seeking young ladies went to Green-wich Village and cast off their repressions. But had Freud been unknown (or known more accurately), the adventure-seekers could have been asserting their emancipation rather than gratifying their impulses, and, indeed, had done just that in an earlier period. (This example was suggested by Waldo Frank, who knew Greenwich Village well, in an interview.) Without attempting to answer probably unanswerable questions, it is still possible to observe that the new psychology was very frequently associated with expressions of new attitudes (regardless of behavior) toward sexual matters.

87. S. C. Kohs, "We've Gone Psychiatric," *The Survey*, 64 (1930), 189–190. See, in general, *Journal of Social Hygiene* for these years.

88. Harvey Wickham, *The Misbehaviorists: Pseudo-Science and the Modern Tem-per* (New York: L. MacVeagh, 1928), p. 130.

89. One of the amusing and perhaps remarkable evidences of the hegemony of narcissistic attitudes in the twenties was the rehabilitation of masturbation in the sex education literature of the times.

90. See the discussion herein.

91. Loren Baritz, *The Servants of Power: A History of the Use of Social Science in American Industry* (Middletown, CT: Wesleyan University Press, 1970), chaps. 1–4.

92. *Ibid*; for example, see Douglas Fryer, review of Strong and Uhrbrock, *Job Analysis and the Curriculum*, in *Mental Hygiene*, 8 (1924), 848–849.

93. F. Z. C. Perrin, "The Psychology of Motivation," *Psychological Review*, 30 (1923), 176.

94. Baritz, *Servants of Power*, p. 6.

95. Ordway Tead, *Instincts in Industry: A Study of Working-Class Psychology* (Boston: Houghton Mifflin Company, 1918), especially chap. 3. See Baritz, *Servants of Power*, chaps. 1–4.

96. See, for the general setting, Otis A. Pease, *The Responsibilities of American Advertising: Private Control and Public Influence, 1920–1940* (New Haven, CT: Yale University Press, 1958), especially chap. 7.

97. Henry C. Link, *The New Psychology of Selling and Advertising* (New York: Macmillan Company, 1932), p. xiii and especially chap. 4. See Birnbaum, "Behaviorism: John Broadus Watson," p. 114.

98. See, for example, Sadie Myers Shellow, review of Watts, *An Introduction to the Psychological Problems of Industry*, in *Mental Hygiene*, 8 (1924), 610.

99. Benjamin Stolberg, "The Degradation of American Psychology," *The Nation*, 131 (1930), 395–398. See, for example, E. E. Southard, "The Modern Specialist in Unrest: A Place for the Psychiatrist in Industry," *Mental Hygiene*, 4 (1920), 550–563. Mary Parker Follett, "The Psychological Foundations: Constructive Conflict," in Henry C. Metcalf, ed., *Scientific Foundations of Business Administration* (Baltimore: Williams and Wilkins Company, 1926), pp. 114–131.

100. See, for example, Stow Persons, *American Minds: A History of Ideas* (New York: Henry Holt and Company, 1958), pp. 431–432.

101. See, for example, Caroline F. Ware, *Greenwich Village, 1920–1930: A Comment on American Civilization in the Post-War Years* (Boston: Houghton Mifflin, 1935), p. 248.

102. V. F. Calverton, "The Rise of Objective Psychology," *Psychological Review*, 31 (1924), 425.

103. William Ernest Hocking, *Human Nature and Its Remaking*, 2d ed. (New Haven, CT: Yale University Press, 1923), p. 13.

104. Frederick Elmore Lumley, *Means of Social Control* (New York: Century Company, 1925), pp. 395–396; Lipsky, *Man the Puppet*, p. 262.

105. Walter Lippmann, *Public Opinion* (New York: Harcourt, Brace and Company, 1922).

106. H. A. Overstreet, *Influencing Human Behavior* (New York: People's Institute Publishing Company, 1925).

107. Lasch, *The New Radicalism*, p. 146, has come to a similar conclusion in a different context: "The study of the inner man could degenerate into a technique of manipulating him in accordance with your own designs"; and Lasch goes on to add that "it could degenerate indeed into a technique of totalitarian control."

108. See, for example, Sievers, *Freud on Broadway*, pp. 76–79; Harvey O'Higgins and Edward H. Reede, *The American Mind in Action* (New York: Harper and Brothers, 1924), pp. 20–25.

109. Roy Lubove, *The Professional Altruist: The Emergence of Social Work as a Career, 1880–1930* (Cambridge, MA: Harvard University Press, 1965), chaps. 2–4. The professionalization process within social work was itself introspective in character, focusing on professional norms and the practitioner's adjustment to them.

110. Daniel R. Miller and Guy E. Swanson, *The Changing American Parent: A Study in the Detroit Area* (New York: John Wiley and Sons, 1958), especially chaps. 2 and 8, provide the conception of the bureaucratic welfare society.
111. Ibid.
112. Dell, *Love in the Machine Age*, pp. 405–407. Schmalhausen, in *Why We Misbehave*, pp. 74–75, epitomized the impact of the new psychology when he observed that "psychologic corrective of economic doctrine is a first-rate contribution to our enlightenment."

Chapter 6

Acknowledgment: Preparation of this paper was supported in part by NIH Grant LM 02539 from the National Library of Medicine. Presented January 22, 1976, at the New York Hospital–Cornell Medical Center.

1. Judd Marmor, "The Current Status of Psychoanalysis in American Psychiatry," *American Journal of Psychiatry*, 125 (1968), 679. Other examples include F. H. Frankel, "Psychiatry Beleaguered: Or the Psychiatric Identity Crisis," *Psychiatric Quarterly*, 43 (1969), 410–413; R. H. Vispo, "Psychiatry: Paradigm of Our Times," *Psychiatric Quarterly*, 46 (1972), 208–219. A particularly well balanced assessment is George Mora, "Recent Psychiatric Developments (Since 1939)," in Silvano Arieti, ed., *American Handbook of Psychiatry*, 2d ed. (New York: Basic Books, Inc., 1974), I, 43–58. One of the most significant attacks was Kate Millett, *Sexual Politics* (Garden City, NY: Doubleday, 1970), *passim.*
2. The various patterns are documented by contributors to Jacques M. Quen and Eric T. Carlson, eds., *American Psychoanalysis: Origins and Development* (New York: Brunner/Mazel, Inc., 1978).
3. Discussion of the sociology of psychoanalytic groups is in John C. Burnham, *Psychoanalysis and American Medicine, 1894–1918: Medicine, Science, and Culture* (New York: International Universities Press, 1967). See also R. P. Knight, "The Present Status of Organized Psychoanalysis in the United States," *Journal of the American Psychoanalytic Association*, 1 (1953), 197–221.
4. The history can be traced in C. P. Oberndorf, *A History of Psychoanalysis in America* (New York: Grune and Stratton, 1953), supplemented by Burnham, *Psychoanalysis and American Medicine*, and by J. A. P. Millet, "Psychoanalysis in the United States," in Franz Alexander, Samuel Eisenstein, and Martin Grotjahn, eds., *Psychoanalytic Pioneers* (New York: Basic Books, Inc., 1966), pp. 547–596. Contemporary observations are in Gregory Zilboorg et al., "Present Trends in Psychoanalytic Theory and Practice," *Bulletin of the Menninger Clinic*, 8 (1944), 3–17.
5. See, for example, Franz Alexander, "Psychoanalysis Comes of Age," *Psychoanalytic Quarterly*, 8 (1939), 299–306; Laura Fermi, *Illustrious Immigrants: The Intellectual Migration from Europe, 1930–41* (Chicago: University of Chicago Press, 1968), especially chap. 6.
6. David A. Hollinger, "Ethnic Diversity, Cosmopolitanism and the Emergence of the American Liberal Intelligentsia," *American Quarterly*, 27 (1975), 133–151. *Perspectives in American History*, 2 (1968).

7.   John C. Burnham, "Psychoanalysis in American Civilization Before 1918" (doc-
      toral dissertation, Stanford University, 1958), chap. 9. It would be easy but to
      some extent in bad taste to assemble the remarkable roster of the analyzed.
8.   Franz Alexander, "Psychoanalysis in Western Culture," *American Journal of
      Psychiatry*, 112 (1956), 694.
9.   In addition to works already cited, see F. H. Matthews, "The Americaniza-
      tion of Sigmund Freud: Adaptations of Psychoanalysis Before 1917," *Journal
      of American Studies*, 1 (1967), 39–62; N. G. Hale, Jr., *Freud and the Ameri-
      cans: The Beginnings of Psychoanalysis in the United States, 1876–1917* (New
      York: Oxford University Press, 1971); John C. Burnham, "The New Psychology:
      From Narcissism to Social Control" (reprinted herein as Chapter 5), in John
      Braeman, Robert H. Bremner, and David Brody, eds., *Change and Continuity
      in Twentieth-Century America: The 1920's* (Columbus: Ohio State University
      Press, 1968), pp. 351–398; and C. L. Covert, "Freud on the Front Page: Trans-
      mission of Freudian Ideas in the American Newspapers of the 1920's" (doctoral
      dissertation, Syracuse University, 1975).
10.   See *Bulletin of the American Psychoanalytic Association*, and B. D. Lewin and
      Helen Ross, *Psychoanalytic Education in the United States* (New York: W. W.
      Norton and Company, 1960).
11.   Karl Menninger, "Present Trends in Psychoanalytic Theory and Practice," *Bul-
      letin of the Menninger Clinic*, 8 (1944), 14–17; Lawrence S. Kubie, "The Di-
      lemma of the Analyst in a Troubled World," *Bulletin of the American Psycho-
      analytic Association*, 6 (1950), 1–4.
12.   Burnham, "The New Psychology"; John C. Burnham, "The Struggle Between
      Physicians and Paramedical Personnel in American Psychiatry, 1917–41," *Jour-
      nal of the History of Medicine and Allied Sciences*, 29 (1974), 93–106. An im-
      portant example of popularization is M. B. Ray, *Doctors of the Mind: The Story
      of Psychiatry* (Boston: Little, Brown and Company, 1942).
13.   F. C. Redlich, "The Psychiatrist in Caricature: An Analysis of Unconscious At-
      titudes Toward Psychiatry," *American Journal of Orthopsychiatry*, 20 (1950),
      560–571; R. Plank, "Portraits of Fictitious Psychiatrists," *American Imago*, 13
      (1956), 259–268; Charles Winick, "The Psychiatrist in Fiction," *Journal of Ner-
      vous and Mental Disease*, 136 (1963), 43–57.
14.   Maxwell Gitelson, "Psychoanalyst, U.S.A., 1955," *American Journal of Psy-
      chiatry*, 112 (1956), 700–701, was one among many who commented on this
      phenomenon. See, too, such discussions as J. D. Benjamin, "Psychoanalysis and
      Psychoanalytic Psychotherapy," *Psychoanalytic Quarterly*, 16 (1947), 169–176.
15.   R. S. Anderson et al., eds., *Neuropsychiatry in World War II*, 2 vols. (Washing-
      ton, DC: Office of the Surgeon General, Department of the Army, 1966–1973).
      Important examples were E. M. Stern, "Don't Let the Big Word Scare You,"
      Reader's Digest, May, 1944, pp. 104–106; E. D. Cooke, *All But Me and Thee:
      Psychiatry at the Foxhole Level* (Washington, DC: Infantry Journal Press, 1946);
      T. A. C. Rennie and L. E. Woodward, *Mental Health in Modern Society* (New
      York: Commonwealth Fund, 1948).
16.   William C. Menninger, "Psychiatry and the Army," *Psychiatry*, 7 (1944), 175–
      181; William C. Menninger, "Psychiatric Objectives in the Army," *American
      Journal of Psychiatry*, 102 (1945), 102–107; R. R. Grinker and J. P. Spiegel,

Men Under Stress (Philadelphia: Blakiston, 1945); Anderson, *Neuropsychiatry in World War II*.

17. Menninger, "Psychiatric Objectives in the Army," p. 102. See, similarly, *Psychoanalytic Quarterly*, 16 (1947), 294.

18. For example, see Abraham Myerson, "The Attitude of Neurologists, Psychiatrists and Psychologists Toward Psychoanalysis," *American Journal of Psychiatry*, 96 (1939), 623–641. One of the important events of the 1930's was the campaign of the Rockefeller Foundation to build up the specialty of psychiatry and fund research in that specialty and cognate disciplines. Although Rockefeller money was extremely important to psychoanalysts in particular cases (especially the Chicago group), most of the funds went to biologically oriented studies and to the older psychiatric establishment.

19. Frederic Wertham, "The Cult of Contentment," *New Republic*, 118 (1948), 22–25.

20. F. S. Wickware, "Psychoanalysis," *Life*, February 3, 1947, p. 98; Ernest Havemann, *The Age of Psychology* (New York: Simon and Schuster, 1957).

21. See such works as F. C. Redlich, "What the Citizen Knows About Psychiatry," *Mental Hygiene*, 34 (1950), 64–79, and the important document, Joint Commission on Mental Illness and Health, *Action for Mental Health* (New York: Basic Books, Inc., 1961); Jeanne L. Brand, "The National Mental Health Act of 1946: A Retrospect," *Bulletin of the History of Medicine*, 39 (1965), 231–245.

22. *Psychoanalytic Quarterly*, 16 (1947), 597. The best-known document is William C. Menninger, *Psychiatry in a Troubled World: Yesterday's War and Today's Challenge* (New York: Macmillan Company, 1948).

23. *The Rockefeller Foundation Annual Report*, 1934, p. 78.

24. Medical acceptance, at least in part, of psychoanalysis was of great importance. Alan Gregg, "The Place of Psychoanalysis in Medicine," in Franz Alexander and Helen Ross, eds., *Twenty Years of Psychoanalysis* (New York: W. W. Norton and Company, 1953), p. 47, made the point this way: "To begin with, medical men have for years regarded psychiatry as an island lying off the coast of the mainland of medicine, doubtless connected geologically with the mainland but not very accessible to less than adventurous spirits. For the past ten years psychiatry has been a sort of St. Michel, an island only when the tides of feeling are at flood. You need no reminder of the somewhat similar status accorded by psychiatrists to psychoanalysts."

25. James McKeen Cattell, "Some Psychological Experiments," *Science*, 63 (1926), 5.

26. Madison Bentley et al., "Dynamical Principles in Recent Psychology," *Psychological Monographs*, 30 (1921), 16.

27. For complete examination see David Shakow and David Rapaport, *The Influence of Freud on American Psychology* (New York: International Universities Press, 1964); Edwin G. Boring, H. S. Langfeld, and H. P. Weld, *Foundations of Psychology* (New York: John Wiley and Sons, 1948), pp. vii–viii; Burnham, "Psychoanalysis in American Civilization," p. 233.

28. Lawrence S. Kubie, "The Pros and Cons of a New Profession: A Doctorate in Medical Psychology," *Texas Reports on Biology and Medicine*, 12 (1954), 692–737.

29. See J. M. Reisman, *The Development of Clinical Psychology* (New York: Appleton-Century-Crofts Company, Inc., 1966); R. S. Garber, "The Relationship of Psychiatry to Medicine," *Psychiatry Digest*, 30 (1969), 11–15. And on Rogers, see H. I. Harris, review of White, *The Abnormal Personality*, in *Psychoanalytic Quarterly*, 17 (1948), 259.

30. The central document is R. W. White, "Motivation Reconsidered: The Concept of Competence," *Psychological Review*, 66 (1959), 297–333. Earlier examples are represented by D. M. Levy, "Animal Psychology in Its Relation to Psychiatry," in Franz Alexander and Helen Ross, eds., *Dynamic Psychiatry* (Chicago: University of Chicago Press, 1952), pp. 483–507.

31. Edwin G. Boring et al., *Psychoanalysis as Seen by Analyzed Psychologists* (Washington, DC: American Psychological Association, 1953); Shakow and Rapaport, *The Influence of Freud*; Reisman, *Development of Clinical Psychology*, pp. 296–303.

32. Henri Ellenberger, "A Comparison of European and American Psychiatry," *Bulletin of the Menninger Clinic*, 19 (1955), 43–44, 51. One well-known illustrative document was Charles Rolo, ed., *Psychiatry in American Life* (New York: Dell Publishing Company, Inc., 1966 [1963]).

33. For example, A. Auerback, "The Anti–Mental Health Movement," *American Journal of Psychiatry*, 120 (1963), 105–111.

34. One collection of typical statements is Benjamin Nelson et al., *Psychoanalysis and the Future: A Centenary Commemoration of the Birth of Sigmund Freud* (New York: National Psychological Association for Psychoanalysis, 1957); Walter Kaufmann, "Freud and the Tragic Virtues," *American Scholar*, 29 (1960), 469.

35. Burnham, "The New Psychology"; Christopher Lasch, *The New Radicalism in America (1889–1963): The Intellectual as a Social Type* (New York: Alfred A. Knopf, 1965), p. 146.

36. The basic document is Erik Erikson, *Childhood and Society* (New York: W. W. Norton and Company, 1950). Erikson himself of course harbored no such conservative ideas.

37. For example, G. J. Hinkle, "The Role of Freudianism in American Sociology" (doctoral dissertation, University of Wisconsin, 1951); R. A. Jones, "Freud and American Sociololgy," *Journal of the History of the Behavioral Sciences*, 10 (1974), 21–39.

38. Examples are H. J. Muller, "The New Psychology in the Old Fiction," *Saturday Review of Literature*, August 21, 1937, pp. 3–4; Bernard De Voto, "Freud's Influence on Literature," *Saturday Review of Literature*, October 7, 1939, pp. 10–11; Frederick J. Hoffman, *Freudianism and the Literary Mind, 1909–1949*, 2d ed. (New York: Grove Press, 1959 [1957]); W. David Sievers, *Freud on Broadway: A History of Psychoanalysis and the American Drama* (New York: Hermitage House Press, 1955); Louis Fraiberg, *Psychoanalysis and American Literary Criticism* (Detroit: Wayne State University Press, 1960).

39. See, for example, H. W. Brosin, "A Review of the Influence of Psychoanalysis on Current Thought," in Alexander and Ross, *Dynamic Psychiatry*, pp. 508–553, and the evidence offered in such works as Lawrence S. Kubie, "Psychiatry and the Films," *Hollywood Quarterly*, 2 (1947), 113–117, and Franklin Fearing, "Psychology and the Films," *Hollywood Quarterly*, 2 (1947), 118–121.

40. Instinctual drive has been discussed in John C. Burnham, "The Medical Origins and Cultural Use of Freud's Instinctual Drive Theory" (reprinted herein as Chapter 4), *Psychoanalytic Quarterly*, 43 (1974), 193–217.
41. Burnham, "Psychoanalysis in American Civilization," pp. 368–371.
42. John C. Burnham, "The Progressive Era Revolution in American Attitudes Toward Sex" (reprinted herein as Chapter 10), *Journal of American History*, 59 (1973), 885–908; Burnham, "The New Psychology." See for example, T. Benedek, review of Kinsey et al., *Sexual Behavior in the Human Female*, in *Psychoanalytic Quarterly*, 23 (1954), 272–279.
43. For example, G. O. Taylor, *The Passages of Thought: Psychological Representation in the American Novel, 1870–1900* (New York: Oxford University Press, 1969); A. Michael Sulman, "The Freudianization of the American Child: The Impact of Psychoanalysis in Popular Periodical Literature in the United States, 1919–1939" (doctoral dissertation, University of Pittsburgh, 1972).
44. Many good examples are discussed in Richard King, *The Party of Eros, Radical Social Thought and the Realm of Freedom* (Chapel Hill: University of North Carolina Press, 1972).
45. For example, Parker Tyler, "An American Theater Motif: The Psychodrama," *American Quarterly*, 15 (1963), 140–151.
46. This problem is discussed in some relevant detail in Burnham, *Psychoanalysis and American Medicine*. See L. L. Havens, *Approaches to the Mind: Movement of the Psychiatric Schools from Sects Toward Science* (Boston: Little, Brown and Company, 1973).
47. Gitelson, "Psychoanalyst, U.S.A., 1955," p. 705. One of the most widely quoted documents was Lionel Trilling, *Freud and the Crisis of Our Culture* (Boston: Beacon Press, 1955). Norman Mailer in 1968 traced the beginnings of disenchantment with psychoanalysis back to a time when "people in analysis began to be subjected to men who were no longer cultivated, poetic, deep and engaged in intellectual activity." Quoted in J. Leo, "Psychoanalysis Reaches a Crossroad," *New York Times*, August 4, 1968.

Chapter 7

Acknowledgment: An earlier version of this paper was read at the annual meeting of the American Historical Association in Boston, December, 1970.

1. This chapter therefore is not to be interpreted as an attempt at anything like an exhaustive survey. Charles E. Rosenberg of the University of Pennsylvania has completed an essay (as yet unpublished) entitled "Sexuality, Class, and Role in Nineteenth-Century America," focusing on historiographical and conceptual problems of that century [later published as "Sexuality, Class and Role in 19th-Century America," *American Quarterly*, 25 (1973), 131–153].
2. Sidney Ditzion, *Marriage, Morals and Sex in America: A History of Ideas* (New York: Bookman Associates, 1953).
3. William Wasserstrom, *Heiress of All the Ages: Sex and Sentiment in the Genteel Tradition* (Minneapolis: University of Minnesota Press, 1959); James R. McGovern, "The American Woman's Pre–World War I Freedom in Manners and

Morals," *Journal of American History*, 55 (1968), 315–333. My generalization is based primarily upon material indexed in American Historical Association, *Writings on American History* (Washington, DC: American Historical Association, 1902–); Margaret Sanger, for example, has received attention primarily because of her female-status interests rather than her contributions to the sexual revolution, and this attention is confirmed in a recent scholarly biography that emphasizes her radicalism: David M. Kennedy, *Birth Control in America: The Career of Margaret Sanger* (New Haven, CT: Yale University Press, 1970).

4. Henry Bamford Parkes, "Morals and Law Enforcement in Colonial New England," *New England Quarterly*, 5 (1932), 431. The original article in this tradition is Charles Francis Adams, "Some Phases of Sexual Morality in Church Discipline in Colonial New England," *Proceedings of the Massachusetts Historical Society*, 2d ser., 6 (1891), 477–516.

5. Emil Oberholzer, Jr., *Delinquent Saints: Disciplinary Action in the Early Congregational Churches of Massachusetts* (New York: Columbia University Press, 1956); Edmund S. Morgan, *The Puritan Family: Essays on Religion and Domestic Relations in Seventeenth-Century New England* (Boston: Trustees of the Public Library, 1944); "The Puritans and Sex," *New England Quarterly*, 15 (1942), 591–607.

6. Standard works include Arthur W. Calhoun, *A Social History of the American Family*, 3 vols. (New York: Barnes and Noble, Inc., 1960 reprint); Alice Felt Tyler, *Freedom's Ferment: Phases of American Social History from the Colonial Period to the Outbreak of the Civil War* (Minneapolis: University of Minnesota Press, 1944).

7. A survey of recent viewpoints is to be found in George P. Rawick, *From Sundown to Sunup: The Making of the Black Community* (Westport, CT: Greenwood Press, 1971).

8. Paul S. Boyer, *Purity in Print: The Vice-Society Movement and Book Censorship in America* (New York: Charles Scribner's Sons, 1968).

9. Some beginnings have been made in two unpublished doctoral dissertations: Stephen W. Nissenbaum, "Careful Love: Sylvester Graham and the Emergence of Victorian Sexual Theory in America, 1830–1840" (University of Wisconsin, 1968); and Graham J. Barker-Benfield, "The Horrors of the Half Known Life: Aspects of the Exploitation of Women by Men" (University of California, Los Angeles, 1968).

10. William L. O'Neill, *Divorce in the Progressive Era* (New Haven, CT: Yale University Press, 1967); another volume representing in places an earlier beginning in this direction is Henry F. May, *The End of American Innocence: A Study of the First Years of Our Own Time, 1912–1917* (New York: Alfred A. Knopf, 1959). Some discussion is to be found in John C. Burnham, "The Progressive Era Revolution in American Attitudes Toward Sex" (reprinted herein as Chapter 10), *Journal of American History*, 59 (1973), 885–908.

11. Sophie D. Aberle and George W. Corner, *Twenty-Five Years of Sex Research: History of the National Research Council Committee for Research in Problems of Sex, 1922–1947* (Philadelphia: W. B. Saunders Company, 1953); James H. Jones, "Origins of the Institute for Sex Research" (doctoral dissertation, Indiana University, 1972).

12. Carl Russell Fish, *The Rise of the Common Man, 1830–1850* (New York: Macmillan Company, 1927), pp. 152–155; William E. Lingelbach, ed., *Approaches to American Social History* (New York: Appleton-Century Company, Inc., 1937), discusses the series.

13. Nelson M. Blake, *The Road to Reno: A History of Divorce in the United States* (New York: Macmillan Company, 1962).

14. Vern L. Bullough has surveyed the European work and put it in a modern context, *The History of Prostitution* (New Hyde Park, NY: University Books, 1964).

15. John Sirjamaki, *The American Family in the Twentieth Century* (Cambridge, MA: Harvard University Press, 1953). Recently groups have been formed within the historical profession to study the family and the child, and these groups give hope that this aspect of historical study will be brought back into the discipline. The fact that a number of non-historians have been drawn into the vacuum means that it is very difficult to know just where it might be advisable to look. For example, in the introduction to a book designed apparently for the popular sex market, Aron M. Krich, a psychotherapist, has provided a quite enlightening overview of aspects of American sex research: Aron M. Krich, ed., *The Sexual Revolution* (New York: Dell Publishing Company, Inc., 1963), pp. vii–xxviii.

16. Herbert Marcuse, *Eros and Civilization* (Boston: Beacon Press, 1966); Norman O. Brown, *Life Against Death: The Psychoanalytical Meaning of History* (Middletown, CT: Wesleyan University Press, 1959). I am interpreting the use that both of these authors make of the putative death instinct as a negation of sex and therefore dependent upon it. See also Robert H. Wiebe, *The Search for Order, 1877–1920* (New York: Hill and Wang, 1967).

17. Two excellent examples are the important papers presented in 1970 at the first session ever held on the subject of sex in history at the annual meetings of the American Historical Association: Edward Shorter, "Sexual Behavior in Nineteenth-Century Europe," and Paul A. Robinson, "Romantic Sexual Theory."

18. Earl E. Thorpe, *Eros and Freedom in Southern Life and Thought* (Durham, NC: Seeman Printery, 1967).

19. Winthrop D. Jordan, *White over Black: American Attitudes Toward the Negro, 1550–1812* (Chapel Hill: University of North Carolina Press, 1968).

20. Using Richard von Krafft-Ebing and his congeners in conjunction with material from legal sources is particularly unfortunate because so much of the exotic in early sexology came from court records. In American history, especially, overtly sexual monographic articles tend overwhelmingly to be based upon legal evidence and indeed often have appeared in law journals. Andrew Sinclair, *The Better Half: The Emancipation of the American Woman* (New York: Harper and Row Publishers, Inc., 1965), has made a beginning at bringing sexual considerations to the history of women's rights and thus reversing the use of women's rights themes for burying sexual matters.

21. Elizabeth Scarborough Goodman, "The History of Marriage Counseling Research: A Quantitative Study" (doctoral dissertation, University of New Hampshire, 1972); Jones, "Origins of the Institute for Sex Research," takes the story

up to 1948, and he has more work under way. The professional, institutional history is an improvement on such popularizations as Edward M. Brecher, *The Sex Researchers* (Boston: Little, Brown and Company, 1969), and recent biographical and memoir material written by former members of Alfred Kinsey's staff.

22. A major history is being written by Vern L. Bullough [published as *Sexual Variance in Society and History* (New York: John Wiley and Sons, 1976)], which includes long sections on the United States. Much of the traditional, popular material is summarized and extended in Arno Karlen's *Sexuality and Homosexuality: A New View* (New York: W. W. Norton and Company, 1971).

23. Peter Gabriel Filene of the University of North Carolina is at present working on this subject [*Him/Her/Self: Sex Roles in Modern America* (New York: Harcourt Brace Jovanovich, 1975)]; see also Rosenberg, "Sexuality, Class and Role."

24. Carroll Smith-Rosenberg, "Beauty, the Beast and the Militant Woman: A Case Study in Sex Roles and Social Stress in Jacksonian America," *American Quarterly*, 23 (1971), 562–584.

25. A series of studies is currently being completed by R. Christian Johnson of the University of Wisconsin, Green Bay, bringing in such factors as social status and social class.

26. Roy Lubove, "The Progressives and the Prostitute," *The Historian*, 24 (1962), 308–330; John C. Burnham, "The Social Evil Ordinance—A Social Experiment in Nineteenth-Century St. Louis," *Missouri Historical Society Bulletin*, 27 (1971), 203–217; John C. Burnham, "Medical Inspection of Prostitutes in America in the Nineteenth Century: The St. Louis Experiment and Its Sequel" (reprinted herein as Chapter 9), *Bulletin of the History of Medicine*, 45 (1971), 203–218; Jeremy P. Felt, "Vice Reform as a Political Technique: The Committee of Fifteen and the Overthrow of the Croker Regime in New York, 1900–1901," *New York History*, 54 (1973), 24–51; and work in progress by Felt on the turn-of-the-century period and by James L. Wunsch of the University of Chicago on the 1870–1900 era [see Chapter 10 herein].

27. David Pivar, *Purity Crusade* (Westport, CT: Greenwood Press, 1973).

Chapter 8

Acknowledgment: The author is grateful to Kevin White for suggestions. The original conference was sponsored by the City University of New York, and my paper is revised and published with the encouragement of Grace Ditzion.

1. John C. Burnham, "American Historians and the Subject of Sex" (reprinted herein as Chapter 7), *Societas*, 2 (1972), 307–316.

2. For example, Carroll Smith-Rosenberg and Charles E. Rosenberg, "The Female Animal: Medical and Biological Views of Woman and Her Role in Nineteenth-Century America," *Journal of American History*, 60 (1973), 332–356.

3. Examples include Charles Rembar, *The End of Obscenity: The Trials of Lady Chatterley, Tropic of Cancer, and Fanny Hill* (New York: Simon and Schuster, 1968); Felice Flanery Lewis, *Literature, Obscenity, and Law* (Carbondale: Southern Illinois University Press, 1976), showing the influence of literary clas-

sics in opening up public acceptance of candid expression; and Paul P. Somers, Jr., and Nancy Pogel, "Pornography," in M. Thomas Inge, ed., *Concise Histories of American Popular Culture* (Westport, CT: Greenwood Press, 1982), pp. 271–279, which includes a bibliography. Richard Christian Johnson, "Anthony Comstock: Reform, Vice, and the American Way" (doctoral dissertation, University of Wisconsin, 1973), shows how a historian can enrich the subject as he rehabilitates Comstock to some extent.

4. The promise of what might follow, for example, since the publication of the excellent survey of material covering the United States before 1900, by Estelle B. Freedman, "Sexuality in Nineteenth-Century America: Behavior, Ideology, and Politics," *Reviews in American History*, 10 (1982), 196–215, it seems to me has not even begun to be fulfilled. In spite of the recent decline in the rate of appearance, the amount of relevant historical writing produced just since the early 1970's is so great that I can of course discuss specifically and cite only a tiny fraction of the whole. A number of bibliographies now exist to open up the subject—and chronicle the growth of historical activity. They include not only references in the monographic works but such special subject works as Vern L. Bullough et al., eds., *An Annotated Bibliography of Homosexuality*, 2 vols. (New York: Garland Publishing, Inc., 1976), I, 37–66; Vern L. Bullough et al., *A Bibliography of Prostitution* (New York: Garland Publishing, Inc., 1977), pp. 128–168. Still another annotated bibliography that, although focused only on women, contains a useful compilation of a substantial part of the literature is Nancy Sahli, *Women and Sexuality in America: A Bibliography* (Boston: G. K. Hall and Company, 1984); these latter annotations unfortunately are not particularly well informed.

5. Robert A. Padgug, "Sexual Matters: On Conceptualizing Sexuality in History," *Radical History Review*, Spring/Summer, 1979, pp. 3–23, struggles in an enlightening way with the tensions between extending sexuality to everything and concentrating on genital activity. Vern L. Bullough, "Teaching the History of Sex," *History Teacher*, 12 (1979), 329–336.

6. See, for example, Daniel Blake Smith, "The Study of the Family in Early America: Trends, Problems, and Prospects," *William and Mary Quarterly*, 39 (1982), 3–28.

7. Ronald G. Walters, "Sexual Matters as Historical Problems: A Framework of Analysis," *Societas*, 6 (1976), 157–175. Thomas L. Altherr, ed., *Procreation or Pleasure?: Sexual Attitudes in American History* (Malabar, FL: Robert E. Krieger Publishing Company, 1983).

8. Vern L. Bullough and Martha Voght, "Homosexuality and Its Confusion with the 'Secret Sin' in Pre-Freudian America," *Journal of the History of Medicine and Allied Sciences*, 28 (1973), 143–155.

9. Arthur N. Gilbert, "Doctor, Patient, and Onanist Diseases in the Nineteenth Century," *Journal of the History of Medicine and Allied Sciences*, 30 (1975), 217–234.

10. H. Tristram Engelhardt, Jr., "The Disease of Masturbation: Values and the Concept of Disease," *Bulletin of the History of Medicine*, 48 (1974), 234–248.

11. A partial exception may be the discussion of the bicycle in the 1890's in James C. Whorton, *Crusaders for Fitness: The History of American Health Reform-*

ers (Princeton, NJ: Princeton University Press, 1982), pp. 327–328. Another possibility, suggested by R. P. Neuman, "Clio, Eros, and Psyche: Separation, Divorce, or Marriage," *Psychohistory Review*, 7 (1978), 11–12, is the electric vibrator, described by sex therapist Virginia Johnson as the only innovation in sexual technique in modern times (as quoted in Janice M. Irvine, "Disorders of Desire: The Professionalization of Sexology" [doctoral dissertation, Brandeis University, 1984], p. 19). A recent work, however, Rachel Maines, "The Vibrator and Its Predecessor Technologies" (paper presented at the meetings of the Society for the Social Study of Science and the Society for the History of Technology, Pittsburgh, October, 1986), discusses the new technology from a social/ideological viewpoint.

12.   Stephen Kern, *Anatomy and Destiny: A Cultural History of the Human Body* (Indianapolis: Bobbs Merrill Company, 1975). Vern L. Bullough, *Sexual Variance in Society and History* (New York: John Wiley and Sons, 1976). Paul A. Robinson, *The Modernization of Sex: Havelock Ellis, Alfred Kinsey, William Masters, and Virginia Johnson* (New York: Harper and Row Publishers, Inc., 1976).

13.   Gordon S. Haight, "Male Chastity in the Nineteenth Century," *Contemporary Review*, 219 (1971), 252–262.

14.   See, for example, John C. Burnham, "The Progressive Era Revolution in American Attitudes Toward Sex" (reprinted herein as Chapter 10), *Journal of American History*, 59 (1973), 885–908.

15.   See, for example, Ronald G. Walters, ed., *Primers for Prudery: Sexual Advice to Victorian America* (Englewood Cliffs, NJ: Prentice-Hall, Inc., 1974).

16.   An epitome of the ambiguous place of sexuality in women's history appears conveniently in a survey, Barbara Sicherman et al., *Recent United States Scholarship on the History of Women* (Washington, DC: American Historical Association, [1983]).

17.   Linda Gordon, *Woman's Body, Woman's Right: A Social History of Birth Control in America* (New York: Grossman Publishers, 1976), especially p. xii.

18.   Freedman, "Sexuality in Nineteenth-Century America." The prescriptive writings issue is taken up again later.

19.   Carroll Smith-Rosenberg, "The New Woman and the New History," *Feminist Studies*, 3 (1975), 185–198. Carroll Smith-Rosenberg, "The Female World of Love and Ritual: Relations Between Women in Nineteenth-Century America," *Signs*, 1 (1975), 1–29.

20.   See, for example, Mary P. Ryan, *Womanhood in America: From Colonial Times to the Present* (New York: New Viewpoints, 1975). Peter Gabriel Filene, *Him/Her/Self: Sex Roles in Modern America* (New York: Harcourt Brace Jovanovich, 1975). And see the even more speculative use of sex role in American history in the extension of James R. McGovern's thesis of the virility impulse in Progressivism, Joe L. Dubbert, "Progressivism and the Masculinity Crisis," *Psychoanalytic Review*, 61 (1974), 443–445.

21.   Rosalind Rosenberg, *Beyond Separate Spheres: Intellectual Roots of Modern Feminism* (New Haven, CT: Yale University Press, 1982); Diana Long Hall, "Biology, Sex Hormones and Sexism in the 1920's," in Carol C. Gould and Marx W. Wartofsky, eds., *Women and Philosophy: Toward a Theory of Liberation* (New York: G. P. Putnam's Sons, 1976), pp. 81–96.

22. See, for example, Joan Kelly, "The Doubled Vision of Feminist Theory: A Postscript to the 'Women and Power' Conference," *Feminist Studies*, 5 (1979), 216–227.

23. Ruth Rosen, *The Lost Sisterhood: Prostitution in America, 1900–1918* (Baltimore: Johns Hopkins University Press, 1982), especially p. 133. Rosen's view is the more curious in that in her book she revises downward from earlier work her estimate of the use of compulsion and depends upon interview records of explicit motivations. The most disturbing omission from the literature on exploitation/autonomy is the good evidence that for generations a large percentage of American prostitutes were mentally retarded.

24. Leslie Fishbein, "Harlot or Heroine? Changing Views of Prostitution, 1870–1920," *The Historian*, 43 (1980), 23–35, for example, focuses on perceptions that changed, rather than actual transformations in the phenomenon that went by the name of prostitution in any particular period.

25. Marion S. Goldman, *Gold Diggers and Silver Miners: Prostitution and Social Life on the Comstock Lode* (Ann Arbor: University of Michigan Press, 1981). Anne M. Butler, *Daughters of Joy, Sisters of Misery: Prostitutes in the American West, 1865–90* (Urbana: University of Illinois Press, 1985). Claudia D. Johnson, "The Guilty Third Tier: Prostitution in Nineteenth-Century American Theaters," *American Quarterly*, 27 (1975), 574–584.

26. John D'Emilio, *Sexual Politics, Sexual Communities: The Making of a Homosexual Minority in the United States, 1940–1970* (Chicago: University of Chicago Press, 1983). The *Journal of Homosexuality* contains a substantial proportion of historical articles but not many on American subjects; bibliographies covering such materials include Bullough et al., *An Annotated Bibliography of Homosexuality*, and William Parker, "Homosexuality in History: An Annotated Bibliography," *Journal of Homosexuality*, 6 (1980–1981), 191–210.

27. Jonathan Katz, ed., *Gay American History: Lesbians and Gay Men in the U.S.A.* (New York: Thomas Y. Crowell Company, 1976). Gregory Sprague, "Male Homosexuality in Western Culture: The Dilemma of Identity and Subculture in Historical Research," *Journal of Homosexuality*, 10 (1984), 29–43; Richard J. Hoffman, "Clio, Fallacies, and Homosexuality," *Journal of Homosexuality*, 10 (1984), 45–51.

28. Martha Vicinus, "Sexuality and Power: A Review of Current Work in the History of Sexuality," *Feminist Studies*, 8 (1982), 133–156. See the gentle comments of James Reed, *The Birth Control Movement and American Society: From Private Vice to Public Virtue*, 2d ed. (Princeton, NJ: Princeton University Press, 1984), pp. xv–xxiii.

29. The line between consciousness-raising and titillation is always a fine one, as witness the current interpretations of publications of the past of the *Maria Monk* variety.

30. A scholarly example is John S. Haller, Jr., and Robin M. Haller, *The Physician and Sexuality in Victorian America* (Urbana: University of Illinois Press, 1974). See also the controversial volume, Graham J. Barker-Benfield, *The Horrors of the Half-Known Life: Male Attitudes Toward Women and Sexuality in Nineteenth-Century America* (New York: Harper and Row Publishers, Inc., 1976).

31. Most have missed the conservative nature of sexual liberation, commented on

historically, for example, by Regina Markell Morantz, "The Scientist as Sex Crusader: Alfred C. Kinsey and American Culture," *American Quarterly*, 29 (1977), 563–589.

32. A notable and enlightening attempt to handle some of this kind of material is found in William R. Leach, *True Love and Perfect Union: The Feminist Reform of Sex and Society* (New York: Basic Books, Inc., 1980).

33. A good example of a scholar's attempt to overcome ahistorical viewpoints is Nancy Sahli, "Smashing: Women's Relationships Before the Fall," *Chrysalis*, no. 8 (1979), 17–27; and see, too, Christina Simmons, "Companionate Marriage and the Lesbian Threat," *Frontiers*, 4 (1979), 54–59. Richard C. Robertiello, "The Decline and Fall of Sex," *Journal of Sex Research*, 12 (1976), 70–73. Herman R. Lantz, "Romantic Love in the Pre-Modern Period: A Sociological Commentary," *Journal of Social History*, 15 (1982), 349–370, surveys some of the problems.

34. Joseph A. McFalls, Jr., and George S. Masnick, "Birth Control and the Fertility of the Black Population, 1880–1980," *Journal of Family History*, 6 (1981), 89–106. Sheldon S. Cohen, " 'To Parts of the World Unknown': The Circumstances of Divorce in Connecticut, 1750–1797," *Canadian Review of American Studies*, 11 (1980), 275–293.

35. Notable examples include Haller and Haller, *The Physician and Sexuality*; James C. Mohr, *Abortion in America: The Origins and Evolution of National Policy, 1800–1900* (New York: Oxford University Press, 1978), who describes the remarkable rise and fall of abortion in the mid–nineteenth century; Reed, *The Birth Control Movement*; and George S. Masnick and Joseph A. McFalls, Jr., "A New Perspective on the Twentieth-Century American Fertility Swing," *Journal of Family History*, 1 (1976), 217–244.

36. Examples include Lawrence Foster, *Religion and Sexuality: The Shakers, the Mormons, and the Oneida Community* (New York: Oxford University Press, 1981); and Louis J. Kern, *An Ordered Love: Sex Roles and Sexuality in Victorian Utopias—The Shakers, the Mormons, and the Oneida Community* (Chapel Hill: University of North Carolina Press, 1981), who uses the communitarians as barometers of Americans' attempts to find a sinless love. Charles A. Cannon, "The Awesome Power of Sex: The Polemical Campaign Against Mormon Polygamy," *Pacific Historical Review*, 43 (1974), 61–82, explores another aspect of the symbolic importance of one group.

37. For example, Hal D. Sears, *The Sex Radicals: Free Love in High Victorian America* (Lawrence: Regents Press of Kansas, 1977); Madeleine B. Stern, "Some Radical Concepts of Sex and Marriage in Nineteenth-Century America," *Prospects*, 2 (1976), 147–166. Taylor Stoehr, *Free Love in America: A Documentary History* (New York: AMS Press, 1979), especially p. 7, notes ironically that ultimately free love won out—but under different guises and bolstered by arguments different from those to which nineteenth-century advocates were accustomed. A particularly important work is Christine Clare Simmons, "Marriage in the Modern Manner: Sexual Radicalism and Reform in America, 1914–1941" (doctoral dissertation, Brown University, 1982).

38. William Simon and John H. Gagnon, "Sex Talk—Public and Private," *Etc.*, 25 (1968), 173–191. In general, American historians continue to be more comfort-

able with cultural rather than biological (or class-associated biological) explanations; see, for example, Daniel Scott Smith and Michael S. Hindus, "Premarital Pregnancy in America, 1640–1971: An Overview Interpretation," *Journal of Interdisciplinary History*, 5 (1965), 537–570. The question of some biological factors is reviewed in Jane Menken, James Trussell, and Susan Watkins, "The Nutrition Fertility Link: An Evaluation of the Evidence," *Journal of Interdisciplinary History*, 11 (1981), 425–441, who conclude that except in famine conditions, social factors such as breast feeding customs, migration, and stress mediated the impact of nutritional factors.

39. See, for example, Herman R. Lantz, Raymond L. Schmitt, and Richard Herman, "The Preindustrial Family in America: A Further Examination of Early Magazines," *American Journal of Sociology*, 79 (1973), 566–588; Stephen W. Nissenbaum, *Sex, Diet, and Debility in Jacksonian America: Sylvester Graham and Health Reform* (Westport, CT: Greenwood Press, 1980); Clara Ann Bowler, "Carted Whores and White Shrouded Apologies: Slander in the County Courts of Seventeenth-Century Virginia," *Virginia Magazine of History and Biography*, 85 (1977), 411–426; and the sophisticated example offered by Lewis Perry, *Childhood, Marriage, and Reform: Henry Clarke Wright 1797–1870* (Chicago: University of Chicago Press, 1980). Still another kind of example, attempting to correlate with behavior, is Steven E. Brown, "Sexuality and the Slave Community," *Phylon*, 42 (1981), 1–10. Perhaps the most notable example is Carroll Smith-Rosenberg, *Disorderly Conduct: Visions of Gender in Victorian America* (New York: Alfred A. Knopf, 1985). Ellen K. Rothman, *Hands and Hearts: A History of Courtship in America* (New York: Basic Books, Inc., 1984).

40. See, among other publications, Larry M. Lance and Christina Y. Berry, "Has There Been a Sexual Revolution? An Analysis of Human Sexuality Messages in Popular Music, 1968–1977," *Journal of Popular Culture*, 15 (1981), 155–164; Ellen Ross, "'The Love Crisis': Couples Advice Books of the Late 1970s," *Signs*, 6 (1980), 109–122. John Modell, "Normative Aspects of American Marriage Timing Since World War II," *Journal of Family History*, 5 (1980), 210–234.

41. Compare the argument made by Roger Thompson, *Sex in Middlesex: Popular Mores in a Massachusetts County, 1649–1699* (Amherst: University of Massachusetts Press, 1986), that his evidence from the seventeenth century, at least, has substantial validity if interpreted correctly.

42. Carl N. Degler, "What Ought to Be and What Was: Women's Sexuality in the Nineteenth Century," *American Historical Review*, 79 (1974), 1467–1490; Clelia Duel Mosher, *The Mosher Survey: Sexual Attitudes of Forty-Five Victorian Women*, James MaHood and Kristine Wenburg, eds. (New York: Arno Press, 1980); and, for example, William G. Shade, "'A Mental Passion': Female Sexuality in Victorian America," *International Journal of Women's Studies*, 1 (1978), 13–29.

43. Martin Bauml Duberman, "'Writhing Bedfellows': 1826; Two Young Men from Antebellum South Carolina's Ruling Elite Share 'Extravagant Delight,'" *Journal of Homosexuality*, 6 (1980–1981), 85–101. Duberman went to much trouble to explore the social setting and significance.

44. Examples include Regina Markell Morantz, "The Lady and Her Physician," in Mary S. Hartman and Lois Banner, eds., *Clio's Consciousness Raised* (New

York: Harper and Row Publishers, Inc., 1974), pp. 38–53; Wilson Yates, "Birth Control Literature and the Medical Profession in Nineteenth Century America," *Journal of the History of Medicine*, 21 (1976), 42–54.

45. Smith-Rosenberg, *Disorderly Conduct*. Part of her work, on the debate over the timing and meaning of ideal female behavior and changes in it, extends another notable contribution, Nancy F. Cott, "Passionlessness: An Interpretation of Victorian Sexual Ideology, 1790–1850," *Signs*, 4 (1978), 219–236.

46. Charles E. Rosenberg, "Sexuality, Class and Role in 19th Century America," *American Quarterly*, 25 (1973), 131–153. Rosenberg of course took account of the complexity of the culture. See, similarly, Shade, "'A Mental Passion.'"

47. David L. Lewis, "Sex and the Automobile: From Rumble Seats to Rockin' Vans," *Michigan Quarterly Review*, 19 (1980–1981), 518–528. Lee A. Gladwin, "Tobacco and Sex: Some Factors Affecting Non-Marital Sexual Behavior in Colonial Virginia," *Journal of Social History*, 12 (1978), 57–75, suggests that sexual institutions were able to withstand economic pressures, at least.

48. Peter Gardella, *Innocent Ecstasy: How Christianity Gave America an Ethic of Sexual Pleasure* (New York: Oxford University Press, 1985).

49. See the excellent pioneer work, Kathy Peiss, "'Charity Girls' and City Pleasures: Historical Notes on Working-Class Sexuality, 1880–1920," in Ann Snitow, Christine Stansell, and Sharon Thompson, eds., *Powers of Desire: The Politics of Sexuality* (New York: Monthly Review Press, 1983), pp. 74–87.

Chapter 9

1. This debate can be found most easily by consulting the publications of the international purity movement, in its late stages in the United States in *The Philanthropist* (continues as *Vigilance*). The confusion over statistics is spelled out in detail in *Conférence internationale pour la prophylaxie de la syphilis et des maladies vénériennes*, 2 vols. (Brussels: H. Lamartin, 1899–1900).

2. A convenient summary of the history of reglementation is to be found in Vern L. Bullough, *The History of Prostitution* (New Hyde Park, NY: University Books, 1964), pp. 166–172. More detailed accounts are in C. J. Lecour, *La prostitution á Paris et á Londres, 1789–1870* (Paris: P. Asselin, 1870); Yves Guyot, *Prostitution under the Regulation System*, trans. by Edgar Beckit Truman (London: G. Redway, 1884).

3. George Rosen, "The Fate of the Concept of Medical Police, 1780–1890," *Centaurus*, 5 (1956), 97–111.

4. It should of course be recognized that many enterprising persons engaged in the prostitution business arranged to have the girls and women in their charge inspected regularly by a physician, simply as a matter of public relations and good business. The subject of the present paper is rather the official attempts to impose inspection of all prostitutes and hospitalization of those ill with venereal disease, by law, as a public health measure. There were a number of cases in which the police of a city, with or without the cooperation of the board of health, enforced an unofficial or unrecognized reglementation, usually by threatening to arrest prostitutes who refused to take medical treatment. See,

for example, Arthur C. Bauer, "The Regulation of Prostitution as a Hygienic Measure," *Cincinnati Lancet-Clinic*, n.s. 33 (1894), 411–416. An even more unofficial effort is described by Julius Rosenstirn, *Our Nation's Health Endangered by Poisonous Infection Through the Social Malady: The Protective Work of the Municipal Clinic of San Francisco and Its Fight for Existence* (San Francisco: Town Talk Press, 1913).

5. A fragmentary account can be found in Aaron M. Powell, *State Regulation of Vice. Regulation Effort in America. The Geneva Congress* (New York: Wood and Holbrook, 1878). A summary history is Howard B. Woolston, *Prostitution in the United States Prior to the Entrance of the United States into the World War* (New York: Century Company, 1921).

6. Sigmund Lustgarten, "The Question of Legal Control of Prostitution in the United States of America," *Conférence internationale pour la prophylaxie de la syphilis*, II, app., p. 42. Two volumes provide general background: Abraham Flexner, *Prostitution in Europe* (New York: Century Company, 1914), and Woolston, *Prostitution in the United States*.

7. Owsei Temkin, "Zur Geschichte von 'Moral und Syphilis,'" *Archiv für Geschichte der Medizin*, 19 (1927), 331–348, especially pp. 346–347. See also Robert E. Riegel, "Changing American Attitudes Toward Prostitution," *Journal of the History of Ideas*, 29 (1968), 437–452.

8. William W. Sanger, *The History of Prostitution: Its Extent, Causes, and Effects Throughout the World* (New York: Medical Publishing Company, 1858; 2d. ed., 1898).

9. William J. Acton, *Prostitution, Considered in Its Moral, Social, and Sanitary Aspects, in London and Other Large Cities: With Proposals for the Mitigation and Prevention of Its Attendant Evils* (London: J. Churchill and Sons, 1857; 2d ed., 1870). A convenient summary of Acton's work is Peter Fryer, "Introduction," in William J. Acton, *Prostitution* (New York: Praeger, 1968 reprint), pp. 7–19.

10. "Venereal Contagion," *California Medical Gazette*, 1 (1869), 171.

11. Howard D. Kramer, "Early Municipal and State Boards of Health," *Bulletin of the History of Medicine*, 24 (1950), 503–529; Wilson G. Smillie, *Public Health, Its Promise for the Future: A Chronicle of the Development of Public Health in the United States, 1607–1914* (New York: Macmillan Company, 1955), sec. 3; John Duffy, *A History of Public Health in New York City, 1625–1866* (New York: Russell Sage Foundation, 1968), chap. 24; *St. Louis Board of Health Annual Report*, 1868–1874. Prostitution was just one among many urban problems with which cities in that period were trying to cope. The distress of San Francisco was typical: "There is occasion for alarm in this city at the spread of the evil. Formerly a few streets contained all of those to whom virtue was a by-word. Now, scarcely a prominent street but is represented by the gilded palaces of sin. . . . Instead of decreasing, the evil is spreading." (*San Francisco Chronicle*, July 6, 1871, p. 2.)

12. William L. Barrett, in *St. Louis Board of Health, Third Annual Report*, 1870, pp. 29-32.

13. See *Missouri Democrat*, July 6, 1870, p. 4; July 7, 1870, p. 4; *Missouri Republican*, July 7, 1870, pp. 2–3.

14.   Some highlights are reported in *Missouri Democrat*, September 1, 1870, p. 4; September 3, 1870, p. 4; January 6, 1872, p. 4; *Missouri Republican*, August 26, 1870, p. 2; *St. Louis Republican*, February 20, 1874, p. 5; March 3, 1874, p. 5; March 19, 1874, p. 1; March 28, 1874, p. 5; April 1, 1874, p. 5; April 3, 1874, p. 8; April 17, 1874, p. 8; May 23, 1874, p. 2; June 10, 1874, p. 5; *St. Louis Globe-Democrat*, January 14, 1876, p. 4; January 21, 1876, p. 3; May 20, 1876, p. 3. See J. Thomas Scharf, *History of Saint Louis City and County* (Philadelphia: L. H. Everts and Company, 1883), II, 1551; William Hyde and Howard L. Conard, eds., *Encyclopedia of the History of St. Louis: A Compendium of History and Biography for Ready Reference*, 4 vols. (New York: The Southern History Company, 1899), IV, 2093; *Laws of Missouri, General and Local Laws Passed at the Adjourned Session of the XXVIIth General Assembly* (Jefferson City, 1874), pp. 384–385. The St. Louis experiment has often been called the only system of compulsory inspection of prostitutes ever set up in the United States. There were other instances, one of which is noted later herein and another of which occurred just after the turn of the century. The latter was the effort of the mayor of Minneapolis, A. A. Ames, a physician, to establish reglementation by police regulations in 1902. The most effective opposition to this scheme was, interestingly enough, that of other physicians. See, for example, *Minneapolis Journal*, March 20, 1902, p. 4; Harold Zink, *City Bosses in the United States: A Study of Twenty Municipal Bosses* (Durham, NC: Duke University Press, 1930), pp. 344–349; Marion D. Shutter et al., *Report of the Vice Commission of Minneapolis* (Minneapolis: H. M. Hall, 1911), pp. 24–25. As is noted later, by the turn of the twentieth century a larger and larger proportion of influential physicians was being enrolled in the purity movement.

15.   Brown, who provides a good example of the advocates of reglementation, was a Scottish-born railroad executive and businessman. Nothing obvious in his background differentiates him from many opponents of the plan. For details on the non-medical politics and local history of the law, see John C. Burnham, "The Social Evil Ordinance—A Social Experiment in Nineteenth Century St. Louis," *Bulletin of the Missouri Historical Society*, 27 (1971), 203–217.

16.   For example, see *Missouri Democrat*, July 21, 1870, p. 4. Interestingly enough, there is no evidence that the important German population in St. Louis, including well-known German physicians, was in any way involved in bringing the Continental system to that city.

17.   See, for example, *Transactions of the Medical Association of the State of Missouri*, 1867–1879, *passim*.

18.   Minutes of the St. Louis Medical Society, Historical Library, St. Louis Medical Society, St. Louis, Missouri, May 21, 1870, p. 705, and June 11, 1870, p. 707. *Missouri Republican*, June 13, 1870, p. 2.

19.   Minutes of the St. Louis Medical Society, June 17, 1871, pp. 758–765; *Missouri Democrat*, June 18, 1871, p. 4.

20.   See, for example, *Missouri Democrat*, August 29, 1870, p. 4; *Missouri Republican*, February 28, 1873, p. 8; April 6, 1873, p. 6; April 9, 1873, p. 5; August 6, 1873, p. 8. Charlotte C. Eliot, *William Greenleaf Eliot: Minister, Educator, Philanthropist* (Boston: Houghton Mifflin, 1904), chap. 12. William Greenleaf Eliot, *A Practical Discussion of the Great Social Question of the Day* (New York: H. J. Hewitt, 1879).

21. See William L. Barrett, in *St. Louis Board of Health, Fourth Annual Report*, 1871, pp. 22–43; idem, *Sixth Annual Report*, 1873, pp. 29–48, reprinted as William L. Barret[t], *Prostitution in Its Relation to Public Health* [St. Louis, 1873].

22. *Medical Gazette*, 5 (1870), 82.

23. For example, see [D. G. Brinton?], "Why Exercise Control over Prostitution?" *Medical and Surgical Reporter*, 32 (1875), 495–496; James E. Washington, "A Social Evil Act Needed," *Nashville Journal of Medicine and Surgery*, 10 (1877), 175–183 (citing the St. Louis experiment); *Chicago Times*, October 29, 1870, p. 2; *San Francisco Chronicle*, July 6, 1871, p. 2; *Missouri Democrat*, August 29, 1870, p. 4; *St. Louis Republican*, February 1, 1874, p. 8; *Lancet* [Cincinnati], quoted in "The Social Evil," *Cincinnati Medical News*, 2 (1873), 122–129.

24. See J. H. Tate, "The Board of Health and Prostitution," *Cincinnati Medical Reporter*, 2 (1869), 97; J. J. Quinn, "The Social Evil," *Cincinnati Medical Advance*, 3 (1876), 579–581.

25. W. M. Chambers, in *Transactions of the American Medical Association*, 26 (1875), 237–238; *Public Health Papers and Reports*, 6 (1880), 411, also quoted in Sanger, *History of Prostitution*, 2d ed., p. 697. See, for example, *New York Tribune*, June 3, 1867, p. 5; *Journal of the Assembly of New York*, 1867, I, 561, 677; II, 1029, 1491, etc. See, in general, Powell, *State Regulation of Vice*.

26. See, for example, the controversy stirred up by the Cleveland Board of Health in 1882–1883; "The Care of Prostitutes in Cleveland," *Medical Record*, 23 (1883), 97–98; *Cleveland Herald*, January 30, 1883, p. 2.

27. Samuel D. Gross, "Syphilis in Its Relation to the National Health," *Transactions of the American Medical Association*, 25 (1874), 249–292.

28. J. Marion Sims, "Address of J. Marion Sims, M.D., President of the Association," *Transactions of the American Medical Association*, 27 (1876), 100–111, also published in part separately as *Legislation and "Contagious Diseases"* (Philadelphia: Collins, 1876). See, for example, J. R. Black, "Preventing the Extension of Syphilis," *Cincinnati Lancet and Observer*, 19 (1876), 1057–1063, who cited Sims's address.

29. See *Transactions of the American Medical Association*, 26 (1875), 226–228, 232–244; 27 (1876), 43.

30. A good example of the American literature on this subject is L. Duncan Bulkley, *Syphilis in the Innocent (Syphilis Insontium), Clinically and Historically Considered, with a Plan for Legal Control of the Disease* (New York: Bailey and Fairchild, 1894); Bulkley, interestingly enough, believed in the inspection of men as well as women.

31. See the discussion herein. A general summary of discoveries regarding syphilis is William Allen Pusey, *The History and Epidemiology of Syphilis* (Springfield, IL: Thomas, 1933), pp. 59–64; Charles C. Norris, *Gonorrhea in Women, Its Pathology, Symptomatology, Diagnosis, and Treatment; Together with a Review of the Rare Varieties of the Disease Which Occur in Men, Women and Children* (Philadelphia: W. B. Saunders Company, 1913), chap. 1, provides an excellent annotated account of discoveries about gonorrhea. For early examples, see Edward L. Keyes, Jr., *Venereal Diseases, Including Stricture of the Male Urethra* (New York: W. Wood and Company, 1880), and the reglementationist plea of Frederic Russell Sturgis, "The Hygiene of Syphilis," in A. H.

Buck, ed., *A Treatise on Hygiene and Public Health* (New York: W. Wood and Company, 1879), II, 537–544. A later summary was offered by James J. Walsh, reported in *Transactions of the American Society of Sanitary and Moral Prophylaxis*, 2 (1907–1908), 54: "We now knew that one out of every five persons who died in our insane asylums went there because of these social diseases. We knew that three fourths of all women operated on gave a history of one of these diseases. It was only within the past two decades that certain grave nervous affections, including locomotor ataxia, had been traced to these social evils." The new knowledge was popularized surprisingly quickly; see, for example, Henry M. Hurd, "The Relation of General Paresis and Syphilitic Insanity," *American Journal of Insanity*, 43 (1886), 1.

32. See, for example, Arne Barkhuus, "The Sanitary Conferences," *Ciba Symposium*, 1–2 (1943), 1563–1579, 1584; M. H. Henry, "The Discussion on the Prevention of Syphilis, with Reference to the Regulation of Prostitution, at the Third International Medical Congress, Held at Vienna, August, 1873—With Additional Remarks," *American Journal of Syphilography and Dermatology*, 5 (1874), 17–28; Louis Chéry, *Syphilis, maladies vénériennes et prostitution, esquisse d'hygiéne sociale, documents récents sur la législation des filles publiques et des maladies sexuelles* (Toulouse, France: Diron, [1911]), p. 72.

33. *Public Health Papers and Reports*, 8 (1882), 281–287, 329–336. Gihon had introduced the subject to the Association three years before, and in 1880 the Association had passed two resolutions calling the attention of public health authorities and legislators to the need for some kind of action; see Albert L. Gihon, "On the Protection of the Innocent and Helpless Members of the Community from Venereal Diseases and Their Consequences," *Public Health Papers and Reports*, 5 (1879), 55–65, and discussion, pp. 177–185; *Public Health Papers and Reports*, 6 (1880), 402–415, 426–431, 437–444; 7 (1881), 411–417, 423–428.

34. See, for example, *IIe Conférence internationale pour la prophylaxie de la syphilis et des maladies vénériennes*, 2 vols. (Brussels: H. Lamartin, 1902–1903).

35. Barrett, *St. Louis Board of Health, Fourth Annual Report*, p. 41. In the case of gonorrhea, technical difficulties inhibited the use of bacteriological techniques for detection and diagnosis. From the first reports of Neisser's discovery of the gonococcus, medical writers took much interest in the pathological and bacteriological issues raised. It was several decades, however, before bacteriological means were considered an essential part of diagnostic procedure. See, for instance, J. L. Milton, *On the Pathology and Treatment of Gonorrhoea and Spermatorrhoea* (New York: William Wood and Company, 1887), in which Neisser's work is recognized, but the discussion of the use of the microscope in diagnosis is limited (p. 19) to its failure as an extension of the usual visual methods of diagnosis. Later even skilled workers found it difficult to stain satisfactorily and to identify the gonococci for certain, and in particular stages of the disease, of course, these pathogens are very scarce. See, for example, Abraham L. Wolbarst, "Observations in the Diagnosis and Treatment of Acute Gonorrhea, with Special Reference to the Value of Protargol as a Therapeutic Agent," *Journal of Cutaneous and Genito-Urinary Diseases*, 19 (1901), 556–558, and the complete review of the technique and literature in David Thomson, *Gonorrhoea* (London:

Oxford Medical Publications, 1923), chaps. 3 and 12. By the 1910's, however, it was customary to demand "microscopic demonstration of the gonococcus . . . in every case." (Ernst Portner, *Genitourinary Diagnosis and Therapy for Urologists and General Practitioners*, trans. by Bransford Lewis [St. Louis: C. V. Mosby Company, 1913], p. 160.) In the late nineteenth century the difficulties of diagnosing gonorrhea in women by bacteriological examination seemed especially forbidding to physicians in the field. See, for example, the discussion in *Journal of Cutaneous and Genito-Urinary Diseases*, 9 (1891), 219–221; George Parker Holden and F. E. Doughty, *A Practical Working Handbook in the Diagnosis and Treatment of Diseases of the Genito-Urinary System, and Syphilis* (Philadelphia: Boericke, 1897), pp. 236–240. In 1895 W. R. Pryor of New York was led to assert that although inspection of public women might limit the spread of syphilis, the difficulties of detecting gonorrhea in prostitutes were so great as to render the procedure profitless; "Latent Gonorrhea in Women," *Journal of Cutaneous and Genito-Urinary Diseases*, 13 (1895), 94–95.

36. "Syphilis in the Female," *Medical Record*, 5 (1871), 538–539.

37. Edmund Andrews, in *Transactions of the American Medical Association*, 26 (1875), 233–236.

38. Edmund Andrews, "Venereal Diseases and Prostitution Under the License System of Europe—The Laws, Statistics, and Results of the System," *Chicago Medical Examiner*, 7 (1867), 603–616.

39. Edmund Andrews, "Prostitution and Its Sanitary Management," *Chicago Medical Examiner*, 12 (1871), 65–97, especially p. 90, also published in part separately (Chicago: n.p., 1871). For an example of the impact of Andrews's work, see "Should Prostitution Be Licensed?" *Pacific Medical and Surgical Journal*, 9 (1867), 294–299. Another example is R. A. Thomas, "A Few Observations on State Regulation of Prostitution," *Maryland Medical Journal*, 8 (1882), 469–472, 9 (1882), 31–37.

40. See, for example, W. L. Mussey, "Syphilis as a Menace to Public Health," *Cincinnati Lancet-Clinic*, n.s. 33 (1894), 133–137; Denslow Lewis, "What Should Be the Policy of the State Toward Prostitution?" *Medical Record*, 48 (1895), 651–653; Salathiel Ewing, reported in *Medical News*, 75 (1899), 346–347.

41. The most convenient source is Josephine E. Butler, *Personal Reminiscences of a Great Crusade* (London: H. Marshall, 1896), in which many letters and documents are reprinted. See especially p. 72, where a letter from Eliot is cited. See Eliot, *William Greenleaf Eliot*, p. 300; Eliot, *A Practical Discussion*, pp. 22–23.

42. Butler, *Personal Reminiscences*, pp. 73, 217.

43. David Jay Pivar, "The New Abolitionism: The Quest for Social Purity, 1876–1900" (doctoral dissertation, University of Pennsylvania, 1965). See, for example, J. Birkbeck Nevins, ed., *An Address to Members of the American Legislature and of the Medical Profession, from the British, Continental, and General Federation for the Abolition of State Regulation of Prostitution, and the National Medical Association (Great Britain and Ireland) for the Abolition of State Regulation of Prostitution, on Recent Proposals to Introduce the System of Regulating or Licensing Prostitution into the United States, with the History and Results of Such Legislation on the Continent of Europe and in England* (London: F. C. Banks, 1877). Often the opposition of physicians on moral

grounds was spontaneous, as in the St. Louis Medical Society; see, for example, the report in *Philadelphia Inquirer*, April 18, 1874, p. 1; *Medical News*, 40 (1882), 310.

44.   This movement is summarized in John C. Burnham, "Medical Specialists and Movements Toward Social Control in the Progressive Era: Three Examples" (reprinted herein as Chapter 13), in Jerry Israel, ed., *Building the Organizational Society: Essays on Associational Activities in Modern America* (New York: Free Press, 1972). See also Joseph Mayer, *The Regulation of Commercialized Vice: An Analysis of the Transition from Segregation to Repression in the United States* (New York: Klebold Press, 1922). Already in the nineteenth century American physicians had shown far greater affinity than Europeans for such ideas as inspection of men and outlawing the act of infecting another person with venereal disease; see, for example, "Zenith, M.D.," in *Medical Record*, 6 (1871), 93. See, in general, Charles Walter Clarke, *Taboo: The Story of the Pioneers of Social Hygiene* (Washington, DC: Public Affairs Press, 1961).

Chapter 10

1.   William L. O'Neill argues that "revolution" is too strong a word because the status of women was left largely unchanged. It is maintained in the present essay that, despite the avowedly conservative goals of the reformers, change in middle-class standards of sexual behavior was revolutionary. O'Neill further contends that the real revolution, insofar as it did occur, was a phenomenon of the 1920's. William L. O'Neill, *Divorce in the Progressive Era* (New Haven, CT: Yale University Press, 1967), pp. vii–viii, 161–167. Arno Karlen, *Sexuality and Homosexuality: A New View* (New York: W. W. Norton and Company, 1971), is explicitly concerned with the existence or non-existence of a "sexual revolution." In summarizing existing literature, Karlen distinguishes between actual sexual behavior and the atmosphere in which sexually mature people grew up. Karlen, *Sexuality and Homosexuality*, pp. xviii–xix, 269–276, 323–324, 448–450. See also John C. Burnham, "The New Psychology: From Narcissism to Social Control" (reprinted herein as Chapter 5), in John Braeman, Robert H. Bremner, and David Brody, eds., *Change and Continuity in Twentieth-Century America: The 1920's* (Columbus: Ohio State University Press, 1968), pp. 351–398; Gilman M. Ostrander, "The Revolution in Morals," ibid., pp. 323–349; Joseph R. Gusfield, "Prohibition: The Impact of Political Utopianism," ibid., pp. 259–308. Gusfield clarifies social levels and forces operating in changing consistencies in styles of life.

2.   The term "conspiracy of silence" originally came into existence in a special context. When English reformers started to agitate for the repeal of sanitary laws regulating and sanctioning prostitution in port cities, the English press, beginning in 1870, refused to give the agitators publicity. The actual term was popularized in a pamphlet by Harriet Martineau and Josephine E. Butler, "Remonstrance Against the Conspiracy of Silence." See Josephine E. Butler, *Personal Reminiscences of a Great Crusade* (London: H. Marshall, 1896), p. 96.

3. Keith Thomas, "The Double Standard," *Journal of the History of Ideas*, 20 (1959), 195–216.

4. William Trufant Foster, ed., *The Social Emergency: Studies in Sex Hygiene and Morals* (Boston: Houghton Mifflin Company, 1914), pp. 5–6. See also Henry Seidel Canby, "Sex and Marriage in the Nineties," *Harper's Monthly Magazine*, 169 (1934), 427–436; Sidney Ditzion, *Marriage, Morals and Sex in America: A History of Ideas* (New York: Bookman Associates, 1953); James R. McGovern, "The American Woman's Pre–World War I Freedom in Manners and Morals," *Journal of American History*, 55 (1968), 315–333.

5. Anthony Comstock wondered, "Why should decent men and women buy and read the sayings of a filthy-minded reporter, or the story of a divorce or contested will case reeking with filthy details? It is bad enough to have these vile details in court. Why admit them into the home?" Anthony Comstock, "How to Guard Our Youth Against Bad Literature," *Chautauquan*, 25 (1897), 520–524. For a typical example of the quack advertisement, see the Kansas City *Star*, March 6, 1903. The seduction theme is treated in Margaret Wyman, "The Rise of the Fallen Woman," *American Quarterly*, 3 (1951), 167–177.

6. Denslow Lewis, *The Gynecologic Consideration of the Sexual Act* (Weston, MA: M and S Press, 1970 [1899]). See also "The Teaching of Sex Hygiene," *New York Medical Journal*, 101 (1915), 850. For an example of openness mixed with prudery, see Irving C. Rosse, "Sexual Hypochondriasis and Perversion of the Generic Instinct," *Journal of Nervous and Mental Disease*, 19 (1892), 795–811.

7. Quoted in William Henry Harbaugh, *Power and Responsibility: The Life and Times of Theodore Roosevelt* (New York: Farrar, Straus and Cudahy, 1961), p. 15.

8. William W. Sanger, *The History of Prostitution: Its Extent, Causes, and Effects Throughout the World*, 2d ed. (New York: Medical Publishing Company, 1898), p. 91; Margaret Deland, "The Change in the Feminine Ideal," *Atlantic Monthly*, 105 (1910), 295–296. See also Robert E. Riegel, "Changing American Attitudes Toward Prostitution (1800–1920)," *Journal of the History of Ideas*, 29 (1968), 437–452; Howard B. Woolston, *Prostitution in the United States Prior to the Entrance of the United States into the World War* (Montclair, NJ: Patterson Smith, 1969 [1921]).

9. Francis P. Weisenburger, *Triumph of Faith: Contributions of the Church to American Life, 1865–1900* (Richmond, VA: William Byrd Press, 1962); Lewis Atherton, *Main Street on the Middle Border* (Bloomington: Indiana University Press, 1954), pp. 86–98; Joseph R. Gusfield, *Symbolic Crusade: Status Politics and the American Temperance Movement* (Urbana: University of Illinois Press, 1963). The purity movement always remained studiously non-sectarian. David Jay Pivar, "The New Abolitionism: The Quest for Social Purity, 1876–1900" (doctoral dissertation, University of Pennsylvania, 1965).

10. The precise connection between feminism and the purity movement is both complex and significant. Butler, *Personal Reminiscences*, pp. 73, 84–85; William L. O'Neill, *Everyone Was Brave: The Rise and Fall of Feminism in America* (Chicago: Quadrangle Books, 1969); Norton Mezvinsky, "An Idea of Female Superiority," *Journal of the Central Mississippi Valley American Studies Association*, 2 (1961), 17–26; Pivar, "The New Abolitionism"; Andrew Sinclair, *The*

Better Half: The Emancipation of the American Woman (New York: Harper and Row Publishers, Inc., 1965), pp. 254–262; John C. Burnham, "Medical Inspection of Prostitutes in America in the Nineteenth Century—The St. Louis Experiment and Its Sequel" (reprinted herein as Chapter 9), *Bulletin of the History of Medicine*, 45 (1971), 203–218.

11. Lavinia L. Dock, *Hygiene and Morality: A Manual for Nurses and Others* (New York: G. P. Putnam's Sons, 1910), pp. 68–81, 104–116. See also Egal Feldman, "Prostitution, the Alien Woman and the Progressive Imagination, 1910–1915," *American Quarterly*, 19 (1967), 192–206. For an example of white-slave literature, see Clifford G. Roe, *The Girl Who Disappeared* (Chicago: American Bureau of Moral Education, 1914).

12. Based on Pivar, "The New Abolitionism." See also Anna Rice Powell, "The American Purity Alliance and Its Work," in Aaron M. Powell, ed., *The National Purity Congress, Its Papers, Addresses, Portraits* (New York: American Purity Alliance, 1896), pp. 130–132; ibid., p. vi. For a summary of the relationship of the purity movement to the social hygiene movement, see Charles Walter Clarke, *Taboo: The Story of the Pioneers of Social Hygiene* (Washington, DC: Public Affairs Press, 1961), pp. 64–65. The repressive forces of the 1920's had a quite different social base. See Paul S. Boyer, *Purity in Print: The Vice-Society Movement and Book Censorship in America* (New York: Charles Scribner's Sons, 1968), especially pp. 167–206. The main journal of the advocates of purity, *The Philanthropist* (later *Vigilance*), for example, continued to the end of its existence in 1914 to include an amazing diversity of opinion on all subjects relating to purity.

13. Roy Lubove, "The Progressives and the Prostitute," *The Historian*, 24 (1962), 308–330. James H. Timberlake, *Prohibition and the Progressive Movement, 1900–1920* (Cambridge, MA: Harvard University Press, 1963); Roy Lubove, *The Professional Altruist: The Emergence of Social Work as a Career, 1880–1930* (Cambridge, MA: Harvard University Press, 1965); Gerd Korman, *Industrialization, Immigrants, and Americanizers: The View from Milwaukee, 1866–1921* (Madison: State Historical Society of Wisconsin, 1967); Robert H. Wiebe, *The Search for Order, 1877–1920* (New York: Hill and Wang, 1967).

14. Contrary to traditional belief, the unitary family, in the urban and industrial society of the late nineteenth century, was becoming increasingly viable as a self-sustaining institution (independent, for example, of economic functions). With the leisure and affluence of the Progressive era, Americans came to demand more of the family than formerly, and, specifically, sexual fulfillment. Benjamin O. Flower, "Prostitution Within the Marriage Bond," *Arena*, 13 (1895), 59–73.

15. O'Neill, *Divorce in the Progressive Era*.

16. McGovern, "The American Woman's Pre–World War I Freedom," pp. 315–333; Kenneth A. Yellis, "Prosperity's Child: Some Thoughts on the Flapper," *American Quarterly*, 21 (1969), 44–64; Freda Kirchwey, ed., *Our Changing Morality: A Symposium* (New York: Albert and Charles Boni, 1924).

17. William Wasserstrom, *Heiress of All the Ages: Sex and Sentiment in the Genteel Tradition* (Minneapolis: University of Minnesota Press, 1959).

18. For the idea that Europe was the source of much of the frankness that Americans detected in the 1890's, see, for example, Leo Markun, *Mrs. Grundy: A History*

of Four Centuries of Morals Intended to Illuminate Present Problems in Great Britain and the United States (New York: D. Appleton and Company, 1930), pp. 315–330; Thomas Beer, *The Mauve Decade: American Life at the End of the Nineteenth Century* (New York: Alfred A. Knopf, 1926), pp. 125–126, 193.

19. O'Neill, *Divorce in the Progressive Era*, pp. 93–99, 114–120, 138–141. See also Ellen Key, *Love and Marriage*, trans. by Arthur G. Chater (New York: Source Book Press, 1911), and Edward Carpenter, *Love's Coming-of-Age: A Series of Papers on the Relations of the Sexes* (New York: M. Kennerley, 1911). Henry F. May, *The End of American Innocence: A Study of the First Years of Our Own Time, 1912–1917* (New York: Alfred A. Knopf, 1959). The eugenics movement and the campaign for birth control (the latter largely within the feminist movement) also involved discussions of sex; both were contemporaneous with the social hygiene movement. For Bohemians and extremists who would have liked to discuss sexual topics in a shocking way, see Moses Harman's magazine, *American Journal of Eugenics* and its predecessor, *Lucifer the Light Bringer*. Ditzion gives a substantial account of such literature. Ditzion, *Marriage, Morals and Sex*, pp. 185–206, 281–316. For advocates of social stability who denounced such evils as white slavery and divorce, see Frederick L. Hoffman, "The Decline in the Birth Rate," *North American Review*, 189 (1909), 675–687, and "The Protection of the Home," *The Independent*, 52 (1900), 2647–2648. Traditional political radicals played but an insignificant role in undermining the conspiracy of silence. David M. Kennedy, *Birth Control in America: The Career of Margaret Sanger* (New Haven, CT: Yale University Press, 1970).

20. Willis B. Hawkins, "The Paris Woman," *Smart Set*, July 1900, p. 47; George Bronson-Howard, "The Sad Awakening of Jekinsby," *Smart Set*, January 1906, pp. 107–108; Louise Winter, "Hearts Aflame," *Smart Set*, June 1900, p. 3. For parallel examples from an unsympathetic observer, see Jean MacArthur Hyde, "Purity in Literature and Art," *The Light*, 11 (1908), 37–39.

21. William A. Gorton, reported in *American Journal of Insanity*, 48 (1891), 86.

22. Charles G. Wagner remarked that general paresis was "the most dreaded disease of modern times," and many experienced physicians shared this view. Charles G. Wagner, "A Case of Trephining for General Paresis," *American Journal of Insanity*, 47 (1890), 59.

23. L. Duncan Bulkley, *Syphilis in the Innocent (Syphilis Insontium), Clinically and Historically Considered, with a Plan for the Legal Control of the Disease* (New York: Bailey and Fairchild, 1894); "New Laws About Drinking Cups," *Life*, 58 (1911), 1152.

24. *Medical News*, 78 (1901), 390; "Report of the Committee on Prophylaxis of Venereal Diseases," *Journal of the American Medical Association*, 40 (1903), 1317–1319.

25. John C. Burnham, "The Social Evil Ordinance—A Social Experiment in Nineteenth Century St. Louis," *Bulletin of the Missouri Historical Society*, 27 (1971), 203–217.

26. Burnham, "Medical Inspection of Prostitutes in America;" Ludwig Weiss, "Venereal Prophylaxis that Is Feasible," *Journal of the American Medical Association*, 40 (1903), 232–238.

27. Edward Bennett Bronson, "Dr. Morrow, the Physician," *Social Diseases*, 4 (1913), 105–111. A detailed necrology is in the possession of the Morrow family.

28. Charles Walter Clarke points out that Prince Albert Morrow lost three of his six children within a few weeks around the turn of the century, and Clarke suggests that Morrow's reform campaign may have represented an attempt to offset his grief. Clarke, *Taboo*, p. 57. Edward L. Keyes, Jr., "Prince Albert Morrow, M.D.," *Venereal Disease Information*, 22 (1941), 39, notes that early in Morrow's campaign he was already betraying signs of a fatal nephritis.

29. Jean-Alfred Fournier, *Syphilis and Marriage*, trans. by Prince Albert Morrow (New York: D. Appleton and Company, 1880), p. iv. See, for example, Prince Albert Morrow, *Atlas of Skin and Venereal Diseases, Comprising Original Illustrations and Selections* (New York: William Wood and Company, 1888–1889).

30. Prince Albert Morrow, *Venereal Memoranda: A Manual for the Student and Practitioner* (New York: William Wood and Company, 1885), pp. 21–22, 197–209.

31. Prince Albert Morrow, "The Prophylaxis of Venereal Diseases. Medical Aspect of the Social Evil in New York," *Philadelphia Medical Journal*, 7 (1901), 663–669. Samuel Treat Armstrong, "Syphilis in Relation to Public Health," in Prince Albert Morrow, ed., *A System of Genito-Urinary Diseases, Syphilology and Dermatology*, 3 vols. (New York: D. Appleton and Company, 1893–1894), II, 813–850.

32. Charles Walter Clarke, "Dr. Prince Albert Morrow and His Aides," *Journal of Social Hygiene*, 40 (1954), 132; *Conférence internationale pour la prophylaxie de la syphilis et des maladies vénériennes*, 2 vols. (Brussels: H. Lamartin, 1899–1900). See also *Preventive Hygiene: An Account of the Brussels International Conference, 1899 and 1902* (London: n.p., 1909), pp. 1–20.

33. Morrow, "Prophylaxis of Venereal Diseases," pp. 663–669; "Medical Inquiry on Social Evil," *Medical News*, 78 (1901), 352; Prince Albert Morrow, "Report of the Committee of Seven on the Prophylaxis of Venereal Disease in New York City, " *Medical News*, 79 (1901), 961–970.

34. Morrow, "Report of the Committee of Seven on the Prophylaxis of Venereal Disease in New York City," p. 967. Morrow's action was typical of Progressive reformers who acted when new scientific and technical information changed their perceptions of what was possible sufficiently to galvanize them into reformers.

35. *IIe conférence internationale pour la prophylaxie de la syphilis et des maladies vénériennes*, 2 vols. (Brussels: H. Lamartin, 1902–1903), I, pt. 2; *Preventive Hygiene*, pp. 21–25.

36. Prince Albert Morrow, "The Society of Sanitary and Moral Prophylaxis: Its Objects and Aims," *Transactions of the American Society of Sanitary and Moral Prophylaxis*, 1 (1905–1906), 27. Morrow was clearly inspired by the now aged Jean-Alfred Fournier. Both had attended the Berlin (1892) and London (1896) meetings.

37. In part Morrow was updating Fournier's volume, which he had translated years before; but he also used the book to explicate many of his own ideas. He felt, for example, that certification of health for marriage licences came too late in the process to be effective; his emphasis on social action already involved sex education and public propaganda. He still believed prostitution to be inevitable. Prince Albert Morrow, *Social Diseases and Marriage: Social Prophylaxis* (New York: Lea Brothers and Company, 1904), pp. vi, 329–385.

38. Prince Albert Morrow, "A Plea for the Organization of a 'Society of Sanitary and Moral Prophylaxis,'" *Transactions of the American Society of Sanitary and Moral Prophylaxis*, 1 (1905–1906), 17–25.

39. Prince Albert Morrow, "Report of Progress," *Social Diseases*, 3 (1912), 1–2; Morrow, "The Society of Sanitary and Moral Prophylaxis," pp. 26–37; New York *Tribune*, April 7, 1912.

40. Morrow, "The Society of Sanitary and Moral Prophylaxis." See also *Transactions of the American Society of Sanitary and Moral Prophylaxis*, 1 (1905–1906).

41. *Transactions of the American Society of Sanitary and Moral Prophylaxis*, 1–3 (1905–1910).

42. Denslow Lewis, "Knowledge as a Factor in Venereal Prophylaxis," *American Journal of Dermatology*, 10 (1906), 67; E. Wood Ruggles, "The Physician's Relation to the Social Evil," *New York Medical Journal*, 85 (1907), 159–161; James M. Anders, "The Role of the Medical Profession in Combating the Social Evil," *Medicine*, 12 (1906), 821–825. See also Maurice A. Bigelow, *Sex-Education: A Series of Lectures Concerning Knowledge of Sex in Its Relation to Human Life* (New York: Macmillan Company, 1916), pp. 231–232.

43. *Transactions of the American Society of Sanitary and Moral Prophylaxis*, 1 (1905–1906), 77; Edward L. Keyes, Jr., "The Sexual Necessity," ibid., pp. 40–45. The American Medical Association refused to pass until 1917 a resolution stating flatly that continence was not detrimental to health. "Report of Reference Committee on Hygiene and Public Health," *Journal of the American Medical Association*, 68 (1917), 1837–1838.

44. A strikingly high proportion of the physicians who had spoken of the dangers of venereal diseases around the turn of the century had advocated education as a preventive measure. For example, see E. W. Allison and W. E. Ashton, "The Failure of Legislation in Limiting the Spread of Venereal Diseases," *Philadelphia County Medical Society Proceedings*, 8 (1885), 311.

45. O. Edward Janney, "The Annual Meeting," *The Philanthropist*, 19 (1904), 1–4; "The Changing Views of Medical Men," ibid., 4.

46. "Societies for Social Hygiene," *The Philanthropist*, 21 (1906), 4. For the official statement of support for Morrow, see O. Edward Janney, "Annual Address," *The Philanthropist*, 22 (1908), 16–19.

47. Copies of incorporation papers, American Social Health Association, New York City; reports in *The Philanthropist, Vigilance, Social Diseases*; "New Federation for Sex Hygiene," *The Survey*, 24 (1910), 501–503. See also Clarke, *Taboo*; Abbie Graham, *Grace H. Dodge: Merchant of Dreams* (New York: Womans Press, 1926), pp. 216–221; Clarke, "Dr. Prince Albert Morrow and His Aides," pp. 188–190. The considerable direct impact of the social hygienists in the World War I period lies beyond the scope of this paper, but it should be noted that they detected considerable resistance to their program in 1914–1915 and suffered financial stringencies because of the concurrent depression. American Social Hygiene Association, *Second Annual Report*, 1914–1915, pp. 5–6. William F. Snow, "The American Social Hygiene Association," *Journal of Social Hygiene*, 32 (1946), 241–249.

48. For example, see Amélie Rives, "Innocence Versus Ignorance," *North American Review*, 155 (1892), 287–292. For a typical bibliography, see Earl Barnes, "Books and Pamphlets Intended to Give Sex-Information," *Stanford Univer-*

sity Studies in Education, 1 (1896–1897), 301–308. For the reasoning of the purity leaders, see Charlton Edholm, *Traffic in Girls and Florence Crittenton Missions* (Chicago: Woman's Temperance Publishing Association, 1893), pp. 87–107; Powell, *The National Purity Congress*. In the Progressive years conservative purity advocates came to attack silence as such but without necessarily advocating anything more than purity training at home. For example, see Orison Swett Marden, *The Crime of Silence* (New York: Physical Culture Publishing Company, 1915); "The Aged Crime of Youth," in R. P. Shuler, ed., *The Anti-Vice Bulletins* (Dallas: n.p. [1914]), p. 5.

49. Mary Wood-Allen, *What a Young Girl Ought to Know*, 2d ed. (Philadelphia: Vir Publishing Company, 1905), p. 21. See also Ernest Edwards, *Personal Information for Boys* (New York: R. F. Fenno and Company, 1909).

50. Prince Albert Morrow, *The Young Man's Problem* (New York: F. H. Hitchcock, 1912); Prince Albert Morrow, *The Boy Problem: For Parents and Teachers* (New York: American Society of Sanitary and Moral Prophylaxis, [1911]), pp. 27–28.

51. L. Duncan Bulkley, "For Young Men of the Working Class?" *Charities*, 15 (1906), 718–721; *Transactions of the American Society of Sanitary and Moral Prophylaxis*, 3 (1909–1910), 156; Frank J. Osborne, "A Health Exhibit for Men," *Social Hygiene*, 3 (1917), 27–49. Irving Kassoy, "A History of the Work of the American Social Hygiene Association in Sex Education" (master's thesis, College of the City of New York, 1931), traces the evolution of the various types of educational programs before and after 1914, when the medical and purity groups completed their partial merger. See also *Vigilance*, 25 (1912), 12–21. At one point insurance companies that lost money on policy holders who died from venereal disease took an interest in the movement. Lee K. Frankel, "The Interest of Life Insurance Companies in Social Hygiene," *Social Hygiene*, 1 (1914), 61–66.

52. *The Light*, 16 (1913), 51. "Announcement," *Journal of the Society of Sanitary and Moral Prophylaxis*, 5 (1914), 2–3; Richard C. Cabot, "Are Sanitary and Moral Prophylaxis Natural Allies?" ibid., 20–30; ibid., 31–44. See also Fred D. Baldwin, "The Invisible Armor," *American Quarterly*, 16 (1964), 432–444.

53. By 1913 former President Charles W. Eliot of Harvard was willing to accept the presidency of the social hygiene organization, and he turned down the ambassadorship to England to do so. Clarke, "Dr. Prince Albert Morrow and His Aides," pp. 193–194.

54. Compare H. D. Sedgwick, Jr., "A Gap in Education," *Atlantic Monthly*, 87 (1901), 68–72, with John L. Elliott, "Education in Sexual Hygiene," *Transactions of the American Society of Sanitary and Moral Prophylaxis*, 1 (1905–1906), 39–40; ibid., 120–121; and Frederick S. Curtis, "Several Years' Practical Experience in Educating Boys in the Hygiene of Sex," ibid., 2 (1907–1908), 205–209. One of the best-known advocates of sex education before Morrow who was occasionally criticized for his advocacy was the psychologist president of Clark University, G. Stanley Hall. G. Stanley Hall, *Life and Confessions of a Psychologist* (New York: D. Appleton and Company, 1923), pp. 406–409.

55. The intrinsic importance of marital love making and training for it is illustrated in a central document of the social hygiene effort. E. B. Lowry and Richard J. Lambert, *Himself—Talks with Men Concerning Themselves* (Chicago: Forbes

and Company, 1912), pp. 131–132; Jane Addams, *A New Conscience and an Ancient Evil* (New York: Macmillan Company, 1912).

56. Compare the typical attitudes in "Municipalities and Vice," *Municipal Affairs*, 4 (1900), 698–707, with the specific changes chronicled in *Social Diseases* and *Social Hygiene*. See also Joseph Mayer, *The Regulation of Commercialized Vice: An Analysis of the Transition from Segregation to Repression in the United States* (New York: Klebold Press, 1922).

57. Perhaps the best known of the many vice commission reports was set off by the discovery that a prostitute had infected four schoolboys. Vice Commission of Chicago, *The Social Evil in Chicago: A Study of Existing Conditions with Recommendations* (Chicago: Gunthorp-Warren Printing Company, 1911). William A. Evans, "The Attack upon Venereal Diseases Through Education and Publicity," *Journal of the Society of Sanitary and Moral Prophylaxis*, 6 (1915), 84. The situation in New York City was particularly complex and involved many of the leaders of social hygiene and Progressive reform. George J. Kneeland, *Commercialized Prostitution in New York City*, 2d ed. (New York: The Century Company, 1917); Willoughby Cyrus Waterman, *Prostitution and Its Repression in New York City, 1900–1931* (New York: the author, 1932); and Edwin R. A. Seligman, ed., *The Social Evil: With Special Reference to Conditions Existing in the City of New York*, 2d ed. (New York: Columbia University Press, 1912). For a fairly complete list of vice commission reports, see Oscar Handlin et al., eds., *Harvard Guide to American History* (Cambridge, MA: Harvard University Press, 1955), p. 469. Morrow's campaign for education, for example, was taken up by the Vice Commission of Philadelphia, *A Report on Existing Conditions with Recommendations to the Honorable Randolph Blankenburg, Mayor of Philadelphia* (Philadelphia: The Commission, 1913), p. 112. See also Marion D. Shutter et al., *Report of the Vice Commission of Minneapolis* (Minneapolis: H. M. Hall, 1911), pp. 103–104. In early 1913 a writer in *The Light*, 16 (1913), 11, noted that opposition to vice commissions had been effective in a number of places, including Cleveland; Philadelphia; and Macon, Georgia.

58. "In an Editorial Way," *Ladies' Home Journal*, May, 1907, p. 5; "The Editor's Personal Page," *Ladies' Home Journal*, January, 1908, p. 1. Edward Bok, *The Americanization of Edward Bok: The Autobiography of a Dutch Boy Fifty Years After* (New York: Charles Scribner's Sons, 1921), pp. 345–351, tells how Lyman Abbott inspired this campaign; although in harmony with the purity movement program, the inspiration was largely medical.

59. Foster, *The Social Emergency*, pp. 6–7. See, for example, McGovern, "The American Woman's Pre–World War I Freedom," pp. 315–333.

60. A compromise position by purity people was represented by Winfield Scott Hall, who rushed into print in order to fill the need for education before the schools were prepared to take over from the home. Winfield Scott Hall, *Sexual Knowledge: The Knowledge of Self and Sex in Simple Language: For the Instruction of Young People, Young Wives and Young Husbands, Fathers and Mothers, Teachers and Nurses, and All Who Feel a Need of Reliable Information on the Best Way and the Best Time to Impart Sexual Knowledge to Boys and Girls* (Philadelphia: International Bible House, 1913), pp. 18–21. By 1914 the volume of writing on sex had become unmanageable, according to Helen

Thompson Woolley, "The Psychology of Sex," *Psychological Bulletin*, 11 (1914), 353.

61. "Dr. Eliot's Plan to Teach Sex Hygiene," *The Survey*, 25 (1911), 803–804. *Journal of Proceedings and Addresses of the Fiftieth Annual Meeting of the National Education Association of the United States*, July 6–12, 1912, p. 43. For example, see *Report of the Sex Education Sessions of the Fourth International Congress on School Hygiene and of the Annual Meeting of the American Federation for Sex Hygiene* (New York, 1913). A full and well-documented account of sex education in the public schools is in Wallace H. Maw, "Fifty Years of Sex Education in the Public Schools of the United States (1900–1950): A History of Ideas" (doctoral dissertation, University of Cincinnati, 1953).

62. See ibid.

63. Clara Schmitt, "The Teaching of the Facts of Sex in the Public School," *Pedagogical Seminary*, 17 (1910), 229–241.

64. "Difficulties of Sex Teaching," *New York Medical Journal*, 101 (1915), 961, referred to the total agglomeration as "an extraordinary collection of literature for the immaturely minded of all ages." A representative anthology of the medical variety of writings of this period is Lee Alexander Stone, ed., *Sex Searchlights and Sane Sex Ethics: An Anthology of Sex Knowledge* (Chicago: Science Publishing Company, 1922). Maw details both problems and controversies. Maw, "Fifty Years of Sex Education." The quote is from "Sex Education," *Vigilance*, 27 (1913), 5.

65. Maw cites much of the conservative literature. Maw, "Fifty Years of Sex Education." *Vigilance* for some time surveyed press comment on the question; Sheppard is quoted from "Sex Education," p. 6. See also *The Nation*, 97 (1913), 200. The more general documentation is illustrated by a well-known article, "Sex O'clock in America," *Current Opinion*, 55 (1913), 113–114, and the indignant answer of William Burgess, "A Wave of Sex Hysteria?" *Vigilance*, 27 (1913), 8–9.

66. For example, Floyd Dell, "Literary Matters," *The Masses*, 8 (1916), 28. It is ironic that Sigmund Freud has so often been blamed for openness about sexual subjects when in fact in America his work became known popularly mainly as a result of the social hygiene movement. For details, see John C. Burnham, "Psychoanalysis in American Civilization Before 1918" (doctoral dissertation, Stanford University, 1958), pp. 313–348.

67. Quoted in May, *End of American Innocence*, p. 339.

68. Walter Lippmann, *Drift and Mastery: An Attempt to Diagnose the Current Unrest* (New York: Michael Kennerley, 1914), pp. 258–259. Not everyone was happy with education and openness. A writer in *Life* asserted (presumably tongue in cheek), "What is most needed today is a society for the prevention of knowledge. No field of ignorance and comfortable obscurity is too sacred for the investigator to invade. . . . It is impossible to be ignorant of anything. . . . The mystery of sex is now unveiled to the toddling infant, and the boy of seventeen is blasé." *Life*, 61 (1913).

69. Eugène Brieux, *Damaged Goods: A Play in Three Acts*, trans. by John Pollock (New York: Brentano's, 1912), was "printed for the Connecticut Society of Social Hygiene." Several lines were omitted on page 21 in the American version; the omitted material deals with a physician's recommending that a young man

who cannot control his passions choose the right kind of older, inspected prostitute. See Edward L. Keyes, Jr., "Report on the Work Accomplished by the French Society of Sanitary and Moral Prophylaxis," *Transactions of the American Society of Sanitary and Moral Prophylaxis*, 1 (1905–1906), 83–85. Clarke, "Dr. Prince Albert Morrow and His Aides," pp. 190–193.

70. *The Stage Year Book*, 1914, p. 239. *Dial* noted that the play was "backed by the 'Medical Review of Reviews' Sociological Fund" in New York. *Dial*, 54 (1913), 288. See "Brieux's Play," *Vigilance*, 26 (1913), 17–18. See also *The Outlook*, 104 (1913), 226; James Shelley Hamilton, "The Sex-Tangled Drama," *Everybody's Magazine*, 29 (1913), 676–687.

71. W. H. Denny, "The Year's Drama in America," *The Stage Year Book*, 1914, p. 59. W. David Sievers notes that European imports of this period dealt more frankly with sex than did American plays. W. David Sievers, *Freud on Broadway: A History of Psychoanalysis and the American Drama* (New York: Hermitage House Press, 1955), pp. 56–57. Yet European works failed to make a great impact prior to Thomas N. Hepburn's and Richard Bennett's work; Frank Wedekind provides an apt comparison. Even after a private production of one of his plays in 1909, his work remained strictly *avant-garde*. See Frank Wedekind, *Tragedies of Sex*, trans. by Samuel A. Eliot, Jr. (New York: Boni and Liveright, 1923), p. xviii; "Wedekind's Tragedy of Pubescence," *Current Literature*, 48 (1910), 429–432.

72. "Reviews of Periodicals," *Vigilance*, 27 (1913), 11–14. Joyce Kilmer, "The Drama as an Instrument of Sex Education," *Journal of the Society of Sanitary and Moral Prophylaxis*, 5 (1914), 54–55. *Life* published a cartoon entitled, "Damaged Goods," depicting two classic women, labelled "Drama" and "Fiction," sitting on the curb in front of a saloon, their white robes soiled and besmirched; the two muses obviously were the damaged ones. *Life*, 62 (1913), 880. William Dean Howells confessed that *Les Avariés* was beyond his tolerance, and he was unable to finish reading it. William Dean Howells, "The Plays of Eugène Brieux," *North American Review*, 201 (1915), 402–411.

73. For a comprehensive discussion, see *Journal of the Society of Sanitary and Moral Prophylaxis*, 5 (1914), 61–77. See also George Cram Cook, in the Chicago *Evening Post Friday Literary Review*, December 20, 1912, p. 6.

74. Edward L. Keyes, Jr., "Society of Sanitary and Moral Prophylaxis, President's Report," *Journal of the Society of Sanitary and Moral Prophylaxis*, 5 (1914), 5. Olive Crosby repeatedly denounced "the present commercialization of the sex-education movement." Olive Crosby, "Annual Report of the Office Secretary," *Journal of the Society of Sanitary and Moral Prophylaxis*, 5 (1914), 141, 143.

75. John Punnet Peters, "Dr. Morrow's Work in Uplift," *Social Diseases*, 4 (1913), 127; Prince Albert Morrow, "The Relations of Social Diseases to the Family," *Papers and Proceedings: Third Annual Meeting, American Sociological Society*, 3 (1908), 46–59.

76. The Progressive implications of generally treating all of the ill are discussed in John C. Burnham, "Medical Specialists and Movements Toward Social Control in the Progressive Era: Three Examples" (reprinted herein as Chapter 13), in Jerry Israel, ed., *Building the Organizational Society: Essays on Associational Activities in Modern America* (New York: Free Press, 1972), pp. 19–30.

77. For example, see the statement, "Prostitution has been proved to be a 'modi-

fiable' phenomenon." Bureau of Social Hygiene, *Commercialized Prostitution in New York City, November 1, 1916: A Comparison Between 1912, 1915, and 1916* (New York: Bureau of Social Hygiene, 1916), p. 2.

Chapter 11

Acknowledgment: Preparation of this paper was facilitated by released time granted by San Francisco State College.

1. James H. Timberlake, *Prohibition and the Progressive Movement, 1900–1920* (Cambridge, MA: Harvard University Press, 1963); Norman H. Clark, *The Dry Years: Prohibition and Social Change in Washington* (Seattle: University of Washington Press, 1965); Norton Mezvinsky, "The Temperance Movement, 1870–1920," paper read at the Organization of American Historians meetings, Kansas City, April, 1965. Even with a very different approach, Paul E. Isaac, *Prohibition and Politics: Turbulent Decades in Tennessee 1885–1920* (Knoxville: University of Tennessee Press, 1965), pp. 139, 262–267, notes the connection between Progressive reform and prohibition.

2. John Higham, "Beyond Consensus: The Historian as Moral Critic," *American Historical Review*, 67 (1962), 610–612, deals with this progressive view of American history. In accordance with his summary, it is amusing to note that most progressive historians deal with prohibition not as evidence of cumulative reform but as one of the "aberrations" that members of this school use to account for non-progressive phenomena; repeal, likewise, then, was a sign that the American people had regained their senses. It is, of course, possible to keep prohibition within this progressive framework but to reverse the way in which it is used: Enactment was a great reform, repeal a great betrayal. See the discussion herein.

3. See especially Timberlake, *Prohibition and the Progressive Movement*; Andrew Sinclair, *Prohibition: The Era of Excess* (Boston: Little, Brown and Company, 1962); Joseph R. Gusfield, *Symbolic Crusade: Status Politics and the American Temperance Movement* (Urbana: University of Illinois Press, 1963); and Clark, *The Dry Years*.

4. It is necessary in this paper to utilize terms denoting social class differences among Americans. For the period, probably the best social classification is that of the Lynds, who distinguished only between business or middle class and working class (Robert S. Lynd and Helen Merrell Lynd, *Middletown: A Study in American Culture* [New York: Harcourt, Brace and World, Inc., 1956 ed.], pp. 22–24). Occasionally some distinction between elements in the business class— between middle and upper classes—is necessary, and so those customary terms are used in explanatory contexts. In general, however, the attempt is made merely to suggest that certain attitudes or patterns of behavior were relatively characteristic of Americans at one end or the other of the social scale. Although the class concept is not as clear and precise as one might hope, yet for crudely empirical research on prohibition it provides both a useful and revealing device, as Clark, *The Dry Years*, has demonstrated well.

5. See, for example, the friendly essay on the saloon by George Ade, *The Old Time*

Saloon; Not Wet—Not Dry, Just History (New York: R. Long and R. R. Smith, 1931); and also the various reports of the pre–World War I vice commissions.

6. Sinclair, *Prohibition*, pp. 72–81.

7. See Timberlake, *Prohibition and the Progressive Movement*, especially pp. 115–120.

8. Robert H. Wiebe, *Businessmen and Reform: A Study of the Progressive Movement* (Cambridge, MA: Harvard University Press, 1962).

9. Timberlake, *Prohibition and the Progressive Movement*, especially pp. 39–66. This emphasis on the class aspect of the Eighteenth Amendment should not obscure the fact that a hard core of support for prohibition in any form continued to come from the religiously oriented social reformers who, without other support, had only very limited success in their political campaigns. For many decades American churches, convinced of the evil nature of liquor, were deeply involved in temperance movements (see Francis P. Weisenburger, *Triumph of Faith: Contributions of the Church to American Life, 1865–1900* [Richmond, VA: William Byrd Press, 1962], pp. 134–157). Gusfield, *Symbolic Crusade*, points out that temperance reform represented an attempt of American middle-class groups to force their own standards and "style of life" upon other Americans, particularly lower classes and immigrants. These homogenous middle-class cultural groups were concentrated in smaller towns and rural areas, but their widespread existence in cities is reflected in Timberlake's discovery of substantial and important urban support of prohibition. Prohibition of both the secular and religious varieties—which were to some extent the same, as it turns out—was merely another aspect of the Progressives' well-known attempts to "Americanize" the immigrants and to transform them and native lower-class elements into middle-class citizens in the image of the dominant group. See especially the work of Clark, *The Dry Years*, in confirming and exploring the points made by Gusfield and Timberlake.

10. Sinclair, *Prohibition*, pp. 99–104.

11. Peter H. Odegard, *Pressure Politics: The Story of the Anti-Saloon League* (New York: Columbia University Press, 1928), p. 265.

12. For years the temperance movement had had successes in legal prohibition on the local and even state levels. Almost—but not quite—equally often these drys had seen their plans defeated and their hard-won legislation rendered ineffective or repealed. This temperance movement has its own history; the present work centers on the version of this reform associated with the Progressive movement. See note 9, above.

13. Timberlake, *Prohibition and the Progressive Movement*, pp. 29, 148 and chap. 6.

14. Sinclair, *Prohibition*, pp. 99–104, 165. Sinclair, p. 347, reprints a cartoon showing two smug-looking factory executives about to have a cocktail; the caption on the cartoon is an ironic "Beer's Bad for our Workers." Sinclair Lewis, in *Babbitt* (New York: New American Library, 1963 ed.), p. 96, has Vergil Gunch, the coal dealer, observe as he sips a cocktail, "Just the same, you don't want to forget prohibition is a mighty good thing for the working-classes. Keeps 'em from wasting their money and lowering their productiveness."

15. Lawrence F. Schmeckebier, *The Bureau of Prohibition: Its History, Activities and Organization* (Washington, DC: Brookings Institution, 1929).

16. Sinclair, *Prohibition*, pp. 148–149, chap. 13.

17. Ibid., pp. 209–214. Details are in National Commission on Law Observance and Enforcement, *Enforcement of Prohibition Laws: Official Records of the National Commission on Law Observance and Enforcement Pertaining to Its Investigation of Facts as to Enforcement, Benefits, and Abuses Under Prohibition Laws, Both Before and Since the Adoption of the Eighteenth Amendment to the Constitution* (Washington, DC: U.S. Government Printing Office, 1931). Occasionally citizens took matters into their own hands. During the upsurge of the Ku Klux Klan in the 1920's, the hooded vigilantes, confronted with passive Negroes and a shortage in the local supply of Jews and Catholics, tended to make bootleggers the objects of their nighttime activities. While this informal enforcement was effective in some localities, the notorious connection between the Klan and the drys tended to confirm in the public mind the connection between rural bigotry and prohibition. See, for example, John Higham, *Strangers in the Land: Patterns of American Nativism* (New Brunswick, NJ: Rutgers University Press, 1955), pp. 268, 295.

18. The Anti-Saloon League had power to elect members of state legislatures and Congressmen, but as the record of local enforcement shows, the League in general did not capture the local party apparatus and so was impotent in naming sheriffs and other local officials. It was a pressure group, by design non-partisan, and so failed at a level where partisan politics and patronage were of overriding importance.

19. Charles Merz, *The Dry Decade* (Garden City, NY: Doubleday, Doran and Company, 1931), pp. 202, 205–207.

20. Sinclair, *Prohibition*, p. 177.

21. Elizabeth Brown, "Enforcement of Prohibition in San Francisco" (master's thesis, University of California, 1940).

22. Clark Warburton, "Prohibition," *Encyclopaedia of Social Sciences*, XII, 507. Warburton's figures were revised from his monograph, *The Economic Results of Prohibition* (New York: Columbia University Press, 1932), in which he made estimates based upon sources of production, death rates, and arrests for drunkenness. The late Dr. E. M. Jellinek informed the writer that he considered Warburton's figures for the prohibition period substantially too high.

23. Thomas C. Cochran, *The Pabst Brewing Company: The History of an American Business* (New York: New York University Press, 1948), p. 180.

24. The best convenient collection of figures is in Warburton, *Economic Results of Prohibition*. See, for example, Carney Landis and Jane Cushman, "The Relation of National Prohibition to Mental Disease," *Scientific Monthly*, 61 (1945), 469ff. Such figures are the more striking in that they emphasize urban units and areas such as New York where prohibition was relatively least effective.

25. James V. May, *Mental Diseases: A Public Health Problem* (Boston: R. G. Badger Company, 1922), pp. 360–362. See Horatio M. Pollock and Frederick W. Brown, "Recent Statistics of Alcoholic Mental Disease," *Mental Hygiene*, 13 (1929), 591–614, and E. M. Jellinek, "Recent Trends in Alcoholism and Alcohol Consumption," *Quarterly Journal of Studies on Alcohol*, 8 (1947), 19–20.

26. E. M. Jellinek, *The Disease Concept of Alcoholism* (New Haven, CT: Hillhouse Press, 1970).

27. Edwin H. Sutherland and C. H. Gehlke, "Crime and Punishment," in *Recent*

Social Trends in the United States: Report of the President's Research Com-mittee on Social Trends (New York: McGraw-Hill Book Company, 1933), II, 1128.

28. Thorstein Sellin, "The Basis of a Crime Index," *Journal of the American Insti-tute of Criminal Law and Criminology*, 22 (1931), 335–356. To date, no research has been published that would improve on or bypass the lack of knowledge of this aspect of American society in the 1920's. For a recent study citing key parts of the literature touching on the problem of historical crime statistics, see Theodore N. Ferdinand, "The Criminal Patterns of Boston Since 1848," *American Journal of Sociology*, 73 (1967), 84–99.

29. Frederick Lewis Allen, *Only Yesterday: An Informal History of the Nineteen-Twenties* (New York: Harper and Brothers, 1931), especially pp. 289–300, is the source of many of our stereotypes of the decade, but Allen was very careful to describe prohibition as only incidental to the rise of the racketeers. Writing about the field that he knew best, journalism, Allen gives throughout his book ample explication of the "ballyhoo" that lay behind the fiction of a crime wave.

30. Traditionally the organization of crime, rather than its mere incidence, has been blamed on the circumstances engendered by the prohibition laws. This conclu-sion ignores two facts: (1) Crime, as Progressives were fond of pointing out, was not unorganized before World War I (see, for example, John Landesco, "Pro-hibition and Crime," *Annals of the American Academy of Political and Social Science*, 163 [1932], 120), and (2) during the 1920's all areas of American society were subject to a striking organization and consolidation of effort. To connect an increase in scale of control and system in illegal activities with nothing but the bootlegging business would be most incautiously to ignore the rest of the social environment of American crime.

31. John R. Meers, "The California Wine and Grape Industry and Prohibition," *California Historical Society Quarterly*, 46 (1967), 19–32.

32. See in general Sinclair, *Prohibition*, chaps. 11 and 16, especially pp. 238, 239.

33. Whiting Williams, quoted in National Commission on Law Observance and Enforcement, *Enforcement of Prohibition Laws*, III, 183–184.

34. Warburton, *Economic Results of Prohibition*, p. 202.

35. Martha Bensley Bruère, *Does Prohibition Work? A Study of the Operation of the Eighteenth Amendment Made by the National Federation of Settlements, Assisted by Social Workers in Different Parts of the United States* (New York: Harper and Brothers, 1927). Clark, *The Dry Years*, especially pp. 136, 144–145, suggests not only that prohibition benefited the lower class but that as workers shared in the prosperity of the 1920's and moved up on the social scale, they had less need for the saloon. This is a novel twist on the common belief of the time, expressed, for example, by Lynd and Lynd, *Middletown*, pp. 256n, 258n, that the money that formerly went to support the saloon now was used to pay for the workers' new automobiles and radios. Warburton, *Economic Results of Prohibition*, chap. 8, is most disappointing in his treatment of what happened to the estimated two billion dollars newly available in the early prohibition years for non-liquor expenditures. He had no detailed information, for instance, on movie attendance, one of the alleged substitutes for saloon patronage, and he does not follow up his own suggestion that inflation might have absorbed all of the economic gains that accrued to former consumers of alcohol.

36. Bartlett Campbell Jones, "The Debate over National Prohibition, 1920–1933" (doctoral dissertation, Emory University, 1961), p. 247.
37. See ibid., in its entirety a useful summary and analysis of the incredible volume of writings dealing with prohibition.
38. Sinclair, *Prohibition*, pp. 309–310; further based on unpublished surveys of editorial and humorous material in newspapers and magazines of the 1920's. What caused such a sudden shift in these public opinion indexes in 1923–1924 is not known at this time. Possibly the noisy repeal of the "Baby Volstead" Act of New York, in 1923, was the critical event that showed that "the public" did not want prohibition, or at least Volsteadism. The new respectability of drinking among Americans at the upper end of the social scale was unquestionably a contributing factor. Also a factor was a recognition, sometime in the period 1921–1923, of the failure of enforcement.
39. Sinclair, *Prohibition*, pp. 226–230, 339.
40. Dayton E. Heckman, "Prohibition Passes: The Story of the Association Against the Prohibition Amendment" (doctoral dissertation, Ohio State University, 1939). Those who are skeptical of the influence of the AAPA and the liquor interests in the defeat of prohibition would do well to read Heckman's unique contemporary work.
41. Ibid.
42. Sinclair, *Prohibition*, especially chap. 21.
43. Ibid.; Jones, "Debate."

Chapter 12

1. For a partial treatment of social control, see Stow Persons, *American Minds: A History of Ideas* (New York: Henry Holt and Company, 1958), chap. 25, and Henry F. May, *The End of American Innocence: A Study of the First Years of Our Own Time, 1912–1917* (New York: Alfred A. Knopf, 1959), pp. 154–158.
2. Each area also had its conservatives analogous to Aldrich and Taft.
3. George E. Mowry, *The Era of Theodore Roosevelt, 1900–1912* (New York: Harper and Brothers, 1958), pp. 17–18, 37.
4. Ibid., pp. 49–51. David W. Noble, *The Paradox of Progressive Thought* (Minneapolis: University of Minnesota Press, 1958), p. 62, summarizes the view of the high priest of Progressivism, Herbert Croly, on the subject.
5. Eric F. Goldman, *Rendezvous with Destiny: A History of Modern American Reform* (New York: Alfred A. Knopf, 1952), p. 94; Mowry, *Era of Theodore Roosevelt*, p. 50. Such thinking was not far distant from other doctrines of the times, such as an economic interpretation of history.
6. Richard Hofstadter, *The Age of Reform: From Bryan to F.D.R.* (New York: Alfred A. Knopf, 1955), has been pre-eminent in suggesting as a major factor in Progressivism the changing status of certain middle-class groups, chap. 4; and Mowry, *Era of Theodore Roosevelt*, pp. 85ff., has documented the middle-class nature of Progressive leadership. (Psychiatrists and psychologists in general belonged to this dominant part of the middle class.) The Progressive reliance on the executive and the cult of the strong man were notable contemporaneous developments; ibid., p. 88; Goldman, *Rendezvous with Destiny*, p. 80;

Noble, *Paradox of Progressive Thought*, p. 74. Even the Progressives' faith in democracy was dependent upon their providing a proper environment for that democracy. See the sophisticated discussion of Progressivism in May, *End of American Innocence*, pp. 21–29.

7. Hofstadter, *Age of Reform*, p. 258; compare the summary in Mowry, *Era of Theodore Roosevelt*, pp. 104–105.

8. Ibid., p. 87; Hofstadter, *Age of Reform*, pp. 204–206, 208–212.

9. The cure rate was about 20 per cent; A. I. Noble, "The Curability of Insanity," *American Journal of Insanity*, 69 (1913), 715–717.

10. For example, H. M. Swift, "Insanity and Race," *American Journal of Insanity*, 70 (1913), 154.

11. See Walter Bromberg, *Man Above Humanity: A History of Psychotherapy* (Philadelphia: J. B. Lippincott Company, 1954), chap. 8.

12. Mark Hughlin Haller, "American Eugenics: Heredity and Social Thought, 1870–1930" (Ann Arbor, MI: University Microfilms, 1960), especially pp. 4, 157–158, shows how Progressives' assumptions of environmentalism did not deter them from supporting the eugenics movement.

13. For somewhat different views, see Louis Filler, *Crusaders for American Liberalism*, 2d ed. (Yellow Springs, OH: Antioch Press, 1950), chap. 22, and Harold Underwood Faulkner, *The Quest for Social Justice, 1898–1914* (New York: Macmillan Company, 1931), pp. 159–162.

14. C. P. Oberndorf, *A History of Psychoanalysis in America* (New York: Grune and Stratton, 1953), p. 152. For example, see the revealing paper, Charles W. Burr, "The Prevention of Insanity and Degeneracy," *American Journal of Insanity*, 74 (1917), 409–424, and especially the discussion, 422–423.

15. Richard C. Cabot, "The Analysis and Modification of Environment," *Psychotherapy*, 3, no. 3 (1909), 5. James V. May, "The Modern Trend of Psychiatry," *Interstate Medical Journal*, 18 (1911), 1098.

16. For example, see the systematic work of Morton Prince, "The Subconscious Setting of Ideas in Relation to the Pathology of the Psychoneuroses," *Journal of Abnormal Psychology*, 11 (1916), 1–18. William L. Russell, "The Widening Field of Practical Psychiatry," *American Journal of Insanity*, 70 (1913), 460. For example, William A. White, *The Principles of Mental Hygiene* (New York: Macmillan Company, 1917), p. 316.

17. For example, C. C. Wholey, in *Journal of the American Medical Association*, 62 (1914), 1036. Thomas W. Salmon, "Some New Fields in Neurology and Psychiatry," *Journal of Nervous and Mental Disease*, 46 (1917), 90–99.

18. For example, William Healy, *The Individual Delinquent: A Text-Book of Diagnosis and Prognosis for All Concerned in Understanding Offenders* (Boston: Little, Brown and Company, 1915); William Healy, *Mental Conflicts and Misconduct* (Boston: Little, Brown and Company, 1917), especially chap. 17. Healy's case affords evidence of a situation in which political Progressives had a direct influence on the development of psychiatry. In an interview with the writer, Dr. Healy remarked that the method of studying children (integrating medical, social, psychometric, and psychiatric studies of a single individual) that yielded him such rich results was suggested in large part by a group of social reformers associated with Hull House and led by Jane Addams and Julia Lathrop, two of the best-known Progressives. The Hull House reformers found financial support for the work and invited Healy to undertake it.

19. George Van Ness Dearborn, *The Influence of Joy* (Boston: Little, Brown and Company, 1916), p. 35. E. W. Taylor, "The Attitude of the Medical Profession Toward the Psychotherapeutic Movement," *Boston Medical and Surgical Journal*, 157 (1907), 845–846. Lewellys F. Barker, "On the Psychic Treatment of Some of the Functional Neuroses," *International Clinics*, 1 (17th ser., 1907), 13, 15, 17.

20. George W. Jacoby, *Suggestion and Psychotherapy* (New York: Charles Scribner's Sons, 1912), chap. 2, especially pp. 207, 218–219.

21. For example, J. T. W. Rowe, "Is Dementia Praecox the 'New Peril' in Psychiatry?" *American Journal of Insanity*, 63 (1907), 389, 393. Even most American psychoanalysts in this early period, it must be admitted, had less regard for theoretical consistency than did their European counterparts.

22. James Jackson Putnam, "The Psychoanalytic Movement," *Scientific American Supplement*, 78 (1914), 391, 402. Freud commented regretfully on Putnam's inclination to make psychoanalysis "the servant of moral aims." Sigmund Freud, *An Autobiographical Study*, trans. by James Strachey, 2d ed. (London: Hogarth Press, 1946), p. 94. Smith Ely Jelliffe and William A. White, *Diseases of the Nervous System: A Text-Book of Neurology and Psychiatry*, 2d ed. (Philadelphia: Lea and Febiger, 1917), p. 98. James Jackson Putnam, "On Some of the Broader Issues of the Psychoanalytic Movement," *American Journal of the Medical Sciences*, 147 (1914), 397–402.

23. For example, Ernest K. Lindley, in *Journal of the Indiana State Medical Association*, 9 (1916), 7; Stephen S. Colvin, "What Dreams Mean," *The Independent*, 72 (1912), 847.

24. Edwin B. Holt, *The Freudian Wish and Its Place in Ethics* (New York: Henry Holt and Company, 1915).

25. The social psychologies of men such as G. H. Mead and J. Mark Baldwin were too close to social philosophy to be properly included here. A case might be made, however, for including G. Stanley Hall and the genetic psychology of that time.

26. John Broadus Watson, "Psychology as the Behaviorist Views It," *Psychological Review*, 20 (1913), 158; see also 168–169, 177. Italics added. For an interesting variation with Freudian elements, see John Broadus Watson and J. J. B. Morgan, "Emotional Reactions and Psychological Experimentation," *American Journal of Psychology*, 28 (1917), 163–174.

27. For example, see M. E. Haggerty, "The Laws of Learning," *Psychological Review*, 20 (1913), 411; Howard C. Warren, "The Mental and Physical," ibid., 21 (1914), 99.

28. For example, see John Broadus Watson, "An Attempted Formulation of the Scope of Behavior Psychology," ibid., 24 (1917), 329–352; A. P. Weiss, "Relation Between Functional and Behavior Psychology," ibid., pp. 353–368.

29. See John Dewey, "The Need for Social Psychology," ibid., pp. 274–275.

30. See Edwin G. Boring, *A History of Experimental Psychology*, 2d ed. (New York: Appleton-Century-Crofts Company, Inc., 1950), pp. 642–643. Carl Rahn, in a review of W. A. White, *Mechanisms of Character Formation*, in *Psychological Bulletin*, 14 (1917), 327. The absence of a British counterpart is especially striking in view of the nearly contemporaneous reform movement there.

31. The intellectual spokesmen for Progressivism were well aware of the possibilities

of the new movements in psychiatry and psychology; for example, see Walter Lippmann, *A Preface to Politics* (New York: Michael Kennerley, 1913).

32. Even though not focusing on Progressivism, May, *End of American Innocence*, gives an idea of the light that can be shed on the movement by an approach such as the one suggested here.

Chapter 13

1. The present essay is related in many ways to the "organizational society" theme of the volume in which it was originally published. To the author, in addition, the reform activity of the physicians illustrates another general point, namely, that there was a Progressive movement—a distinguishable reform movement, but one that, unlike many other reform movements, operated primarily through non-governmental institutions and left more lasting effects upon non-political than upon political sectors of American society. The political bias of many historians has rendered them blind to the non-political and very real existence of Progressivism as it is discussed in the present essay and as it affected the lives of millions of people early in the twentieth century. See, for example, Peter Gabriel Filene's very premature "An Obituary for 'The Progressive Movement,'" *American Quarterly*, 22 (1970), 20–34.

2. See, for example, Committee on the Prevention of Tuberculosis, Charity Organization Society of the City of New York, *A Handbook on the Prevention of Tuberculosis* (New York, 1903).

3. See Richard Harrison Shryock, *National Tuberculosis Association, 1904–1954: A Study of the Voluntary Health Movement in the United States* (New York: National Tuberculosis Association, 1957), chaps. 2–3. For a contemporary example, see Henry Phipps Institute for the Study, Treatment, and Prevention of Tuberculosis, *Second Annual Report* (Philadelphia, 1906), especially pp. 8–11.

4. See, for example, Ernest Poole, "The Lung Block," *Charities and the Commons*, 11 (1903), 193–199.

5. See, for example, a well-known pioneer publicity piece by a New York physician, T. Mitchell Prudden, "Tuberculosis and Its Prevention," *Harper's*, 88 (1894), 630–637.

6. Ohio Society for the Prevention of Tuberculosis, *The Cause, Prevention and Cure of Tuberculosis (Consumption)* (Columbus, OH, 1904), p. 4.

7. Shryock, *National Tuberculosis Association*.

8. Much of the early propaganda was devoted to breaking this conspiracy of silence; see, for example, Lawrence F. Flick, *Consumption a Curable and Preventable Disease: What a Layman Should Know About It* (Philadelphia: D. McKay, 1903).

9. E. O. Otis, "Measures for Stamping Out Consumption," *Journal of Tuberculosis*, 3 (1901), 152.

10. Christopher Easton, "End of Tuberculosis," *The Survey*, 26 (1911), 726–728.

11. The foregoing two paragraphs are based on Shryock, *National Tuberculosis Association*.

12. Livingston Farrand, "Strategy in Tuberculosis," *The Survey*, 26 (1911), 693–694; Philip Peter Jacobs, "Eight Million Dollars to Prevent Tuberculosis," *The*

Survey, 22 (1909), 821–822; Philip Peter Jacobs, "Trend of the Anti-Tuberculosis Crusade," *The Survey*, 22 (1909), 710–713.

13. See Shryock, *National Tuberculosis Association*.

14. See, for example, the classic statement of William Trufant Foster, in William Trufant Foster, ed., *The Social Emergency: Studies in Sex Hygiene and Morals* (Boston: Houghton Mifflin Company, 1914), p. 5, and similarly, an editorial, "The Teaching of Sex Hygiene," *New York Medical Journal*, 101 (1915), 850.

15. See, for example, L. Duncan Bulkley, "Syphilis as a Non-Venereal Disease," *Journal of the American Medical Association*, 11 (1888), 865–873.

16. See, for example, Jean-Alfred Fournier, *The Prophylaxis of Syphilis*, trans. by C. F. Marshall (London: Rebman, 1906).

17. Charles Walter Clarke, *Taboo: The Story of the Pioneers of Social Hygiene* (Washington, DC: Public Affairs Press, 1961), especially chap. 7.

18. David Jay Pivar, "The New Abolitionism: The Quest for Social Purity, 1876–1900" (doctoral dissertation, University of Pennsylvania, 1965). The evolution of the movement is best traced in its journals such as *Vigilance*, *The Philanthropist*, and *The Light*. For a convenient summary, see Aaron M. Powell, ed., *The National Purity Congress, Its Papers, Addresses, Portraits* (New York: American Purity Alliance, 1896).

19. Henry F. May, *The End of American Innocence: A Study of the First Years of Our Own Time, 1912–1917* (New York: Alfred A. Knopf, 1959), covers the subject generally. For an example of contemporary comment, see George Cram Cook, in the Chicago *Evening Post Friday Literary Review*, December 20, 1912, p. 6.

20. See, for example, the short stories in *Smart Set* in the early years of the new century.

21. See, for example, Norton Mezvinsky, "An Idea of Female Superiority," *Journal of the Central Mississippi Valley American Studies Association*, 2 (1961), 17–26; and a contemporary example, Anna Garlin Spencer, "The Double Standard of Morals: The Last Refuge of Human Slavery," *Vigilance*, September, 1912, pp. 6–9.

22. See *Transactions of the American Society of Sanitary and Moral Prophylaxis*, *passim*. and particularly Prince Albert Morrow, "A Plea for the Organization of a 'Society of Sanitary and Moral Prophylaxis,'" 1 (1905–1906), 17–25, and Prince Albert Morrow, "The Society of Sanitary and Moral Prophylaxis: Its Objects and Aims," 1 (1905–1906), 26–37.

23. See, for example, ibid. and Edward L. Keyes, Jr., "The Sexual Necessity," *Transactions of the American Society of Sanitary and Moral Prophylaxis*, 1 (1905–1906), 40–45.

24. The most convenient summary is Lavinia L. Dock, *Hygiene and Morality: A Manual for Nurses and Others* (New York: G. P. Putnam's Sons, 1910). A contemporary example is Denslow Lewis, "The Prophylaxis and Management of Prostitution," *St. Paul Medical Journal*, 8 (1906), 591–600. The movement can be followed in detail in the magazine, *Social Hygiene*. For scholarly analysis, see Roy Lubove, "The Progressives and the Prostitute," *The Historian*, 24 (1962), 308–330.

25. See, for example, Edward L. Keyes, Jr., "Society of Sanitary and Moral Pro-

phylaxis, President's Report," *Journal of the Society of Sanitary and Moral Prophylaxis*, 5 (1914), 4–8.

26. See, for example, *The Stage Year Book*, 1914, pp. 59, 239.

27. William L. O'Neill, *Divorce in the Progressive Era* (New Haven, CT: Yale University Press, 1967).

28. John C. Burnham, *Psychoanalysis and American Medicine, 1894–1918: Medicine, Science, and Culture* (New York: International Universities Press, 1967), especially chaps. 2–3.

29. See, for example, C. L. Dana, in *Journal of Nervous and Mental Disease*, 35 (1908), 783. See, too, Richard Weiss, *The American Myth of Success: From Horatio Alger to Norman Vincent Peale* (New York: Basic Books, Inc., 1969).

30. George C. Smith, in *Journal of the American Medical Association*, 49 (1907), 267; "Psychotherapy," *Interstate Medical Journal*, 13 (1906), 952–954.

31. R. J. Cunningham, "The Emmanuel Movement: A Variety of American Religious Experience," *American Quarterly*, 14 (1962), 47–63; Weiss, *The American Myth of Success*.

32. See Barbara Sicherman, "The Quest for Mental Health in America, 1880–1917" (doctoral dissertation, Columbia University, 1967), especially p. 290.

33. John C. Burnham, "Psychiatry, Psychology and the Progressive Movement" (reprinted herein as Chapter 12), *American Quarterly*, 12 (1960), 457–465.

34. James V. May, "The Modern Trend of Psychiatry," *Interstate Medical Journal*, 18 (1911), 1098.

35. An early example was Lewellys F. Barker, "On the Psychic Treatment of Some of the Functional Neuroses," *International Clinics*, 1 (17th series, 1907), 1–22.

36. Smith Ely Jelliffe and William A. White, *Diseases of the Nervous System: A Text-Book of Neurology and Psychiatry*, 2d ed. (Philadelphia: Lea and Febiger, 1917), p. 98. See, too, Burnham, "Psychiatry, Psychology and the Progressive Movement," and Weiss, *The American Myth of Success*.

37. See, for example, Donald R. Hooker, "Social Hygiene—Another Great Social Movement," *Social Hygiene*, 2 (1916), 5–10.

38. See in general Harold M. Cavins, *National Health Agencies: A Survey with Especial Reference to Voluntary Associations* (Washington, DC: Public Affairs Press, 1945).

39. See, for example, Woods Hutchinson, "The Conquest of the Great Diseases," *World's Work*, 21 (1911), 13881–13883; Ida M. Cannon, *Social Work in Hospitals: A Contribution to Progressive Medicine* (New York: Survey Associates, Inc., 1913).

40. Jacobs, "Trend of the Anti-Tuberculosis Crusade," p. 712.

Chapter 14

Acknowledgment: Particular thanks for suggestions are owed to Gary Reichard, Gerd Korman, and Gerald D. Nash. Writing was supported in part by assigned research duty from the Ohio State University.

1. Peter Gabriel Filene, "An Obituary for 'The Progressive Movement,'" *American Quarterly*, 22 (1970), 20–34.

2. Samuel P. Hays, "The Politics of Reform in Municipal Government in the Progressive Era," *Pacific Northwest Quarterly*, 55 (1964), 157–169.

3. Just such local work convinced one historian that generalizations that Progressives neglected the oppression of blacks are not viable; Gilbert Osofsky, "Progressivism and the Negro: New York, 1900–1915," *American Quarterly*, 16 (1964), 153–168.

4. Arthur M. Schlesinger, Jr., *The Age of Jackson* (Boston: Little, Brown and Company, 1945).

5. Otis L. Graham, Jr., *An Encore for Reform: The Old Progressives and the New Deal* (New York: Oxford University Press, 1967); Richard S. Kirkendall, "The New Deal as Watershed: The Recent Literature," *Journal of American History*, 54 (1968), 843–847.

6. Clyde Griffen, "The Progressive Ethos," in Stanley Coben and Lorman Ratner, eds., *The Development of an American Culture* (Englewood Cliffs, NJ: Prentice-Hall, Inc., 1970), pp. 120–149. Attempts at elucidating conservative opposition during this period have been unfruitful; see, for example, Richard W. Leopold, *Elihu Root and the Conservative Tradition* (Boston: Little, Brown and Company, 1954), showing an apparent conservative to be only an unsystematic legalist.

7. Maxwell H. Bloomfield, *Alarms and Diversions: The American Mind Through American Magazines, 1900–1914* (The Hague, Netherlands: Mouton, 1967), p. 11. Cf. Dorothy M. Brown, "The Quality Magazines in the Progressive Era," *Mid-America*, 53 (1971), 139–159. Louis Filler, *Crusaders for American Liberalism*, 2d ed. (Yellow Springs, OH: Antioch Press, 1950), chap. 28, and others associate the end of muckraking with business pressure. But other evidence indicates that merely negative exposés were already passé and that the muckrakers for their own reasons were turning to other types of publications; for example, Robert C. Bannister, Jr., *Ray Stannard Baker: The Mind and Thought of a Progressive* (New Haven, CT: Yale University Press, 1966), especially 108–110, and Charles Forcey, *The Crossroads of Liberalism: Croly, Weyl, Lippmann, and the Progressive Era* (New York: Oxford University Press, 1961). Warren I. Titus, "The Progressivism of the Muckrakers: A Myth Re-Examined Through Fiction," *Journal of the Central Mississippi Valley American Studies Association*, 1 (1960), 10–16.

8. Dewey W. Grantham, Jr., "The Progressive Era and the Reform Tradition," *Mid-America*, 46 (1964), 227–251. Scott M. Cutlip, *Fund Raising in the United States: Its Role in Philanthropy* (New Brunswick, NJ: Rutgers University Press, 1965).

9. Robert H. Wiebe, *Businessmen and Reform: A Study of the Progressive Movement* (Cambridge, MA: Harvard University Press, 1962). A striking specific example is discussed in Anthony Raymond Travis, "The Impulse Toward the Welfare State: Chicago, 1890–1932" (doctoral dissertation, Michigan State University, 1971), pp. 28–29.

10. Thomas A. Edison to Henry Ford, quoted in Allan Nevins and Frank Ernest Hill, *Ford: The Times, the Man, the Company* (New York: Charles Scribner's Sons, 1954), I, 531–532. Winston Allen Flint, *The Progressive Movement in Vermont* (Washington, DC: American Council on Public Affairs, 1941), shows that even in politics in a one-party, conservative state there was Progressive

agitation and change that was recognized as part of a national movement. Aaron
I. Abell, *American Catholicism and Social Action: A Search for Social Justice,
1865–1950* (Garden City, NY: Hanover House, 1960), especially pp. 140–141,
181, describes how even anti-environmentalist Jesuits talked about "the social
regeneration of our country."

11. Harry A. Wheeler, quoted in Paul W. Glad, "Progressives and the Business
Culture of the 1920s," *Journal of American History*, 53 (1966), 80. John D.
Buenker, *Urban Liberalism and Progressive Reform* (New York: Charles Scrib-
ner's Sons, 1973), pp. 46–48; Melvin Holli, "Urban Reformation in the Progres-
sive Era," in Louis L. Gould, ed., *The Progressive Era* (Syracuse, NY: Syracuse
University Press, 1974), pp. 133–151.

12. Herbert Croly, *Progressive Democracy* (New York: Macmillan Company, 1914),
p. 426. Joel A. Tarr, "The Urban Politician as Entrepreneur," *Mid-America*, 49
(1967), 55–67, shows that reformers attacked the bosses for using politics for private purposes. See, similarly, Hays, "The Politics of Reform," p. 163. Theodore
Lowi, "The Public Philosophy: Interest-Group Liberalism," *American Political
Science Review*, 61 (1967), 19, comments wryly on later developments exalting interest groups so as to make "conflict-of-interest a principle of government
rather than a criminal act."

13. John Braeman, "Seven Progressives," *Business History Review*, 35 (1961), 581–
592. Daniel Levine, *Varieties of Reform Thought* (Madison: University of Wisconsin Press, 1964) concluded that no generalization about Progressivism is
possible.

14. Graham, *Encore for Reform*, pp. 55–56; for a non-political example see Lloyd
C. Taylor, Jr., *The Medical Profession and Social Reform, 1885–1945* (New
York: St. Martin's Press, 1974), especially chap. 2; Eric Anderson, "Prostitution
and Social Justice: Chicago, 1910–15," *Social Service Review*, 48 (1974), 216–
218.

15. Filene, "An Obituary," made the error of saying that because no disciplined and
clearly identifiable leadership existed, there was no Progressive movement—
using movement in the narrow sense of the Communist party, U.S.A. The Progressive movement in fact meets the standards for a social movement set forth
by Roberta Ash, *Social Movements in America* (Chicago: Markham Publishers,
1972), p. 2, especially the distinction between movement organization and social
movements proper. See, for example, Robert H. Wiebe, *The Search for Order,
1877–1920* (New York: Hill and Wang, 1967), pp. 128–129; C. Roland Marchand, *The American Peace Movement and Social Reform, 1898–1918* (Princeton, NJ: Princeton University Press, 1972), pp. 90–98; Travis, "Impulse Toward
the Welfare State;" Nancy J. Weiss, *The National Urban League, 1910–1940*
(New York: Oxford University Press, 1974), chap. 4.

16. Norman N. Wilensky, *Conservatives in the Progressive Era: The Taft Republi-
cans of 1912* (Gainesville: University of Florida Press, 1965).

17. David Thelen, *The New Citizenship: Origins of Progressivism in Wisconsin,
1885–1900* (Columbia: University of Missouri Press, 1972).

18. Jean B. Quandt, *From the Small Town to the Great Community: The Social
Thought of Progressive Intellectuals* (New Brunswick, NJ: Rutgers University
Press, 1970); R. Jackson Wilson, *In Quest of Community: Social Philosophy in
the United States, 1860–1920* (New York: John Wiley and Sons, 1968); Wiebe,

The Search for Order. Graham, *Encore for Reform,* p. 65n., suggests that pre-1900 reformers felt economic injustices more keenly than those who joined reform ranks later.

19. David M. Chalmers, *The Social and Political Ideas of the Muckrakers* (New York: Citadel Press, 1964), p. 104.

20. Roy Lubove, "The Twentieth Century City: The Progressive as Municipal Reformer," *Mid-America,* 41 (1959), 199, 200–201, 207–208. Quandt, *From the Small Town;* Wilson, *In Quest of Community;* Edward Stevens, Jr., "Social Centers, Politics, and Social Efficiency in the Progressive Era," *History of Education Quarterly,* 12 (1972), 16–33.

21. James R. McGovern, "David Graham Phillips and the Virility Impulse of Progressives," *New England Quarterly,* 39 (1966), 334–355; James Penick, Jr., "The Progressives and the Environment," in Gould, *The Progressive Era,* pp. 115–131.

22. John Higham, "The Reorientation of American Culture in the 1890's," in John Weiss, ed., *The Origins of Modern Consciousness* (Detroit: Wayne State University Press, 1965), pp. 25–48.

23. Wiebe, *Businessmen and Reform,* chap. 4; Allen F. Davis, *Spearheads for Reform: The Social Settlements and the Progressive Movement,* 1890–1914 (New York: Oxford University Press, 1967); Travis, "Impulse Toward the Welfare State."

24. James Oppenheim, "And the Greatest of These?" in *War and Laughter* (New York: Century Company, 1916), p. 176. See, for example, William L. Bowers, "County Life Reform, 1900–1920: A Neglected Aspect of 'Progressive' Era History," *Agricultural History,* 45 (1961), 211–221.

25. Walter Lippmann, *Drift and Mastery: An Attempt to Diagnose the Current Unrest* (New York: Michael Kennerley, 1914), p. 325.

26. It is only fair to add that earlier efforts at reform and cooperation had sometimes been successful and provided both experience and continuity between earlier reform and later uplift. Examples include Timothy L. Smith, "Progressivism in American Education, 1880–1900," *Harvard Educational Review,* 31 (1961), 168–193; and K. Austin Kerr, "Labor-Management Cooperation: An 1897 Case," *Pennsylvania Magazine of History and Biography,* 99 (1975), 45–71.

27. Edgar Gardner Murphy, quoted in Levine, *Varieties of Reform Thought,* p. 92. Walter Rauschenbusch, *Christianizing the Social Order* (New York: Macmillan Company, 1912), pp. 126–127.

28. Among others, Forcey, *Crossroads of Liberalism,* discusses this problem at length. Arthur Mann, "British Social Thought and American Reformers of the Progressive Era," *Mississippi Valley Historical Review,* 42 (1956), 672–692, suggests the influence of English elitism.

29. The most relevant treatment is Richard Weiss, *The American Myth of Success: From Horatio Alger to Norman Vincent Peale* (New York: Basic Books, Inc., 1969), chaps. 5–7; the quotes are from pp. 179 and 215.

30. Forcey, *Crossroads of Liberalism,* discusses some of the tensions in the formal writings of politically oriented Progressive intellectuals. See, similarly, David W. Noble, *The Paradox of Progressive Thought* (Minneapolis: University

of Minnesota Press, 1958). Romantic individualism is of course related to the virility impulse discussed previously.

31. Herbert Croly, *The Promise of American Life*, 1965 ed. (Cambridge, MA: Harvard University Press, 1965), p. 270. See Graham, *Encore for Reform*, p. 38, and Arthur A. Ekirch, *The Decline of American Liberalism*, 2d ed. (New York: Atheneum, 1967), chap. 11. David W. Southern, *The Malignant Heritage: Yankee Progressives and the Negro Question, 1901–1914* (Chicago: Loyola University Press, 1968), suggests that in so far as blacks were excluded from American nationalism, so they were excluded from Progressivism.

32. Frederick A. Cleveland, *Organized Democracy: An Introduction to the Study of American Politics* (New York: Longmans, Green, and Company, 1913), p. 438. Ellis W. Hawley et al., *Herbert Hoover and the Crisis of American Capitalism* (Cambridge, MA: Schenkman Publishing Company, 1973).

33. *World's Work*, 17 (1908), 10860. See, similarly, the evidence in John Lee Eighmy, "Religious Liberalism in the South During the Progressive Era," *Church History*, 38 (1969), 359–372.

34. Arnold M. Rose, "Voluntary Associations Under Conditions of Competition and Conflict," *Social Forces*, 34 (1955), 159–163, found that at a later time the voluntary groups were greatly stimulated by both competition from other groups and opposition, a phenomenon that would help explain the mutual reinforcement of the Progressives. The voluntary group phenomenon itself in the context of other American institutions has long been recognized as fulfilling important social functions; for specific examples of group coalescence, see Marchand, *The American Peace Movement*.

35. Daniel Fox, "Social Policy and City Politics: Tuberculosis Reporting in New York, 1889–1900," *Bulletin of the History of Medicine*, 49 (1975), 169. Obviously such revision by principals has misled later historians.

36. See, for example, Davis, *Spearheads for Reform*, p. 314.

37. Suggestive discussions are Louis Galambos, *Competition and Cooperation: The Emergence of a National Trade Association* (Baltimore: Johns Hopkins Press, 1966); Jonathan Lurie, "Private Associations, Internal Regulation and Progressivism: The Chicago Board of Trade, 1880–1923, as a Case Study," *American Journal of Legal History*, 16 (1972), 215–238; Jerry Israel, ed., *Building the Organizational Society: Essays on Associational Activities in Modern America* (New York: Free Press, 1972). Gregory H. Singleton, "Protestant Voluntary Organizations and the Shaping of Victorian America," *American Quarterly*, 27 (1975), 549–560, suggests that church organization of the late nineteenth century was an important influence on other voluntary organizations.

38. See, for example, Gerd Korman, *Industrialization, Immigrants, and Americanizers: The View from Milwaukee, 1866–1921* (Madison: State Historical Society of Wisconsin, 1967); Manicus S. Hutton, "Progress of the Safety Movement," *Scientific American Supplement*, 77 (1914), 90–91; Edward L. Tinker, "The Man Who Is Father of the 'Safety First' Movement, Ralph C. Richards," *American Magazine*, 76 (1913), 44–45.

39. Richard Harrison Shryock, *National Tuberculosis Association, 1904–1954: A Study of the Voluntary Health Movement in the United States* (New York: National Tuberculosis Association, 1957); John C. Burnham, "Medical Specialists

and Movements Toward Social Control in the Progressive Era: Three Examples" (reprinted herein as Chapter 13), in Israel, *Building the Organizational Society*, pp. 19–30.

40.   Manfred J. Waserman, "Henry L. Coit and the Certified Milk Movement in the Development of Modern Pediatrics," *Bulletin of the History of Medicine*, 46 (1972), 359–390.

41.   William L. O'Neill, *Divorce in the Progressive Era* (New Haven, CT: Yale University Press, 1967); John C. Burnham, "The Progressive Era Revolution in American Attitudes Toward Sex" (reprinted herein as Chapter 10), *Journal of American History*, 59 (1973), 885–908; Annie S. Daniel, "The Wreck of the Home," *Charities*, 14 (1905), 624–629.

42.   Griffen, "The Progressive Ethos," p. 149; see especially Ferenc M. Szasz, "The Progressive Clergy and the Kingdom of God," *Mid-America*, 55 (1973), 3–20.

43.   Rush Welter, *Popular Education and Democratic Thought in America* (New York: Columbia University Press, 1962), especially chaps. 15 and 16; Lawrence A. Cremin, *The Transformation of the School: Progressivism in American Education, 1876–1957* (New York: Alfred A. Knopf, 1961); William H. Issel, "Teachers and Educational Reform During the Progressive Era: A Case Study of the Pittsburgh Teachers' Association," *History of Education Quarterly*, 7 (1967), 220–233; and many other publications dealing with educational reform.

44.   Korman, *Industrialization, Immigrants, and Americanizers*; and such statements as Arthur Jerome Eddy, *The New Competition*, 5th ed. (Chicago: A McClurg, 1916), and Edward N. Hurley, *Awakening of Business* (Garden City, NY: Doubleday, Page and Company, 1917). Milton Derber, "The Idea of Industrial Democracy in America, 1898–1915," *Labor History*, 7 (1966), 259–286.

45.   Samuel Haber, *Efficiency and Uplift: Scientific Management in the Progressive Era, 1890–1920* (Chicago: University of Chicago Press, 1964). George V. Thompson, "Intercompany Technical Standardization in the Early American Automobile Industry," *Journal of Economic History*, 14 (1954), 1–20.

46.   Raymond E. Callahan, *Education and the Cult of Efficiency: A Study of the Social Forces that Have Shaped the Administration of the Public Schools* (Chicago: University of Chicago Press, 1962); Cremin, *Transformation of the School*; Roy Lubove, *The Professional Altruist: The Emergence of Social Work as a Career, 1880–1930* (Cambridge, MA: Harvard University Press, 1965); Edwin T. Layton, Jr., *The Revolt of the Engineers: Social Responsibility and the American Engineering Profession* (Cleveland, OH: Press of Case Western Reserve University, 1971).

47.   Samuel P. Hays, *Conservation and the Gospel of Efficiency: The Progressive Conservation Movement, 1890–1920* (Cambridge, MA: Harvard University Press, 1959); Joel Spring, "Education and Progressivism," *History of Education Quarterly*, 10 (1970), 53–71; Roy Lubove, *The Progressives and the Slums: Tenement House Reform in New York City, 1890–1917* (Pittsburgh: University of Pittsburgh Press, 1962). Even in the arts there appeared to be counterpart movements parallel with Progressivism. According to William H. Jordy, *American Buildings and Their Architects: Progressive and Academic Ideas at the Turn of the Twentieth Century* (Garden City, NY: Doubleday and Company, 1972), pp. 219–220, 373–375, in architecture Charles McKim wanted to lead and inspire with neoclassical designs, while the craftsman's movement

used the adjectives "sincere, liberating, democratic, functional, organic." Even music was involved in the ethos of the day; see Robert M. Crunden, "Charles Ives' Innovative Nostalgia," *Choral Journal*, 15 (1974), 5–12.

48. "Social Forces," *The Survey*, 25 (1911), 893.

49. Gerald Kurland, *Seth Low: The Reformer in an Urban and Industrial Age* (New York: Twayne Publishers, 1971). Lewis L. Gould, *Progressives and Prohibitionists: Texas Democrats in the Wilson Era* (Austin: University of Texas Press, 1973), especially p. 38, shows how Southerners, because of attitudes left over from Reconstruction, wanted to keep government at all levels as weak as possible, and how this worked out in the prohibition controversy of the Progressive era.

50. Thelen, *The New Citizenship*, is one work describing the disillusionment with politics.

51. David Jay Pivar, *Purity Crusade: Sexual Morality and Social Control, 1868–1900* (Westport, CT: Greenwood Press, 1973).

52. Korman, *Industrialization, Immigrants, and Americanizers*.

53. David Graham Phillips, *The Reign of Gilt* (New York: J. Pott and Company, 1905), p. 191.

54. James H. Cassedy, "The 'Germ of Laziness' in the South, 1900–1915: Charles Wardell Stiles and the Progressive Paradox," *Bulletin of the History of Medicine*, 45 (1971), 159–169. Perhaps the most conspicuously influential group is described by Marguerite Green, *The National Civic Federation and the American Labor Movement, 1900–1925* (Washington, DC: Catholic University of America Press, 1956).

55. W. Brooke Graves, *Uniform State Action: A Possible Substitute for Centralization* (Chapel Hill: University of North Carolina Press, 1934), pp. 33–34. Kurland, *Seth Low*, p. 203, quotes the *Review of Reviews*: "Tammany Hall binds together, not by ties of disinterested and patriotic political conviction, but rather of private interest, something like half of all the voters who lived in New York City." Lloyd Sponholtz, "The Initiative and Referendum: Direct Democracy in Perspective, 1898–1920," *American Studies*, 14 (1973), 43–64. Arthur Lipow, "Plebiscitarian Politics and Progressivism: The Direct Democracy Movement," unpublished paper presented to the American Historical Association, December, 1973. Norbert Brockman, "The National Bar Association, 1888–1893: The Failure of Early Bar Federation," *American Journal of Legal History*, 5 (1961), 125. Opposition to Progressives in the political sphere tended to appear as partisanship, or regularity or defense of the traditional institutions the Progressives were attempting to bypass, such as seniority. See, for a case history, Peter Romanofsky, " 'The Public Is Aroused': The Missouri Children's Code Commission 1915–1919," *Missouri Historical Review*, 28 (1973), 204–222.

56. Griffen, "The Progressive Ethos."

57. Pivar, *Purity Crusade*; the quote is from Griffen, "The Progressive Ethos," p. 133; John A. Garraty, *Right-Hand Man: The Life of George W. Perkins* (New York: Harper and Row Publishers, 1960); Benjamin O. Flower, "A Civil Leader of the New Time," *Arena*, 25 (1901), 400. W. D. P. Bliss, "The Church and Social Reform Workers," *The Outlook*, 82 (1906), 122–125. See, too, Robert M. Crunden, "George D. Herron in the 1890's: A New Frame of Reference for the Study of the Progressive Era," *Annals of Iowa*, 42 (1973), 81–113, and

John B. Clark, "Reform Currents in Polite Monthly Magazines, 1880–1900," *Mid-America*, 47 (1965), 3–23.

58.   Gregory H. Singleton, "The Dynamics of 'WASP' Culture: From Ethnic Cohesion to Organization Man," unpublished paper. Joseph R. Gusfield, *Symbolic Crusade: Status Politics and the American Temperance Movement* (Urbana: University of Illinois Press, 1963), works out one example. Paul Kleppner, *The Cross of Culture: A Social Analysis of Midwestern Politics, 1850–1900* (New York: Free Press, 1970). John Milton Cooper, Jr., "Progressivism and American Foreign Policy: A Reconsideration," *Mid-America*, 51 (1969), 260–277; Jerry Israel, *Progressivism and the Open Door: America and China, 1905–1921* (Pittsburgh: University of Pittsburgh Press, 1971).

59.   Wiebe, *The Search for Order*; Gerald D. Nash, *State Government and Economic Development: A History of Administrative Policies in California, 1849–1933* (Berkeley: Institute of Governmental Studies, University of California, 1964).

60.   Layton, *Revolt of the Engineers*; Lubove, *Professional Altruist*; Otis A. Pease, *The Responsibilities of American Advertising: Private Control and Public Influence, 1920–1940* (New Haven, CT: Yale University Press, 1958), especially pp. 44–45.

61.   Carl Resek, "Introduction," in Carl Resek, ed., *The Progressives* (Indianapolis: Bobbs-Merrill, 1967), p. xx; Samuel Hynes, *The Edwardian Turn of Mind* (Princeton, NJ: Princeton University Press, 1968), chap. 3.

62.   Roy Lubove, "The Progressives and the Prostitute," *The Historian*, 24 (1962), 308–330.

63.   This latter point was suggested by Gerd Korman.

64.   Ronald C. Tobey, *The American Ideology of National Science, 1919–1930* (Pittsburgh: University of Pittsburgh Press, 1971), pp. 4–5, 18–19.

65.   Haber, *Efficiency and Uplift*, pp. ix–x and *passim*; Callahan, *Education and the Cult of Efficiency*, pp. 15–46. An excellent and largely non-political example is William Harvey Allen, *Efficient Democracy* (New York: Dodd, Mead and Company, 1907).

66.   Croly, *Promise of American Life*, p. 434.

67.   William English Walling, *Progressivism—And After* (New York: Macmillan Company, 1914), pp. xx–xxi.

68.   This is a distinction not made in the pioneer study by Peter H. Odegard, *Pressure Politics: The Story of the Anti-Saloon League* (New York: Columbia University Press, 1928).

69.   Rauschenbusch, *Christianizing the Social Order*, p. 156. Yet one should be careful not to underestimate the impact of the Progressive ethos even on apparently selfish groups; see, for example, Lurie, "Private Associations, Internal Regulation and Progressivism."

70.   Burnham, "Medical Specialists."

71.   Charles Hirschfeld, "Nationalist Progressivism and World War I," *Mid-America*, 45 (1963), 139–156; Sidney Kaplan, "Social Engineers as Saviors: Effects of World War I on Some American Liberals," *Journal of the History of Ideas*, 17 (1956), 347–369; Paul F. Bourke, "Culture and the Status of Politics, 1909–1917: Studies in the Social Criticism of Herbert Croly, Walter Lippmann, Randolph Bourne and Van Wyck Brooks" (doctoral dissertation, University of Wisconsin,

1967). Allen F. Davis, "Welfare, Reform and World War I," *American Quarterly*, 19 (1967), 516–533.

72. Nicholas Joost, "The Dial in Transition: The End of the Browne Family's Control, 1913–1916," *Illinois History*, 22 (1965), 240–270. Travis, "Impulse Toward the Welfare State," pp. 55–56.

73. Harold Stearns, *Liberalism in America: Its Origin, Its Temporary Collapse, Its Future* (New York: Boni and Liveright, 1919).

74. Richard H. Pells, *Radical Visions and American Dreams: Culture and Social Thought in the Depression Years* (New York: Harper and Row Publishers, Inc., 1973), pp. 22–23; Robert M. Crunden, *From Self to Society, 1919–1941* (Englewood Cliffs, NJ: Prentice-Hall, Inc., 1972), pp. 1–75; Hawley, in *Herbert Hoover and the Crisis of American Capitalism*, pp. 3–27.

75. Clarke A. Chambers, *Seedtime of Reform: American Social Service and Social Action, 1918–1933* (Minneapolis: University of Minnesota Press, 1963). William E. Leuchtenburg, *Franklin D. Roosevelt and the New Deal, 1932–1940* (New York: Harper and Row Publishers, Inc., 1963), pp. 338–340; Rexford G. Tugwell, "The New Deal—The Progressive Tradition," *Western Political Quarterly*, 3 (1958), 390–427.

76. W. Lloyd Warner, *American Life: Dream and Reality* (Chicago: University of Chicago Press, 1953), p. 194.

77. The most perceptive of these critiques is Jeremy P. Felt, "The Progressive Era in America: 1900–1917," *Societas*, 3 (1973), 103–114.

78. Richard Hofstadter, *The Age of Reform: From Bryan to F.D.R.* (New York: Alfred A. Knopf, 1955), pp. 202–212; Samuel P. Hays, *The Response to Industrialism: 1885–1914* (Chicago: University of Chicago Press, 1957), p. 76; Lubove, "The Twentieth Century City," p. 206.

79. Randolph S. Bourne, *Youth and Life* (Boston: Houghton Mifflin Company, 1913), p. 292.

Conclusion

1. Elsewhere (pp. 128–129) in the volume in which the last chapter originally appeared, I commented further on the Progressive movement: "The unifying ingredient was unselfishness. A traditional ideal, it was new in the Progressive Era in the public form that it took and the scale on which people encountered consciousness of it. Even religion that was essentially selfish was not acceptable to progressives. The businessmen and bosses were attacked not particularly because of institutional defect but because—and when—they utilized institutions for selfish purposes. Progressives were aware of the growing tension between personal goals and bureaucratic, societal constraints. Voluntarism, as Ellis Hawley points out, was designed to mediate between increasing social demands and individual autonomy. The search for autonomy continues today, but it is not clear that any recent program designed to achieve it has been superior to that of the progressives. It behooves their descendants to take them seriously."

2. Taylor Stoehr, *Hawthorne's Mad Scientists: Pseudoscience and Social Science in Nineteenth-Century Life and Letters* (Hampden, CT: Archon Books, 1978). Mary O. Furner, *Advocacy and Objectivity: A Crisis in the Professionalization*

of American Social Science, 1865–1905 (Lexington: University Press of Kentucky, 1975). Thomas L. Haskell, *The Emergence of Professional Social Science: The American Social Science Association and the Nineteenth-Century Crisis of Authority* (Urbana: University of Illinois Press, 1977). Another important stream is noted in Dorothy Ross, "Socialism and American Liberalism: Academic Social Thought in the 1880's," *Perspectives in American History*, 11 (1977–1978), 7–79. A general account is Paul S. Boyer, *Urban Masses and Moral Order in America, 1820–1920* (Cambridge, MA: Harvard University Press, 1978).

3. David Thelen, *The New Citizenship: Origins of Progressivism in Wisconsin, 1885–1900* (Columbia: University of Missouri Press, 1972). Christopher Lasch, *The Culture of Narcissism: American Life in an Age of Diminishing Expectations* (New York: W. W. Norton and Company, 1979); I have cited this book in other contexts herein. See, similarly, on the same theme as my essay, Robert M. Crunden, *From Self to Society, 1919–1941* (New York: Prentice-Hall, 1972).

4. The key works at present are Warren I. Susman, *Culture as History: The Transformation of American Society in the Twentieth Century* (New York: Pantheon Books, 1984), and Richard Wightman Fox and T. J. Jackson Lears, eds., *The Culture of Consumption: Critical Essays in American History, 1880–1980* (New York: Pantheon Books, 1983).

5. William R. Leach, *True Love and Perfect Union: The Feminist Reform of Sex and Society* (New York: Basic Books, Inc., 1980), pp. 213–237. William R. Leach, "Transformations in a Culture of Consumption: Women and Department Stores, 1890–1925," *Journal of American History*, 71 (1984), 319–342.

6. A pioneer investigation was Michael Gordon, "From an Unfortunate Necessity to a Cult of Mutual Orgasm: Sex in American Marital Education Literature," in James M. Henslin, ed., *Studies in the Sociology of Sex* (New York: Appleton-Century-Crofts Company, Inc., 1971), pp. 53–77. Peter Gardella, *Innocent Ecstasy: How Christianity Gave America an Ethic of Sexual Pleasure* (New York: Oxford University Press, 1985), is mentioned in chapter 8 above. See, for example, the story—which I only summarize—as it has been developed in Gary S. Luter, "Sexual Reform on the American Stage in the Progressive Era, 1900–1915" (doctoral dissertation, University of Florida, 1981).

7. Kerry W. Buckley, "The Selling of a Psychologist: John Broadus Watson and the Application of Behavioral Techniques to Advertising," *Journal of the History of the Behavioral Sciences*, 18 (1982), 207–221. Elaine S. Abelson, "The Invention of Kleptomania: Women as Consumers in the Nineteenth-Century Department Store," paper read at the meetings of the American Historical Association, December, 1986. Roland Marchand, *Advertising the American Dream: Making Way for Modernity, 1920–1940* (Berkeley: University of California Press, 1985), especially pp. 358–359.

Index

AMERICAN CIVILIZATION
A series edited by Allen F. Davis

Gospel Hymns and Social Religion: The Rhetoric of Nineteenth-Century Revivalism,   by Sandra S. Sizer

Social Darwinism: Science and Myth in Anglo-American Social Thought,   by Robert C. Bannister

Twentieth Century Limited: Industrial Design in America, 1925–1939, by Jeffrey L. Meikle

Charlotte Perkins Gilman: The Making of a Radical Feminist, 1860–1896,   by Mary A. Hill

Inventing the American Way of Death, 1830–1920,   by James J. Farrell

Anarchist Women, 1870–1920,   by Margaret S. Marsh

Woman and Temperance: The Quest for Power and Liberty, 1873–1900,   by Ruth Bordin

Hearth and Home: Preserving a People's Culture,   by George W. McDaniel

The Education of Mrs. Henry Adams,   by Eugenia Kaledin

Class, Culture, and the Classroom: The Student Peace Movement in the 1930s,   by Eileen Eagan

Fathers and Sons: The Bingham Family and the American Mission, by Char Miller

An American Odyssey: Elia Kazan and American Culture,   by Thomas H. Pauly

Silver Cities: The Photography of American Urbanization, 1839–1915, by Peter B. Hales

Actors and American Culture, 1800–1920,   by Benjamin McArthur

Saving the Waifs: Reformers and Dependent Children, 1890–1917, by LeRoy Ashby

A Woman's Ministry: Mary Collson's Search for Reform as a Unitarian Minister, a Hull House Social Worker, and a Christian Science Practitioner, by Cynthia Grant Tucker

Depression Winters: New York Social Workers and the New Deal,   by William W. Bremer

Forever Wild: Environmental Aesthetics and the Adirondack Forest Preserve,   by Philip G. Terrie

Art and Labor: Ruskin, Morris, and the Craftsman Ideal in America, by Eileen Boris

Paths into American Culture: Psychology, Medicine, and Morals,   by John C. Burnham